Author's
Message:

NOBUYUKI ANZAI
安西信行
PRESENTS

Art: Hiroshi Matsunobu

We've been turned into an
anime!
I'm so happy!

MÄR
Vol. 10
Story and Art by Nobuyuki Anzai

English Adaptation/Gerard Jones
Translation/Kaori Inoue
Touch-up Art & Lettering/James Gaubatz
Design/Izumi Evers
Editor/Andy Nakatani

Managing Editor/Annette Roman
Editorial Director/Elizabeth Kawasaki
Editor in Chief/Alvin Lu
Sr. Director of Acquisitions/Rika Inouye
Sr. VP of Marketing/Liza Coppola
Exec. VP of Sales & Marketing/John Easum
Publisher/Hyoe Narita

Printed in the U.S.A.

Published by VIZ Media, LLC
P.O. Box 77010
San Francisco, CA 94107

10 9 8 7 6 5 4 3 2 1
First printing, November 2006

www.viz.com
store.viz.com

PARENTAL ADVISORY
MÄR is rated T for Teen and is recommended for ages 13 and up. It contains fantasy violence.

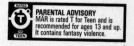

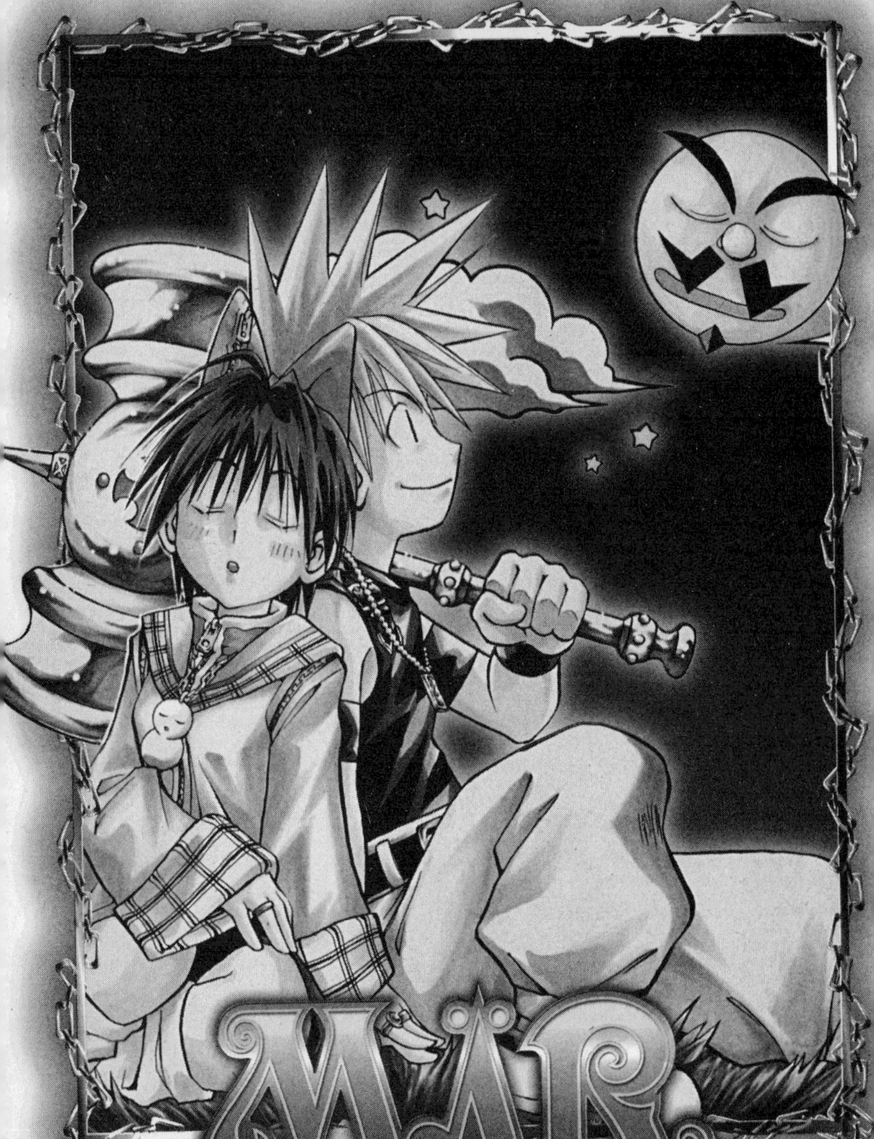
MÄR

MÄRCHEN AWAKENS ROMANCE

Vol. 10

Nobuyuki Anzai

Characters

Alan

A warrior who played a major role in the war six years ago. For a while, a curse trapped him in the form of Edward.

Snow

The Princess of the Kingdom of Lestava. Now participating in the War Games after completing 180 days of training with Ginta.

Edward

The dog who devotedly serves Princess Snow.

Nanashi

Leader of the Thieves Guild, Luberia. Detests the Chess Pieces.

Alviss

He brought Ginta to MÄR Heaven with the Dimensional ÄRM called the "Gate Keeper Clown."

Ginta Toramizu

A second-year middle school student who dreams about the world of fairy tales—and suddenly finds himself there! Now in order to save that world, he must fight the Chess Pieces.

Babbo

A rare talking ÄRM, who by synchronizing with Ginta is able to change shape—now up to version five. He once belonged to Phantom.

Jack

A farmboy who left his mother and his farm to go on adventures with Ginta.

Previous Volume

Ginta jumps through a "door" that suddenly appears in his class-room and finds himself in Märchen, the magical world of his dreams. Now, at the "request" of the Chess Pieces, the War Games have begun—and Ginta and his friends, calling themselves Mär, must battle the Chess warriors. The members of Mär have steadily increased their skills, winning the first four battles. Now they arrive on a desert stage for the fifth round—as Snow and Emokis face off!!

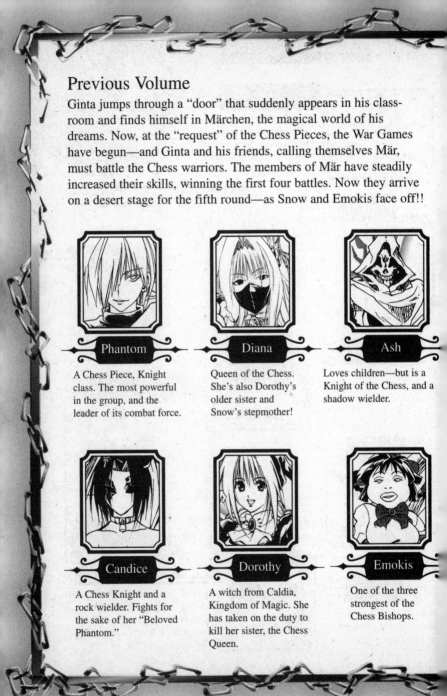

Phantom

A Chess Piece, Knight class. The most powerful in the group, and the leader of its combat force.

Diana

Queen of the Chess. She's also Dorothy's older sister and Snow's stepmother!

Ash

Loves children—but is a Knight of the Chess, and a shadow wielder.

Candice

A Chess Knight and a rock wielder. Fights for the sake of her "Beloved Phantom."

Dorothy

A witch from Caldia, Kingdom of Magic. She has taken on the duty to kill her sister, the Chess Queen.

Emokis

One of the three strongest of the Chess Bishops.

CONTENTS

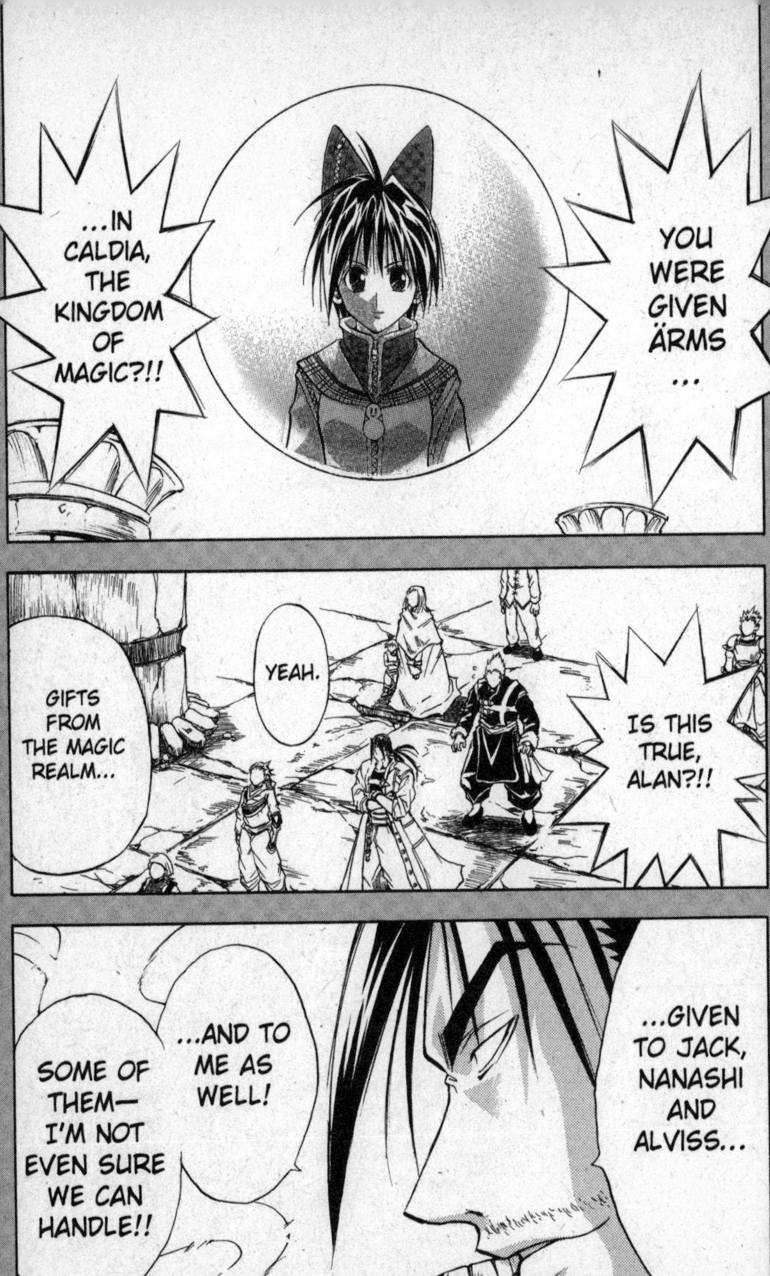
YOU WERE GIVEN ÄRMS ...
...IN CALDIA, THE KINGDOM OF MAGIC?!!
IS THIS TRUE, ALAN?!!
YEAH.
GIFTS FROM THE MAGIC REALM...
...GIVEN TO JACK, NANASHI AND ALVISS...
...AND TO ME AS WELL!
SOME OF THEM— I'M NOT EVEN SURE WE CAN HANDLE!!

AKT.97/SNOW VS. EMOKIS③

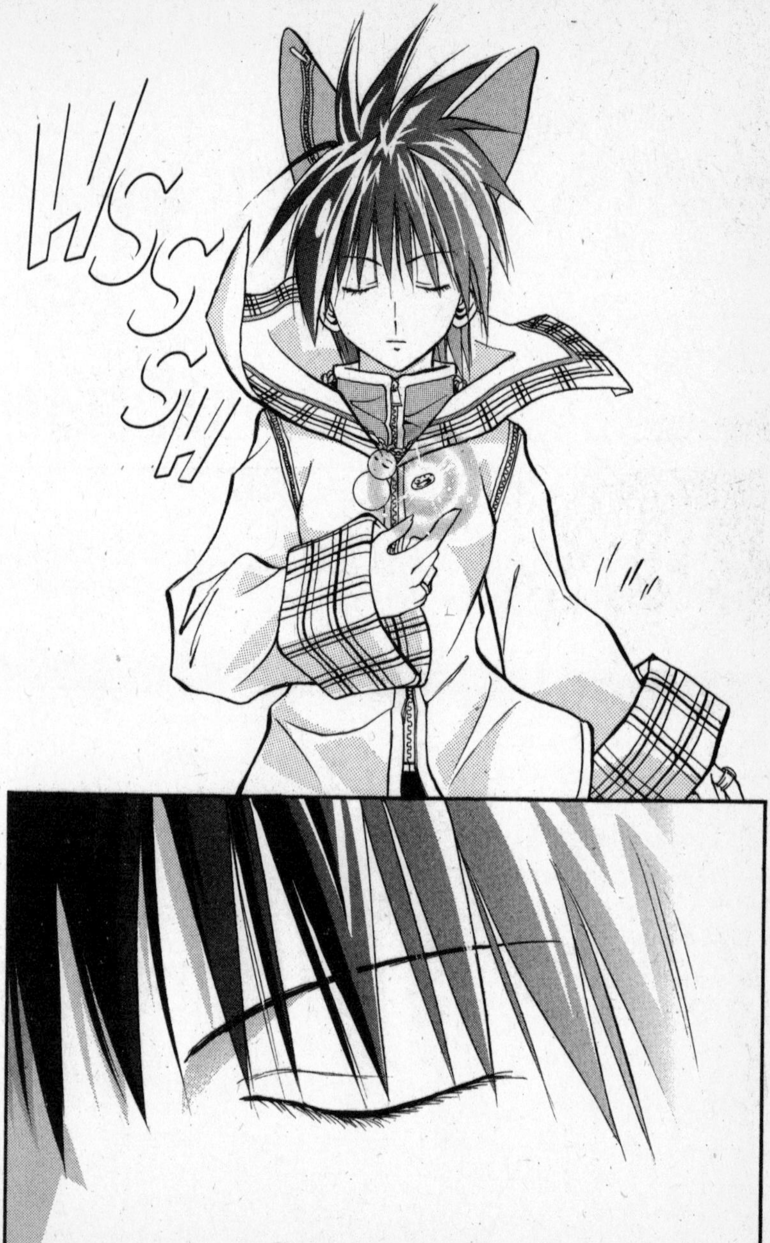
WSSSH

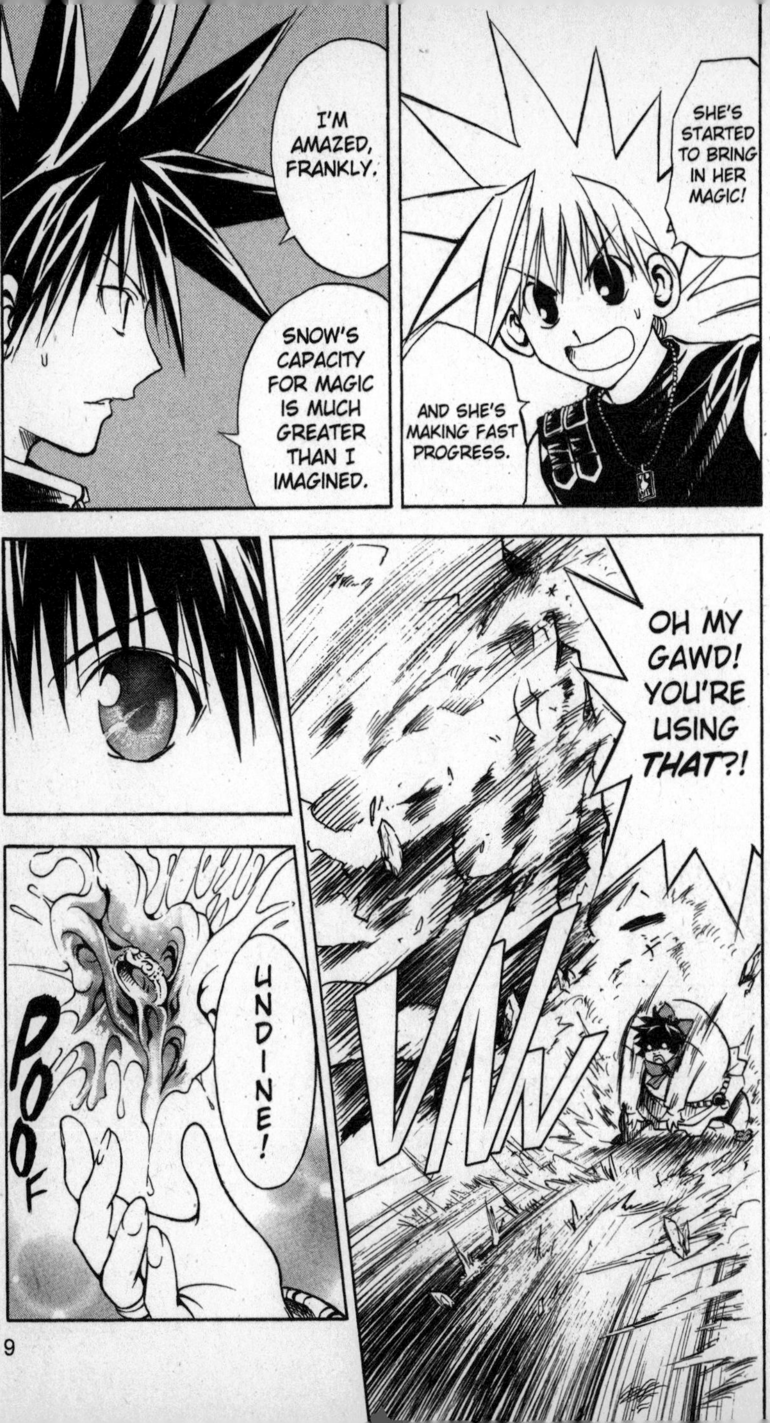
SHE'S STARTED TO BRING IN HER MAGIC!
AND SHE'S MAKING FAST PROGRESS.
I'M AMAZED, FRANKLY.
SNOW'S CAPACITY FOR MAGIC IS MUCH GREATER THAN I IMAGINED.
OH MY GAWD! YOU'RE USING *THAT*?!
UNDINE!
POOF

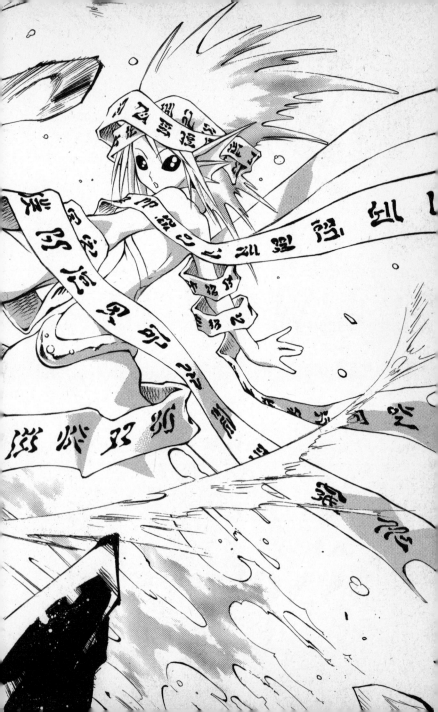

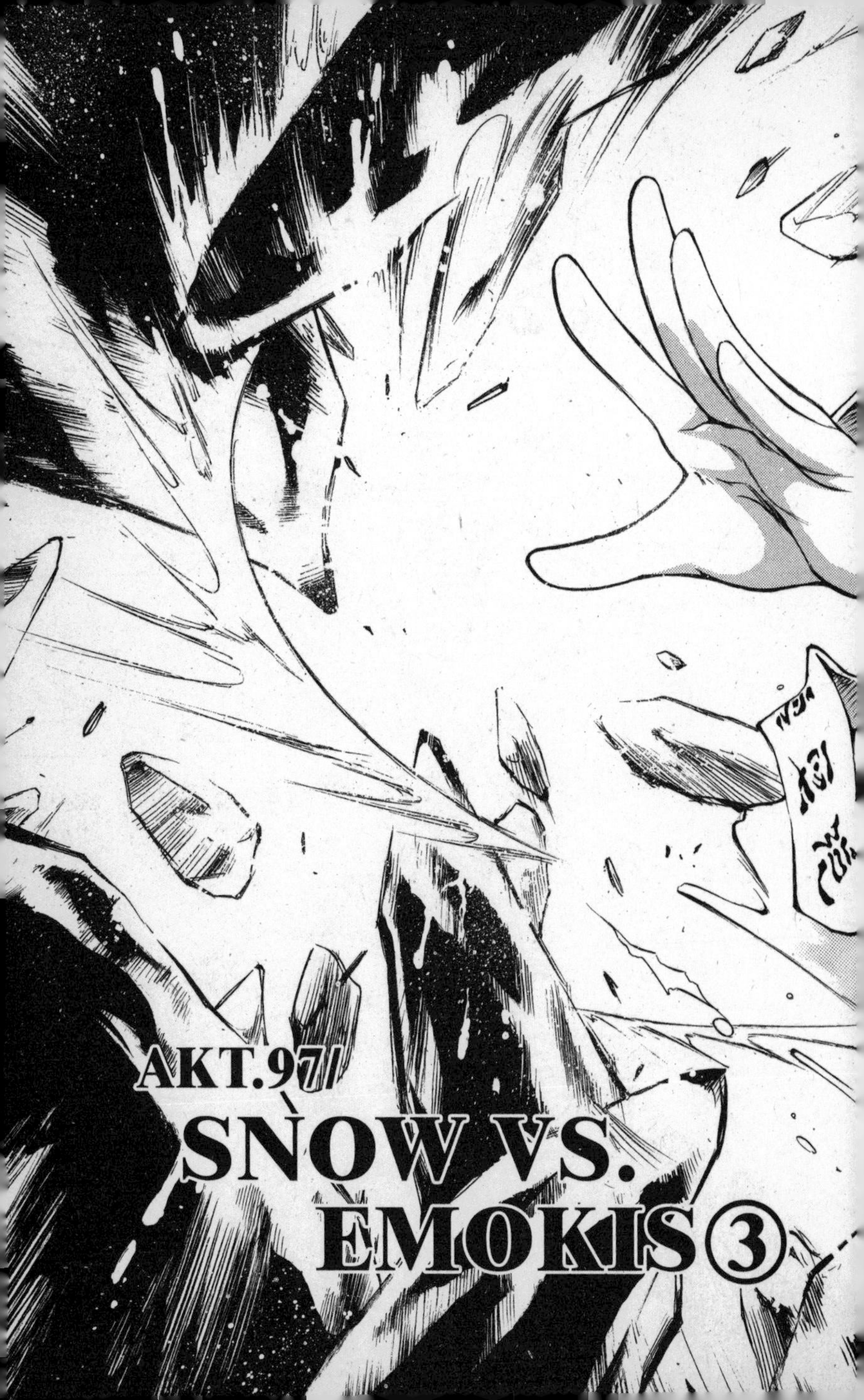
AKT.97/
SNOW VS. EMOKIS③

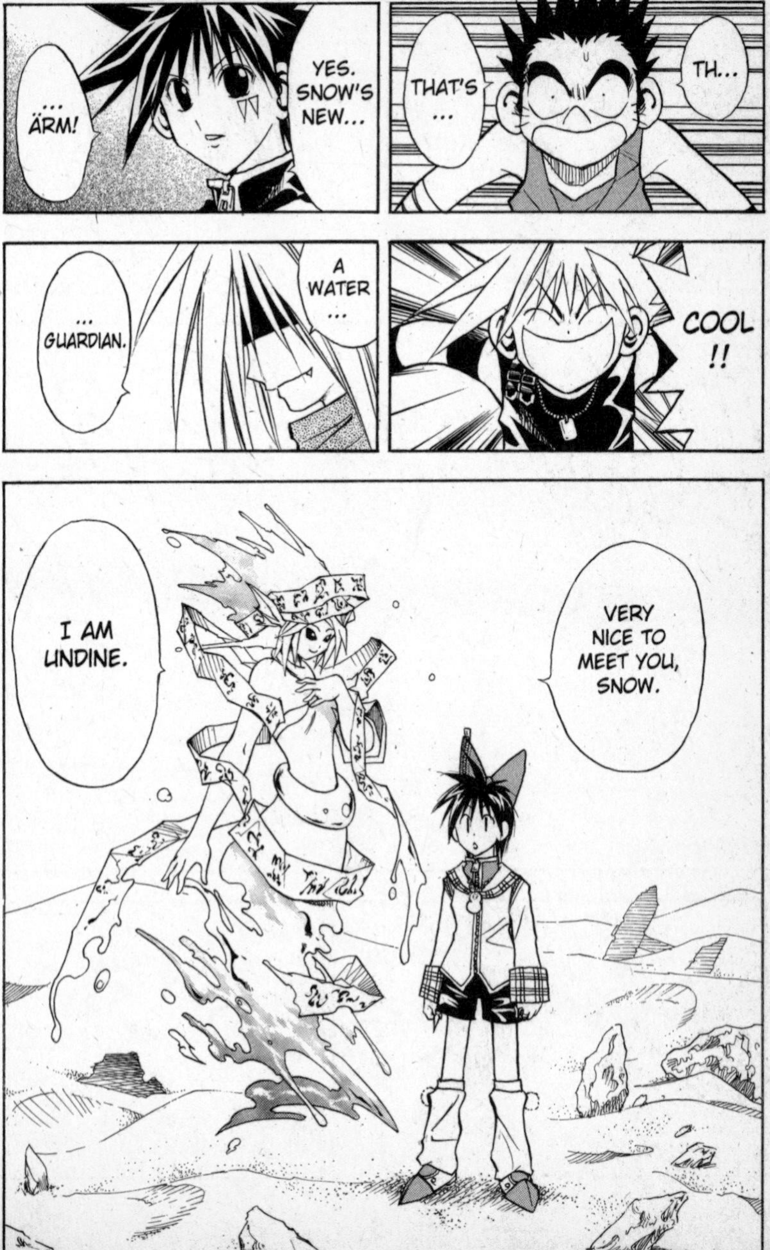
TH...
THAT'S ...
YES. SNOW'S NEW...
... ÄRM!
COOL !!
A WATER ...
... GUARDIAN.
VERY NICE TO MEET YOU, SNOW.
I AM UNDINE.

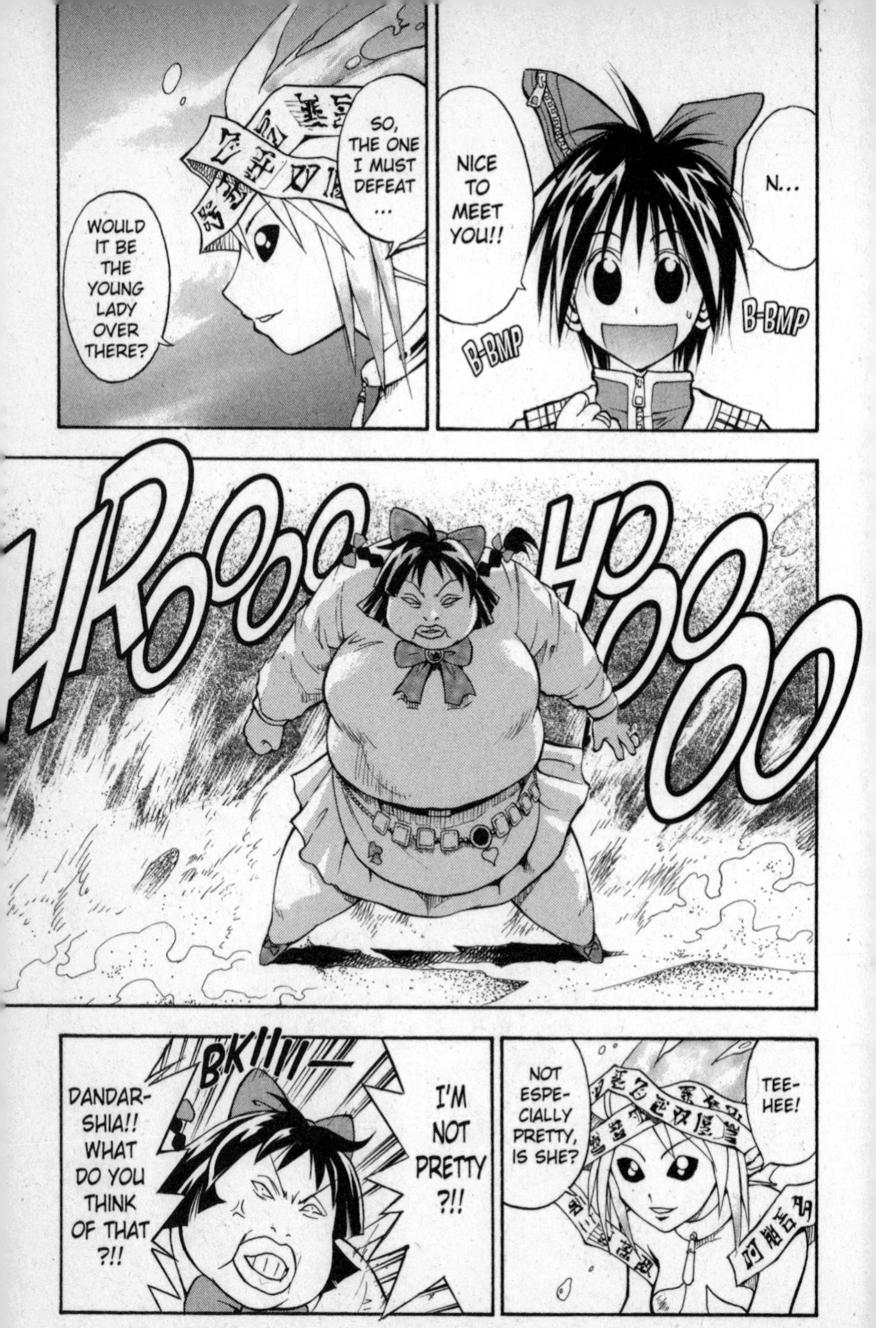
N...
NICE TO MEET YOU!!
B-BMP
B-BMP
SO, THE ONE I MUST DEFEAT...
WOULD IT BE THE YOUNG LADY OVER THERE?
HROOOO
HROOOOO
TEE-HEE!
NOT ESPECIALLY PRETTY, IS SHE?
BKIIII—
I'M NOT PRETTY?!!
DANDARSHIA!! WHAT DO YOU THINK OF THAT?!!

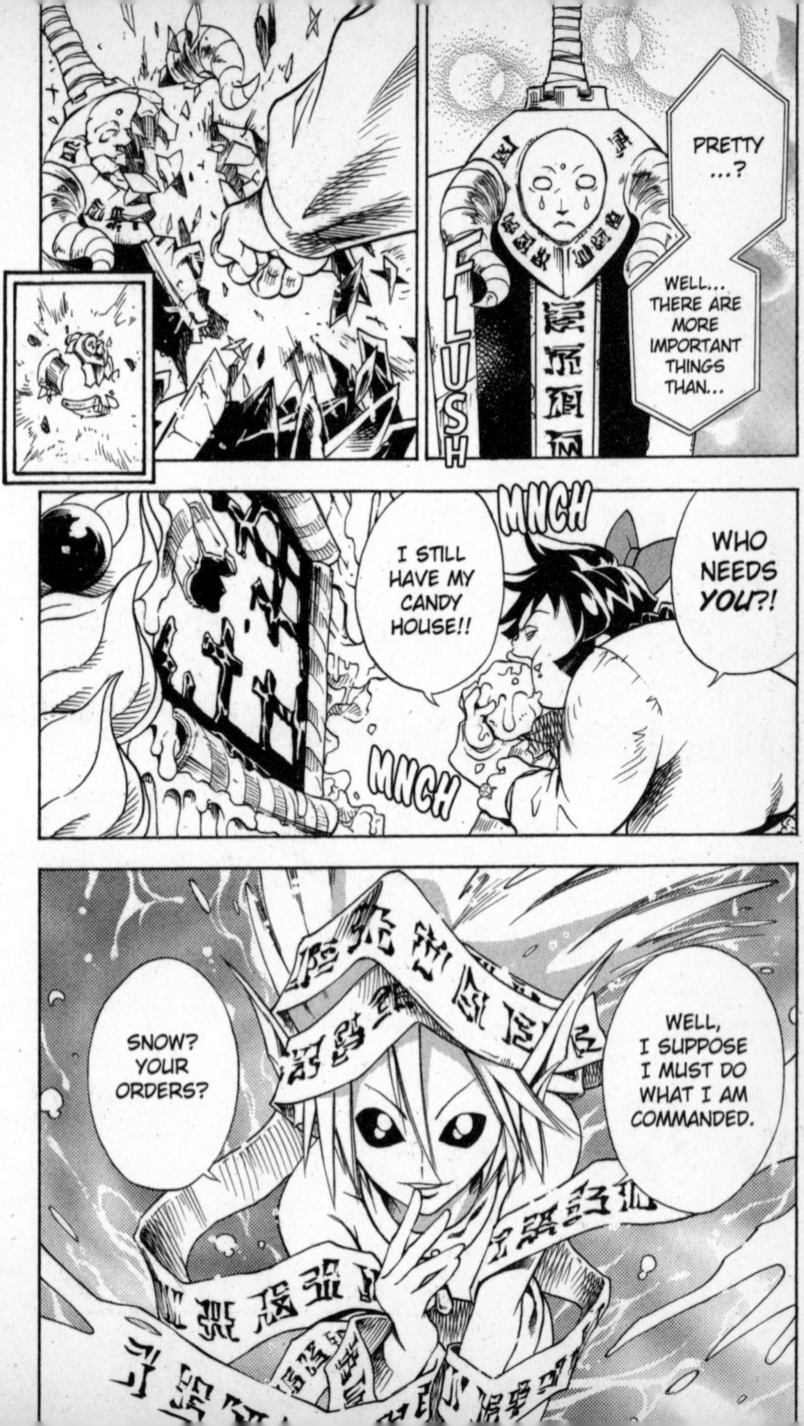
PRETTY ...?
WELL... THERE ARE MORE IMPORTANT THINGS THAN...
FLUSH
MNCH
WHO NEEDS YOU?!
I STILL HAVE MY CANDY HOUSE!!
MNCH
WELL, I SUPPOSE I MUST DO WHAT I AM COMMANDED.
SNOW? YOUR ORDERS?

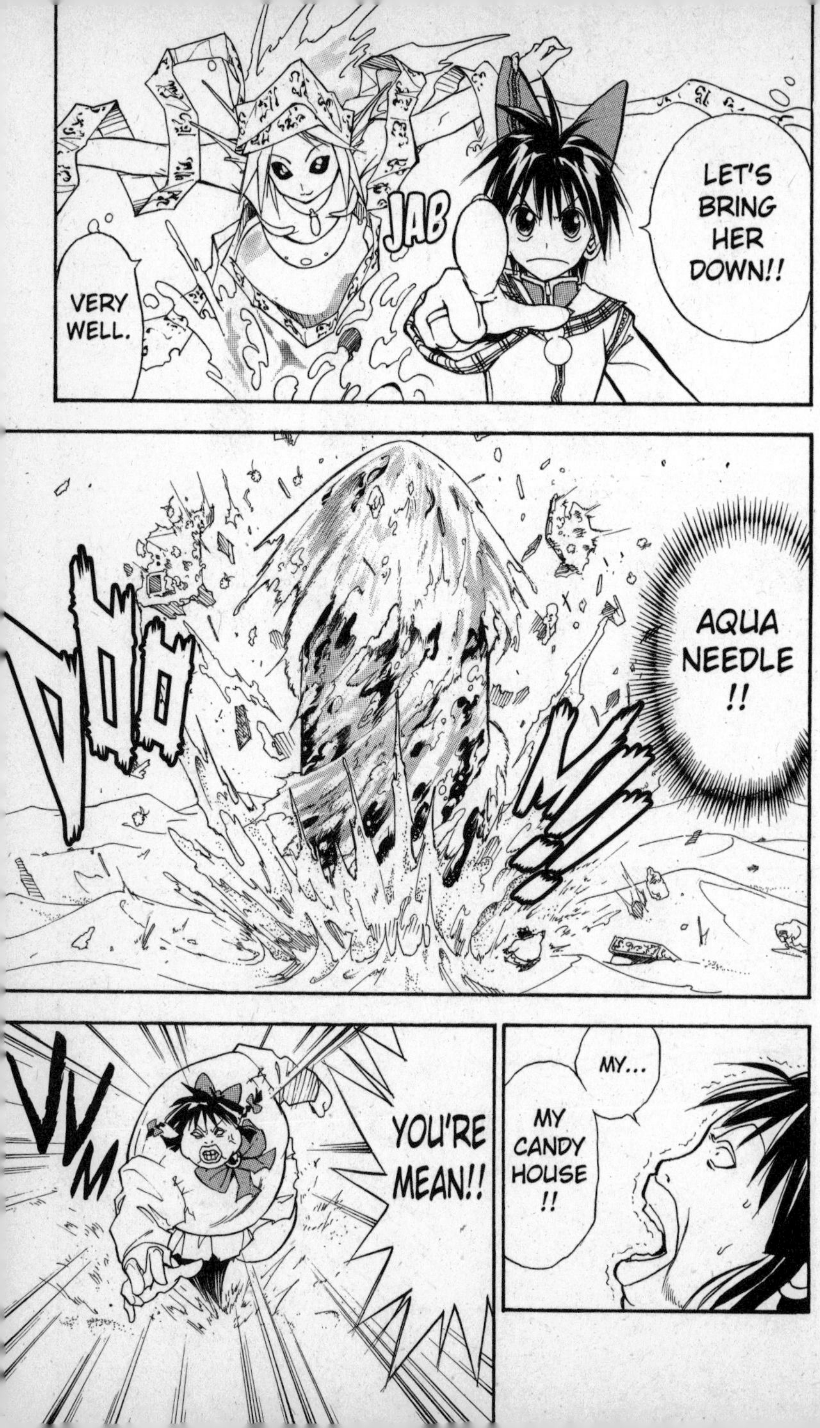
LET'S BRING HER DOWN!!
JAB
VERY WELL.
AQUA NEEDLE !!
MY...
MY CANDY HOUSE !!
YOU'RE MEAN!!

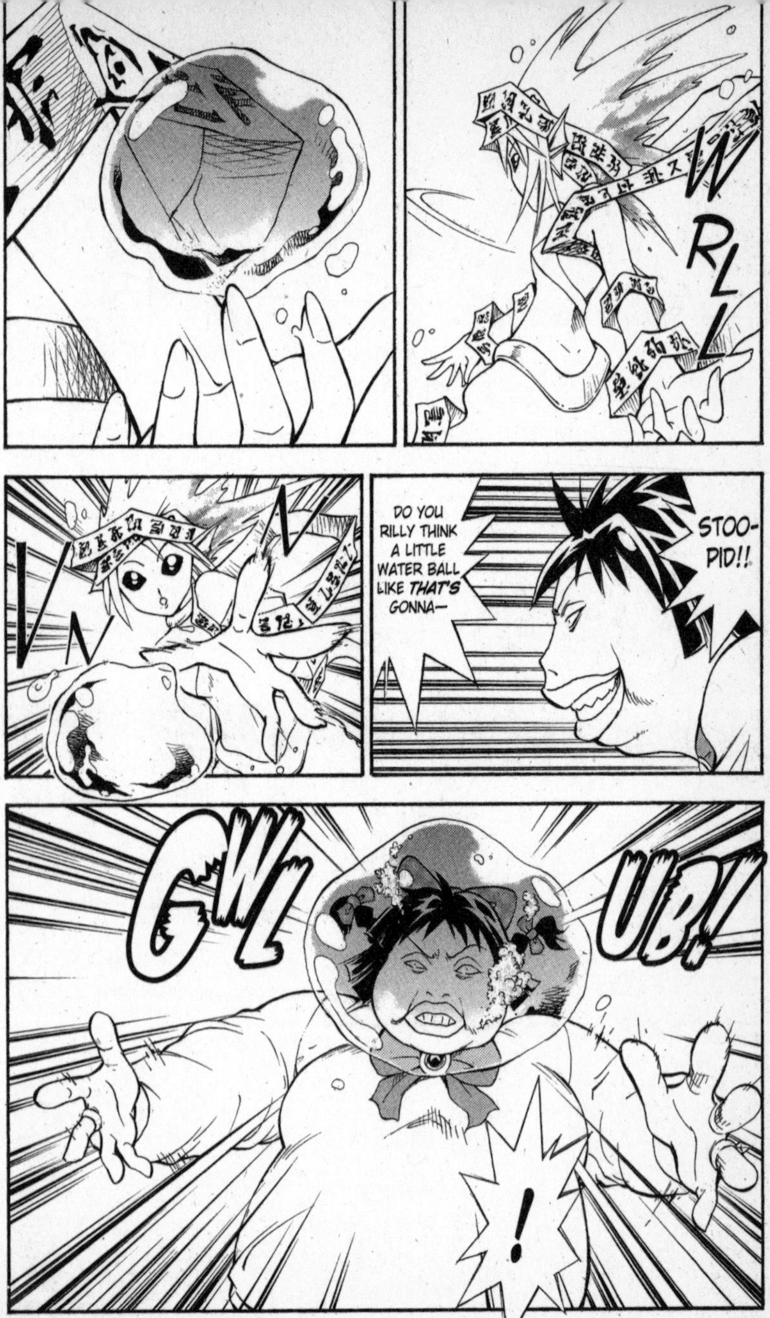
WRLL
STOO-PID!!
DO YOU RILLY THINK A LITTLE WATER BALL LIKE *THAT'S* GONNA—
GWUB!
!

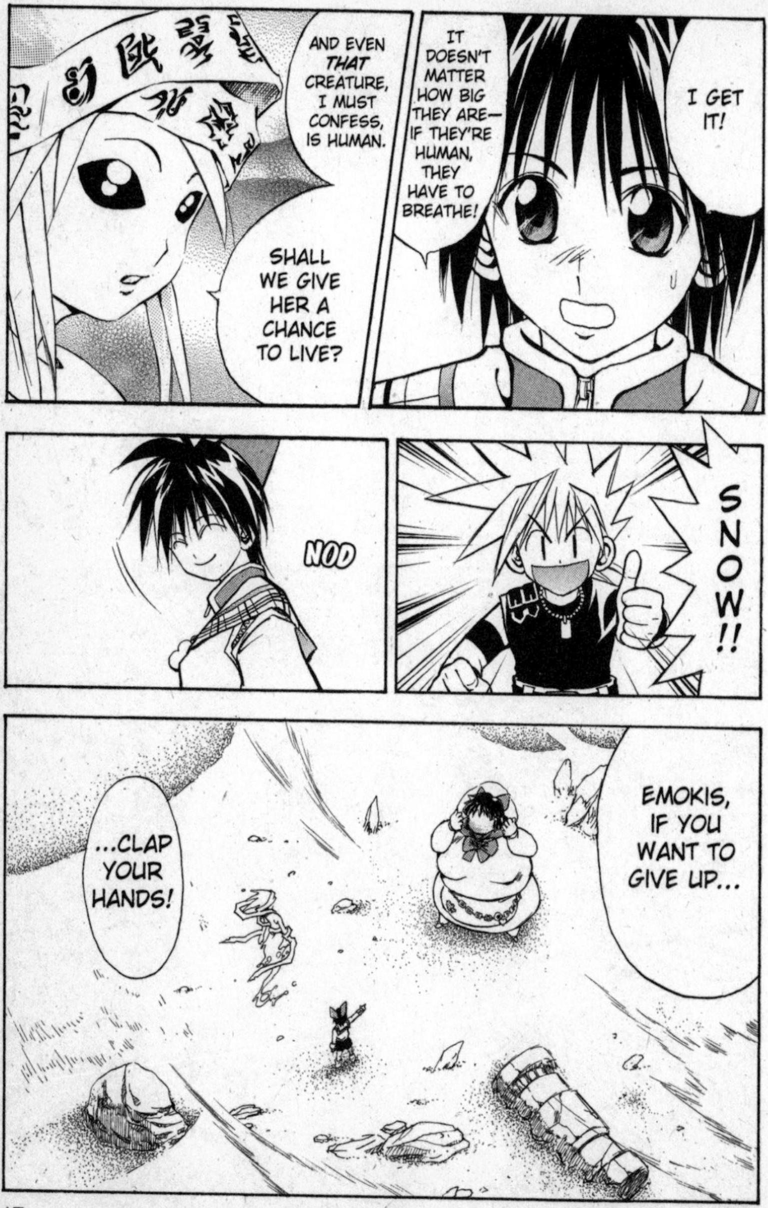
I GET IT!
IT DOESN'T MATTER HOW BIG THEY ARE— IF THEY'RE HUMAN, THEY HAVE TO BREATHE!
AND EVEN *THAT* CREATURE, I MUST CONFESS, IS HUMAN.
SHALL WE GIVE HER A CHANCE TO LIVE?
SNOW!!
NOD
EMOKIS, IF YOU WANT TO GIVE UP...
...CLAP YOUR HANDS!

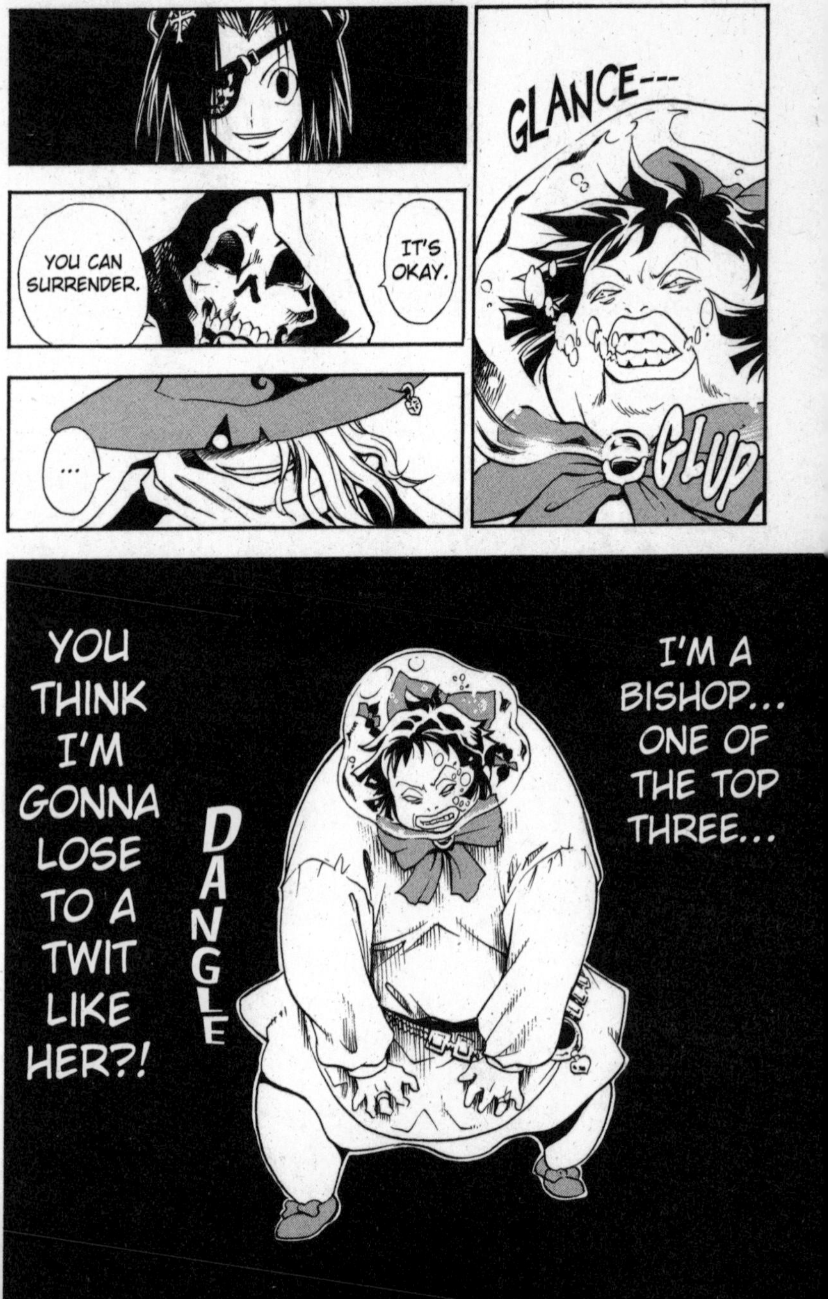
GLANCE---
GLUP
IT'S OKAY.
YOU CAN SURRENDER.
...
I'M A BISHOP... ONE OF THE TOP THREE...
DANGLE
YOU THINK I'M GONNA LOSE TO A TWIT LIKE HER?!

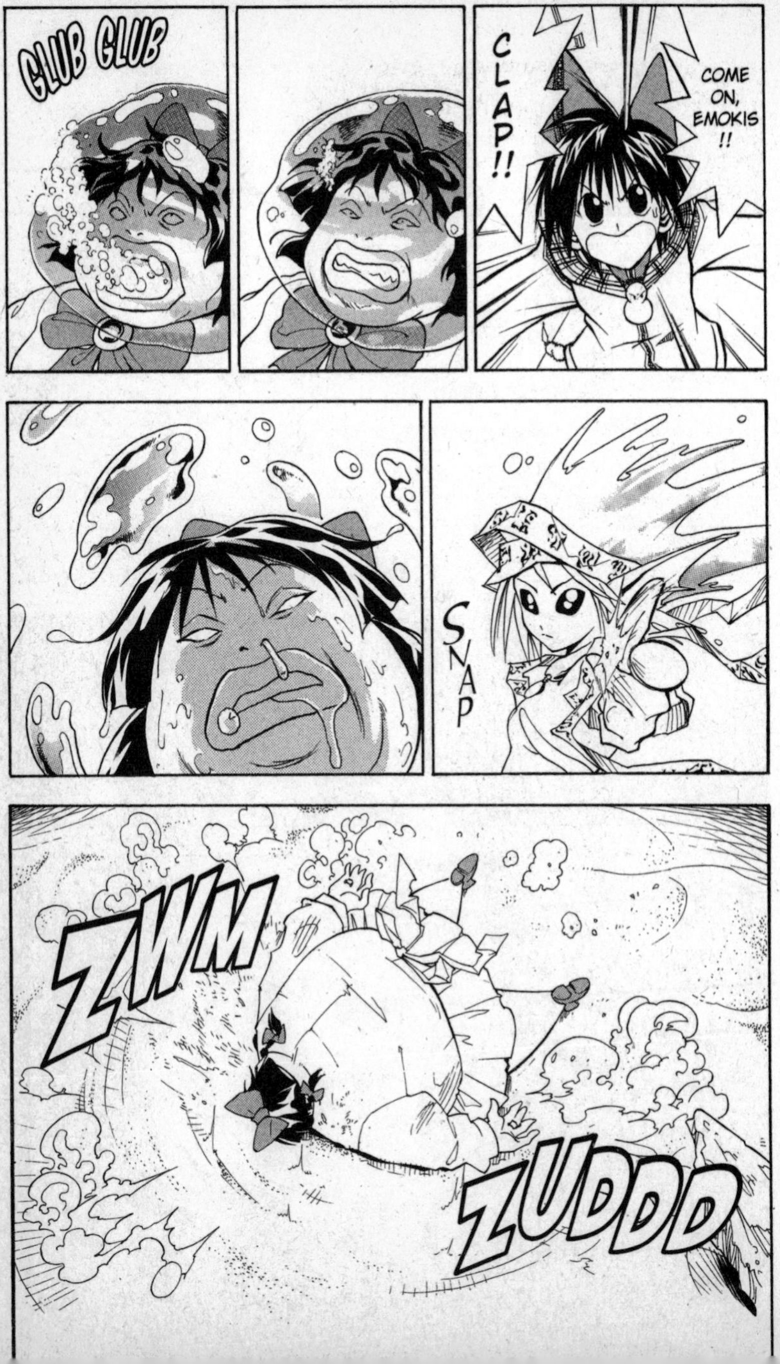
COME ON, EMOKIS!!
CLAP!!
GLUB GLUB
SNAP
ZWM
ZUDDD

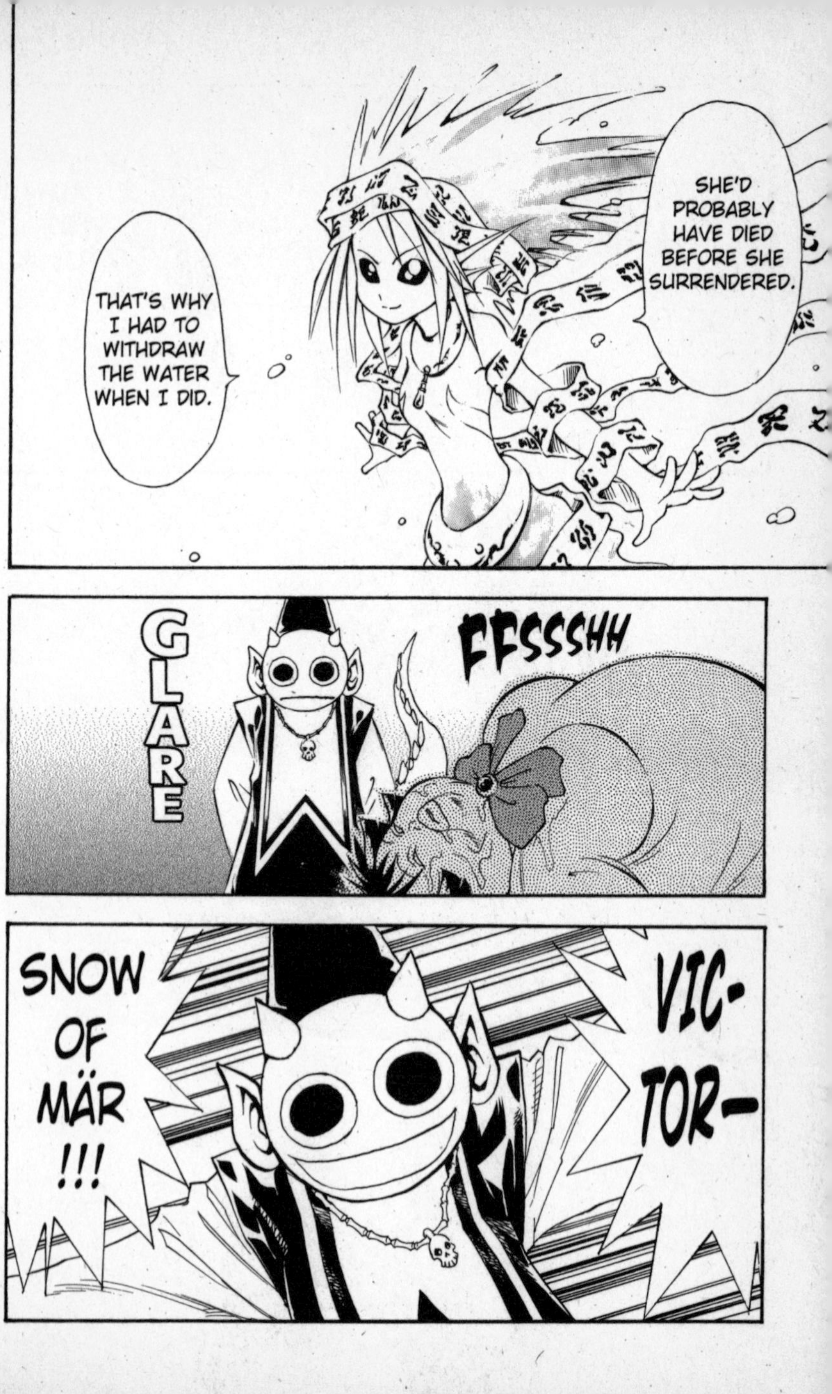
SHE'D PROBABLY HAVE DIED BEFORE SHE SURRENDERED.
THAT'S WHY I HAD TO WITHDRAW THE WATER WHEN I DID.
FFSSSHH
GLARE
VIC-TOR-
SNOW OF MÄR !!!

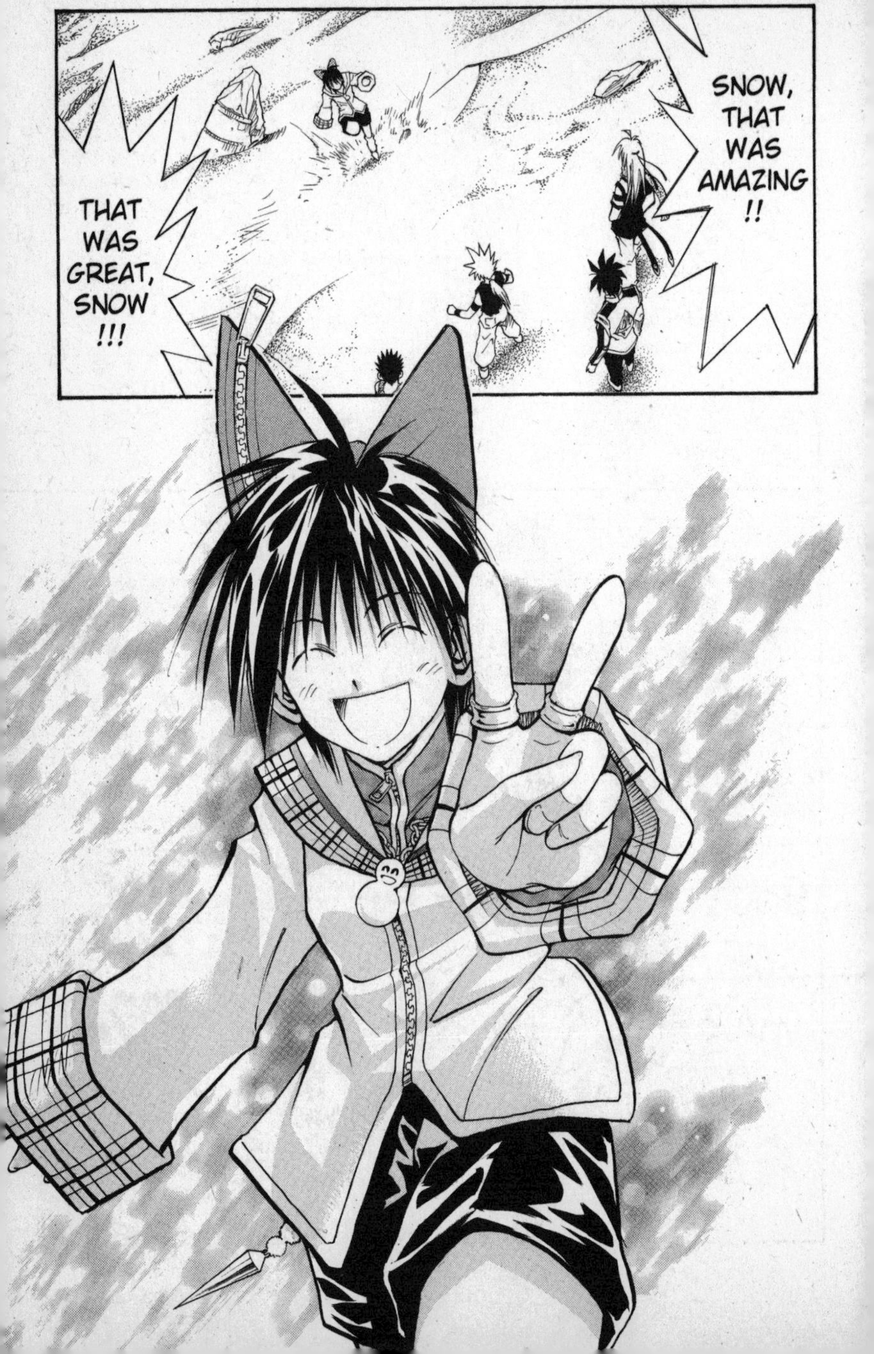
SNOW, THAT WAS AMAZING!!
THAT WAS GREAT, SNOW!!!

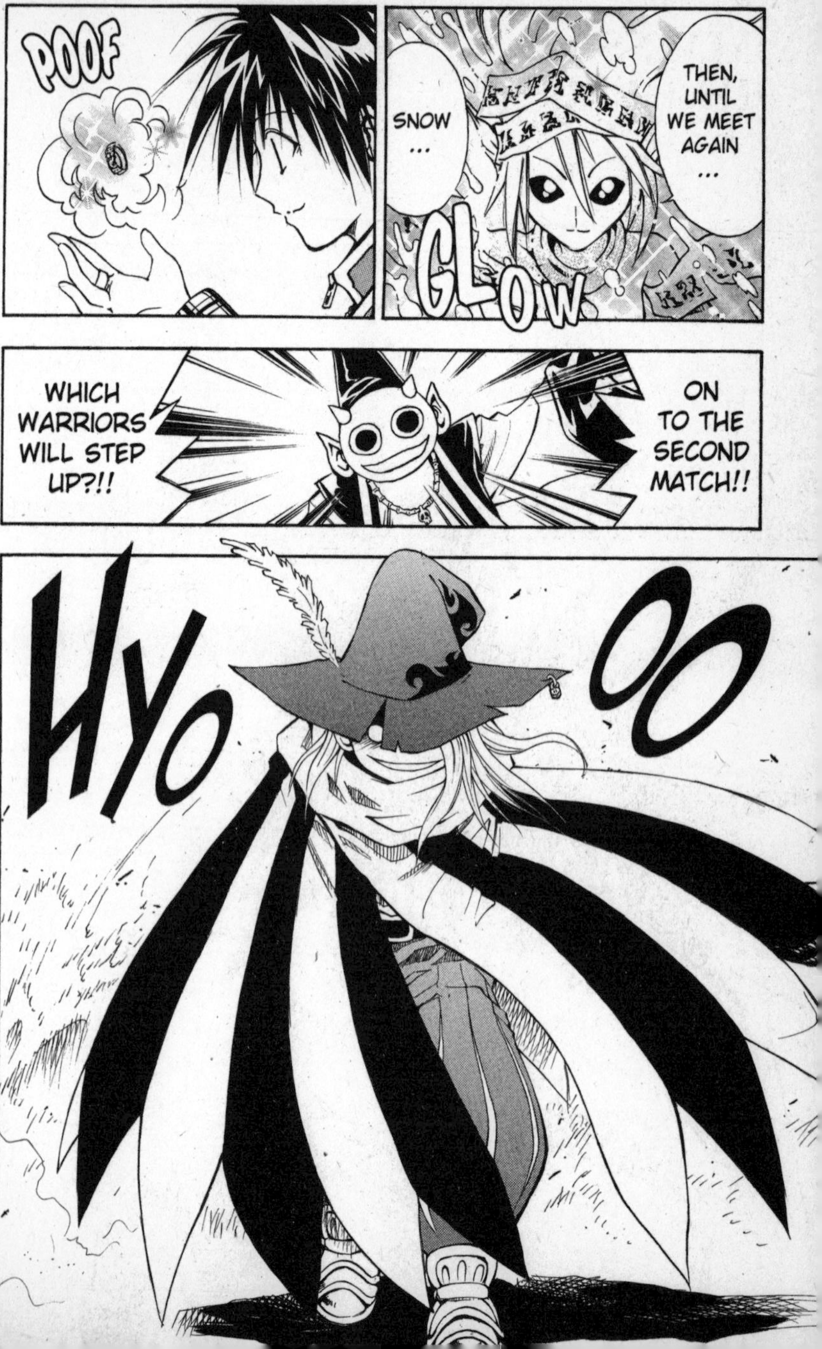
THEN, UNTIL WE MEET AGAIN ...
SNOW ...
GLOW
POOF
ON TO THE SECOND MATCH!!
WHICH WARRIORS WILL STEP UP?!!
HYOOO

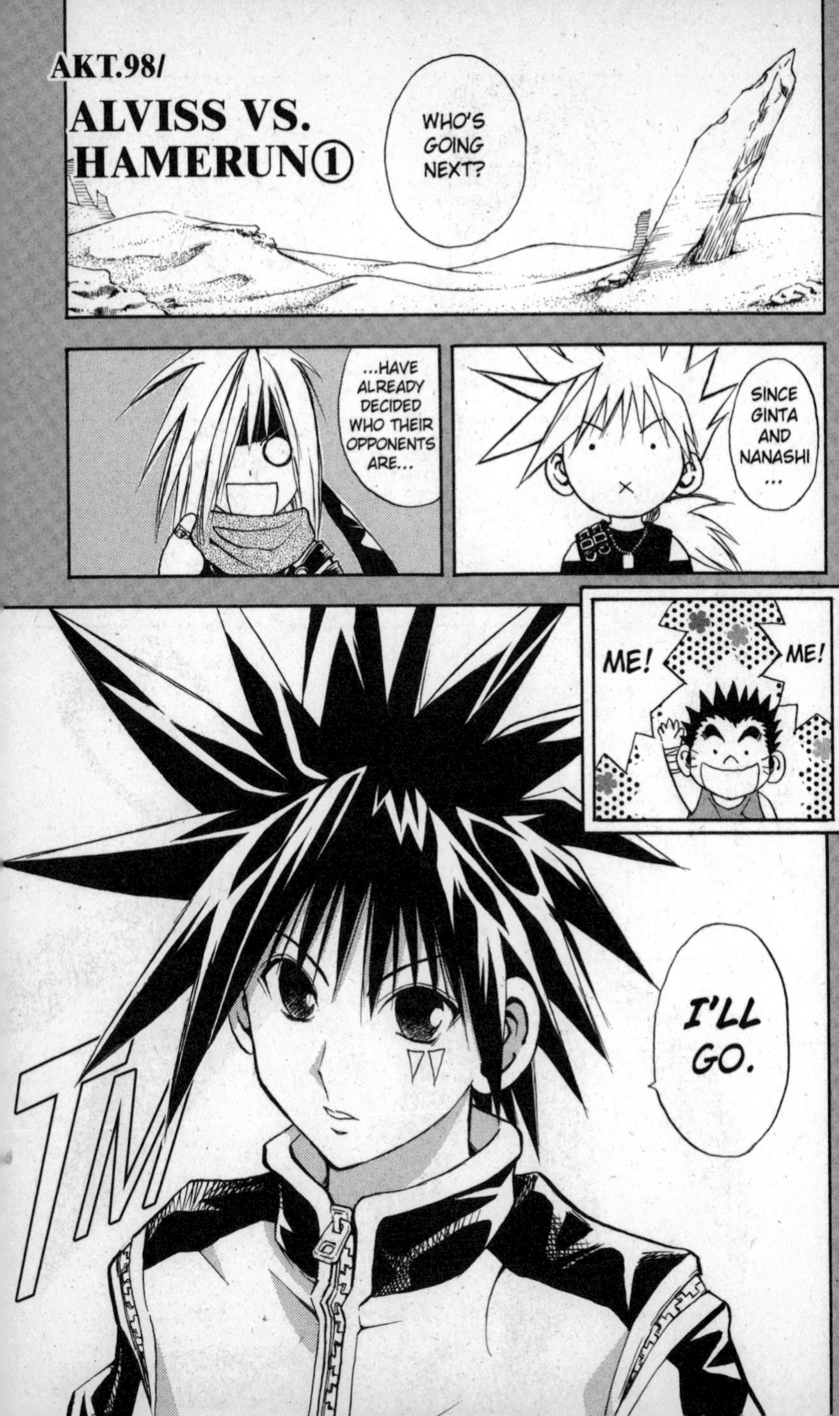
AKT.98/
ALVISS VS. HAMERUN①
WHO'S GOING NEXT?
SINCE GINTA AND NANASHI ...
...HAVE ALREADY DECIDED WHO THEIR OPPONENTS ARE...
ME!
ME!
I'LL GO.
TM

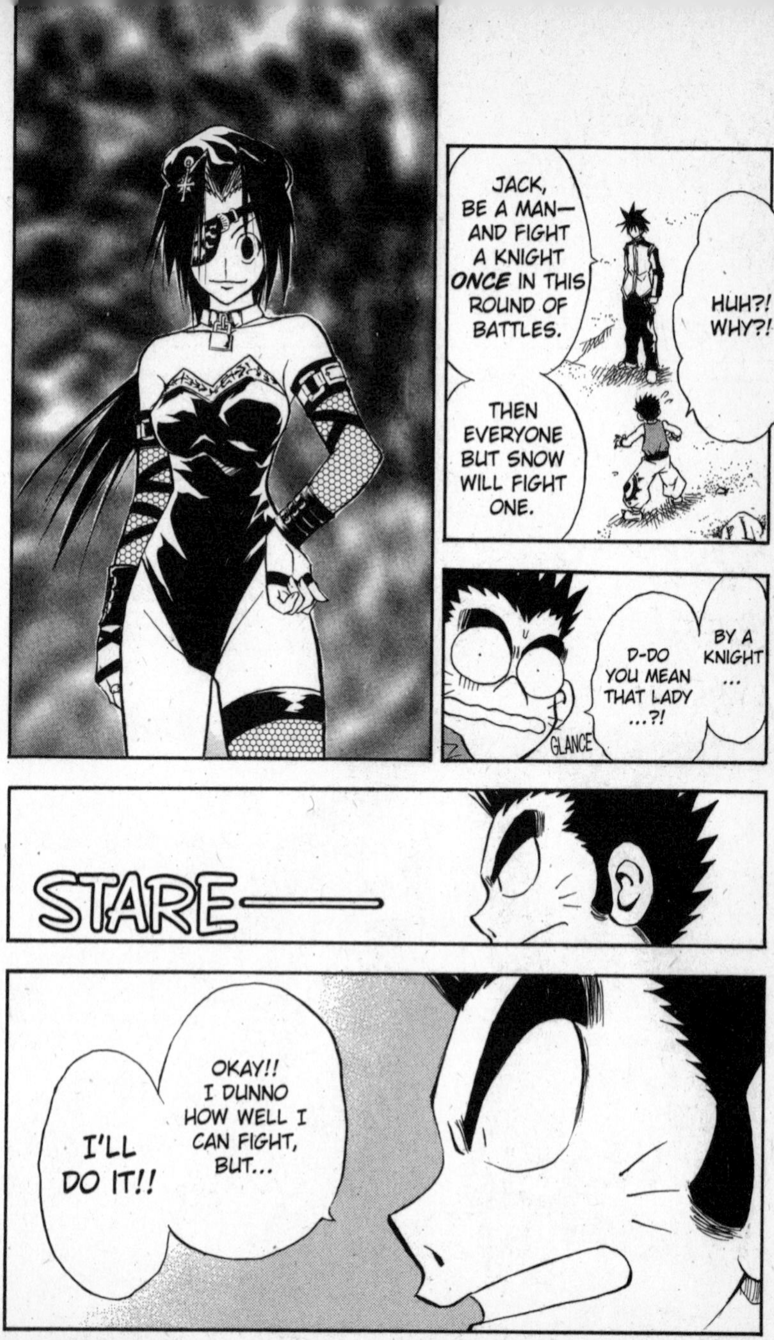
JACK, BE A MAN— AND FIGHT A KNIGHT ONCE IN THIS ROUND OF BATTLES.
HUH?! WHY?!
THEN EVERYONE BUT SNOW WILL FIGHT ONE.
BY A KNIGHT ...
D-DO YOU MEAN THAT LADY ...?!
GLANCE
STARE——
OKAY!! I DUNNO HOW WELL I CAN FIGHT, BUT...
I'LL DO IT!!

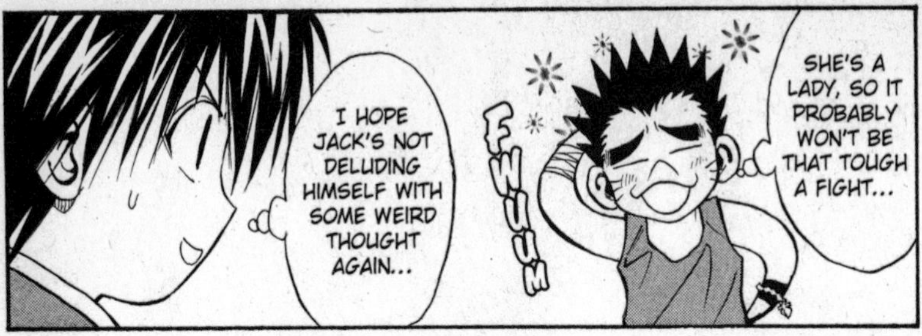
SHE'S A LADY, SO IT PROBABLY WON'T BE THAT TOUGH A FIGHT...
FWUUM
I HOPE JACK'S NOT DELUDING HIMSELF WITH SOME WEIRD THOUGHT AGAIN...

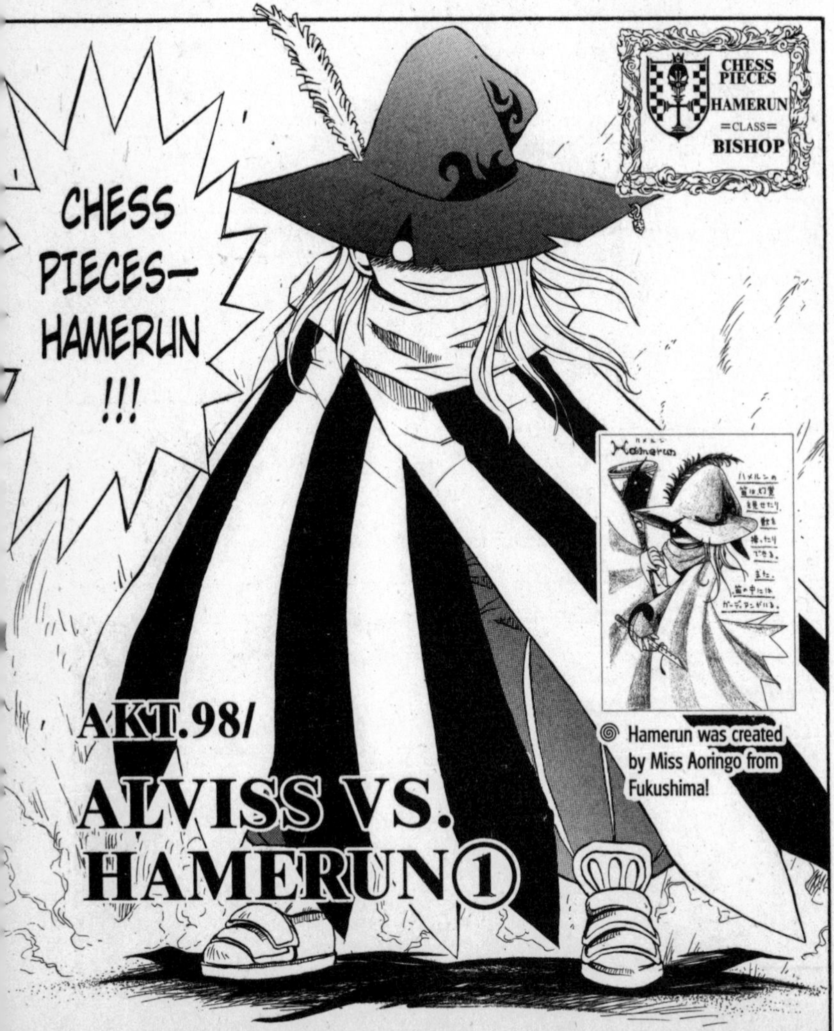
CHESS PIECES
HAMERUN
=CLASS=
BISHOP
CHESS PIECES—HAMERUN!!!
Hamerun
Hamerun was created by Miss Aoringo from Fukushima!
AKT.98/
ALVISS VS. HAMERUN①

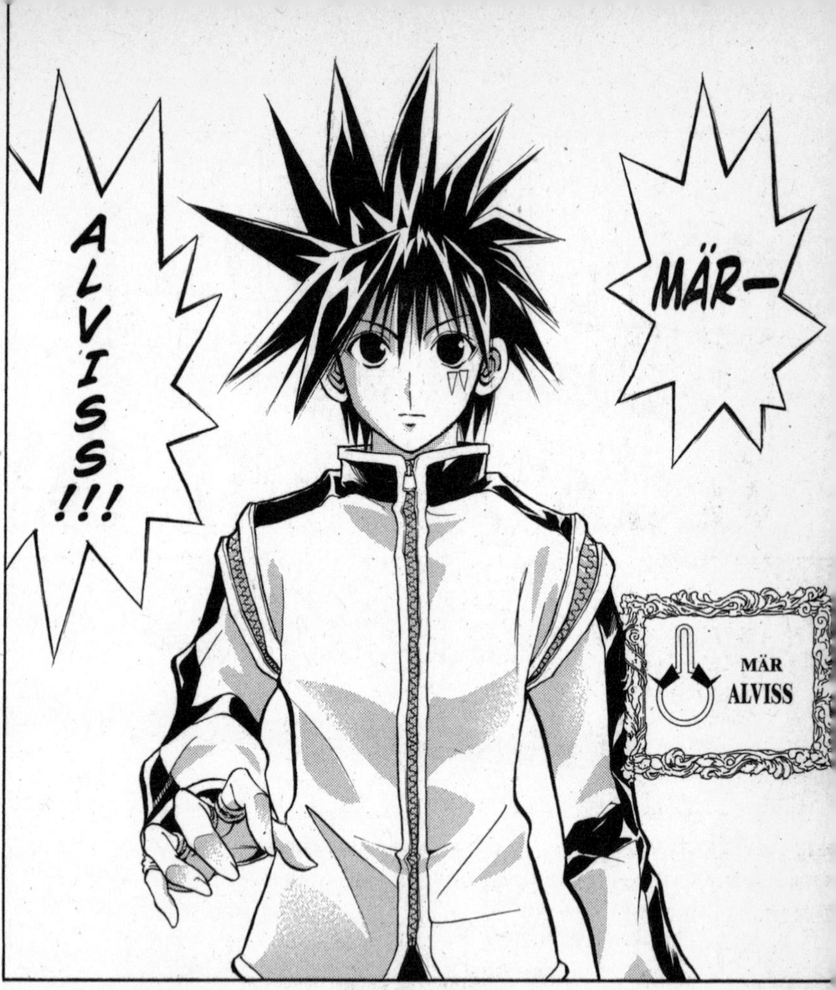
MÄR–
ALVISS!!!
MÄR
ALVISS

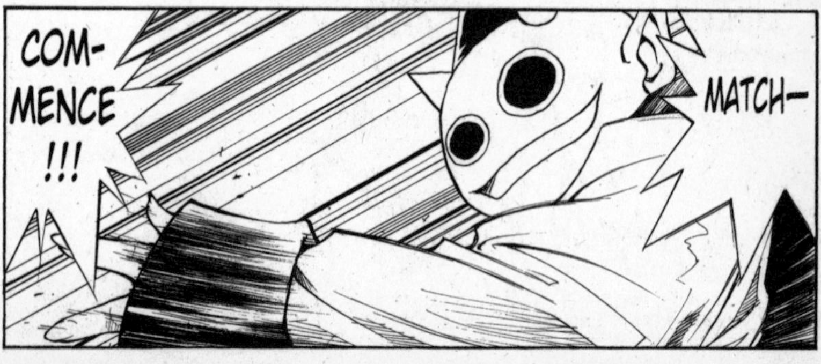
MATCH–
COM-
MENCE
!!!

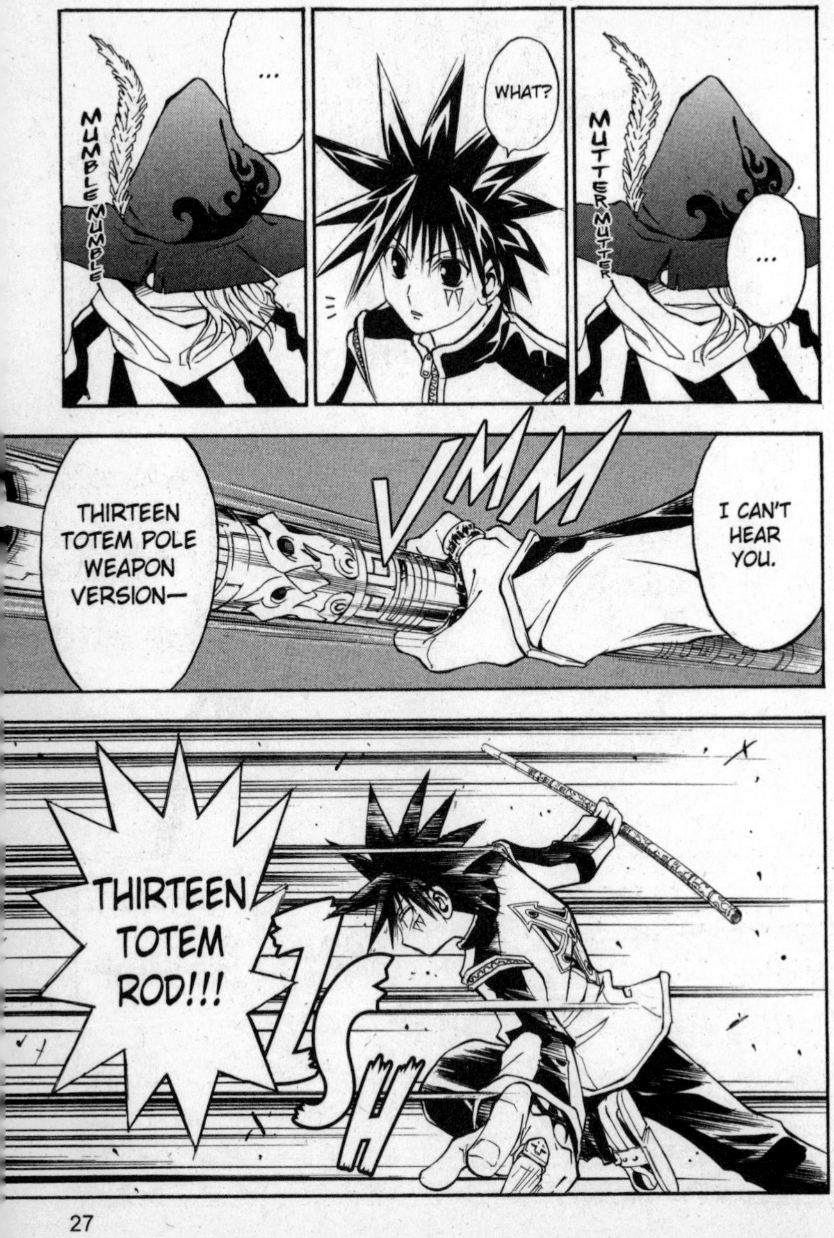
MUTTER MUTTER
...
WHAT?
MUMBLE MUMBLE
...
I CAN'T HEAR YOU.
VMM
THIRTEEN TOTEM POLE WEAPON VERSION—
THIRTEEN TOTEM ROD!!!

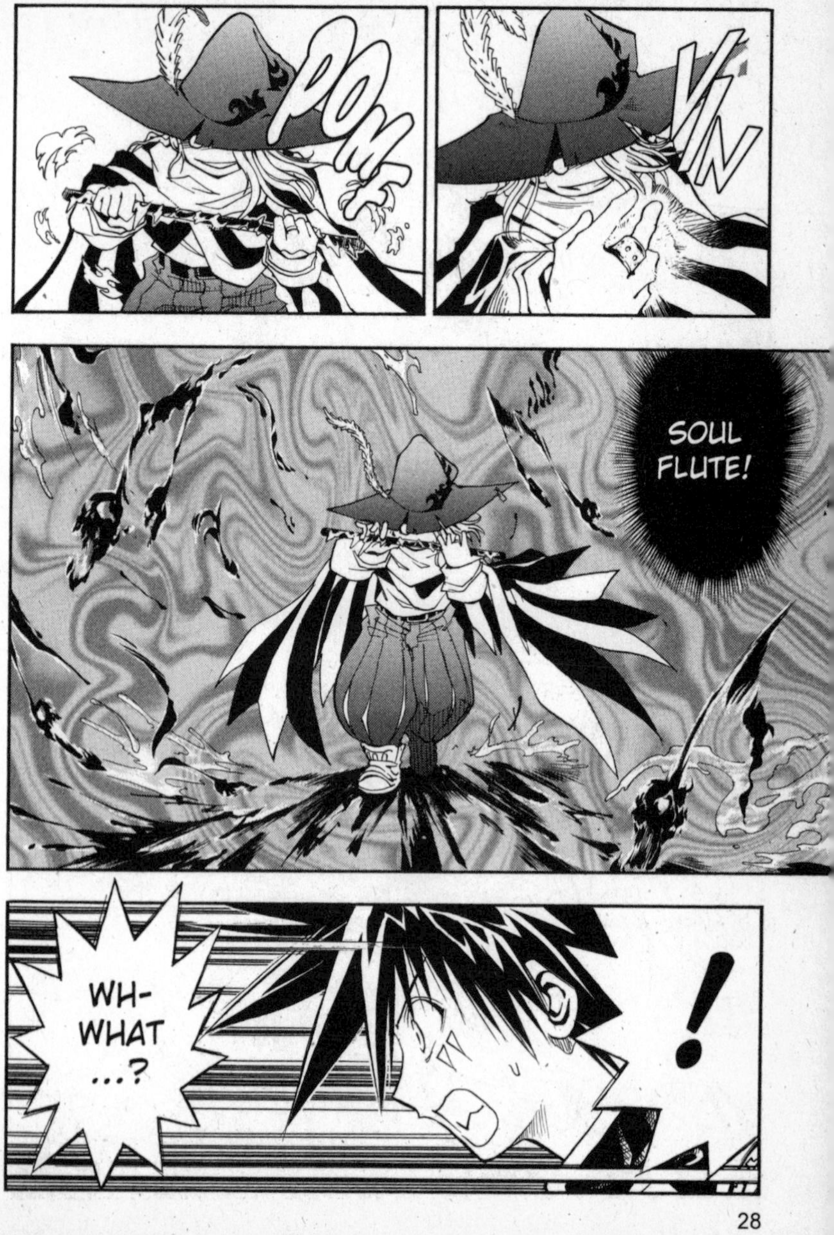
VIN
POM
SOUL FLUTE!
WH- WHAT ...?
!

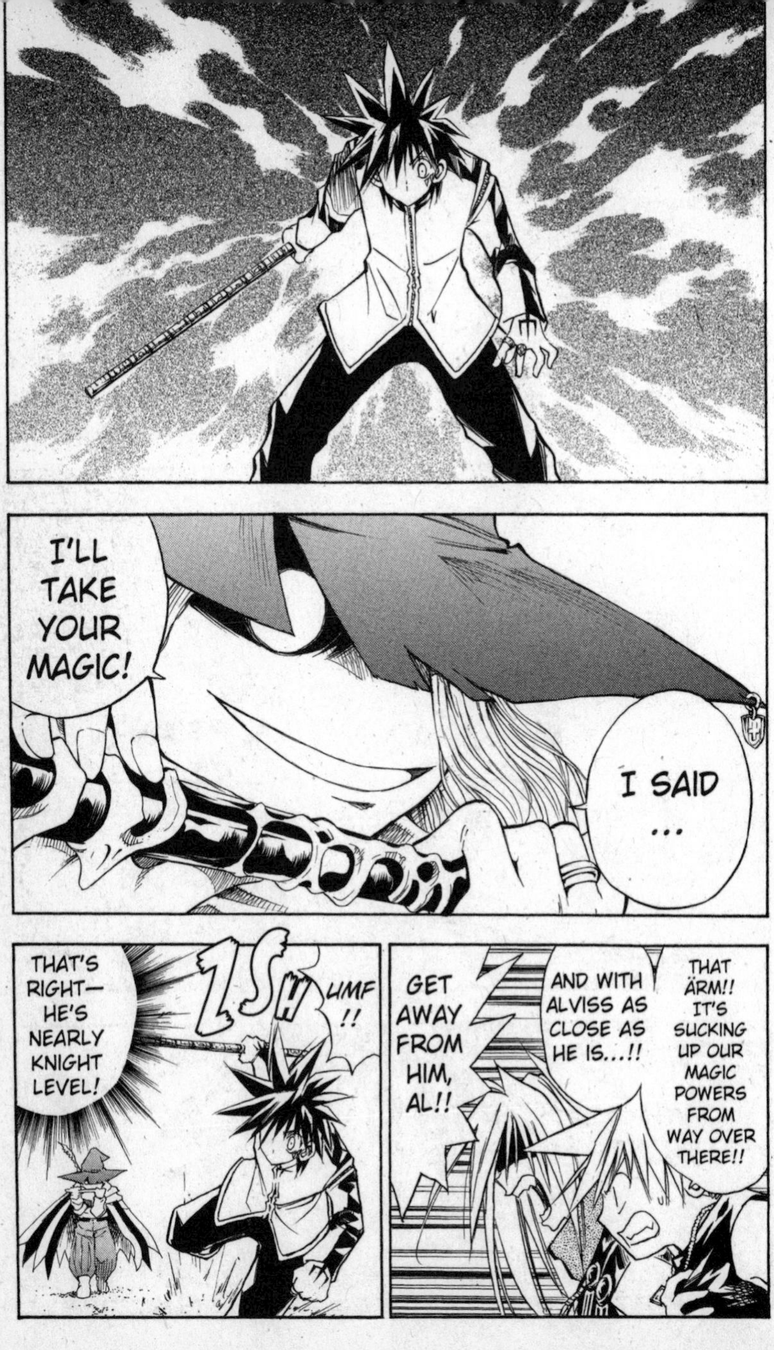
I SAID ...
I'LL TAKE YOUR MAGIC!
THAT ÄRM!! IT'S SUCKING UP OUR MAGIC POWERS FROM WAY OVER THERE!!
AND WITH ALVISS AS CLOSE AS HE IS...!!
GET AWAY FROM HIM, AL!!
UMF!!
THAT'S RIGHT— HE'S NEARLY KNIGHT LEVEL!

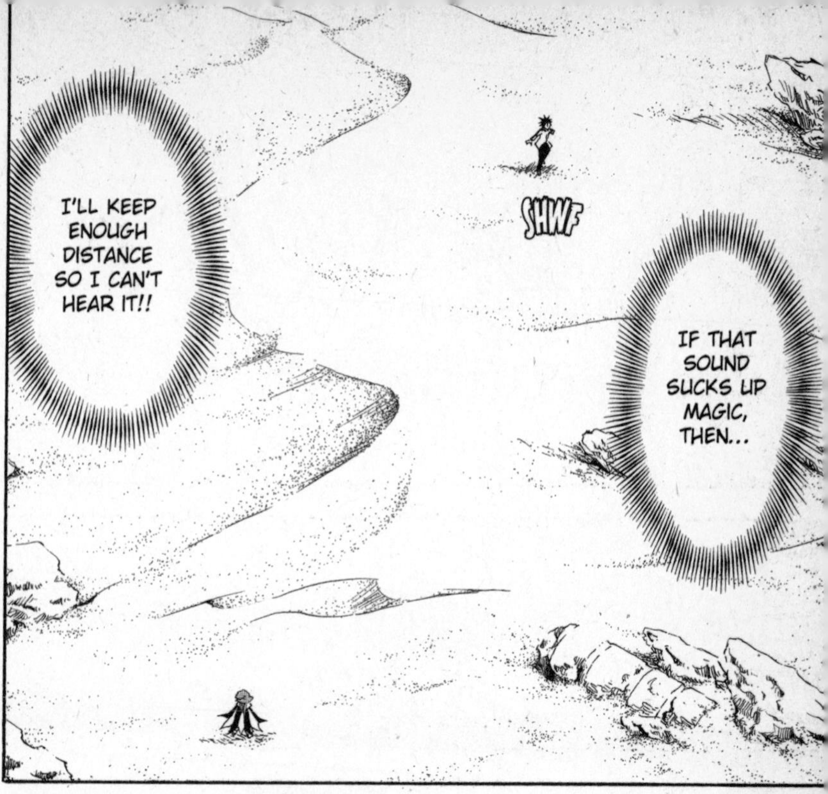
IF THAT SOUND SUCKS UP MAGIC, THEN...
SHWF
I'LL KEEP ENOUGH DISTANCE SO I CAN'T HEAR IT!!
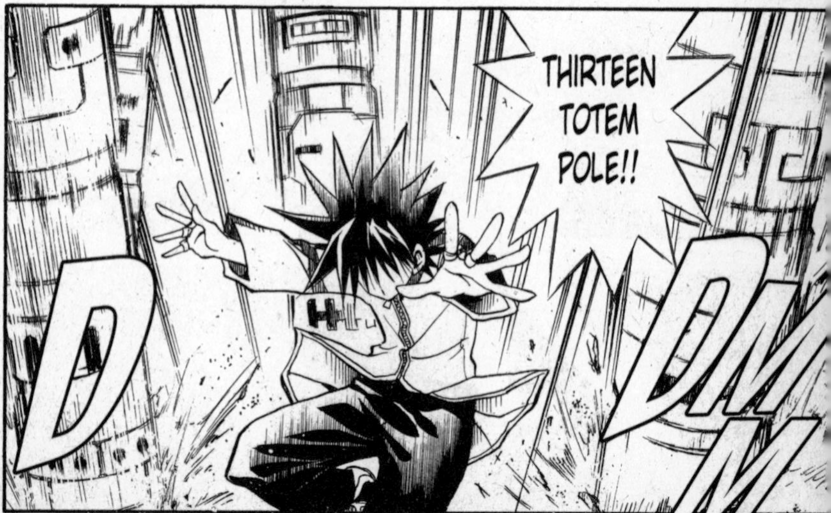
THIRTEEN TOTEM POLE!!
DMM
D

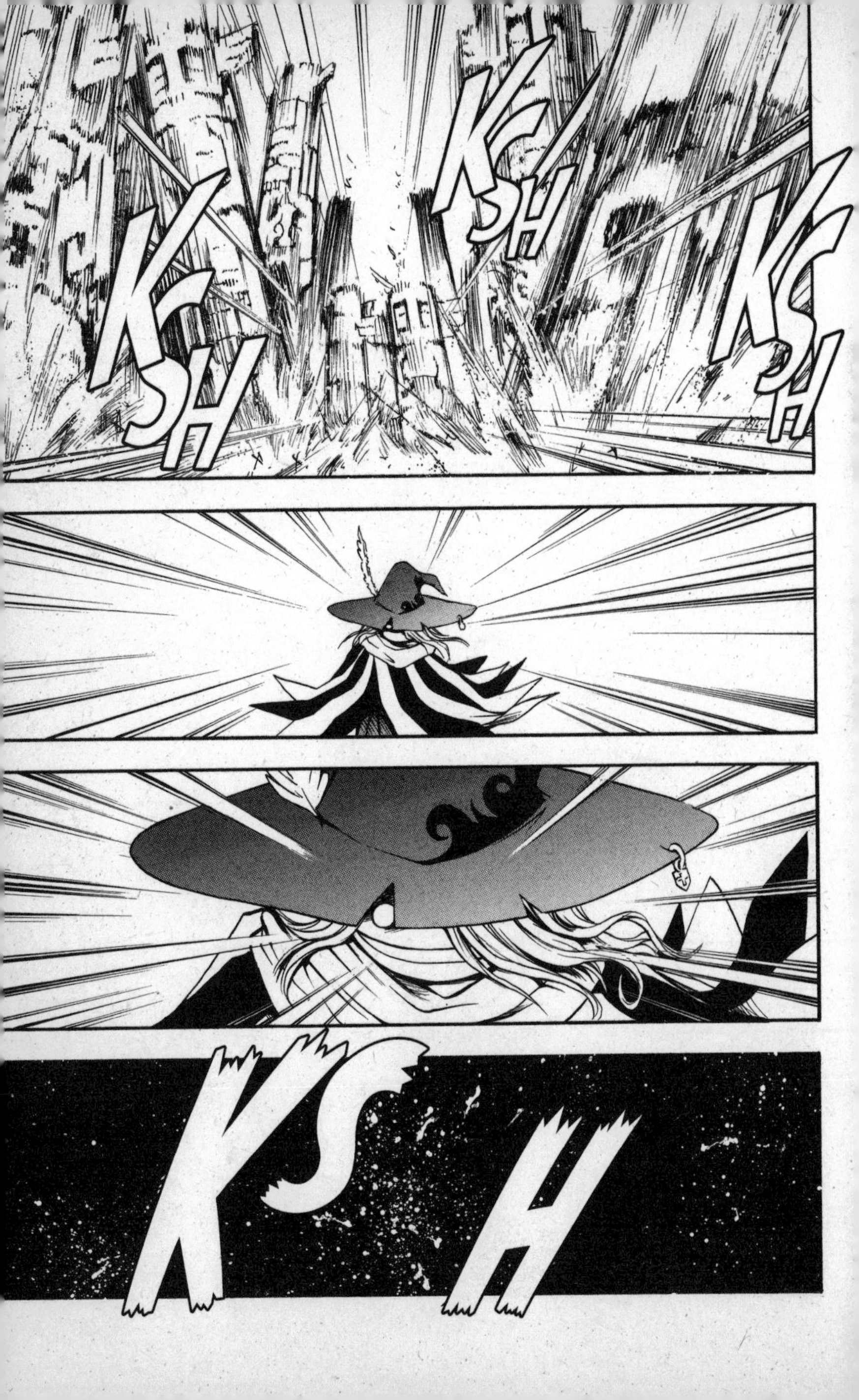
KSH
KSH
KSH
KSH

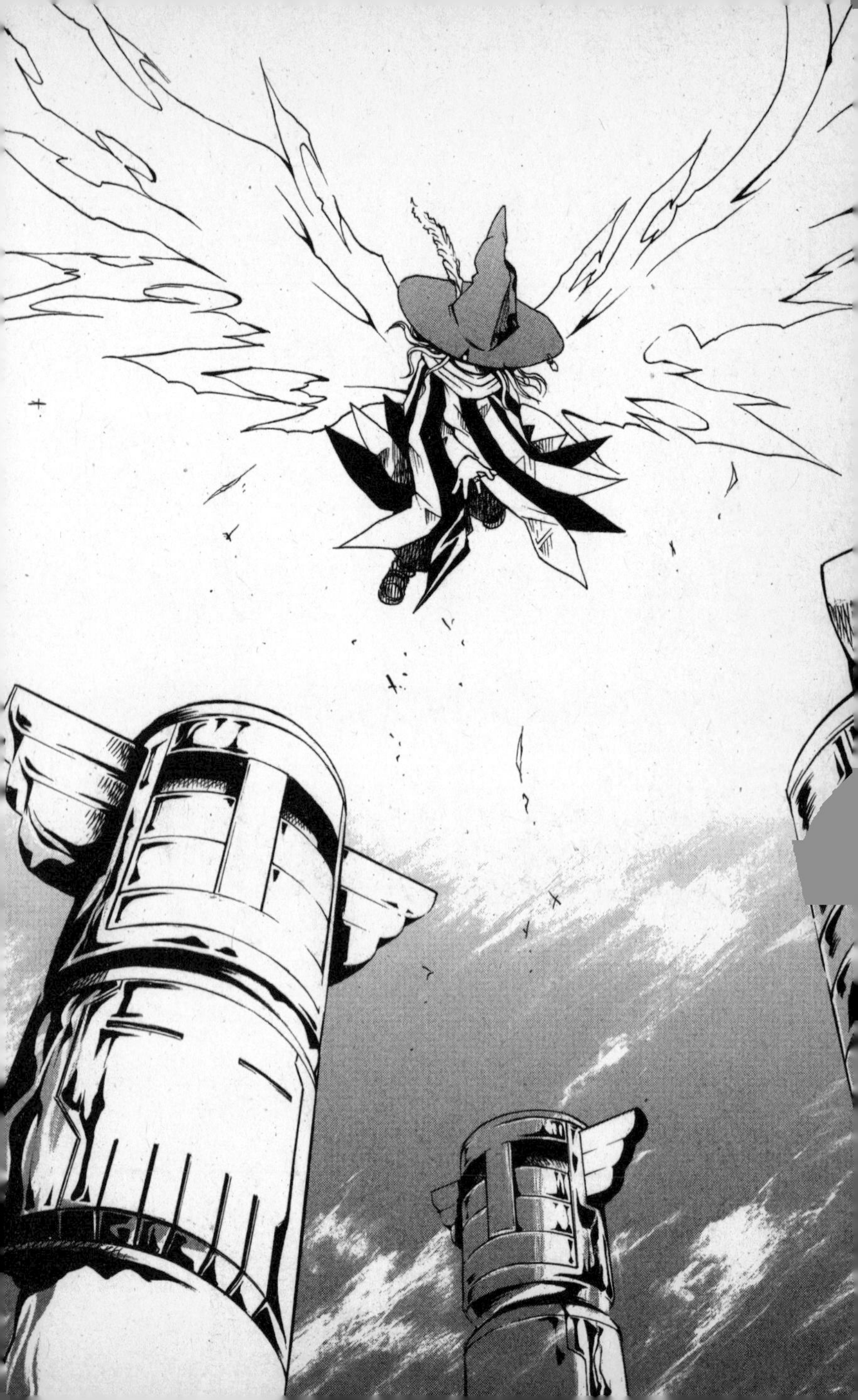

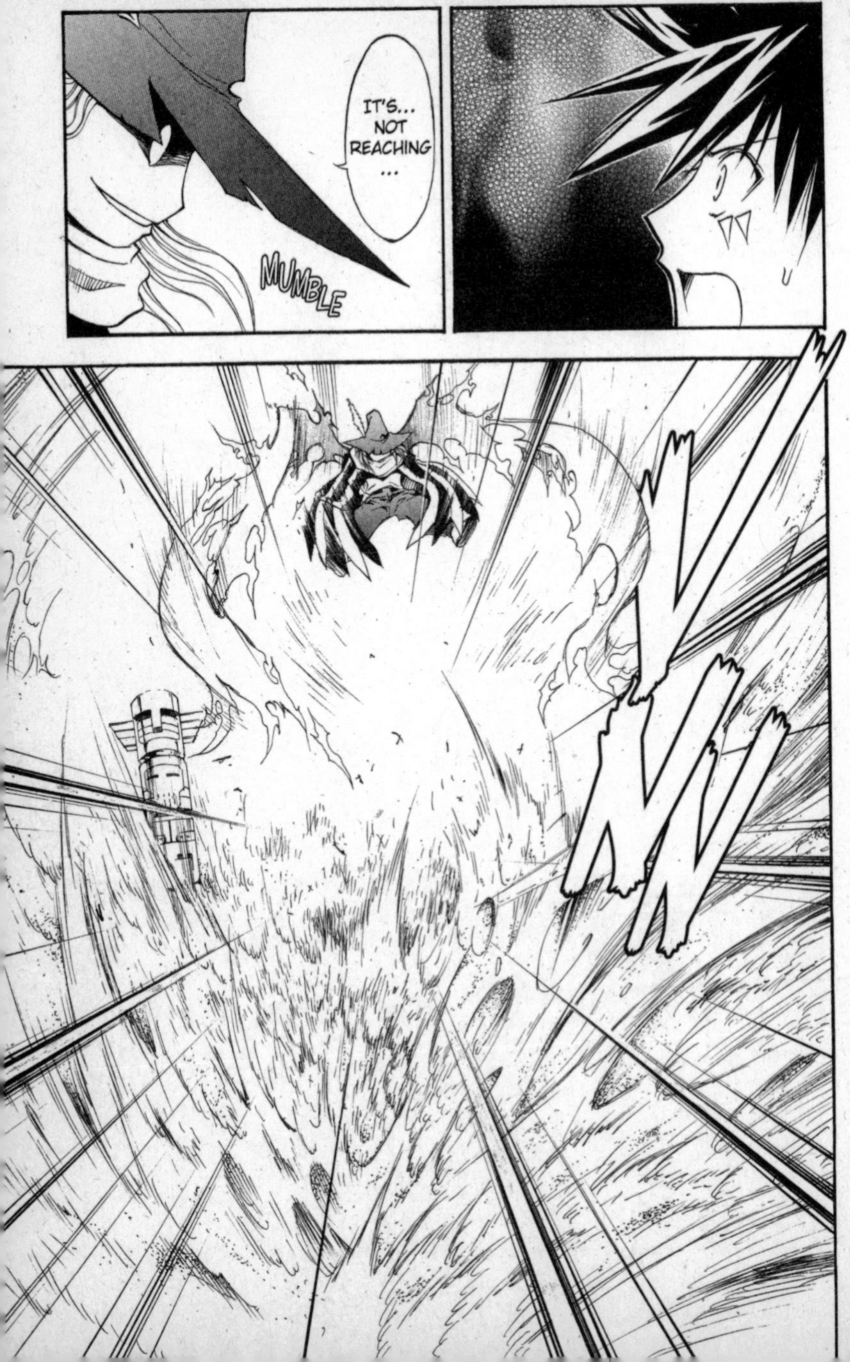
IT'S... NOT REACHING ...
MUMBLE

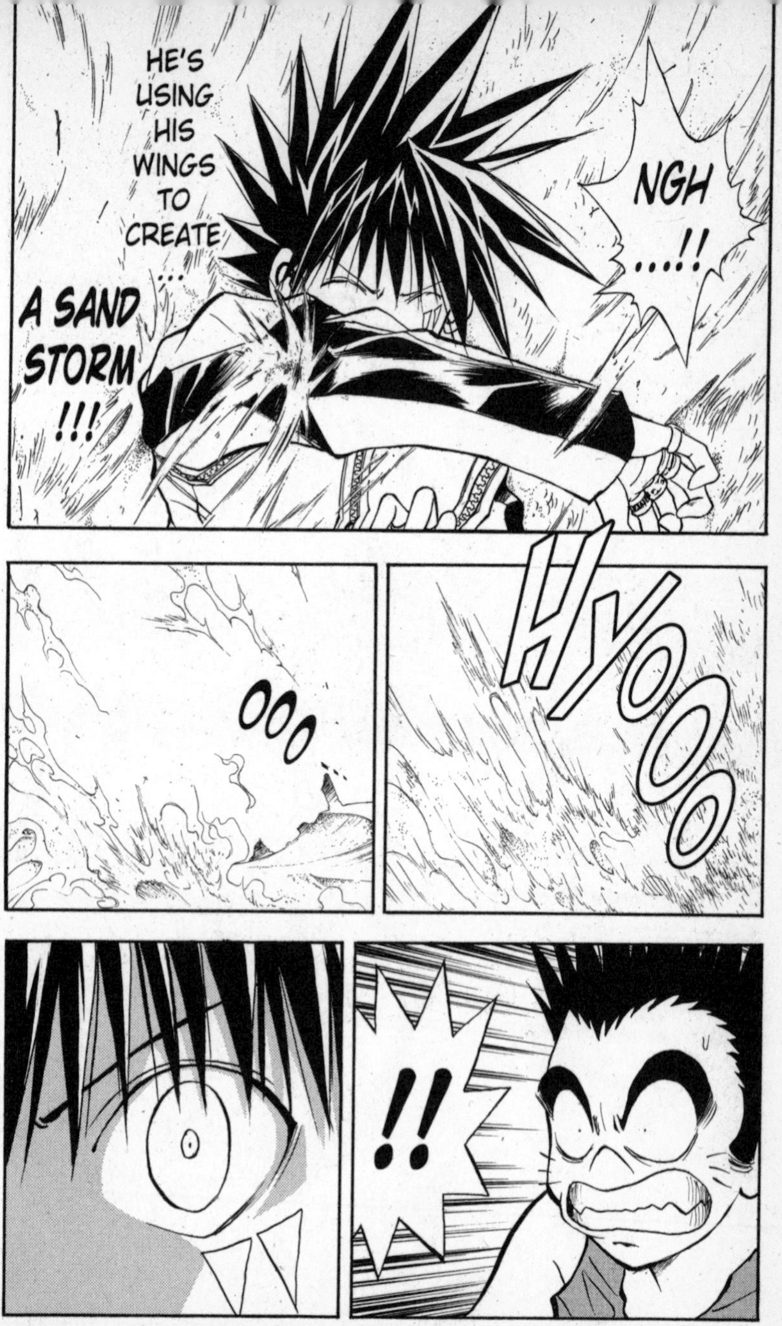
NGH ...!!
HE'S USING HIS WINGS TO CREATE ...
A SAND STORM !!!
HYOOO
OOO
!!

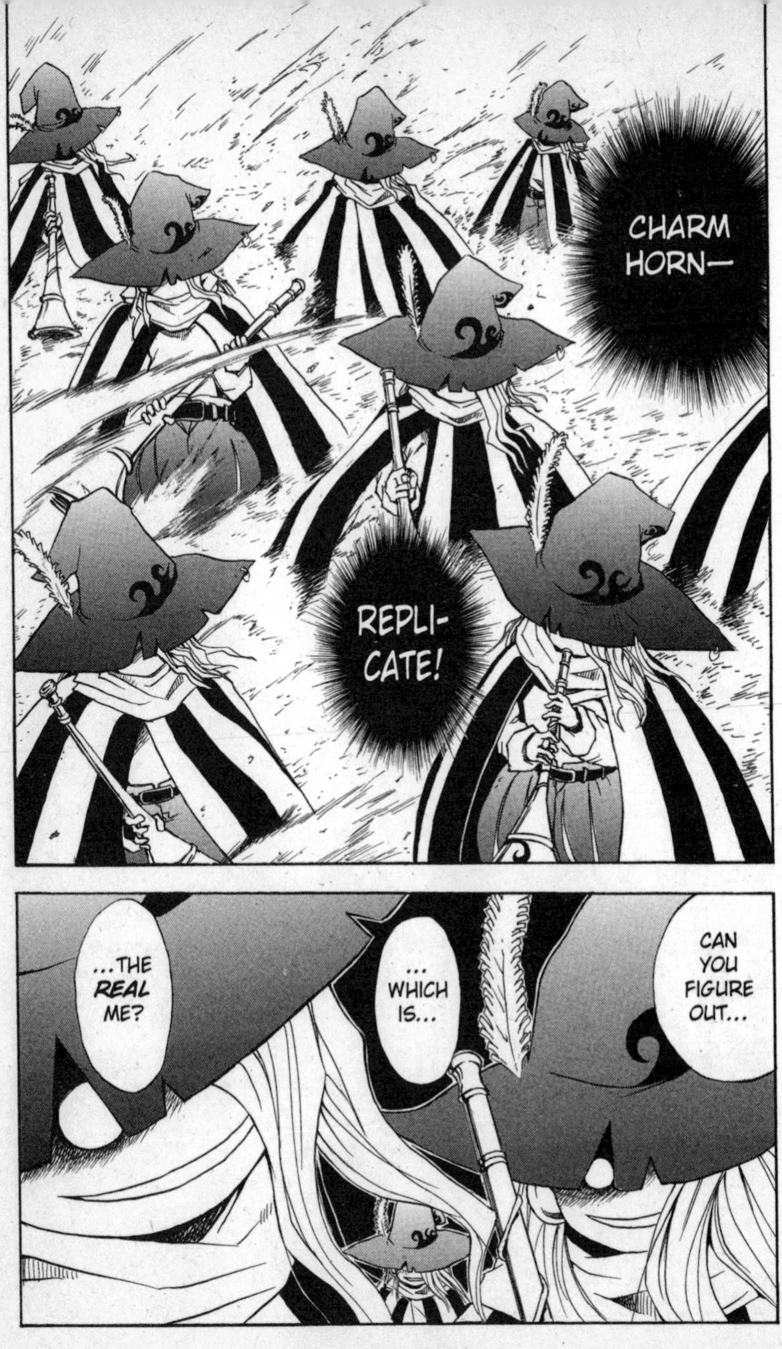
CHARM HORN—
REPLI-CATE!
CAN YOU FIGURE OUT...
...WHICH IS...
...THE *REAL* ME?

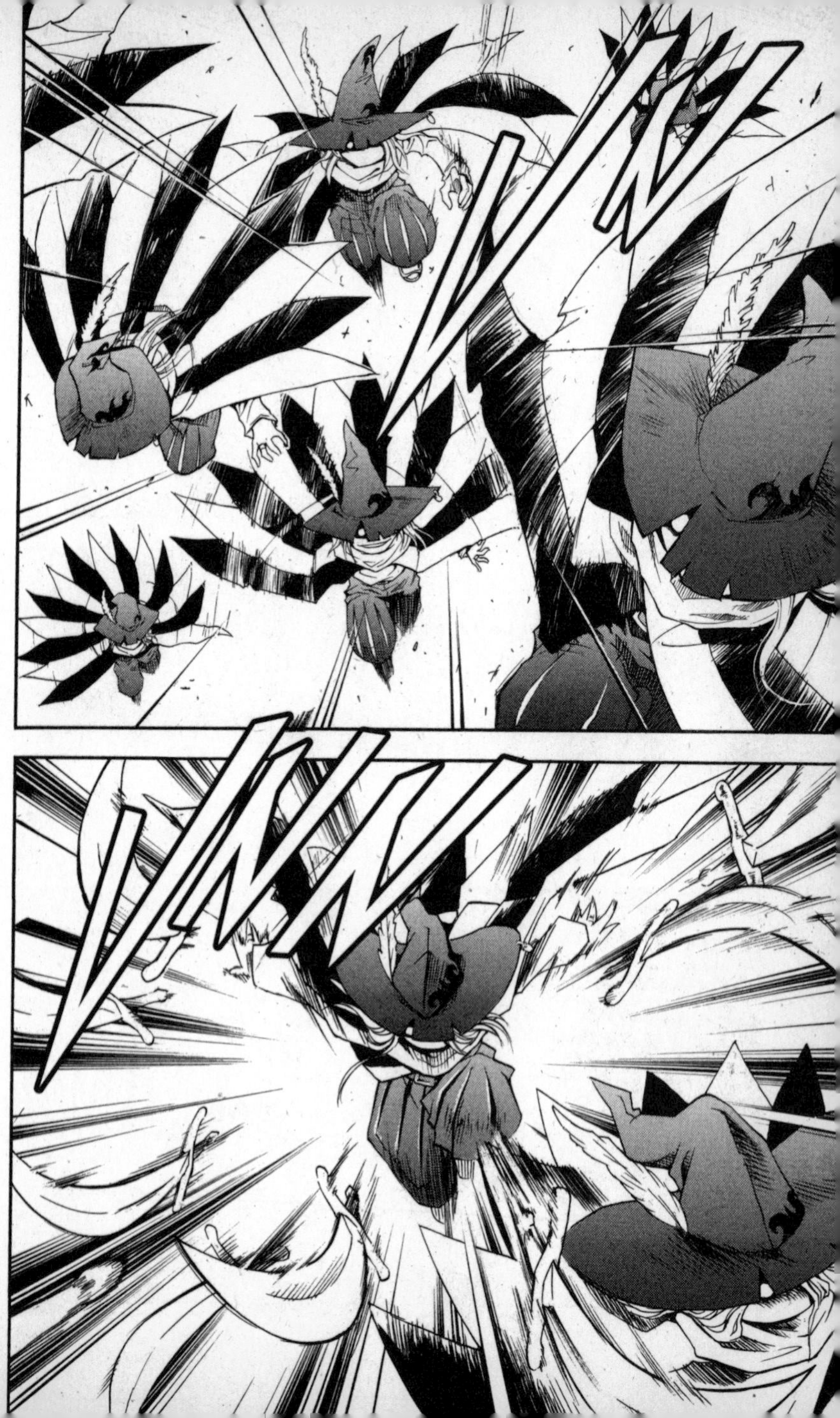

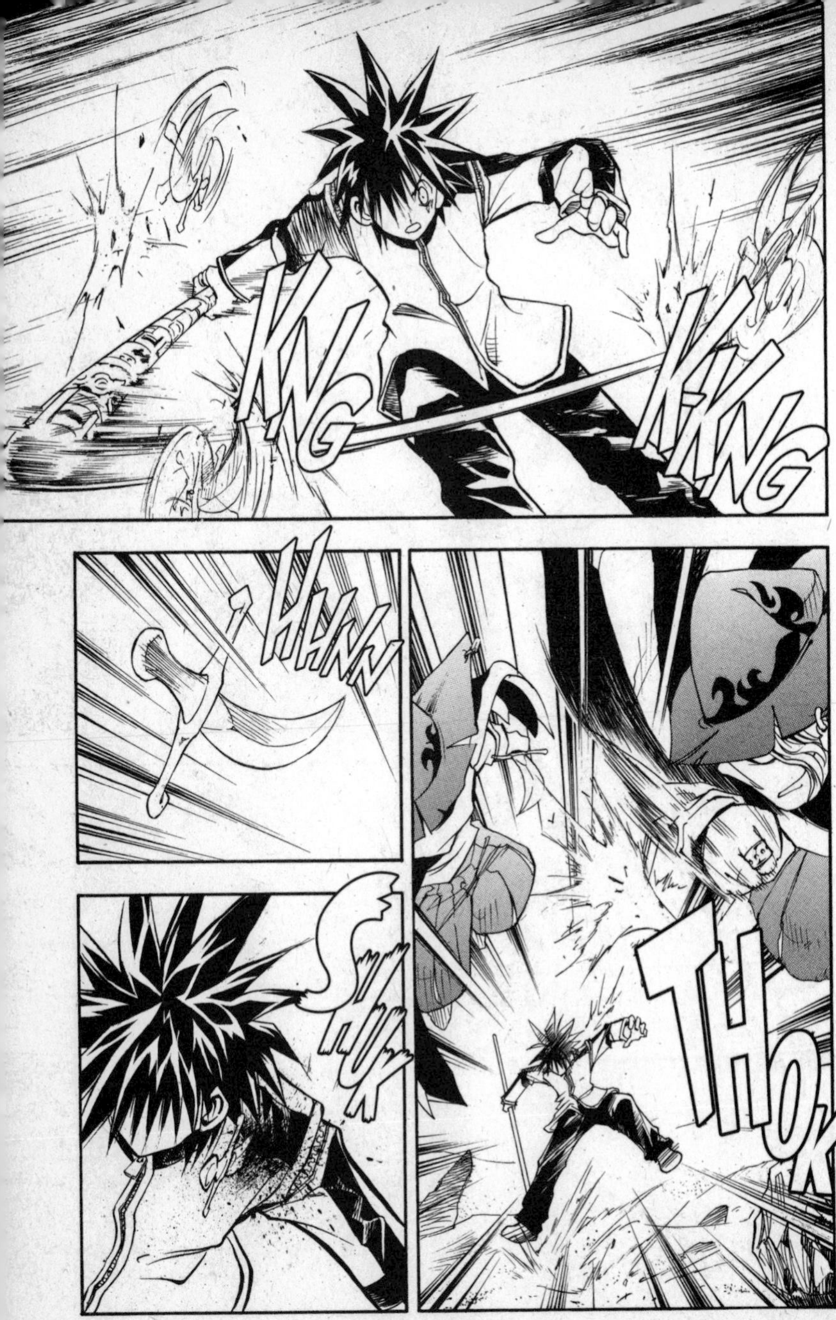
KING
KING
KING
THOK
VWANN
SHUK

DIRECT HIT!
HYA HAHA!
HEH ...
HEH HEH ...
NOW YOU'VE DONE IT.
YOU GOT ME MAD.
SHWP

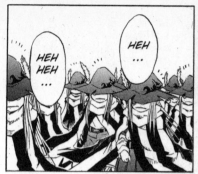

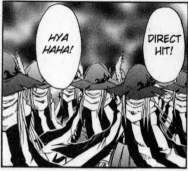

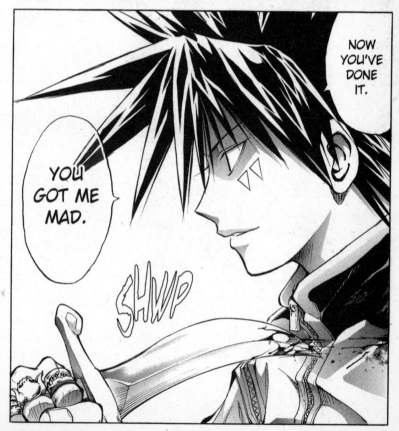

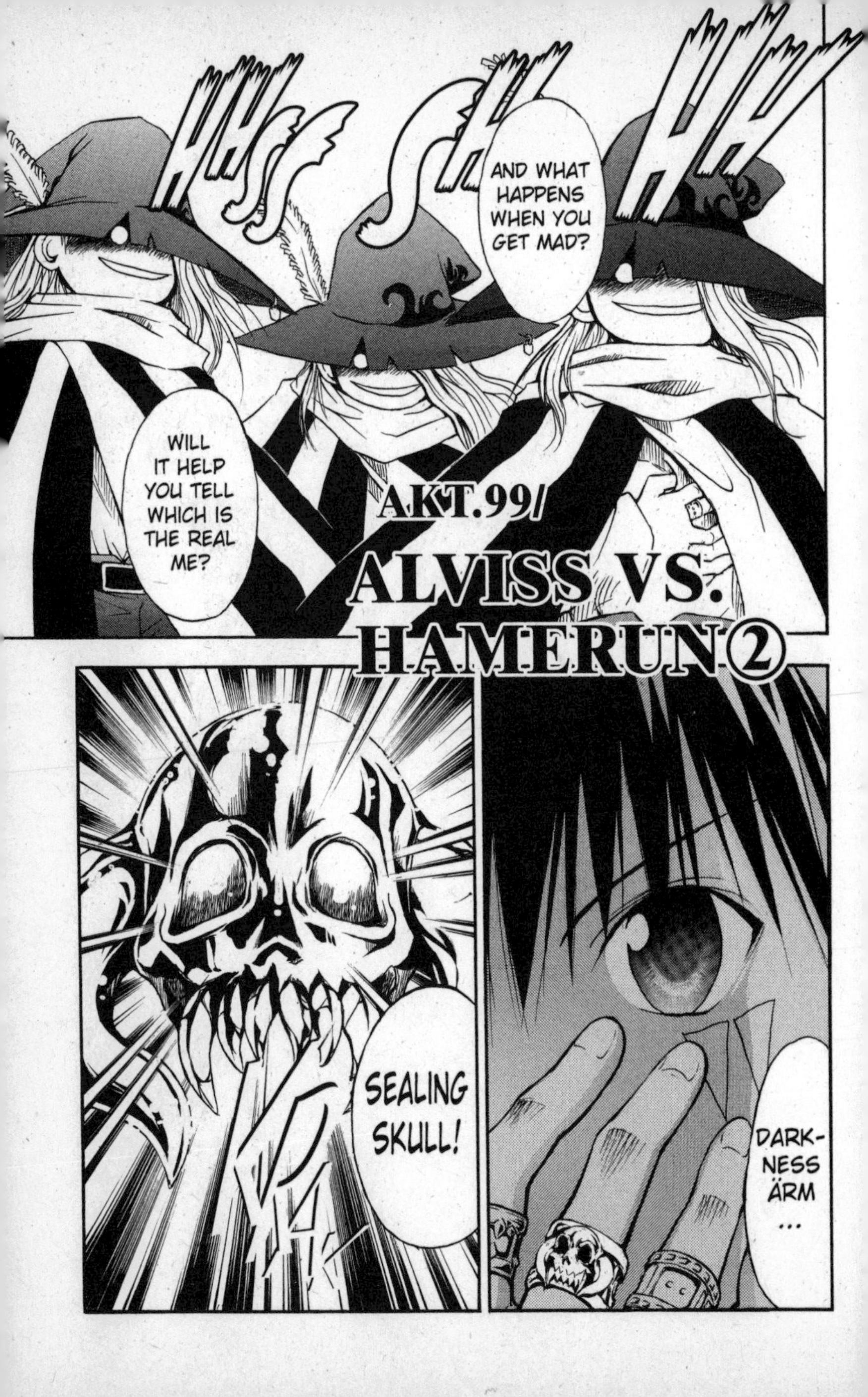
AND WHAT HAPPENS WHEN YOU GET MAD?
WILL IT HELP YOU TELL WHICH IS THE REAL ME?
AKT.99/
ALVISS VS. HAMERUN②
DARK-NESS ÄRM ...
SEALING SKULL!

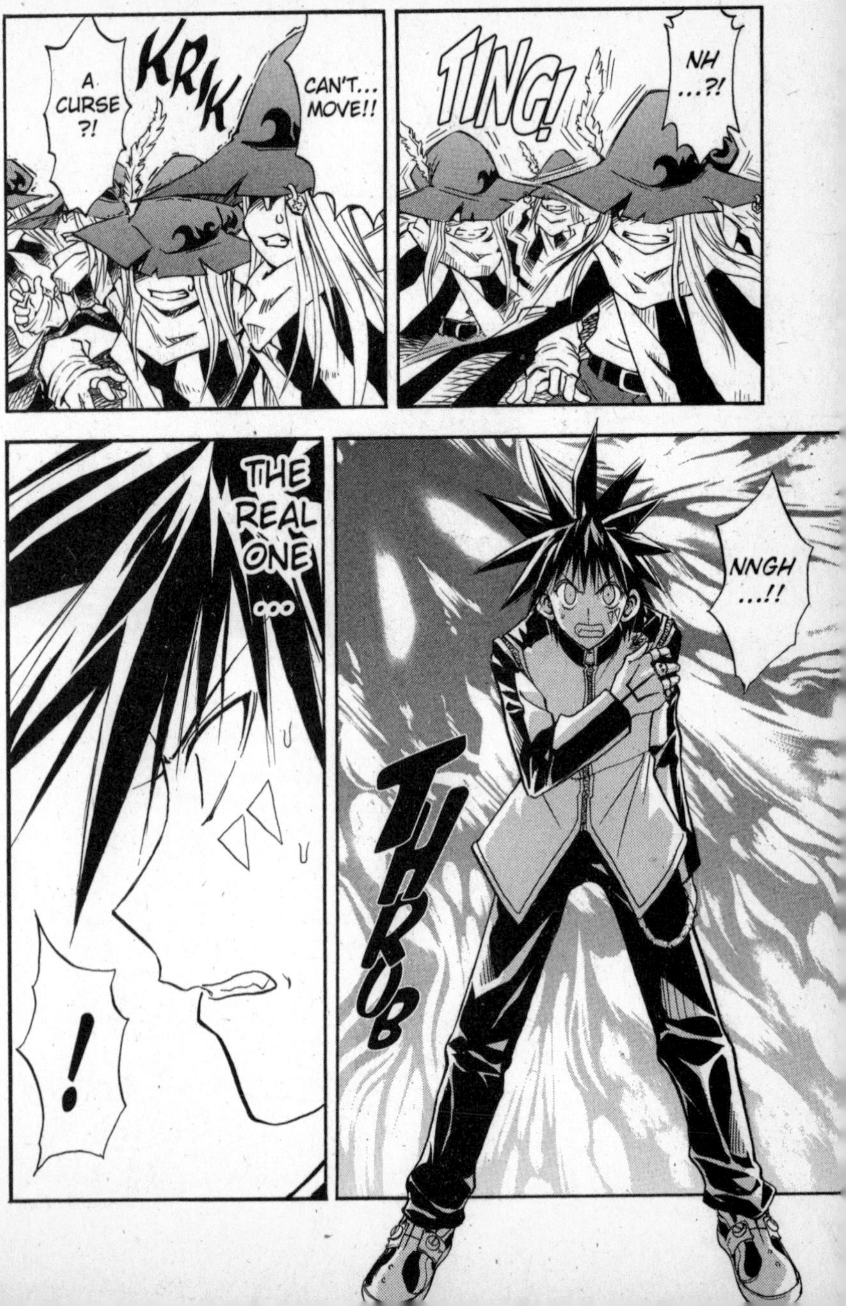
TING!
NH ...?!
CAN'T... MOVE!!
KRIK
A CURSE ?!
NNGH ...!!
THROB
THE REAL ONE ...
!

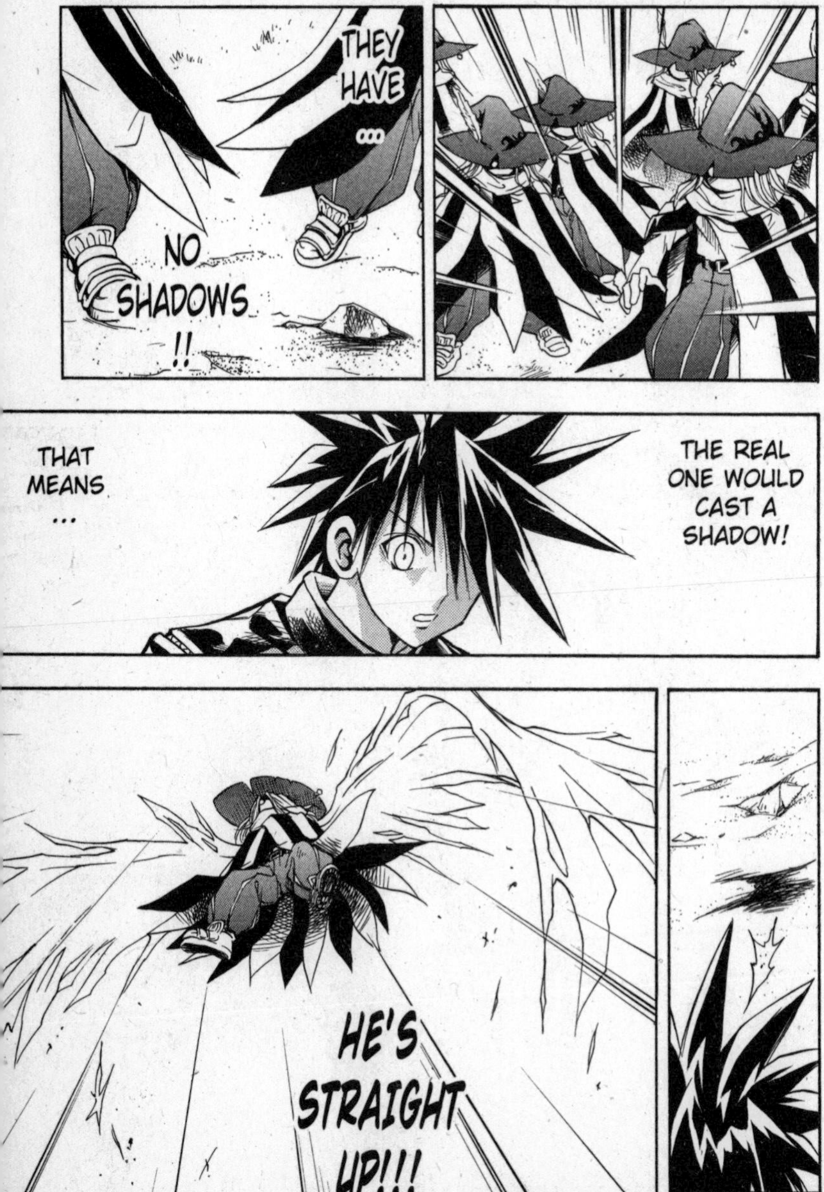
THEY HAVE ...
NO SHADOWS !!
THE REAL ONE WOULD CAST A SHADOW!
THAT MEANS ...
HE'S STRAIGHT UP!!!

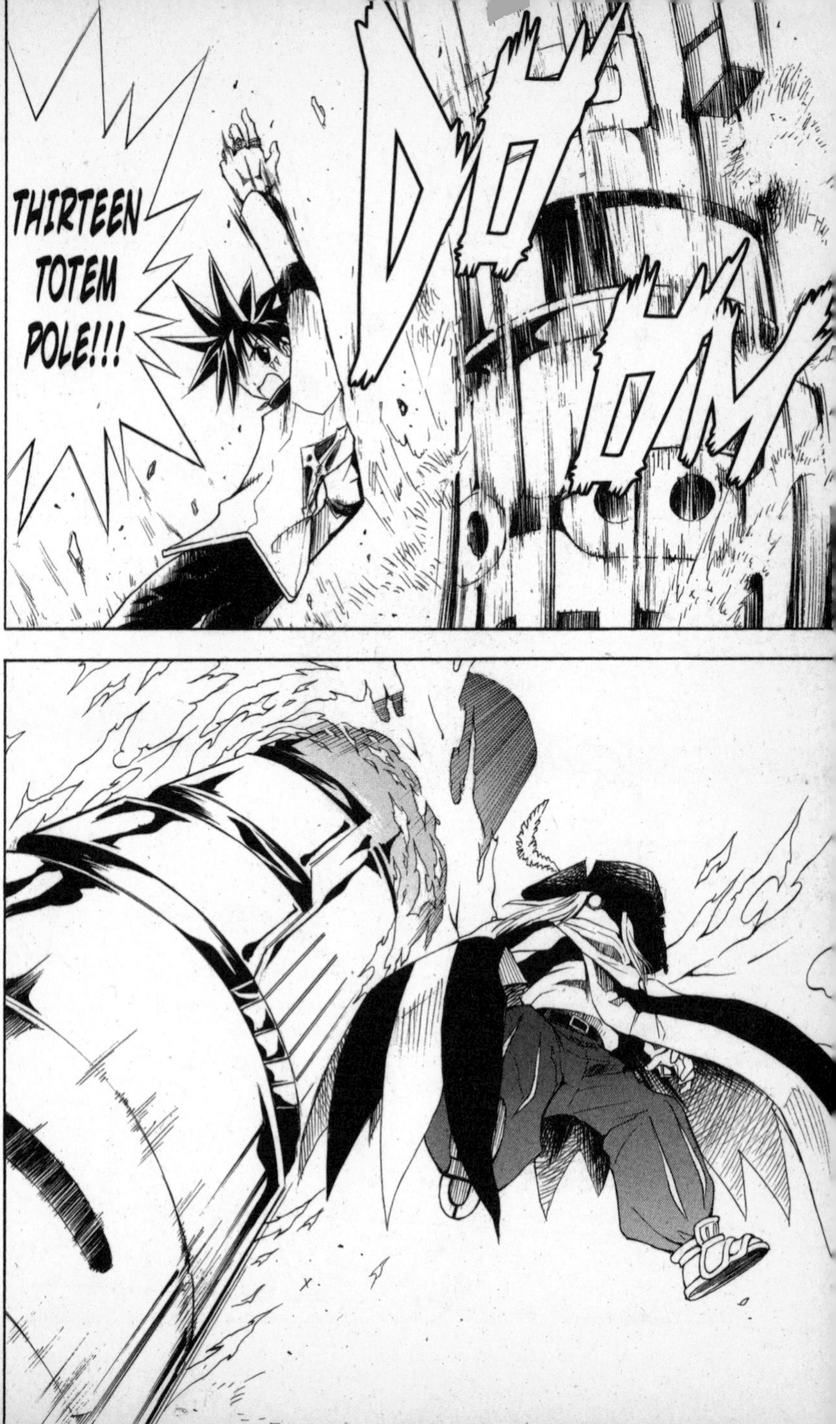
THIRTEEN TOTEM POLE!!!

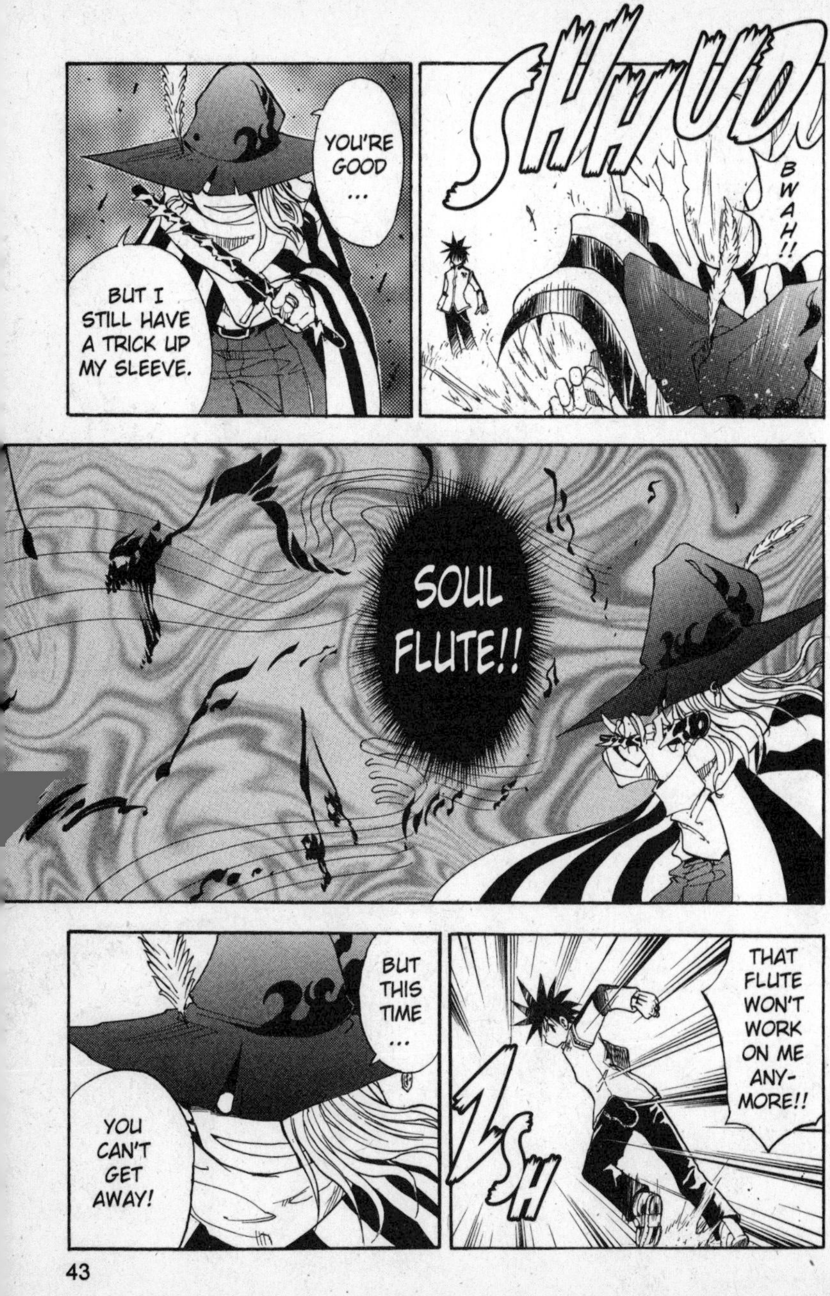
YOU'RE GOOD ...
BUT I STILL HAVE A TRICK UP MY SLEEVE.
SHHUO
BWAH!!
SOUL FLUTE!!
BUT THIS TIME ...
YOU CAN'T GET AWAY!
ZSH
THAT FLUTE WON'T WORK ON ME ANY-MORE!!

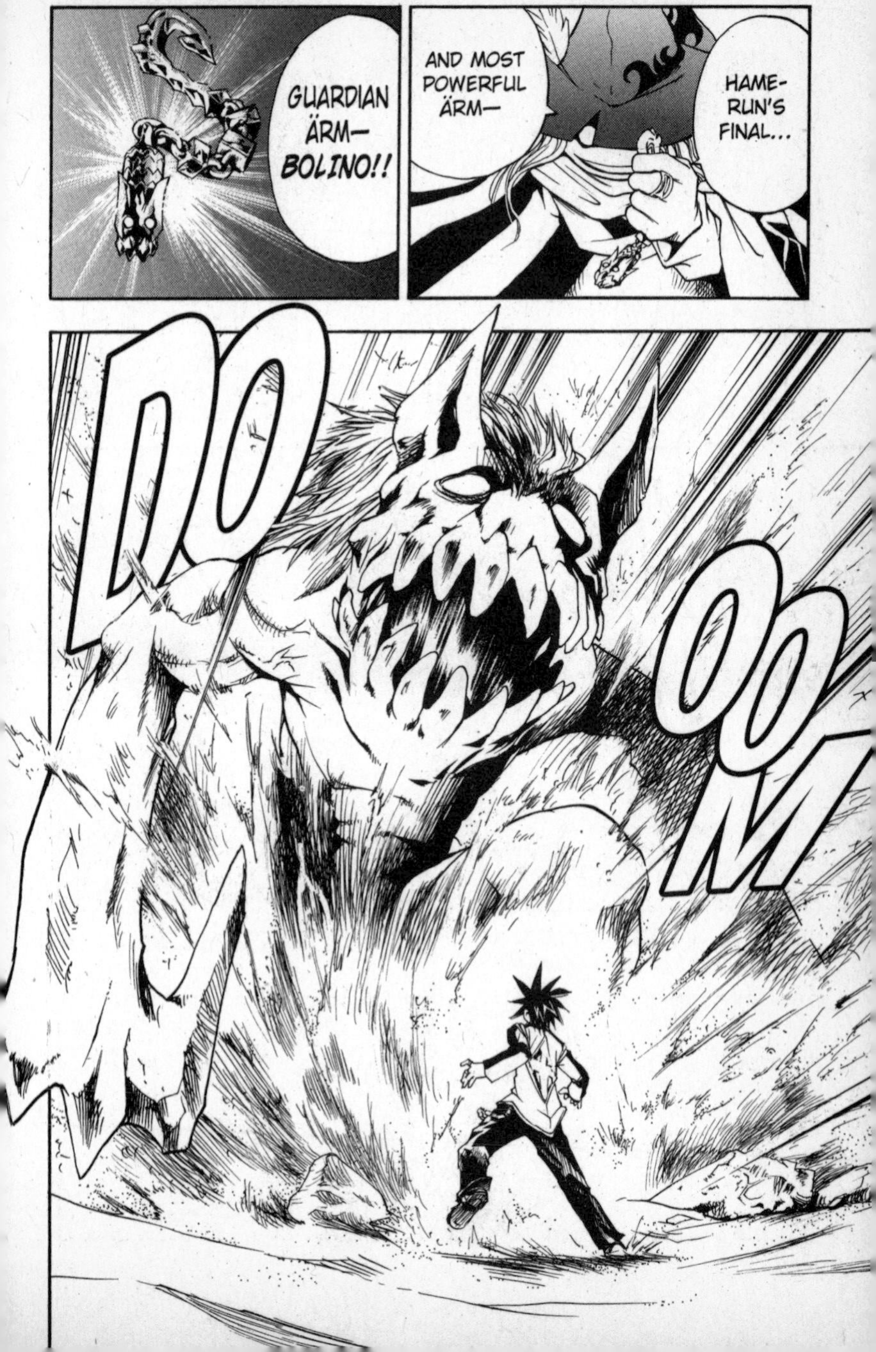
HAME-RUN'S FINAL...
AND MOST POWERFUL ÄRM—
GUARDIAN ÄRM— BOLINO!!
DOOOOM

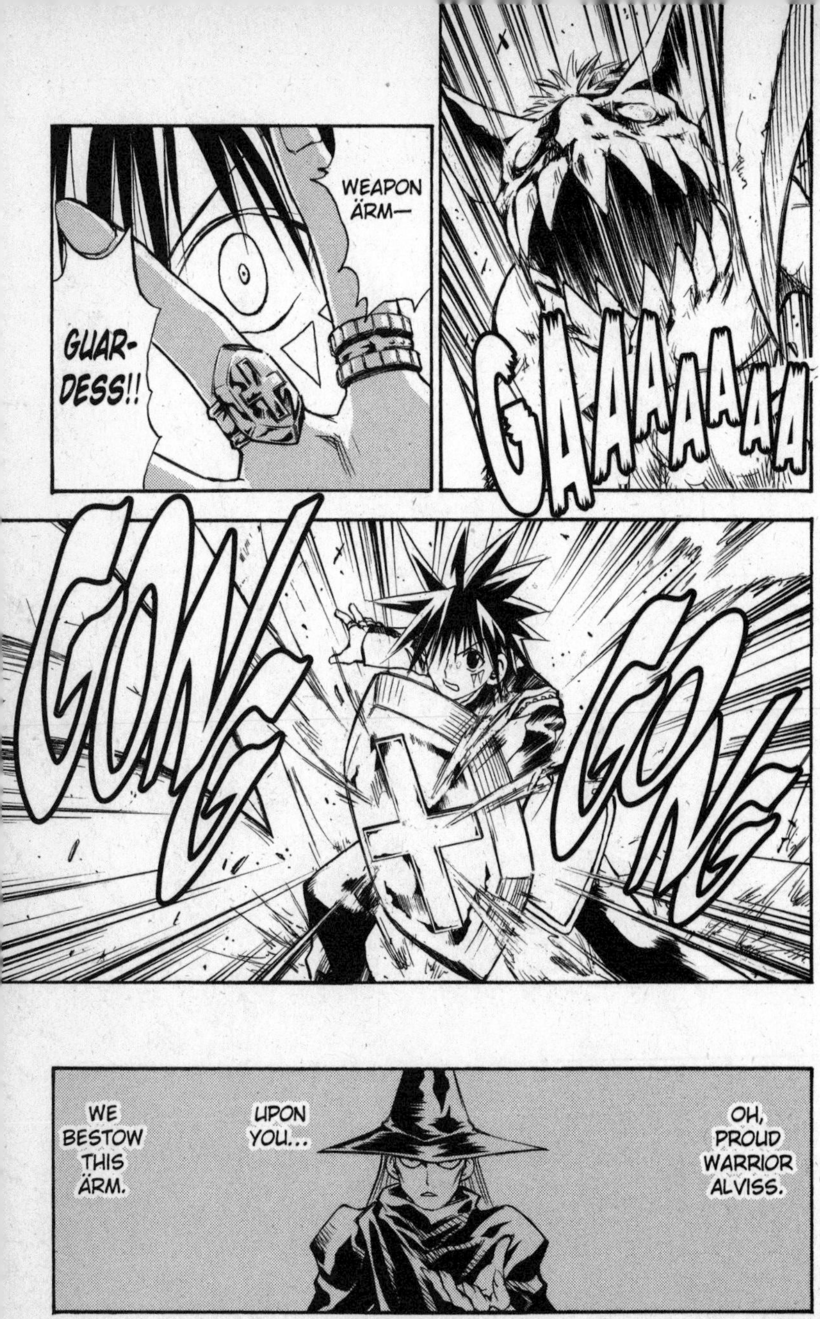
GAAAAAA
WEAPON ÄRM—
GUAR-DESS!!
GON
GON
OH, PROUD WARRIOR ALVISS.
UPON YOU...
WE BESTOW THIS ÄRM.

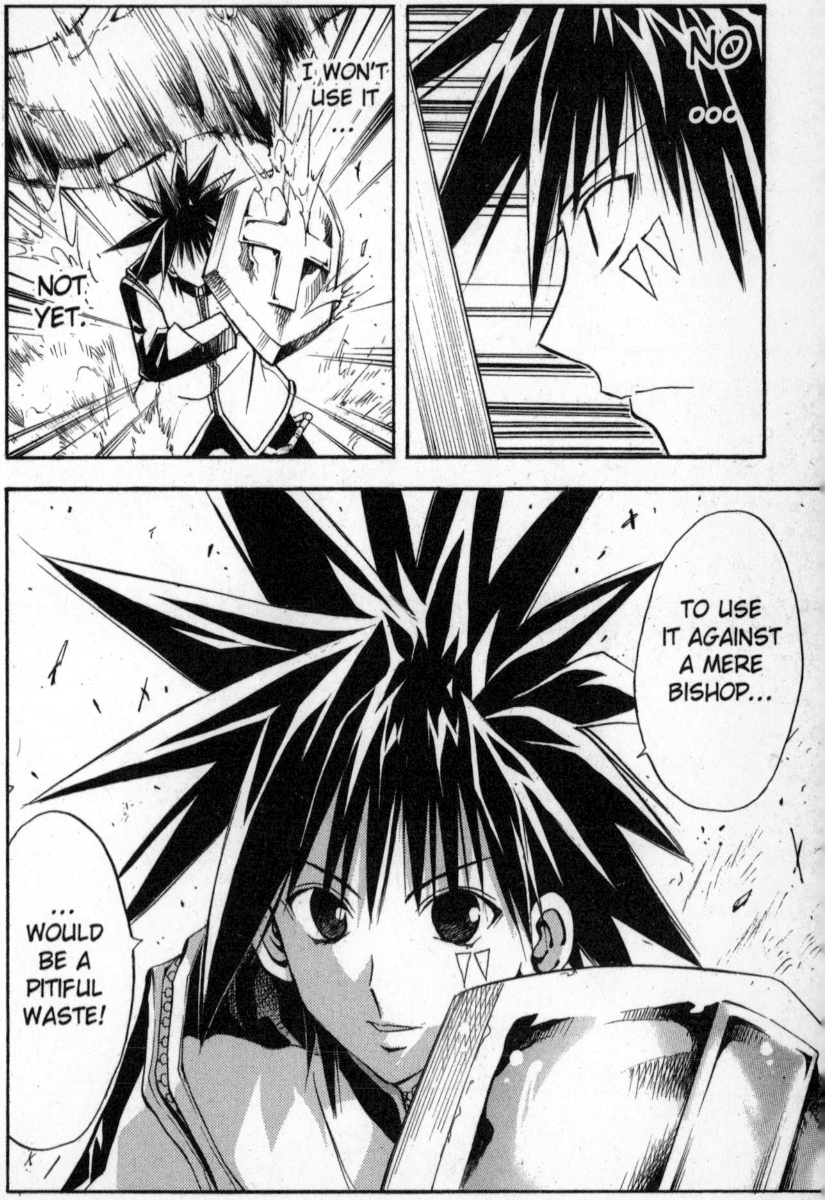
NO ...
I WON'T USE IT ...
NOT YET.
TO USE IT AGAINST A MERE BISHOP...
... WOULD BE A PITIFUL WASTE!

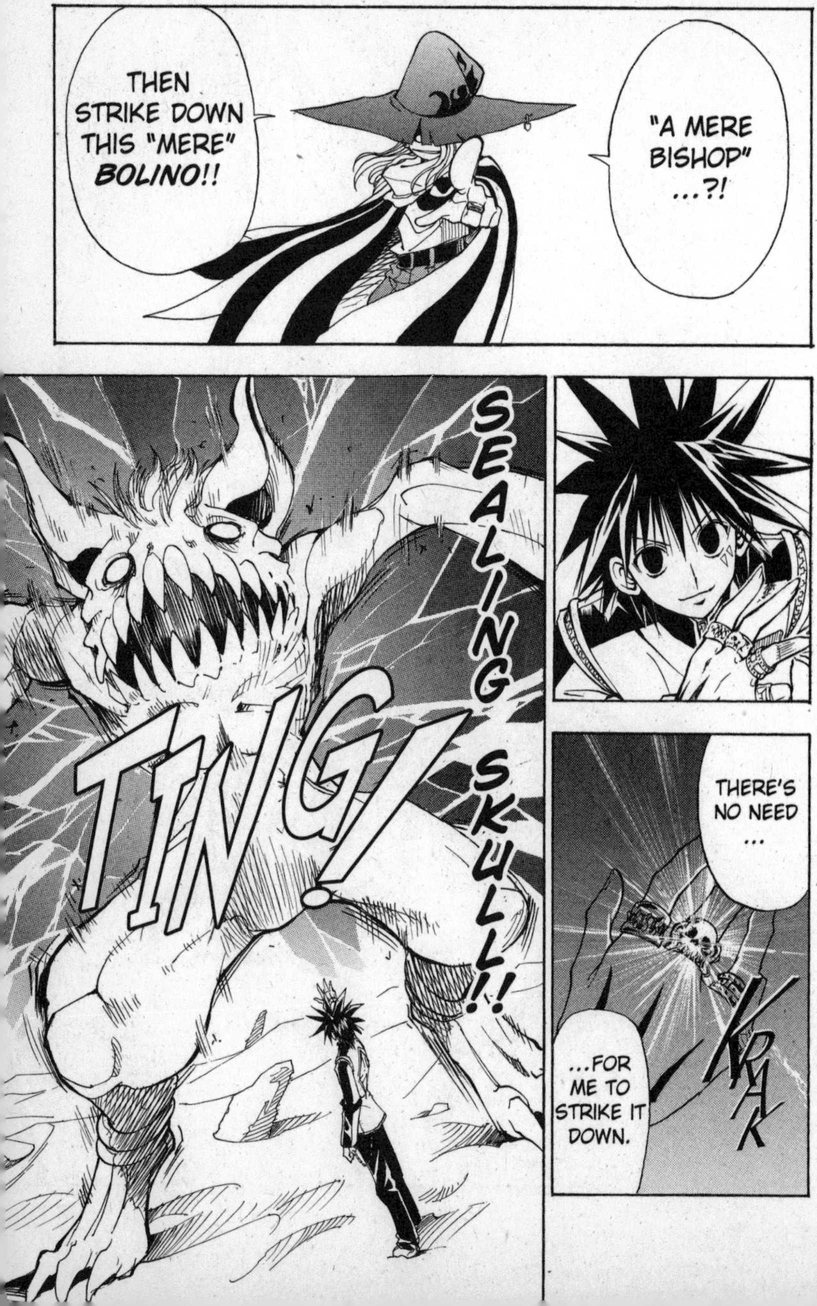
"A MERE BISHOP" ...?!
THEN STRIKE DOWN THIS "MERE" BOLINO!!
THERE'S NO NEED ...
...FOR ME TO STRIKE IT DOWN.
KRAK
SEALING SKULL!!
TING!

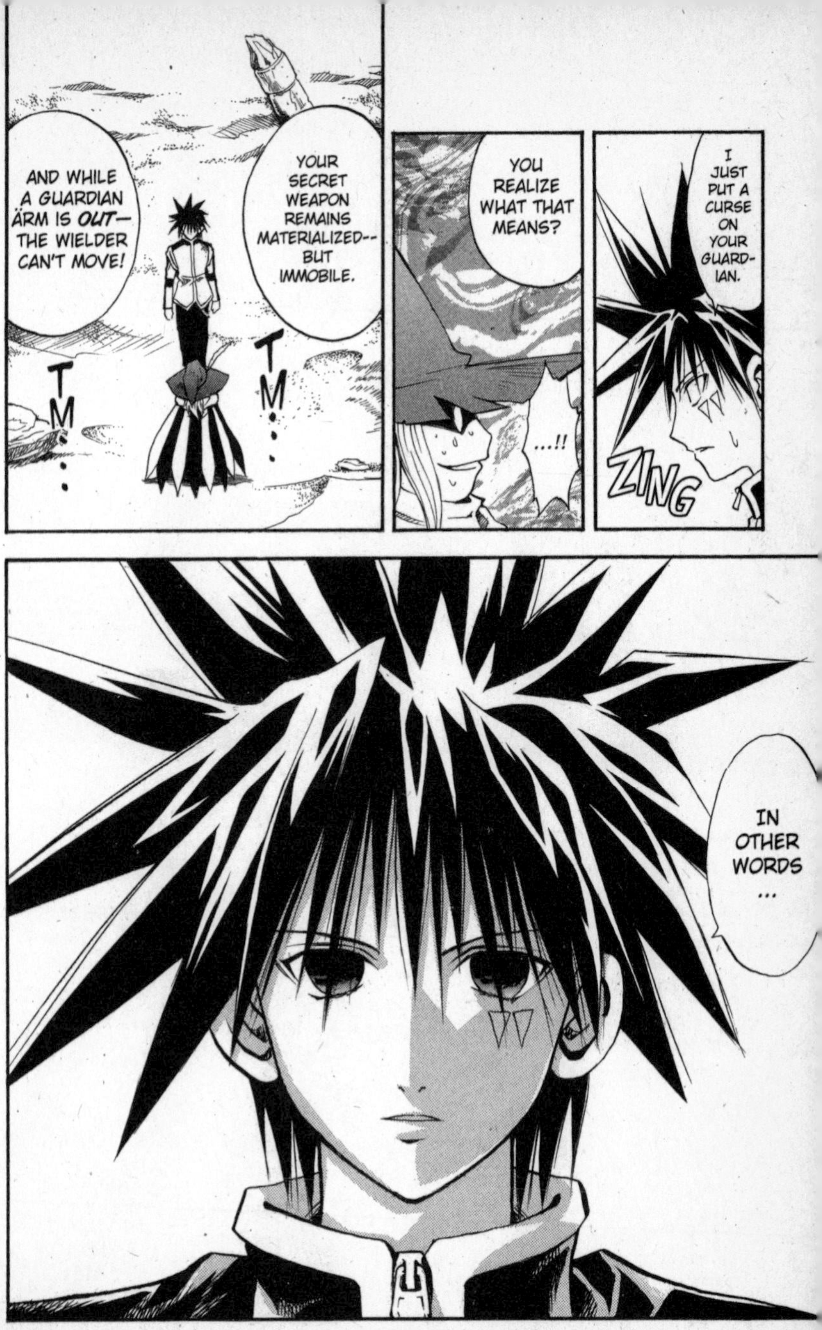
I JUST PUT A CURSE ON YOUR GUARDIAN.
ZING
YOU REALIZE WHAT THAT MEANS?
...!!
YOUR SECRET WEAPON REMAINS MATERIALIZED--BUT IMMOBILE.
TM...
AND WHILE A GUARDIAN ÄRM IS *OUT*—THE WIELDER CAN'T MOVE!
TM...
IN OTHER WORDS ...

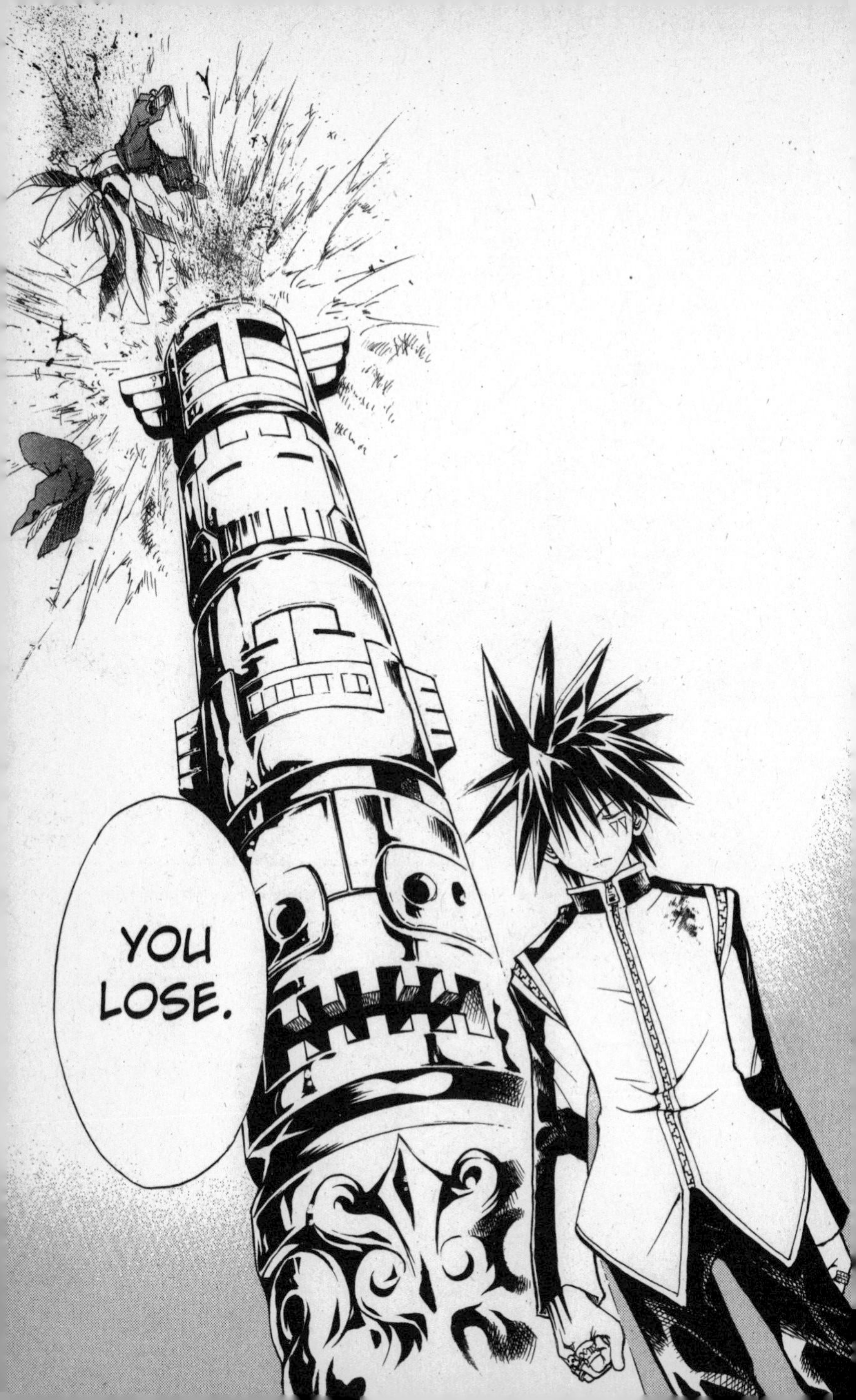
YOU LOSE.

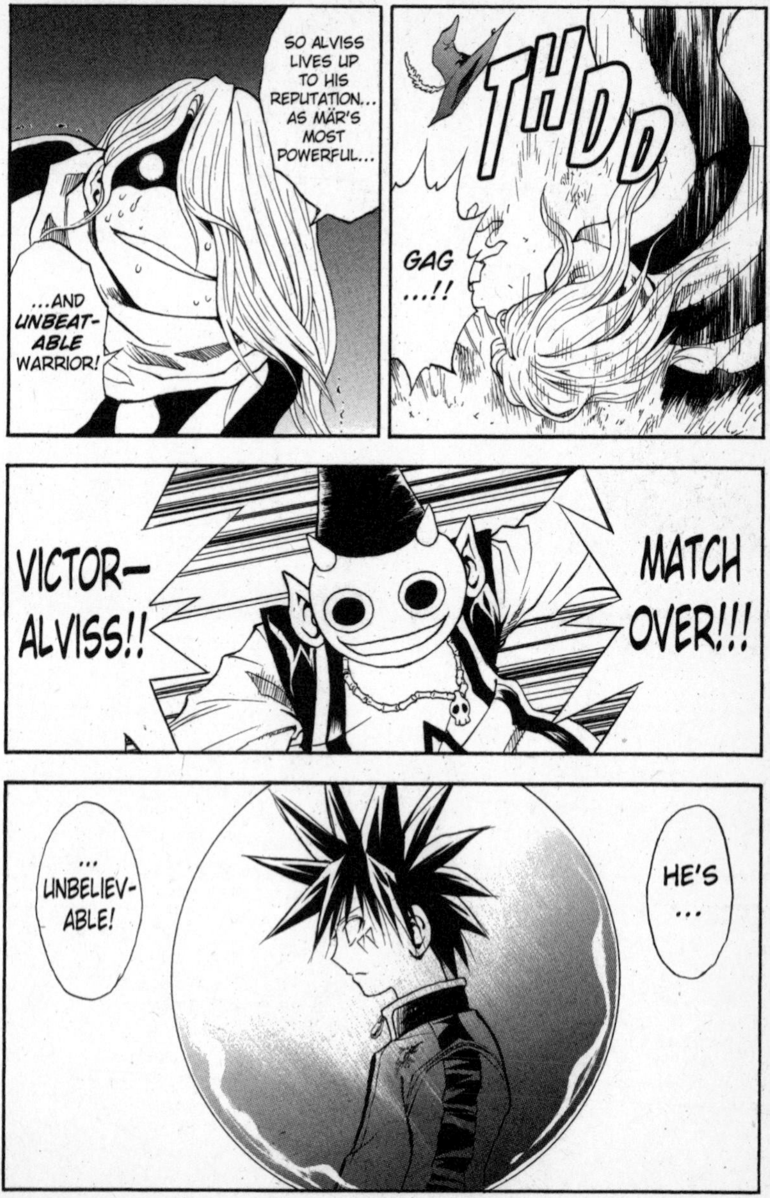
THDD
GAG ...!!
SO ALVISS LIVES UP TO HIS REPUTATION... AS MÄR'S MOST POWERFUL...
...AND UNBEAT-ABLE WARRIOR!
MATCH OVER!!!
VICTOR— ALVISS!!
HE'S ...
... UNBELIEV-ABLE!

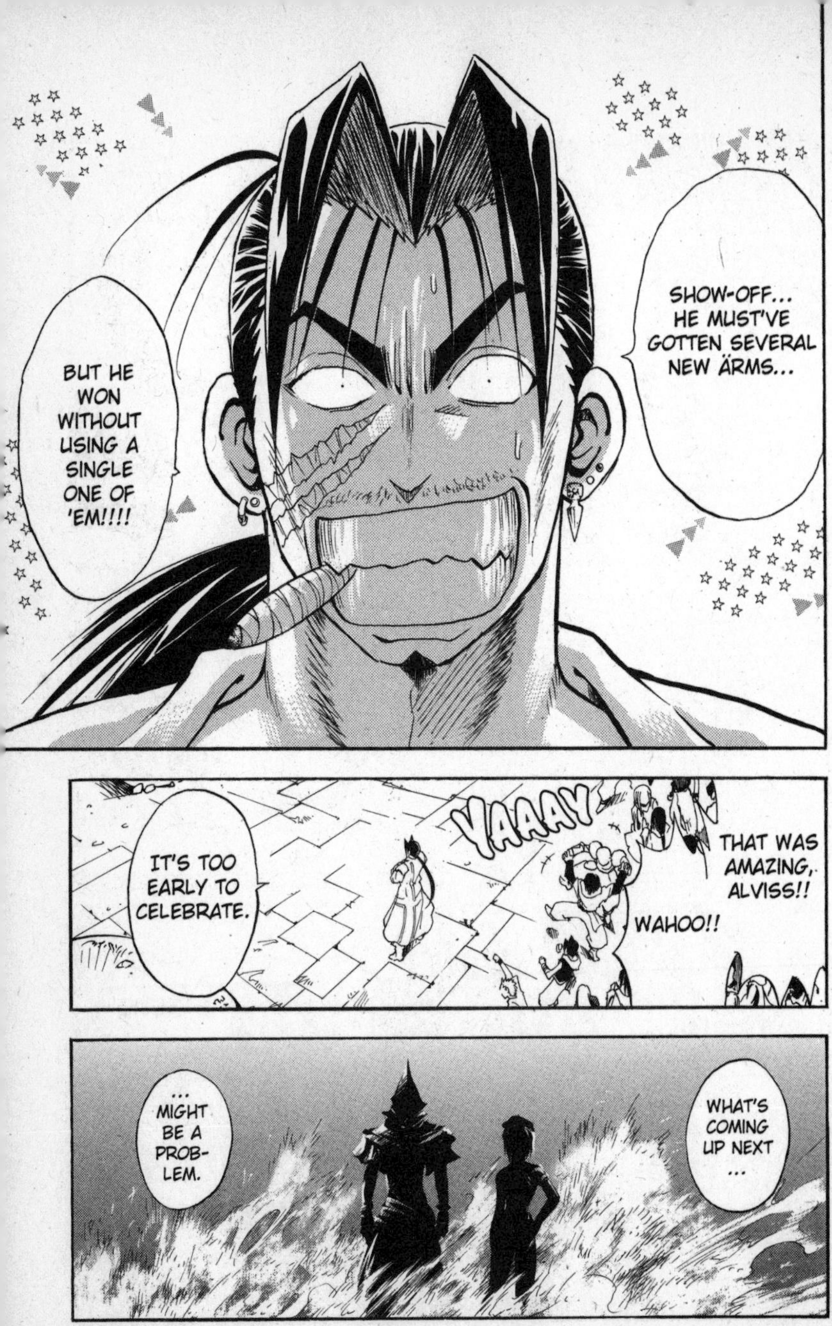
SHOW-OFF... HE MUST'VE GOTTEN SEVERAL NEW ÄRMS...
BUT HE WON WITHOUT USING A SINGLE ONE OF 'EM!!!!
THAT WAS AMAZING, ALVISS!!
WAHOO!!
YAAAY
IT'S TOO EARLY TO CELEBRATE.
WHAT'S COMING UP NEXT ...
... MIGHT BE A PROB-LEM.

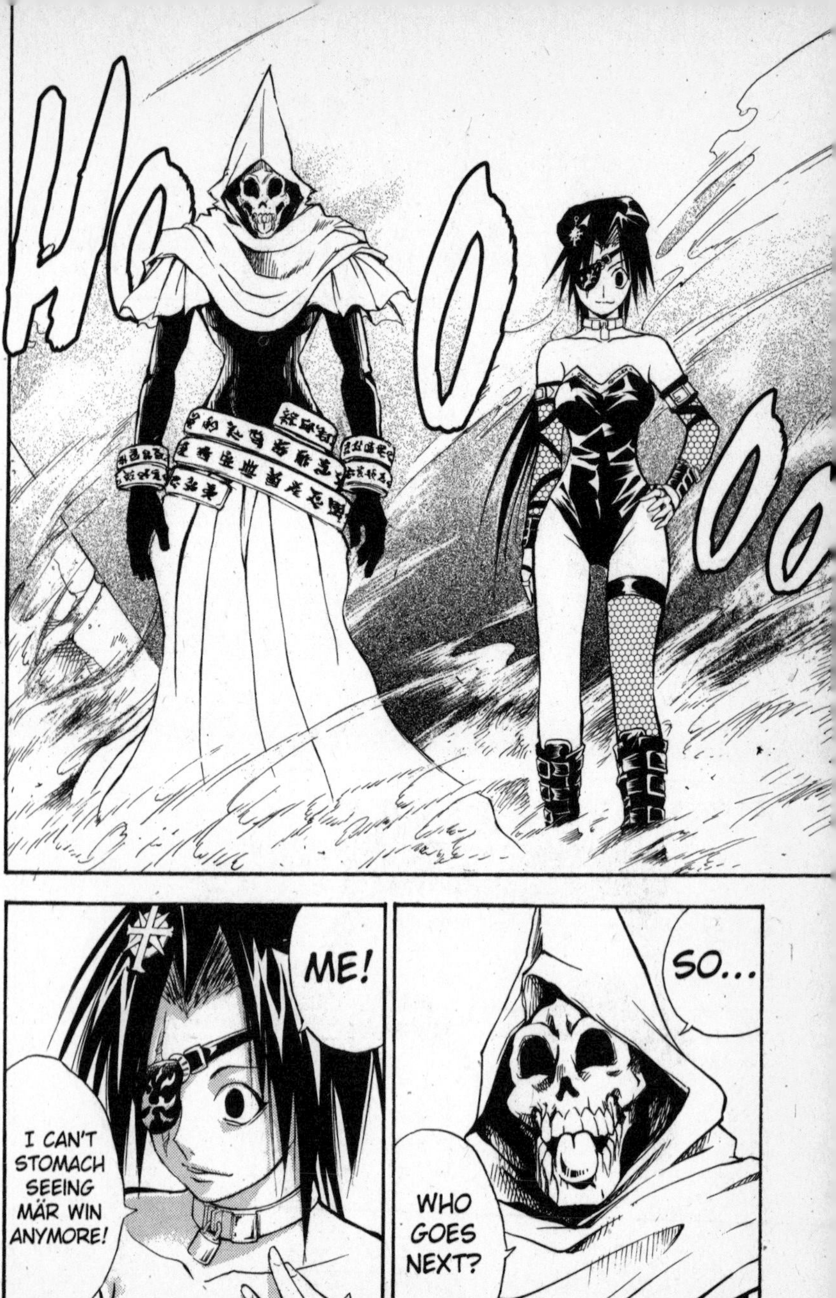
HOOOOO
SO...
WHO GOES NEXT?
ME!
I CAN'T STOMACH SEEING MÄR WIN ANYMORE!

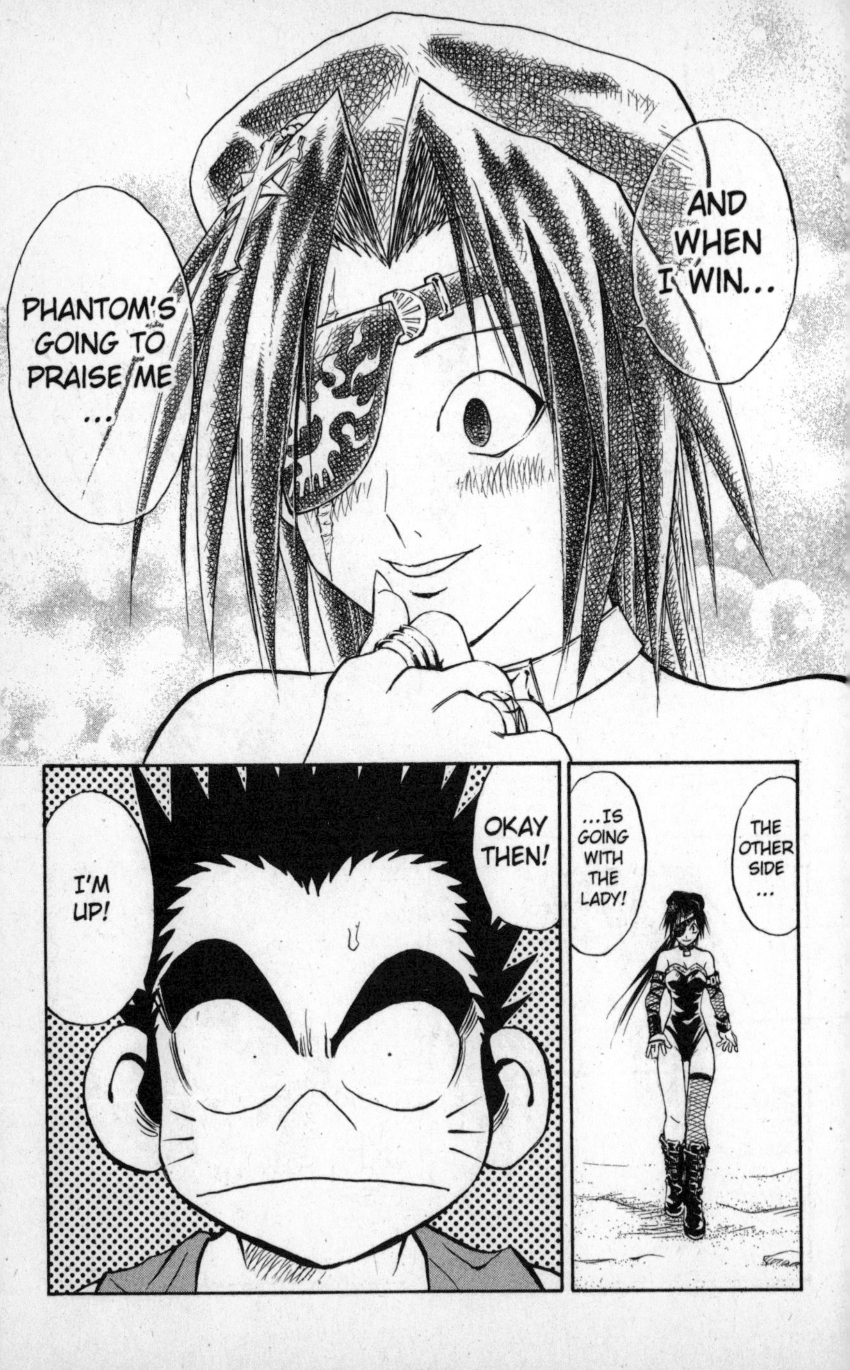
AND WHEN I WIN...
PHANTOM'S GOING TO PRAISE ME ...
THE OTHER SIDE ...
...IS GOING WITH THE LADY!
OKAY THEN!
I'M UP!

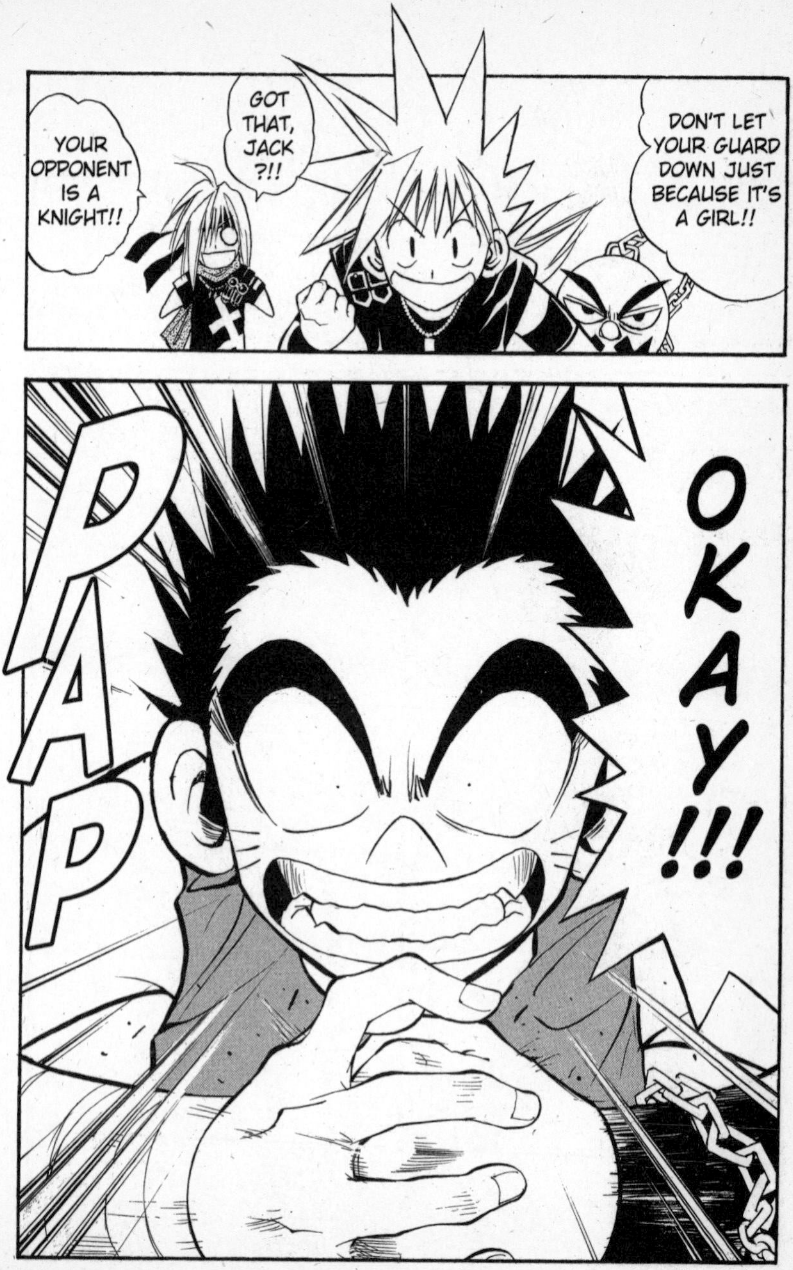
DON'T LET YOUR GUARD DOWN JUST BECAUSE IT'S A GIRL!!
GOT THAT, JACK?!!
YOUR OPPONENT IS A KNIGHT!!
OKAY!!!
PAP

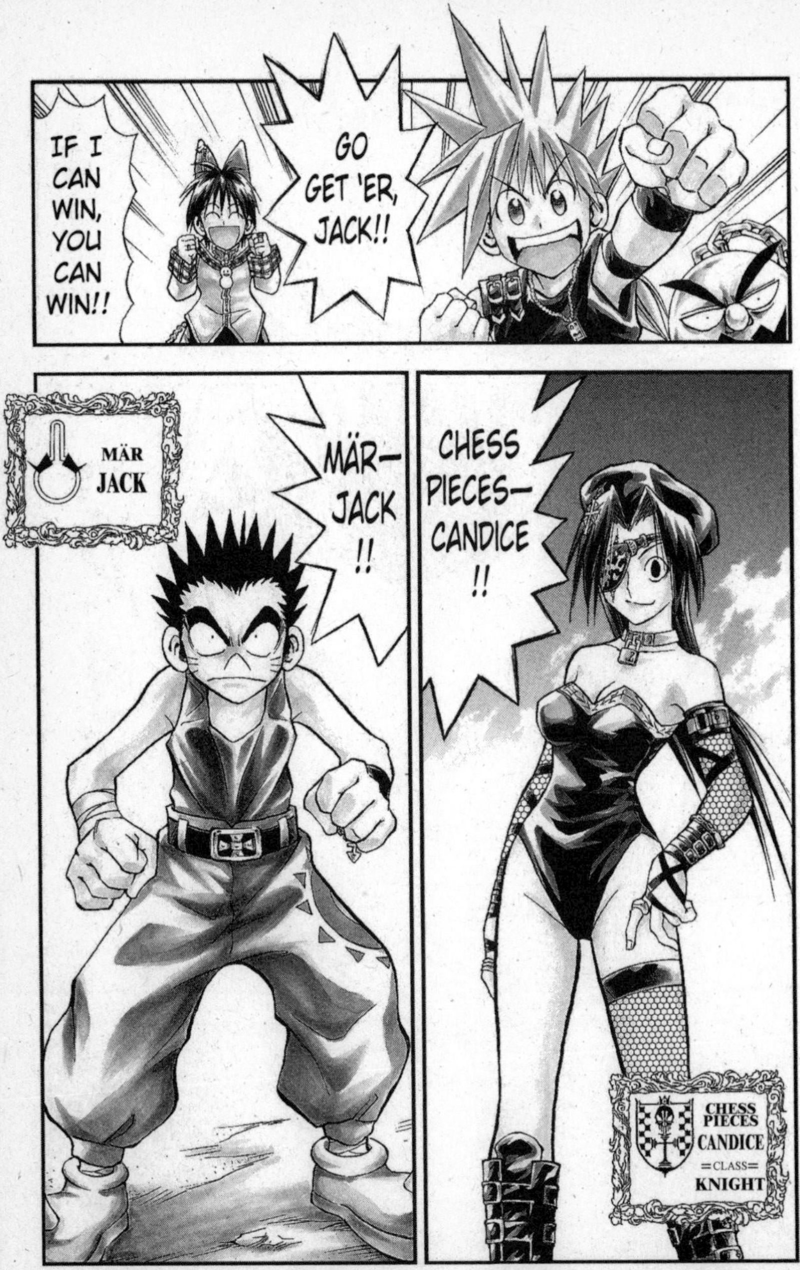
GO GET 'ER, JACK!!
IF I CAN WIN, YOU CAN WIN!!
CHESS PIECES—CANDICE!!
CHESS PIECES CANDICE
=CLASS=
KNIGHT
MÄR—JACK!!
MÄR JACK

AKT.100/ JACK VS. CANDICE ①

AKT.100/ JACK VS. CANDICE ①

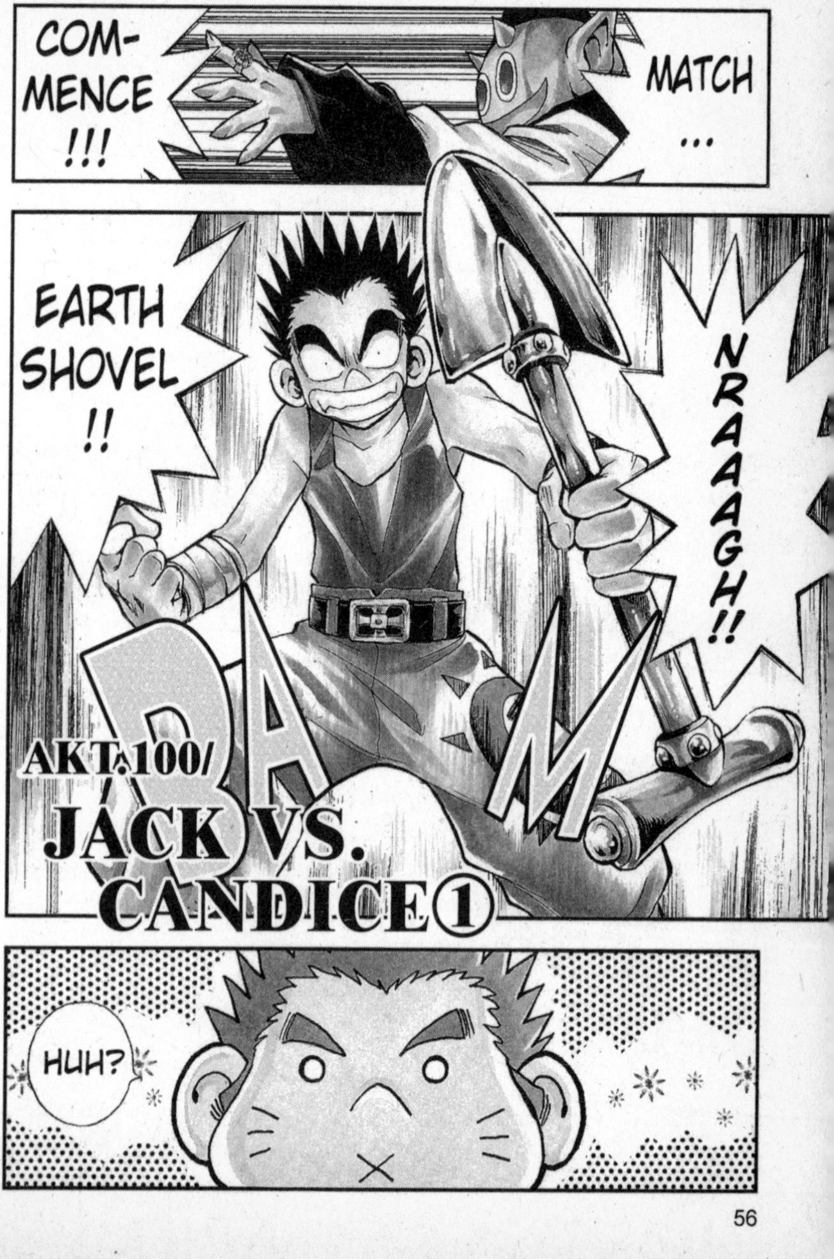
MATCH ...
COM-MENCE !!!
NRAAAAGH!!
EARTH SHOVEL !!
DAM
HUH?

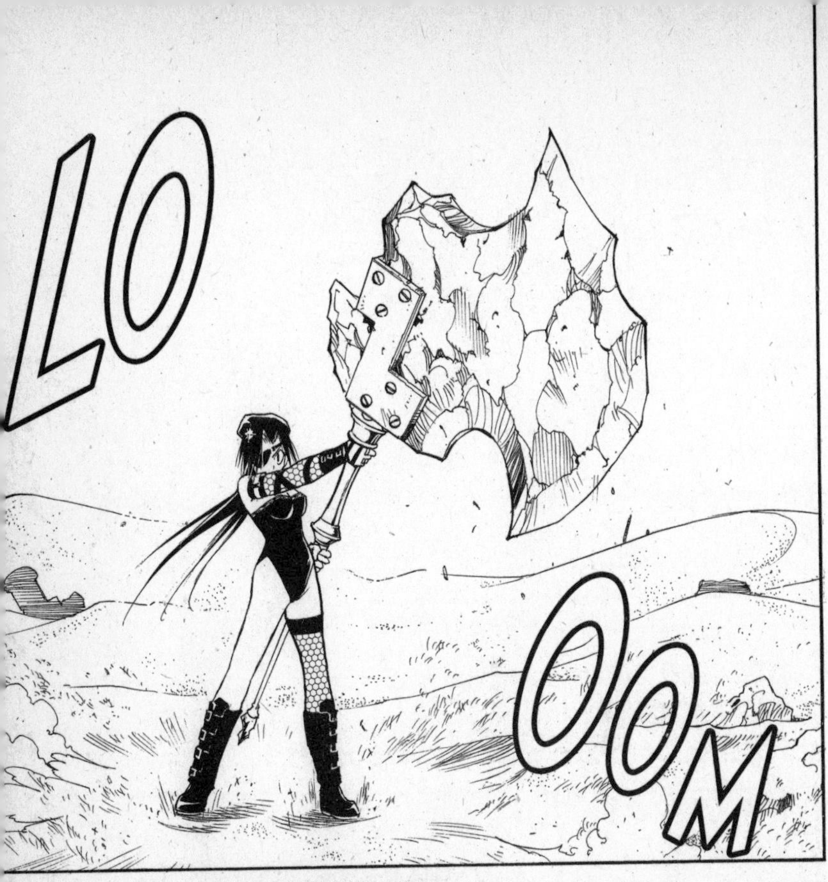
LO
OOOM
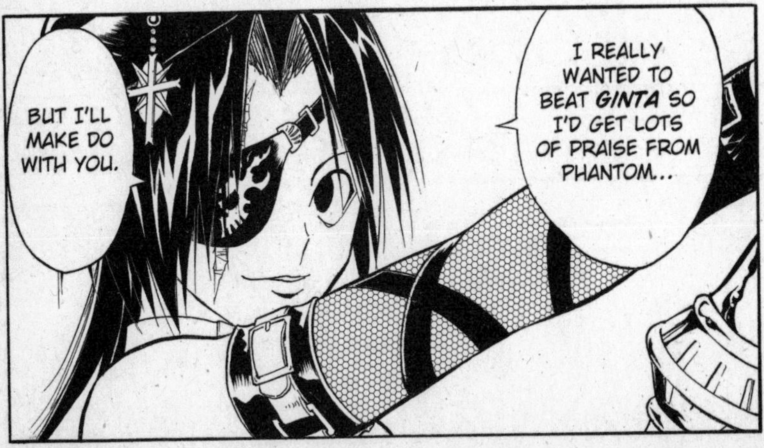
I REALLY WANTED TO BEAT GINTA SO I'D GET LOTS OF PRAISE FROM PHANTOM...
BUT I'LL MAKE DO WITH YOU.

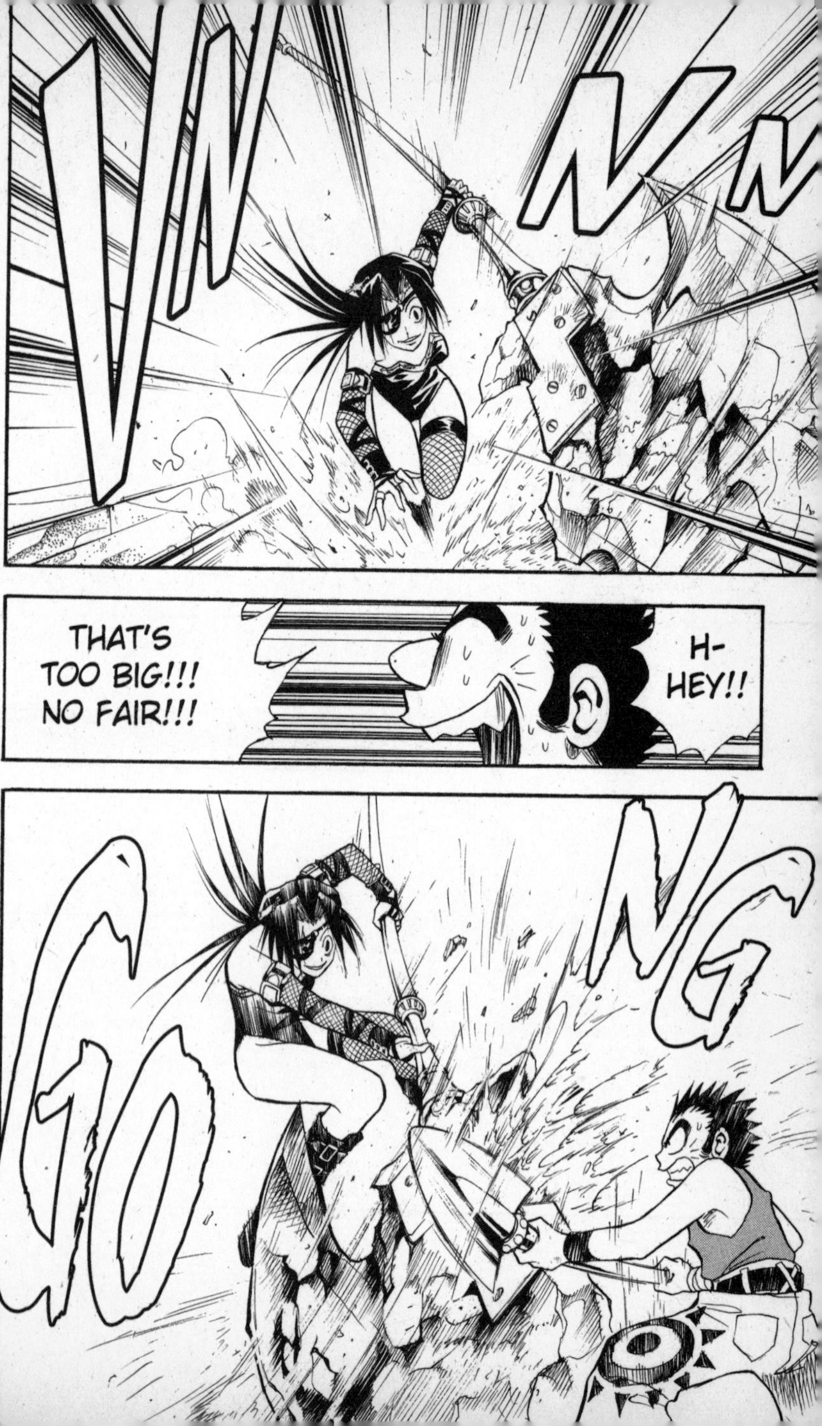
VNNN
H- HEY!!
THAT'S TOO BIG!!! NO FAIR!!!
GONG

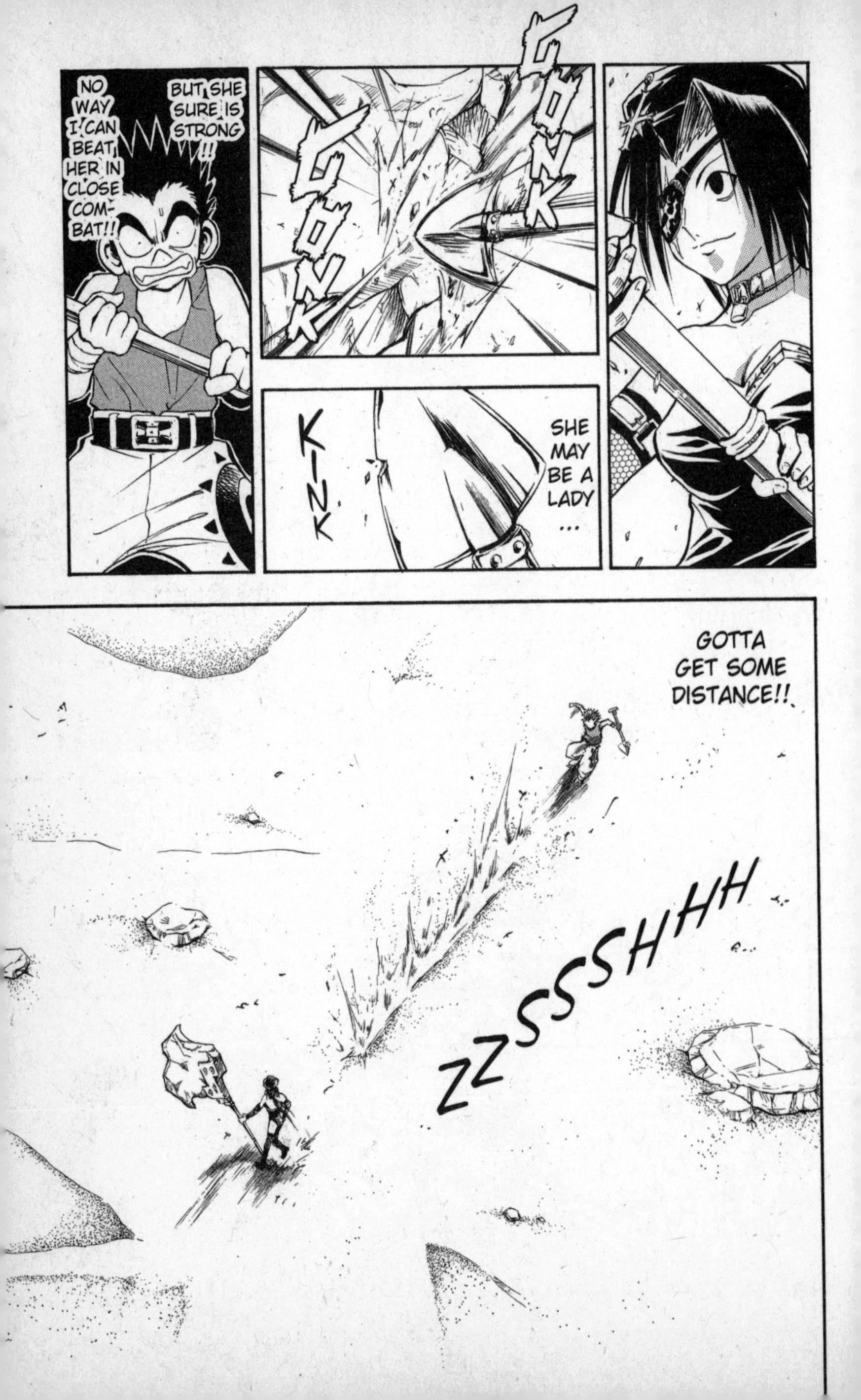
GONK
GONK
SHE MAY BE A LADY...
KINK
BUT SHE SURE IS STRONG!!
NO WAY I CAN BEAT HER IN CLOSE COMBAT!!
GOTTA GET SOME DISTANCE!!
ZZSSSHHH

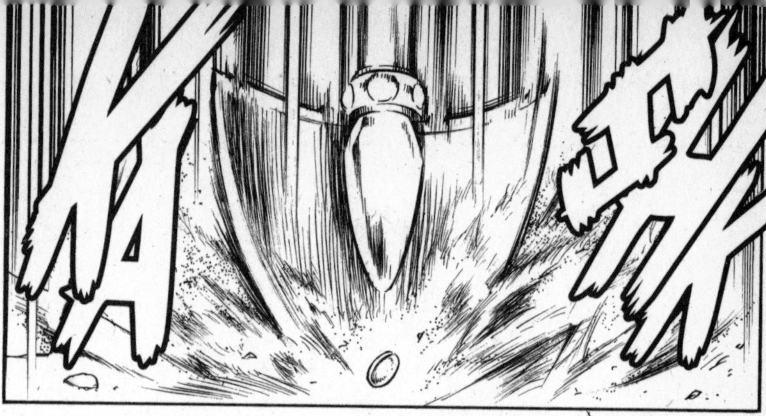
KA

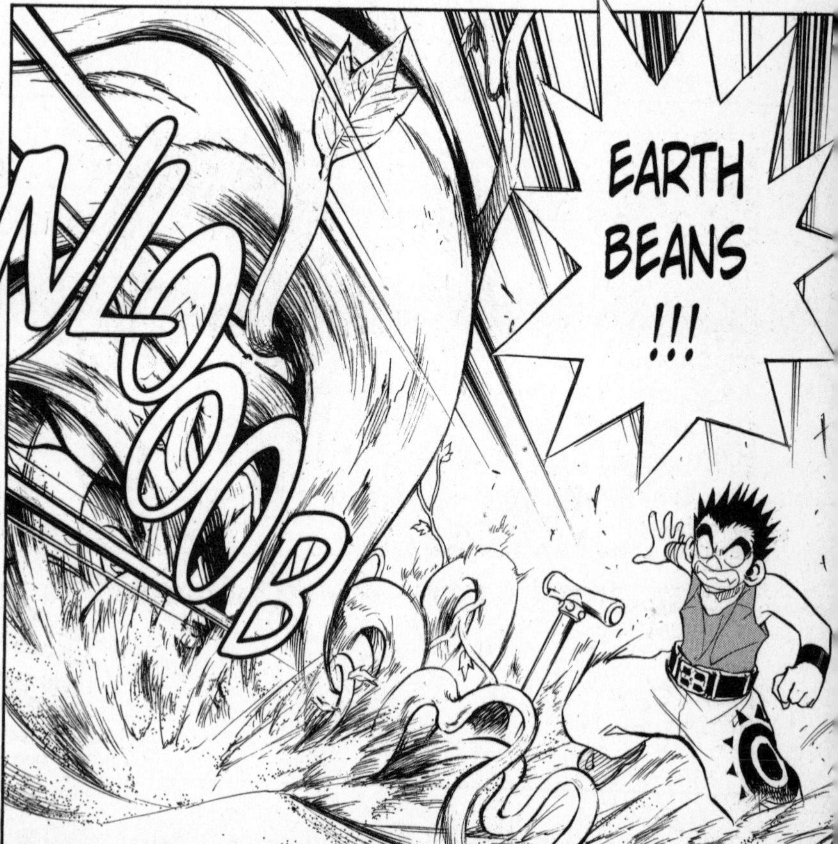
EARTH
BEANS
!!!

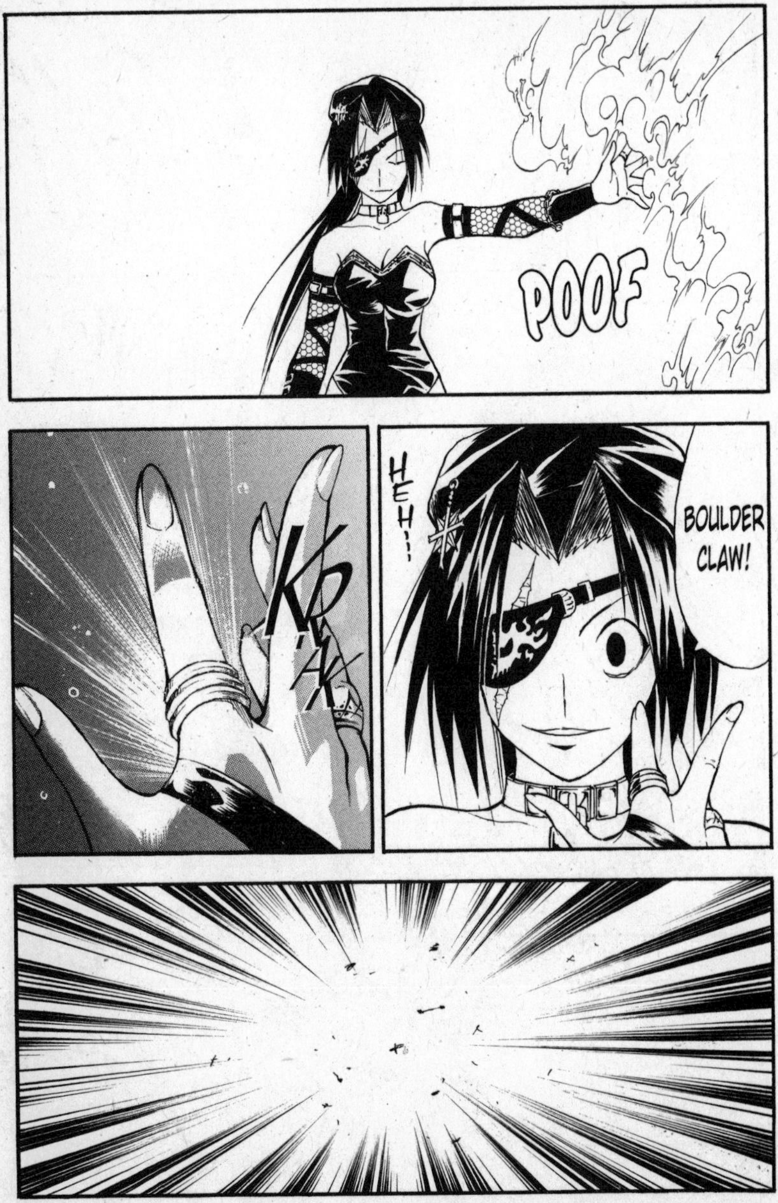
POOF
HEH!!
BOULDER CLAW!
KRAK

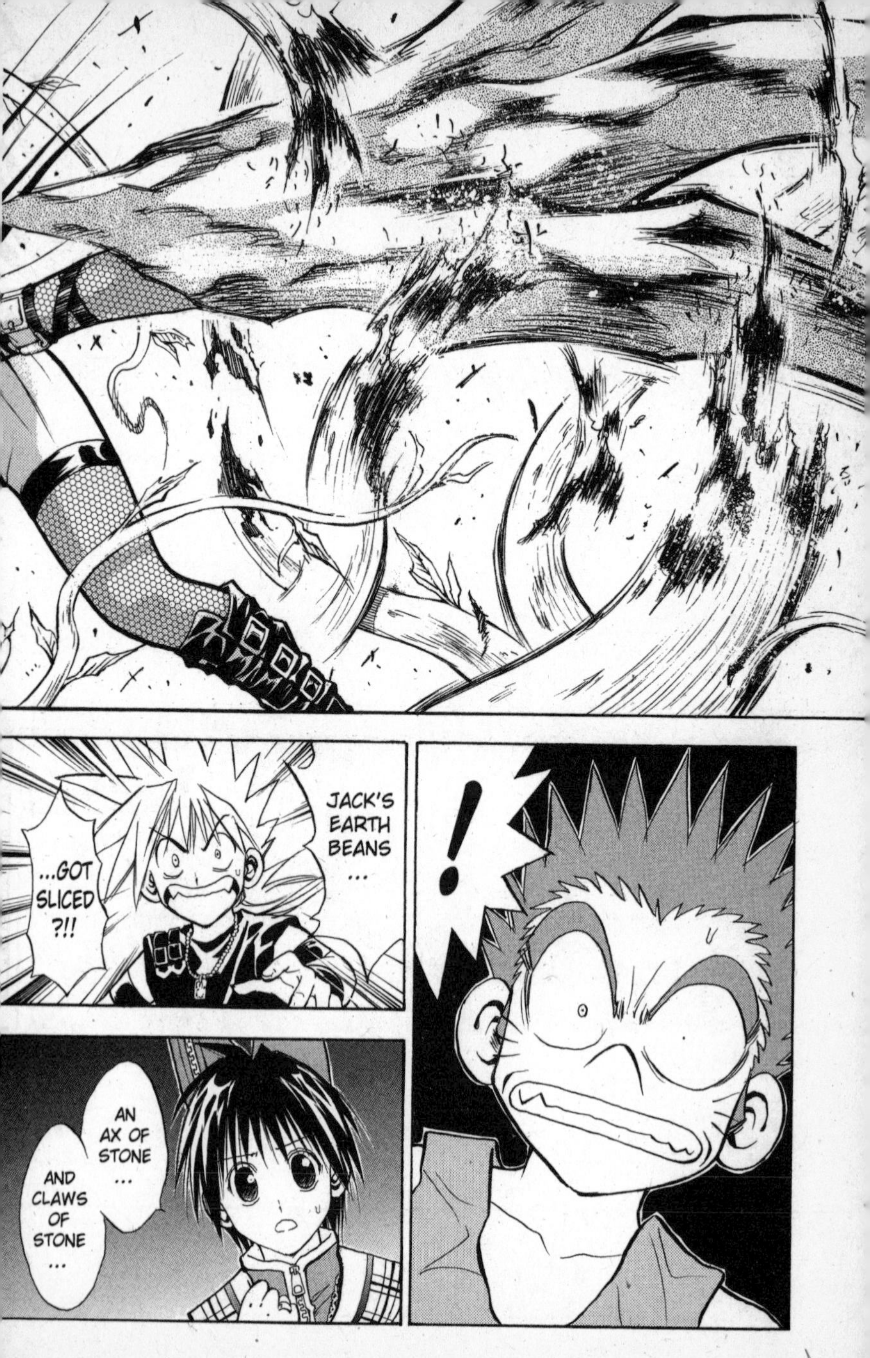
!
JACK'S EARTH BEANS ...
...GOT SLICED ?!!
AN AX OF STONE ...
AND CLAWS OF STONE ...

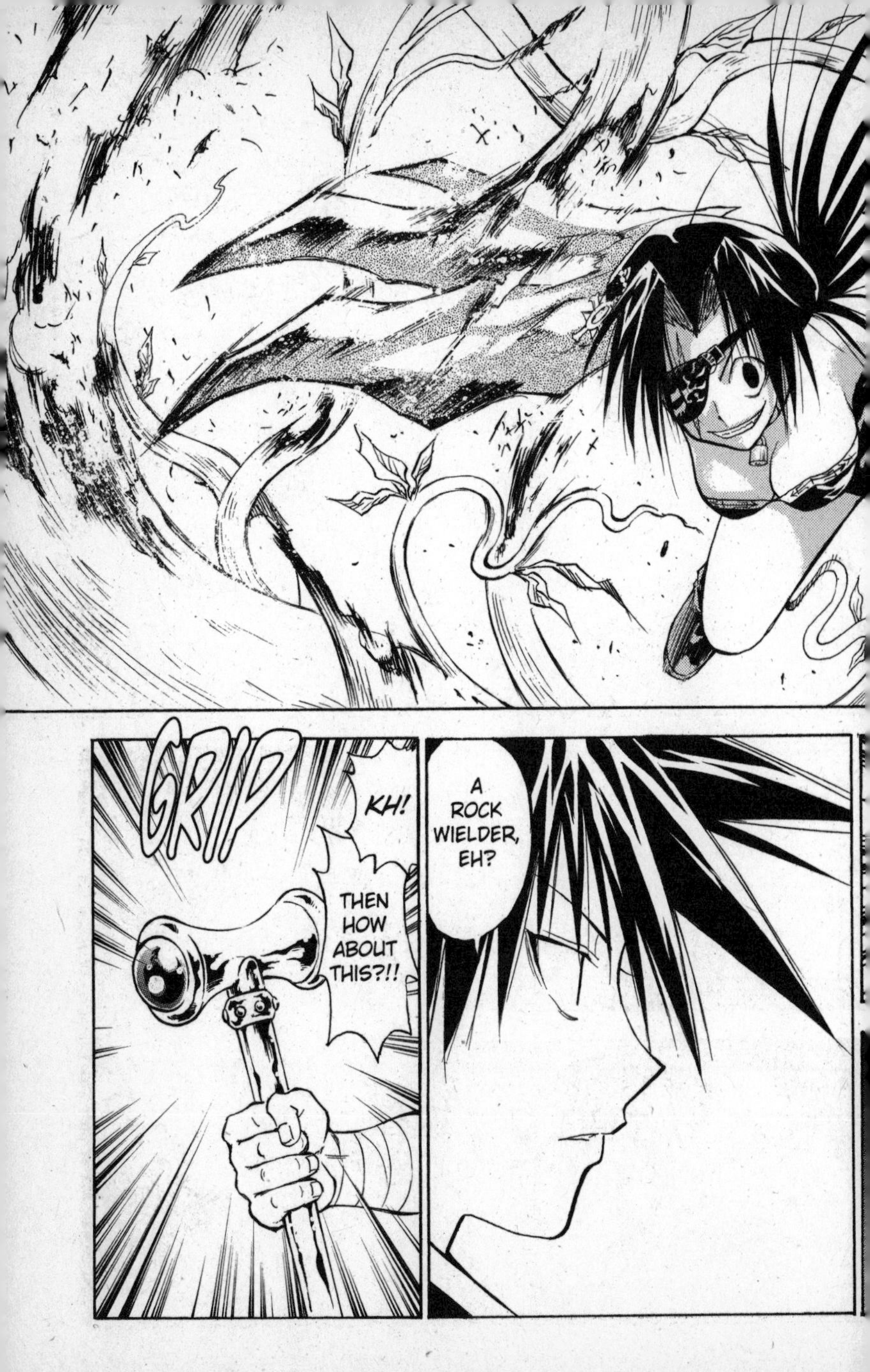
A ROCK WIELDER, EH?
GRIP
KH!
THEN HOW ABOUT THIS?!!

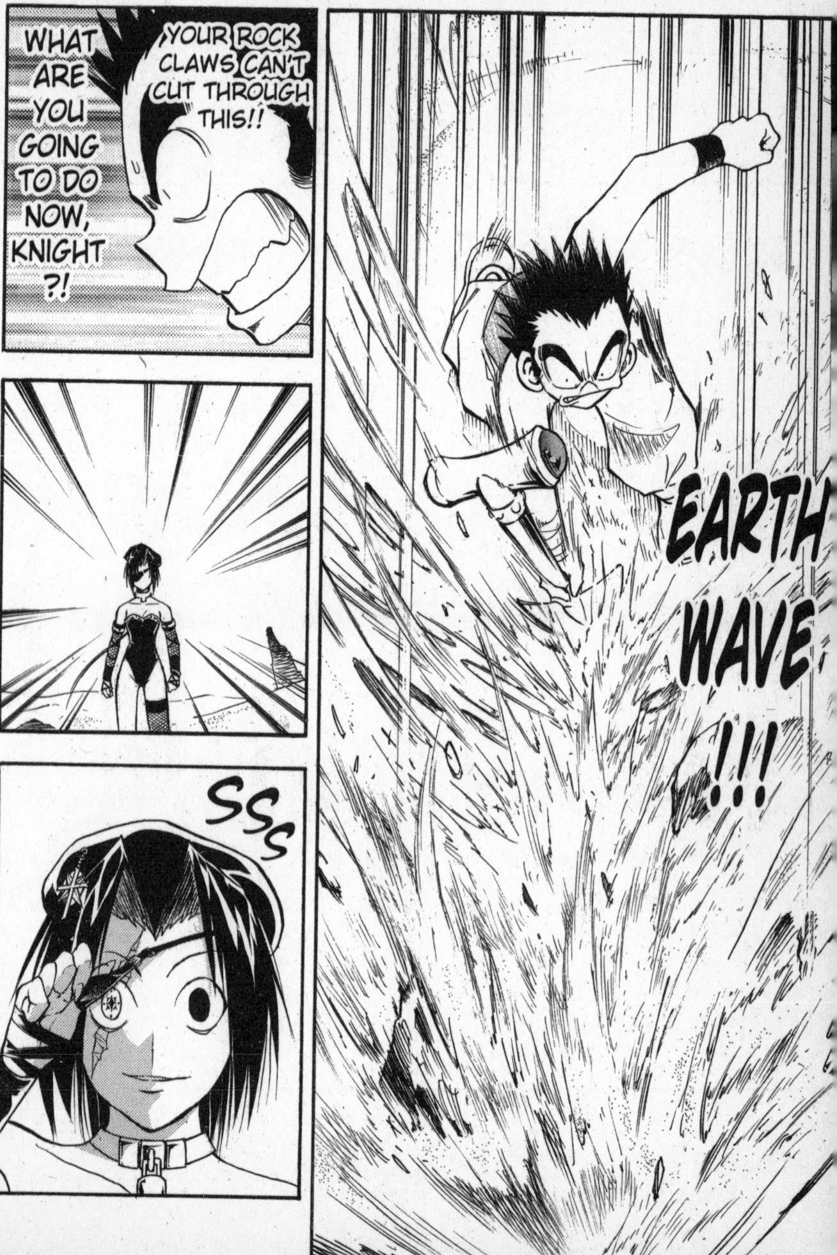
EARTH WAVE!!!
YOUR ROCK CLAWS CAN'T CUT THROUGH THIS!!
WHAT ARE YOU GOING TO DO NOW, KNIGHT?!
SSS

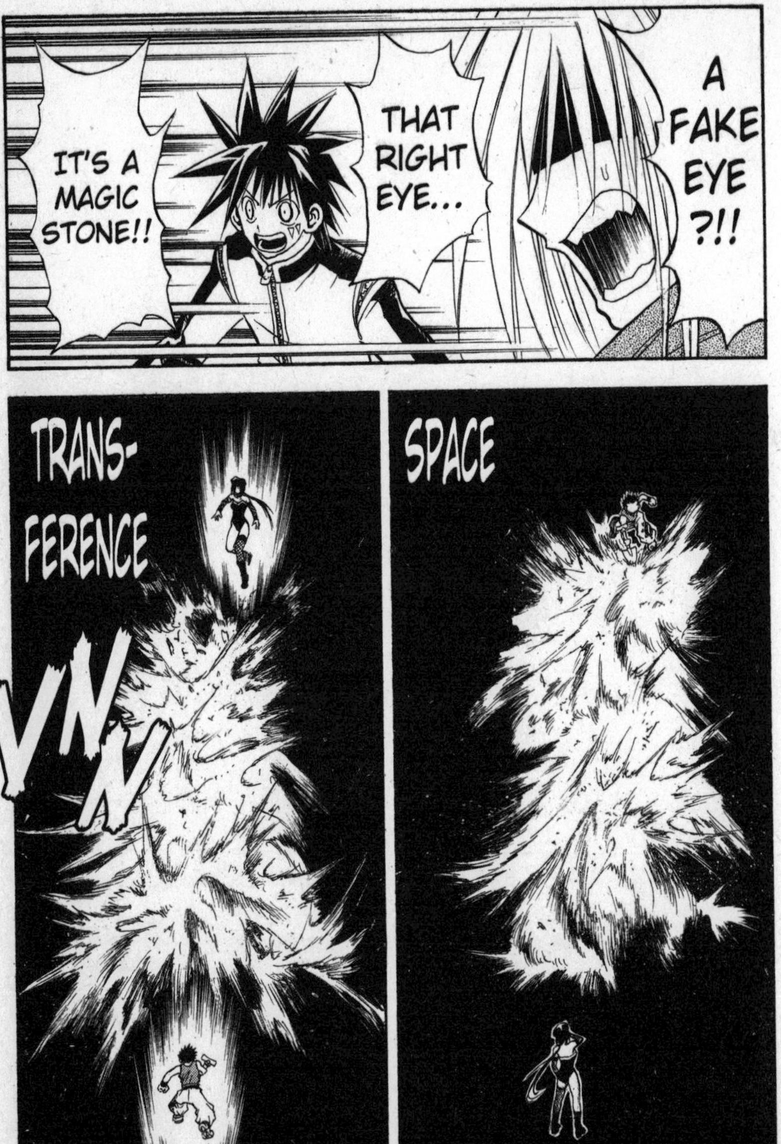
A FAKE EYE ?!!
THAT RIGHT EYE...
IT'S A MAGIC STONE!!
SPACE
TRANS-FERENCE
VN

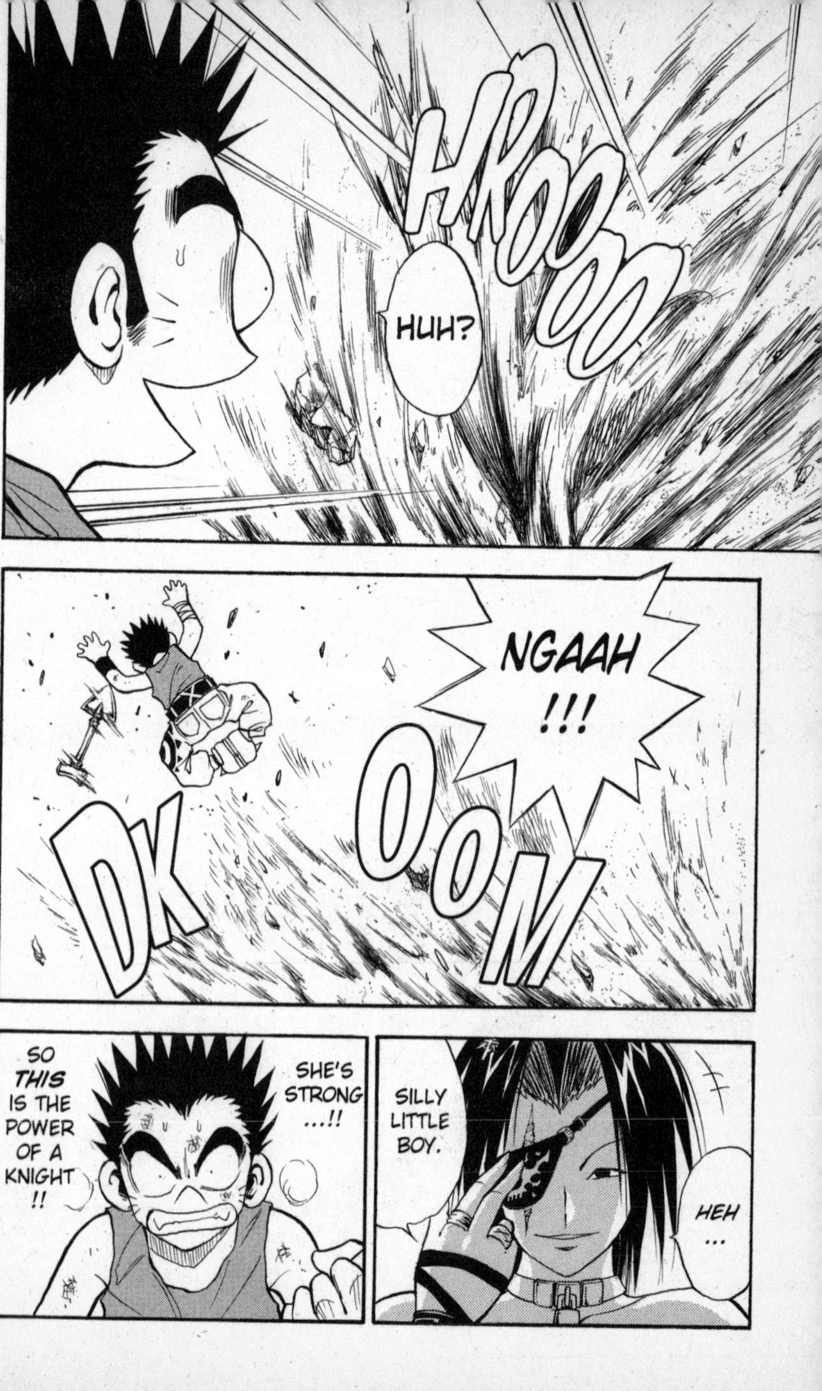
HROOOOO
HUH?
NGAAH !!!
DKOOOM
HEH ...
SILLY LITTLE BOY.
SHE'S STRONG ...!!
SO *THIS* IS THE POWER OF A KNIGHT !!

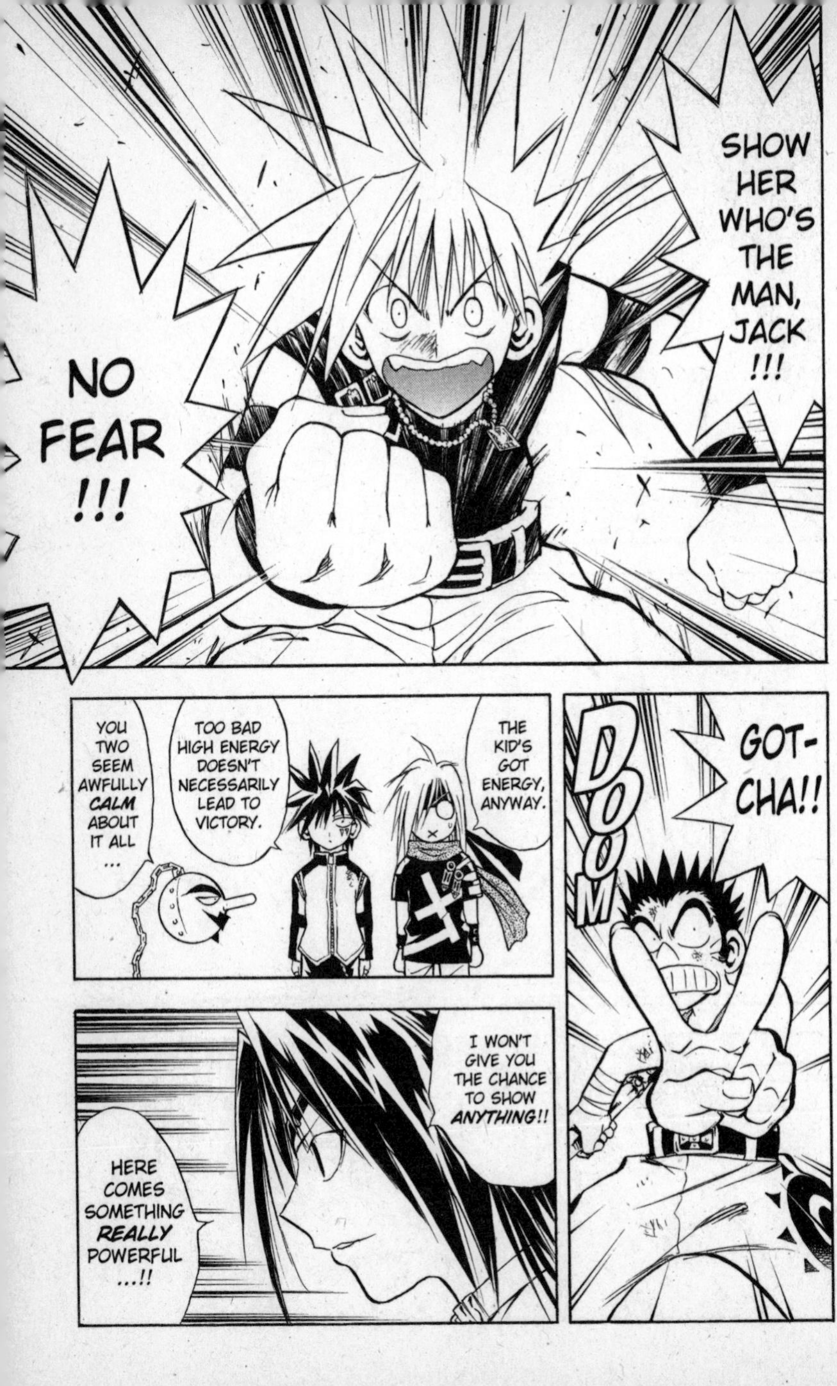
SHOW HER WHO'S THE MAN, JACK!!!
NO FEAR!!!
GOT-CHA!!
DOOM
THE KID'S GOT ENERGY, ANYWAY.
TOO BAD HIGH ENERGY DOESN'T NECESSARILY LEAD TO VICTORY.
YOU TWO SEEM AWFULLY CALM ABOUT IT ALL...
I WON'T GIVE YOU THE CHANCE TO SHOW ANYTHING!!
HERE COMES SOMETHING REALLY POWERFUL...!!

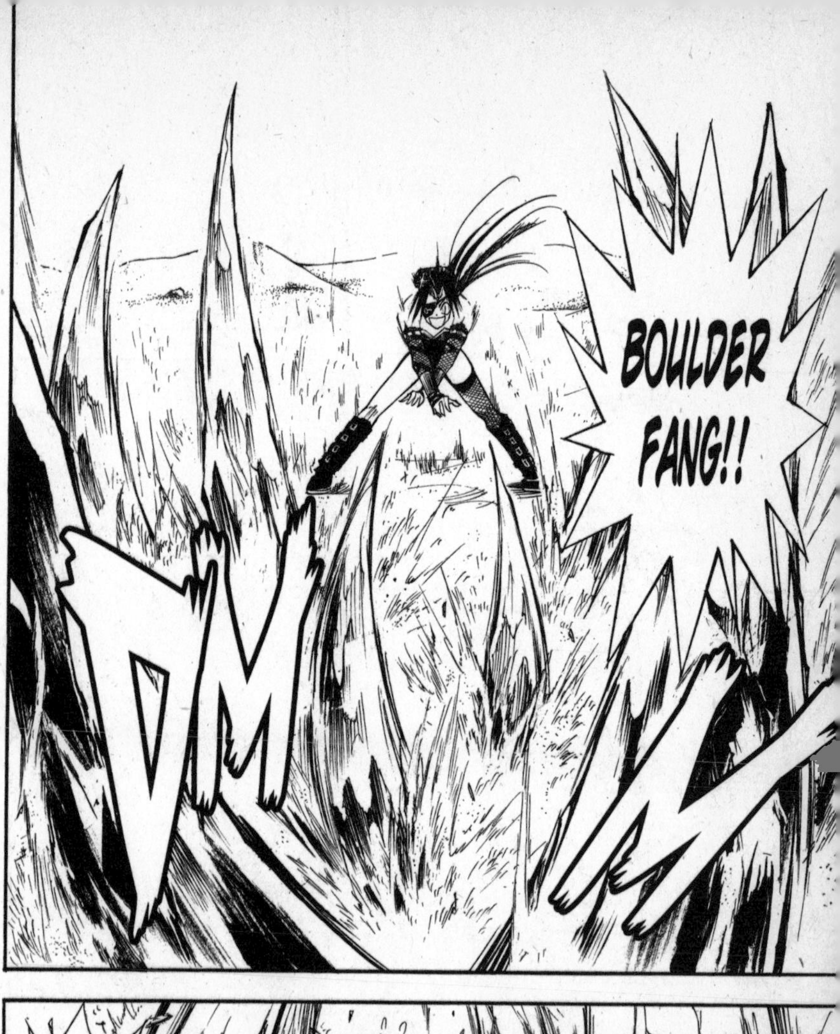
BOULDER FANG!!

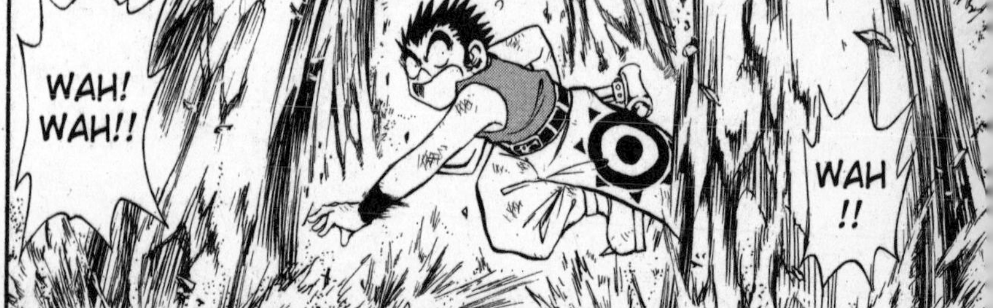
WAH !!
WAH! WAH!!

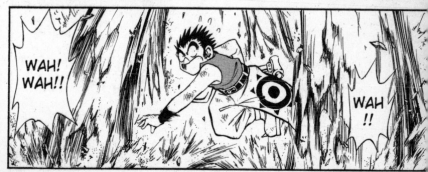

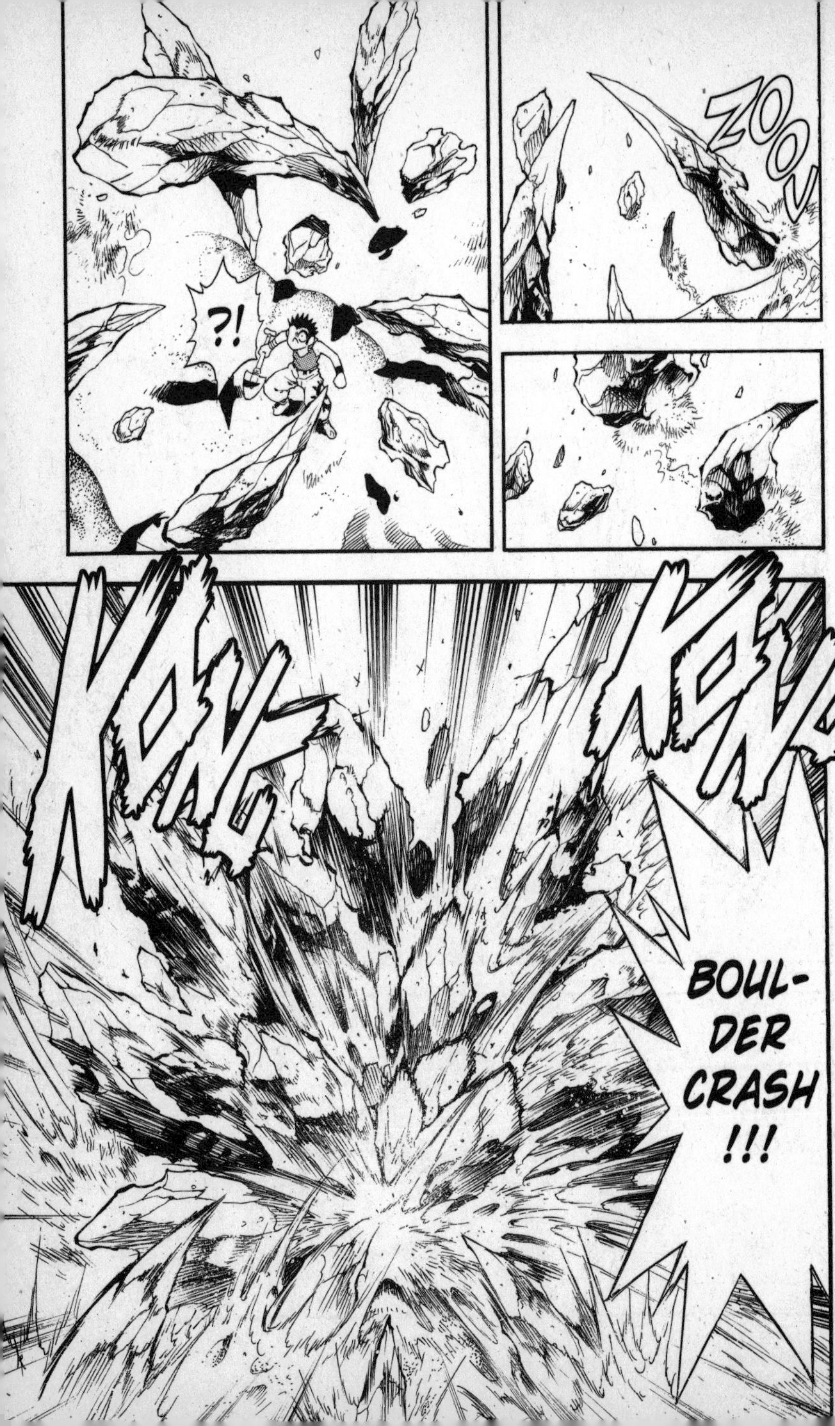
ZOOOV
?!
KONK
KONK
BOUL-
DER
CRASH
!!!

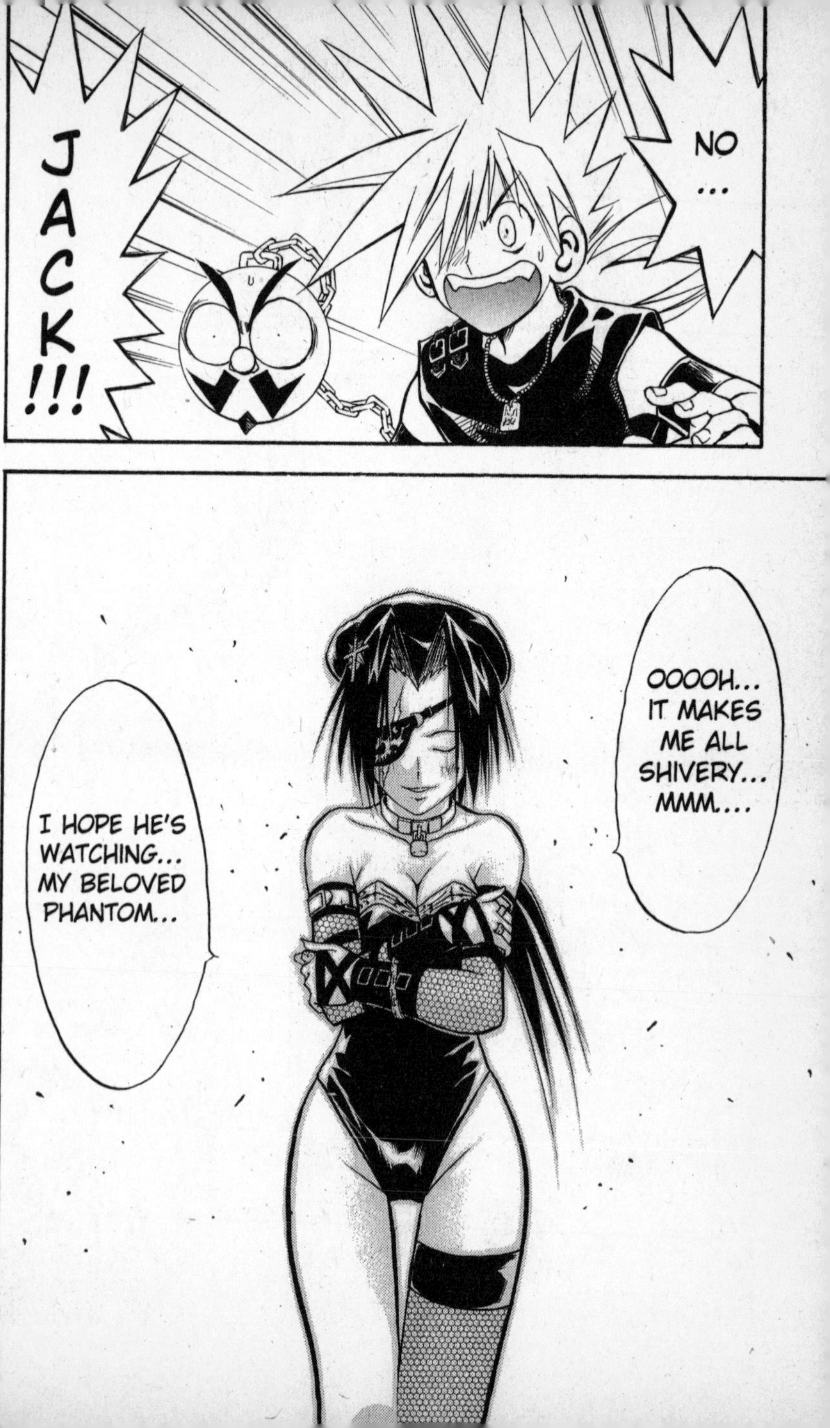
NO ...
JACK!!!
OOOOH... IT MAKES ME ALL SHIVERY... MMM...
I HOPE HE'S WATCHING... MY BELOVED PHANTOM...

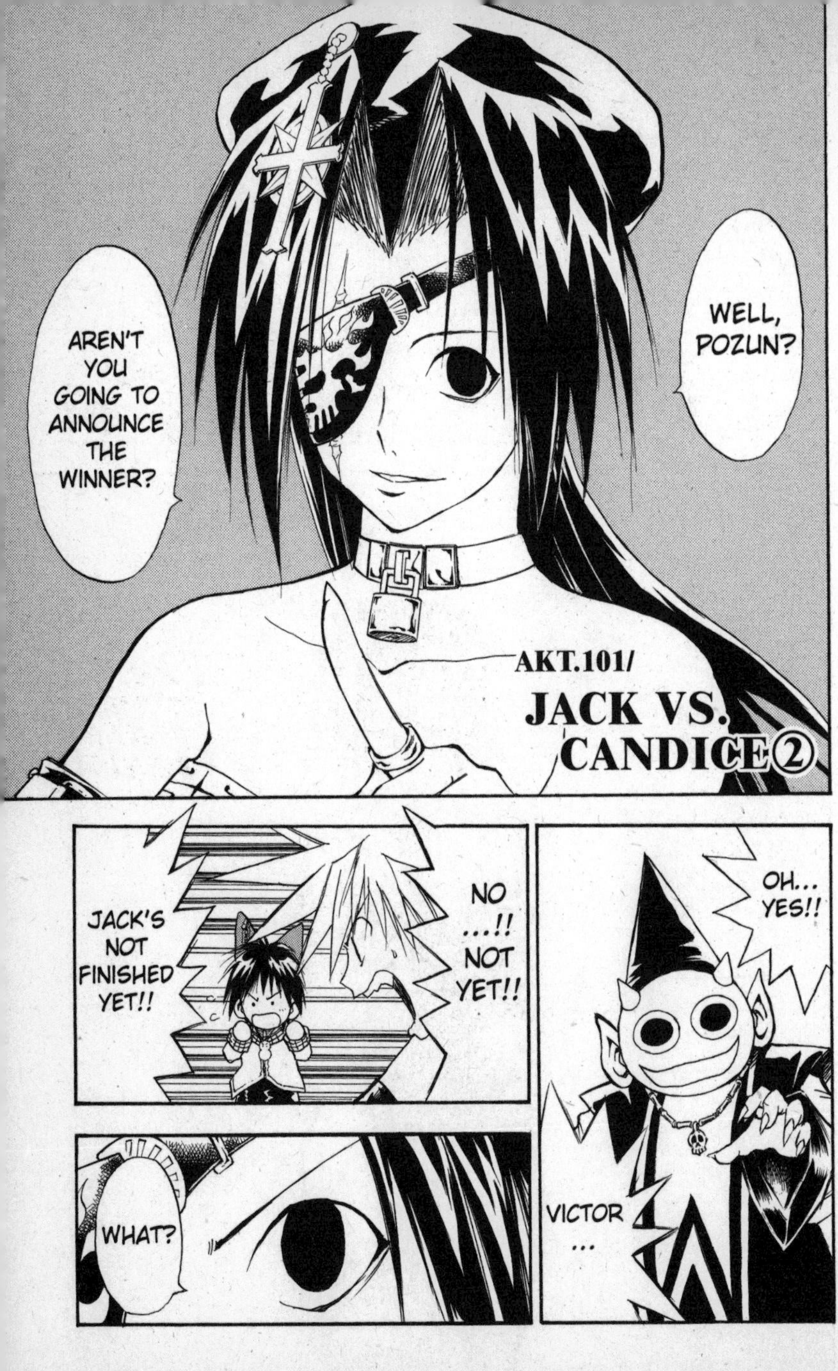
WELL, POZUN?
AREN'T YOU GOING TO ANNOUNCE THE WINNER?
AKT.101/
JACK VS. CANDICE②
OH... YES!!
VICTOR ...
NO ...!! NOT YET!!
JACK'S NOT FINISHED YET!!
WHAT?

AKT.101/ JACK VS. CANDICE ②

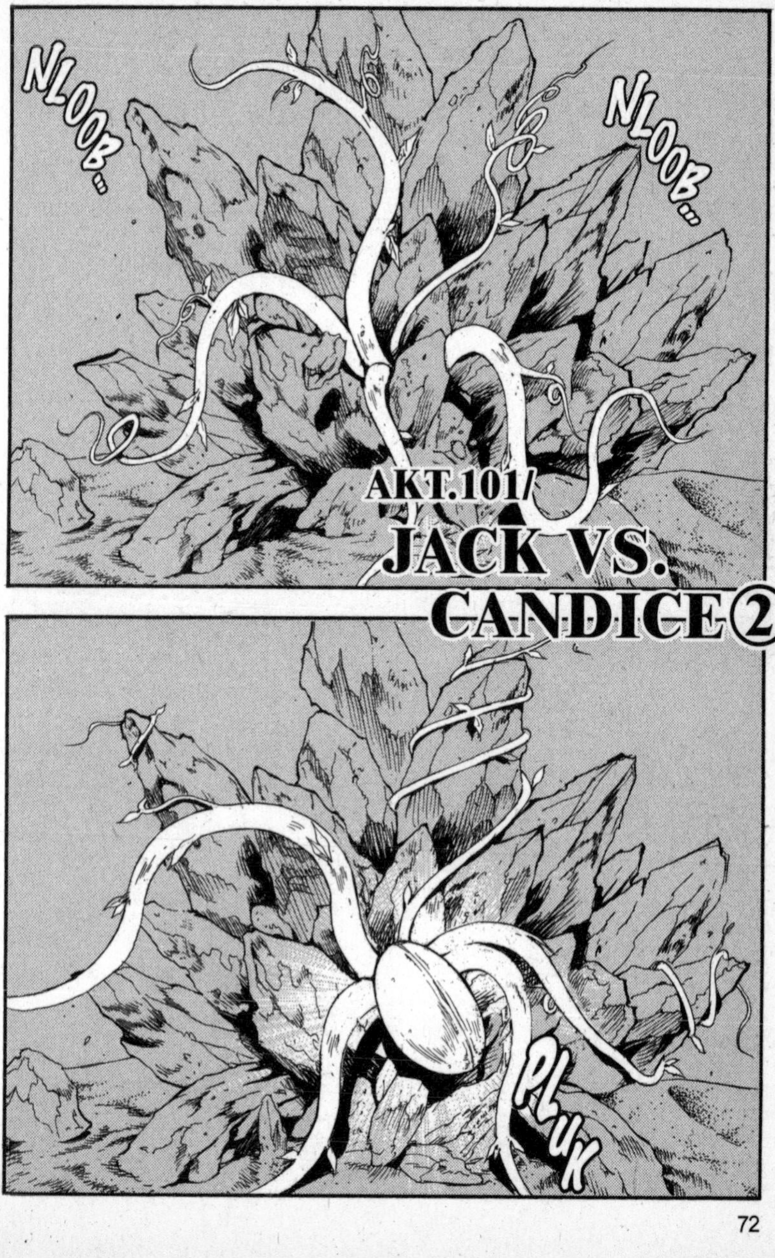
NLOOB...
NLOOB...
PLUK

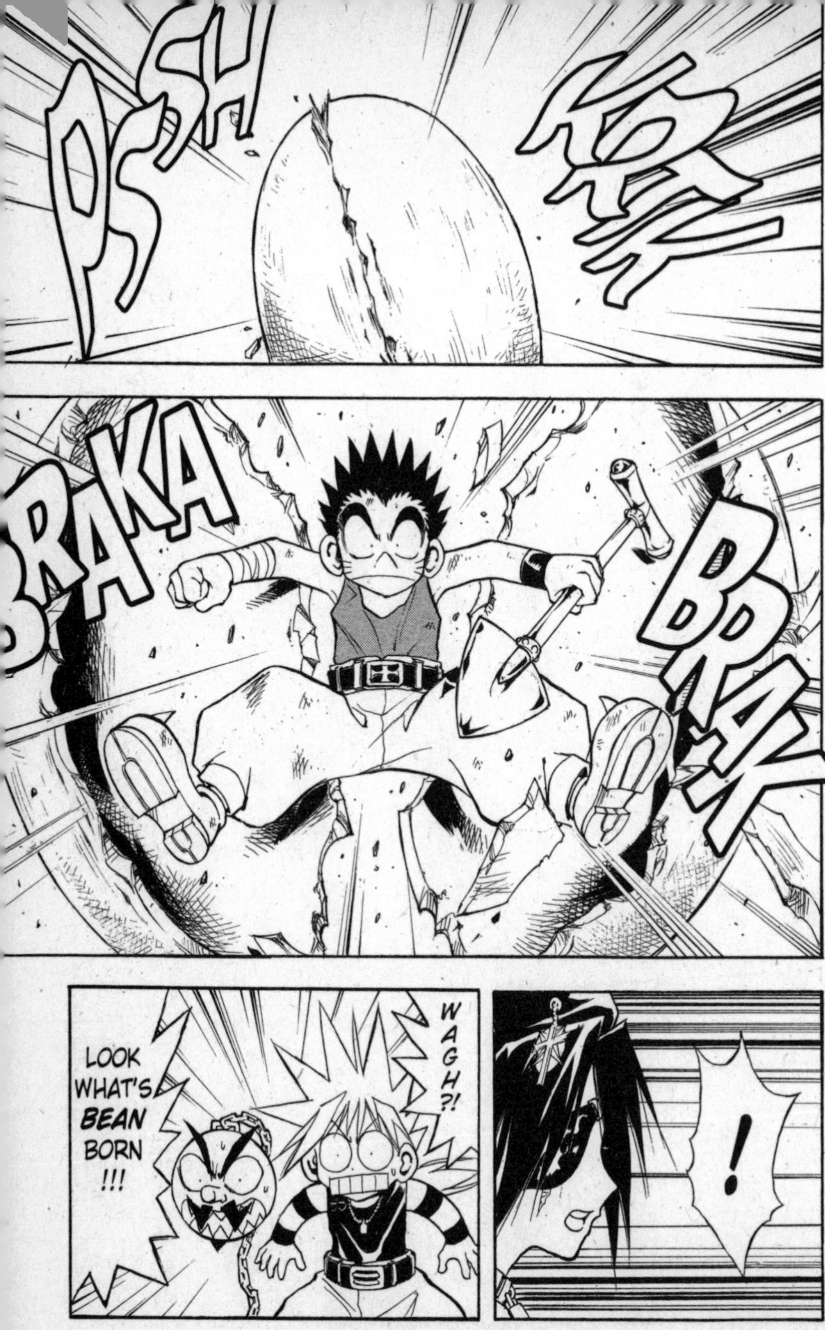
KRIK
PSSH
BRAK
BRAKA
!
WAGH?!
LOOK WHAT'S BEAN BORN !!!

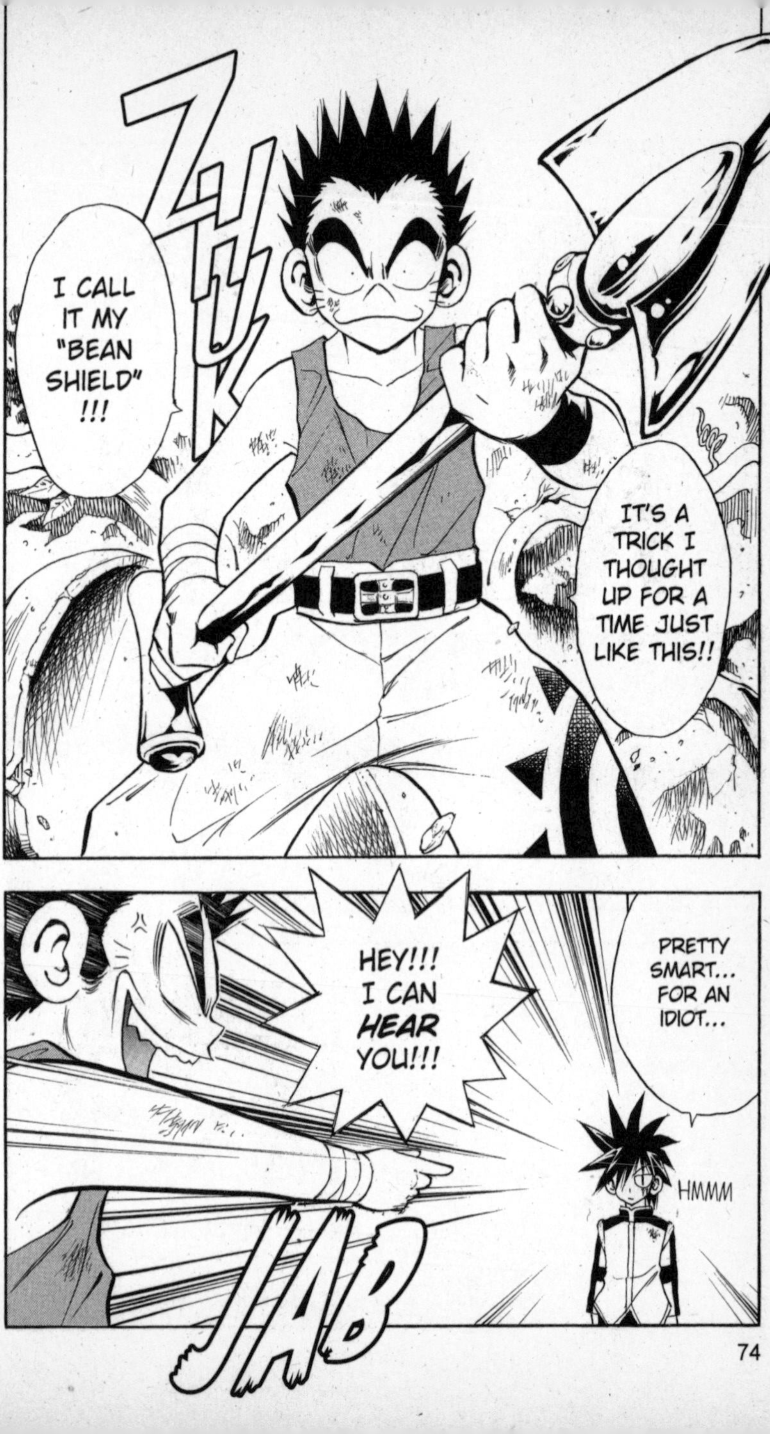
ZHUK
I CALL IT MY "BEAN SHIELD" !!!
IT'S A TRICK I THOUGHT UP FOR A TIME JUST LIKE THIS!!
PRETTY SMART... FOR AN IDIOT...
HMMM
HEY!!! I CAN HEAR YOU!!!
JAB

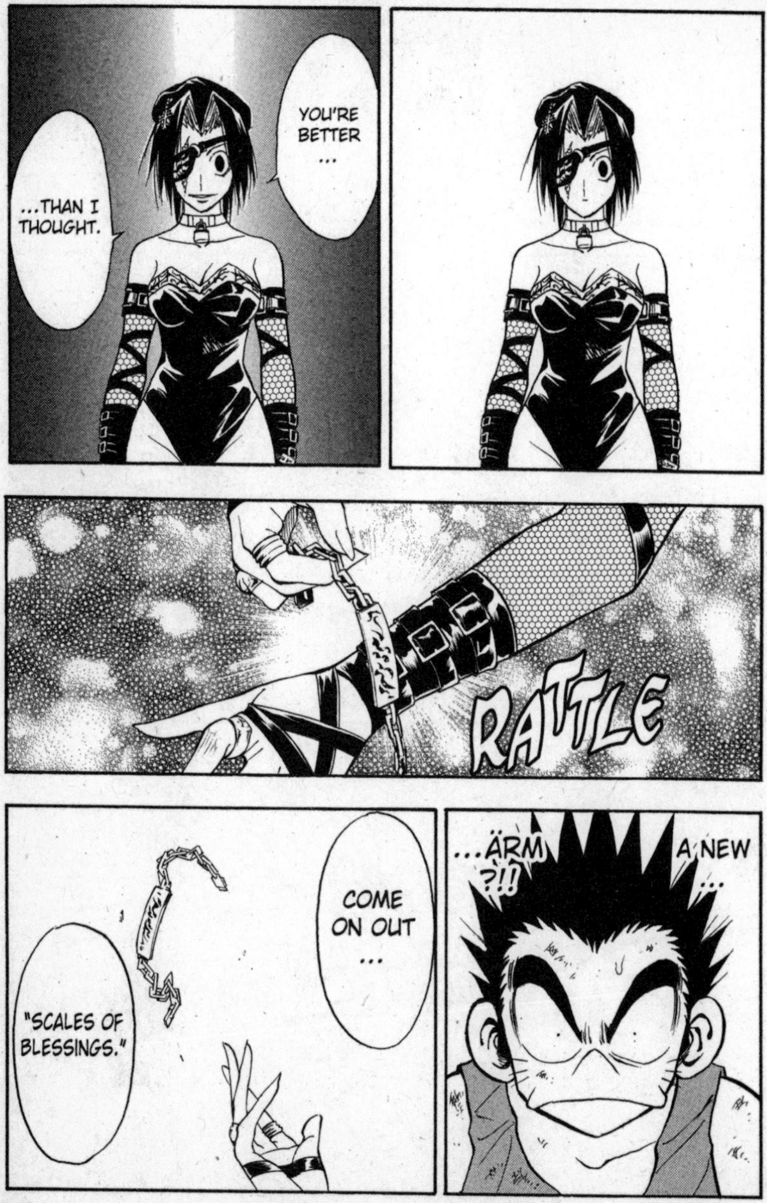
YOU'RE BETTER ...
...THAN I THOUGHT.
RATTLE
A NEW ...
...ÄRM ?!!
COME ON OUT ...
"SCALES OF BLESSINGS."

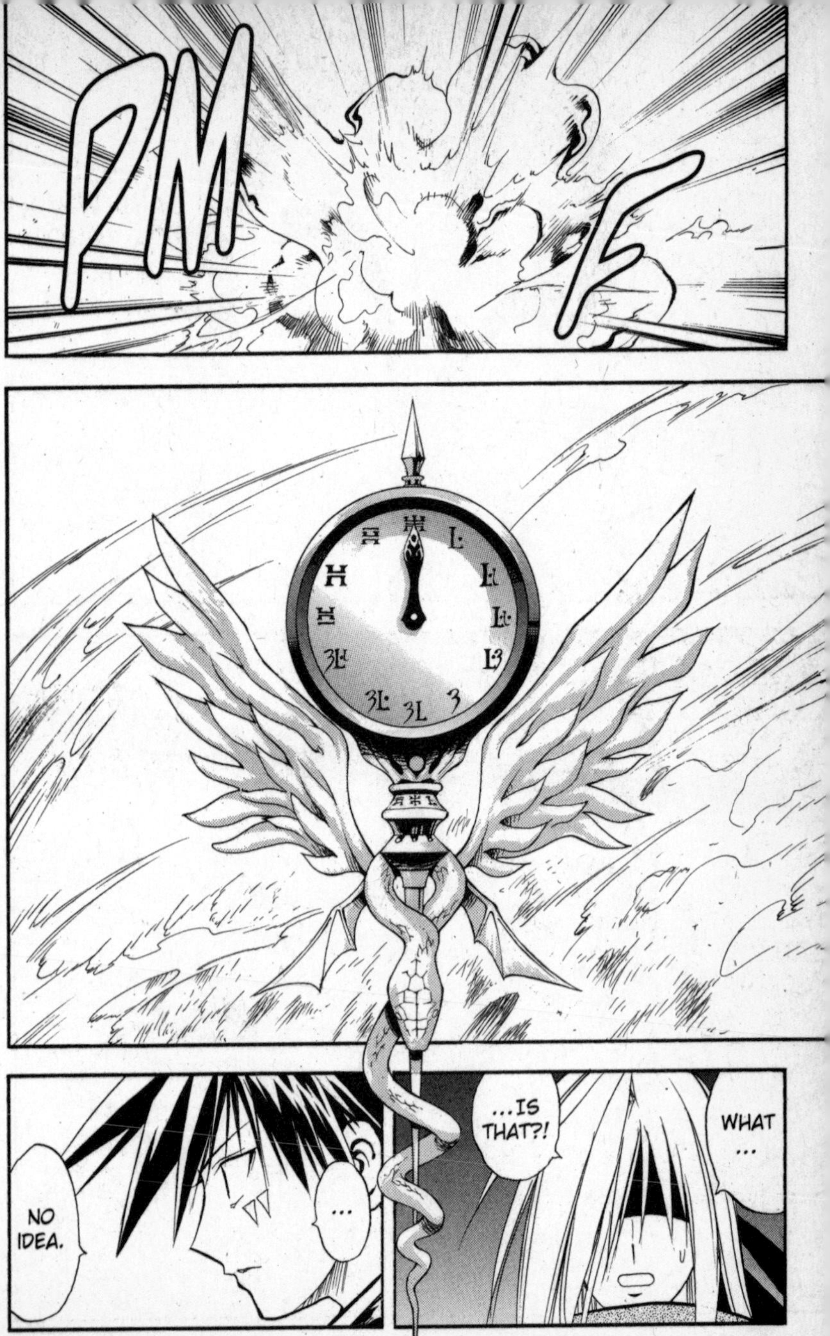
WHAT ...
...IS THAT?!
...
NO IDEA.

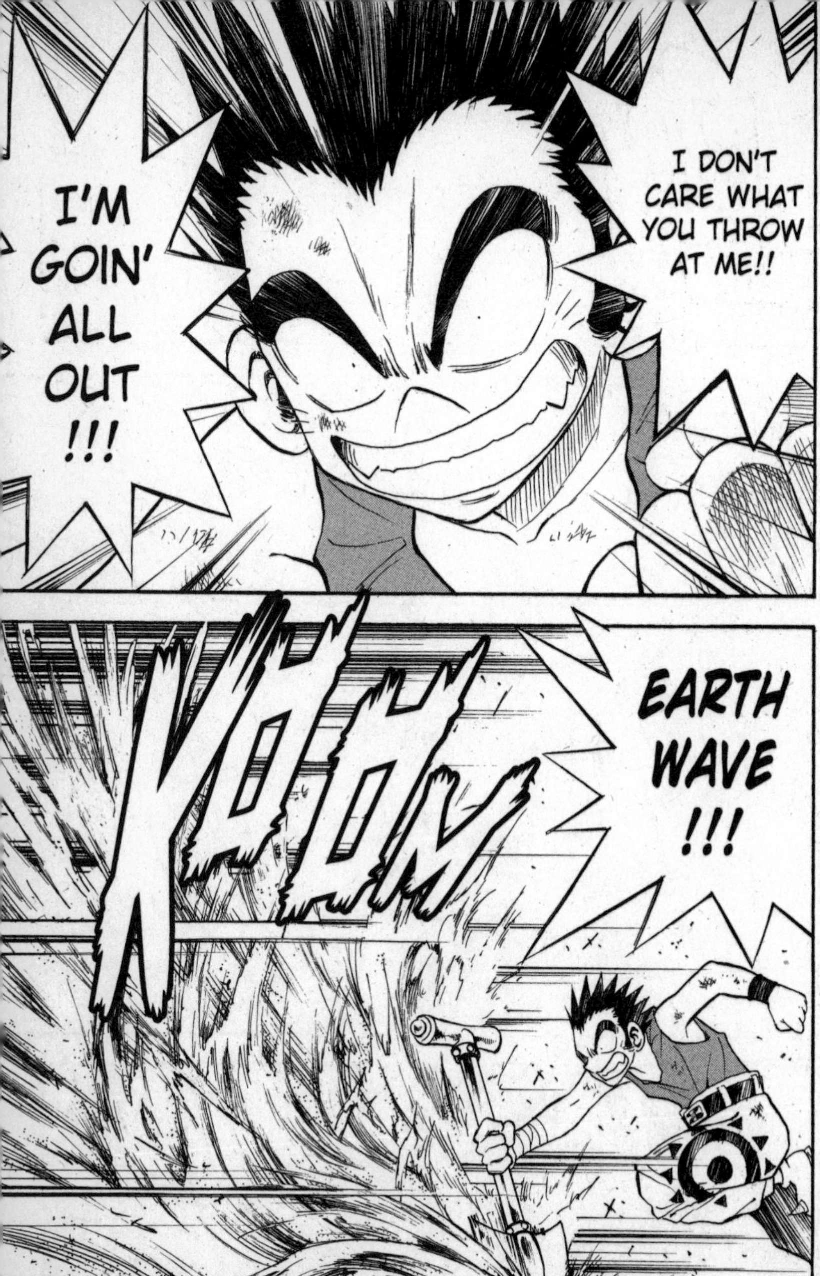
I DON'T CARE WHAT YOU THROW AT ME!!
I'M GOIN' ALL OUT!!!
EARTH WAVE!!!

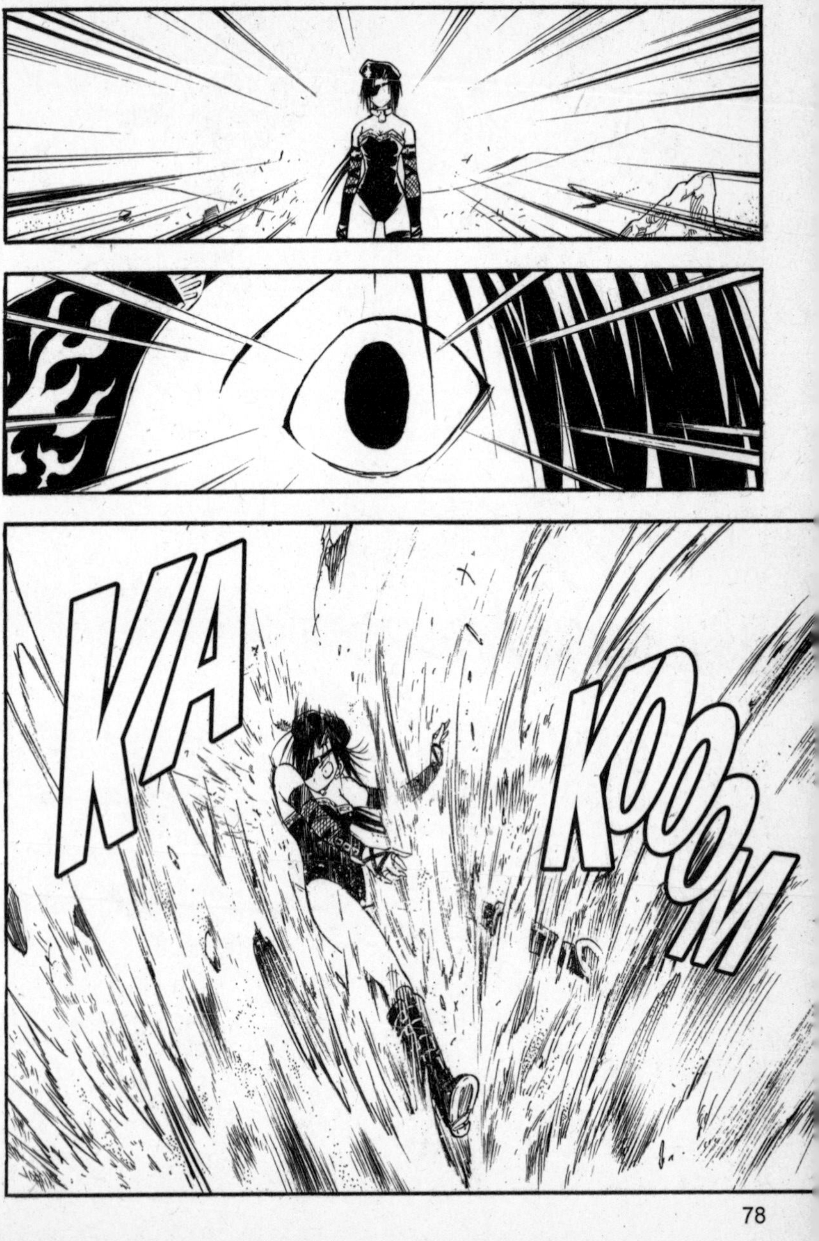
KA
KOOOM

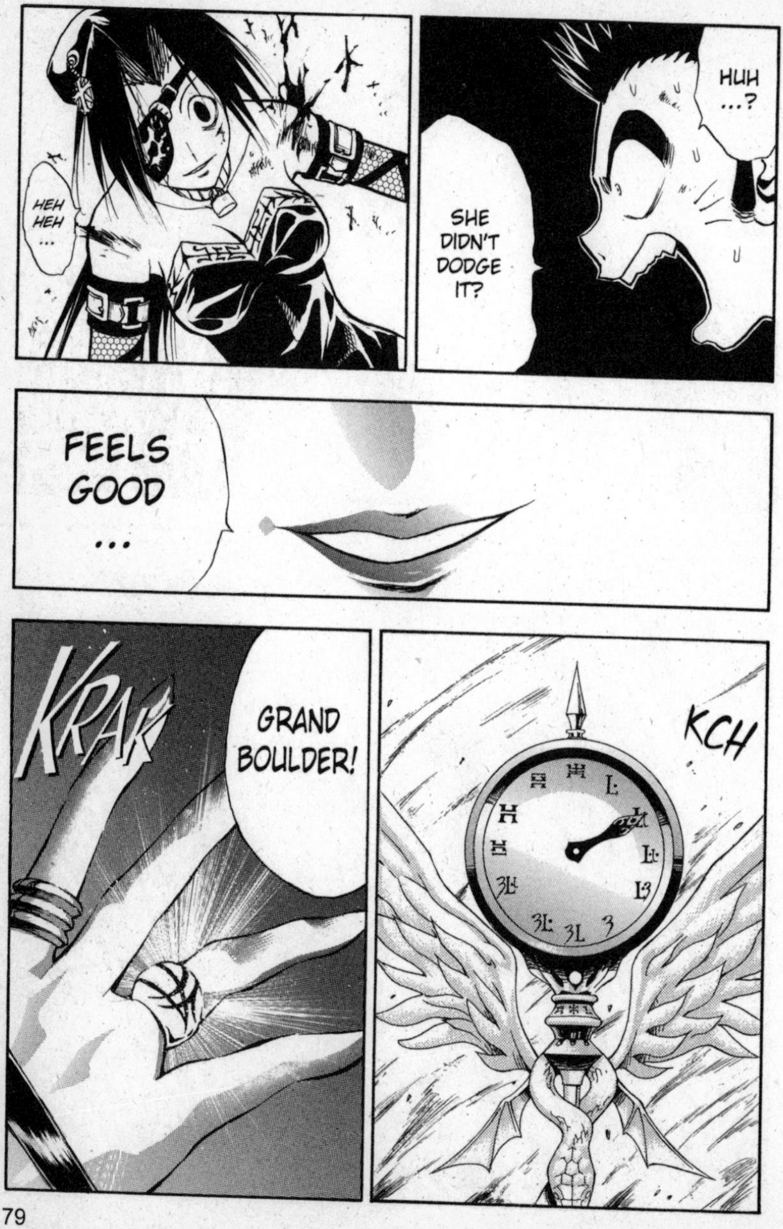
HUH ...?
SHE DIDN'T DODGE IT?
HEH HEH ...
FEELS GOOD ...
KCH
GRAND BOULDER!
KRAK

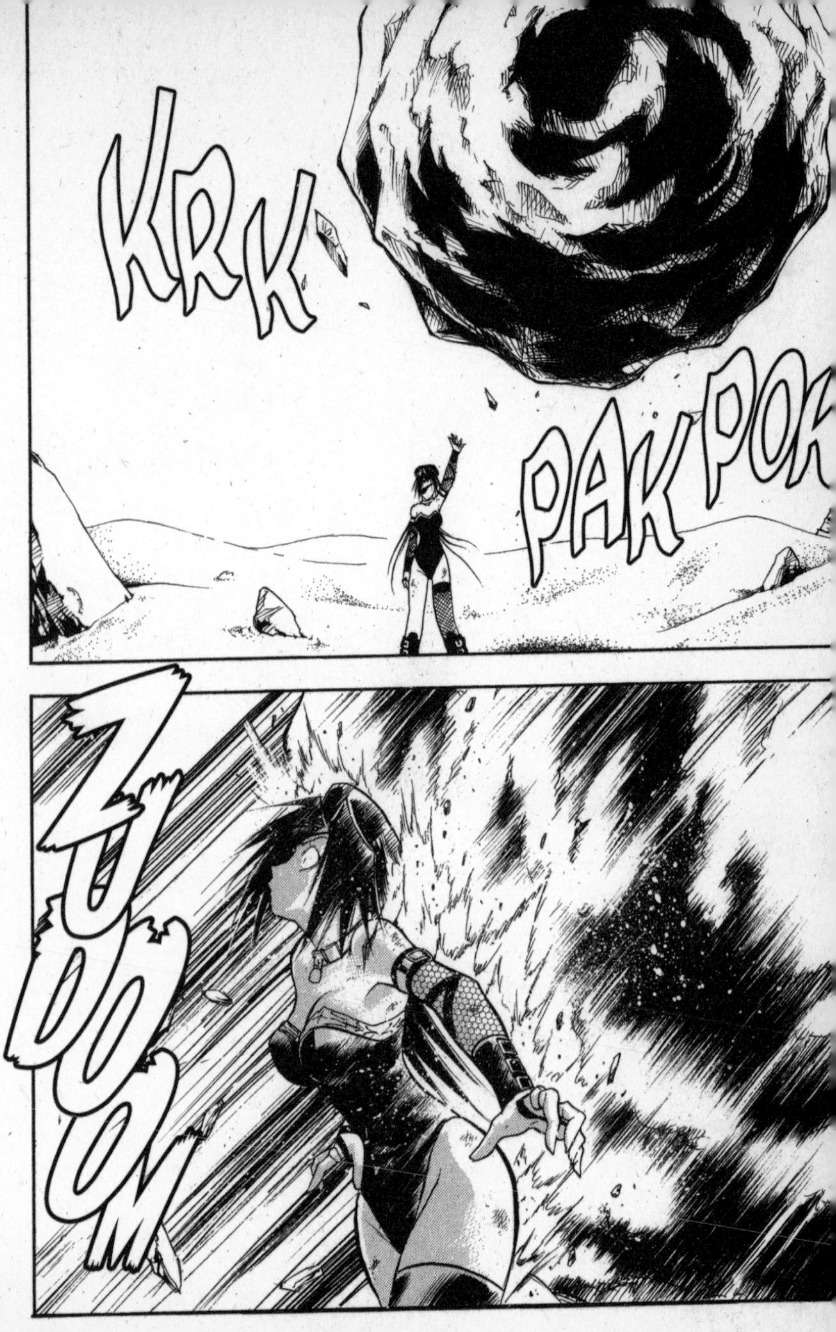
KRK
PAK POK
ZUDOOM

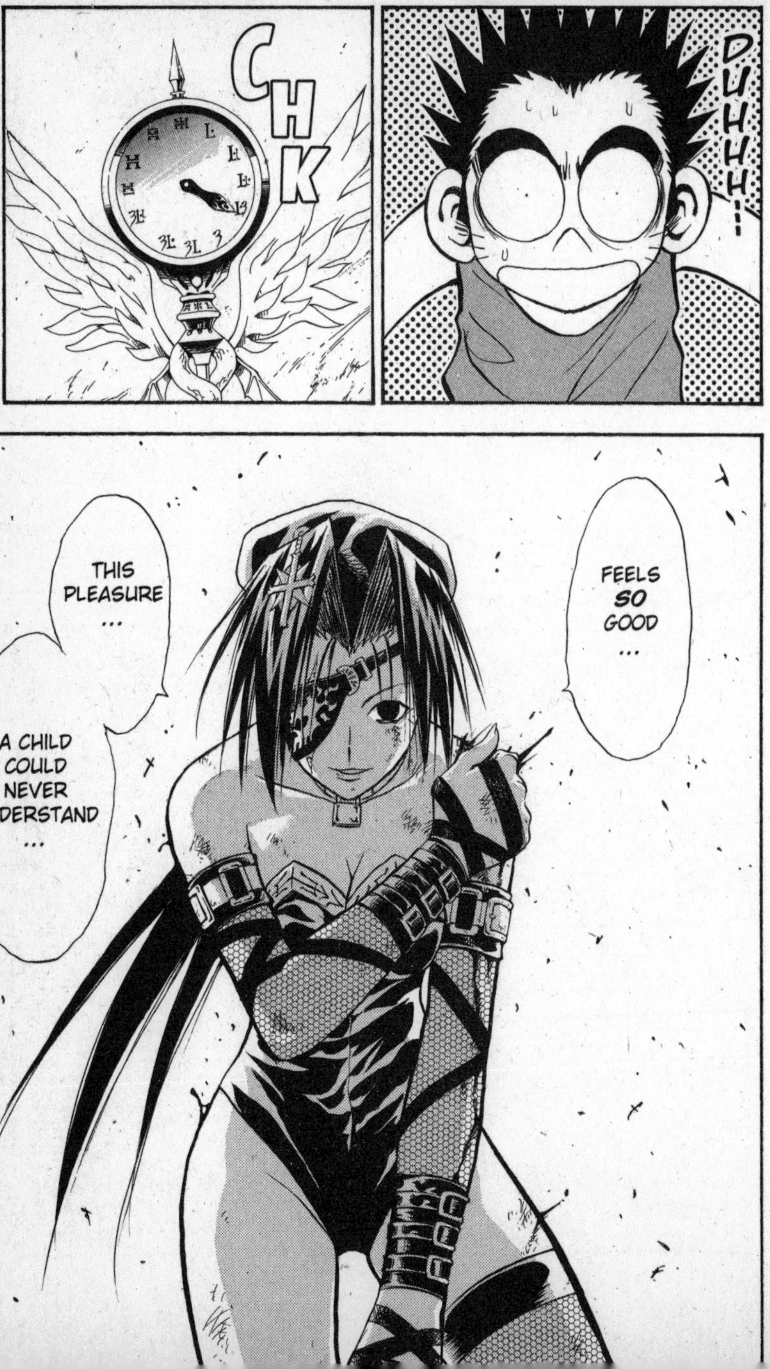
DUHHH!!
CHK
FEELS SO GOOD ...
THIS PLEASURE ...
A CHILD COULD NEVER UNDERSTAND ...

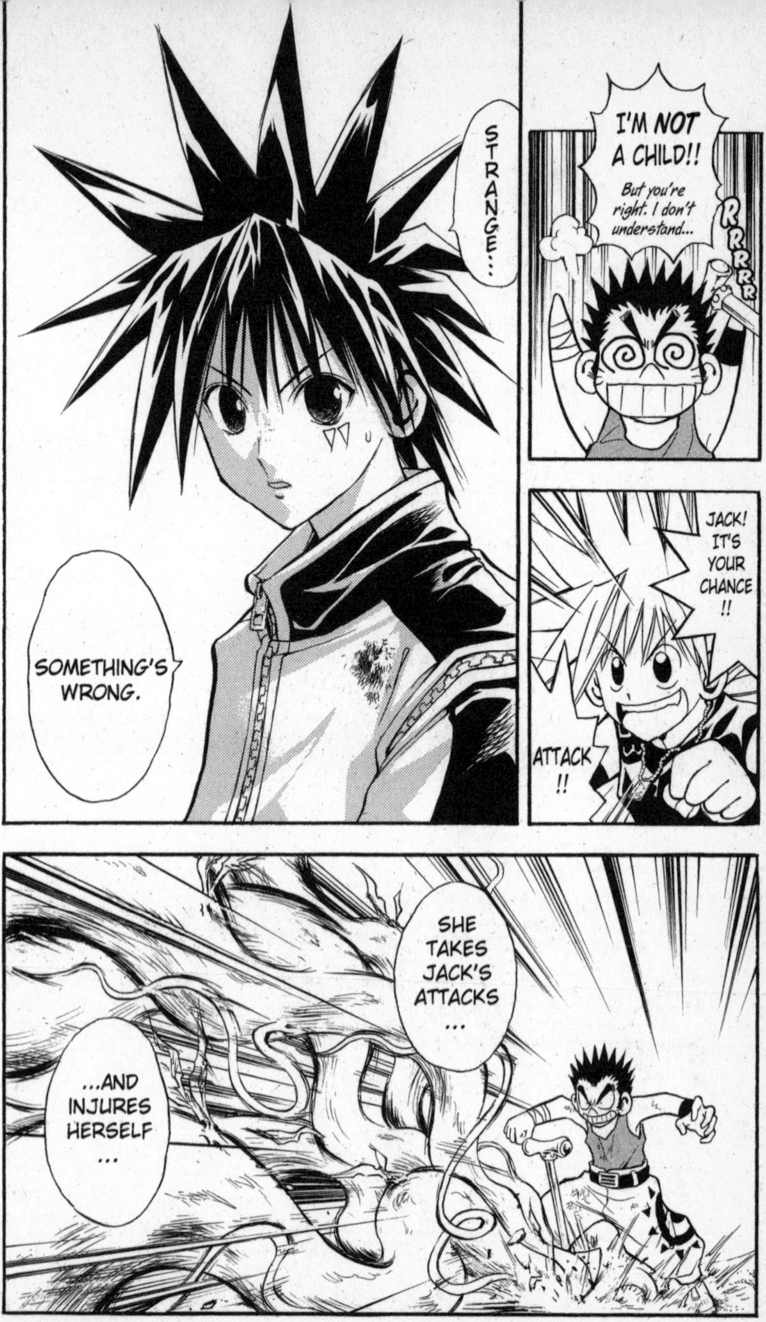
I'M NOT A CHILD!!
But you're right. I don't understand...
RRRRR
JACK! IT'S YOUR CHANCE!!
ATTACK!!
STRANGE...
SOMETHING'S WRONG.
SHE TAKES JACK'S ATTACKS...
...AND INJURES HERSELF...

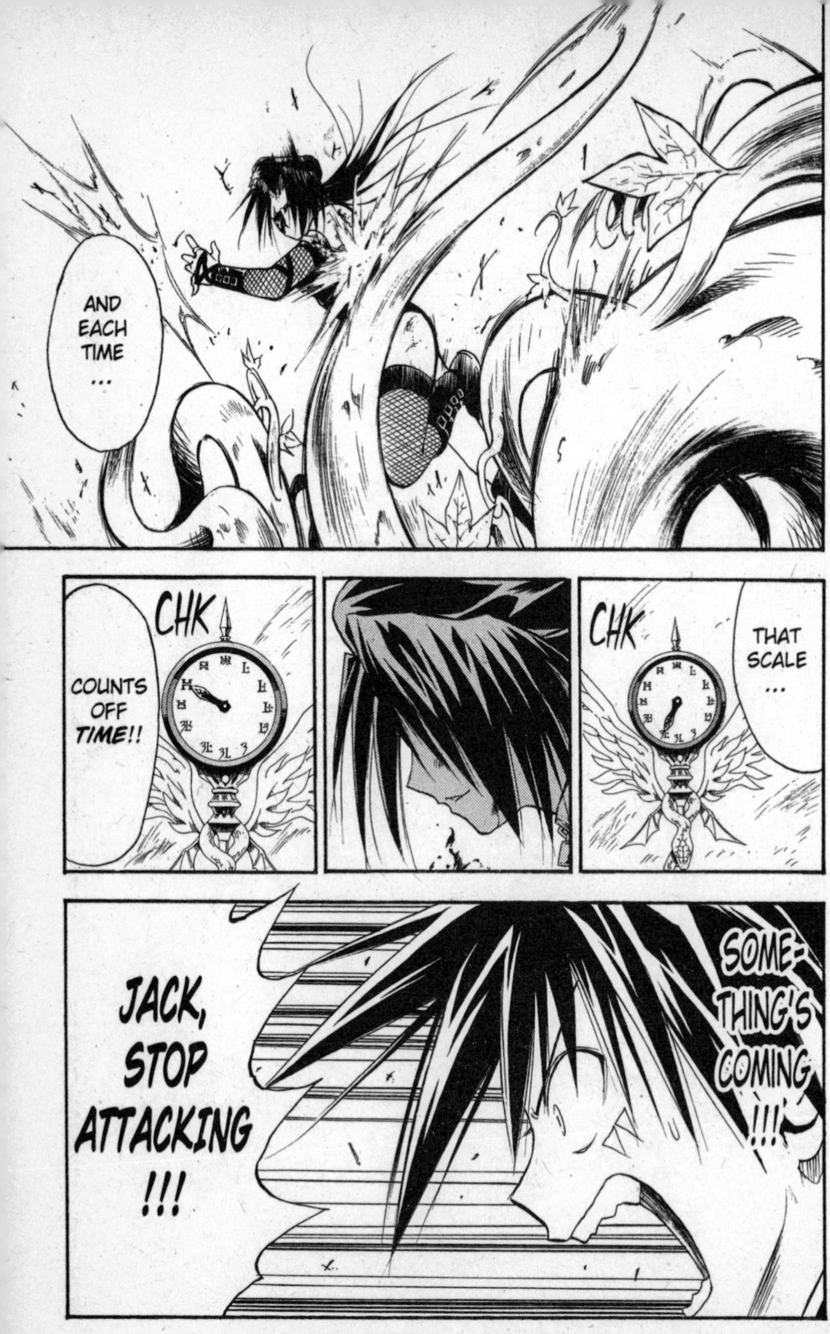
AND EACH TIME ...
CHK
THAT SCALE ...
CHK
COUNTS OFF *TIME!!*
SOME-THING'S COMING !!!
JACK, STOP ATTACKING !!!

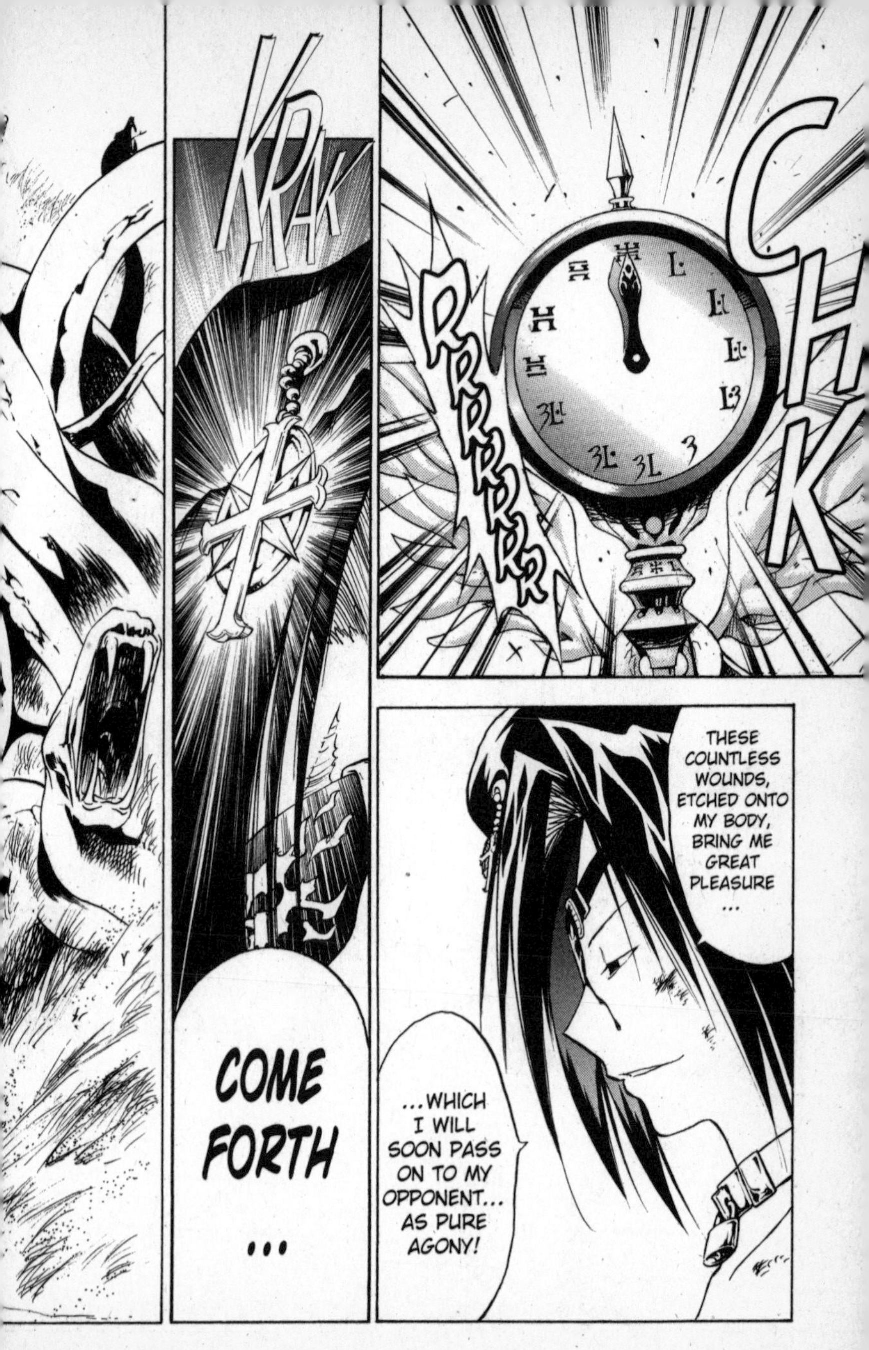
CHAK
RRRRRRRRR
THESE COUNTLESS WOUNDS, ETCHED ONTO MY BODY, BRING ME GREAT PLEASURE ...
...WHICH I WILL SOON PASS ON TO MY OPPONENT... AS PURE AGONY!
KRAK
COME FORTH ...

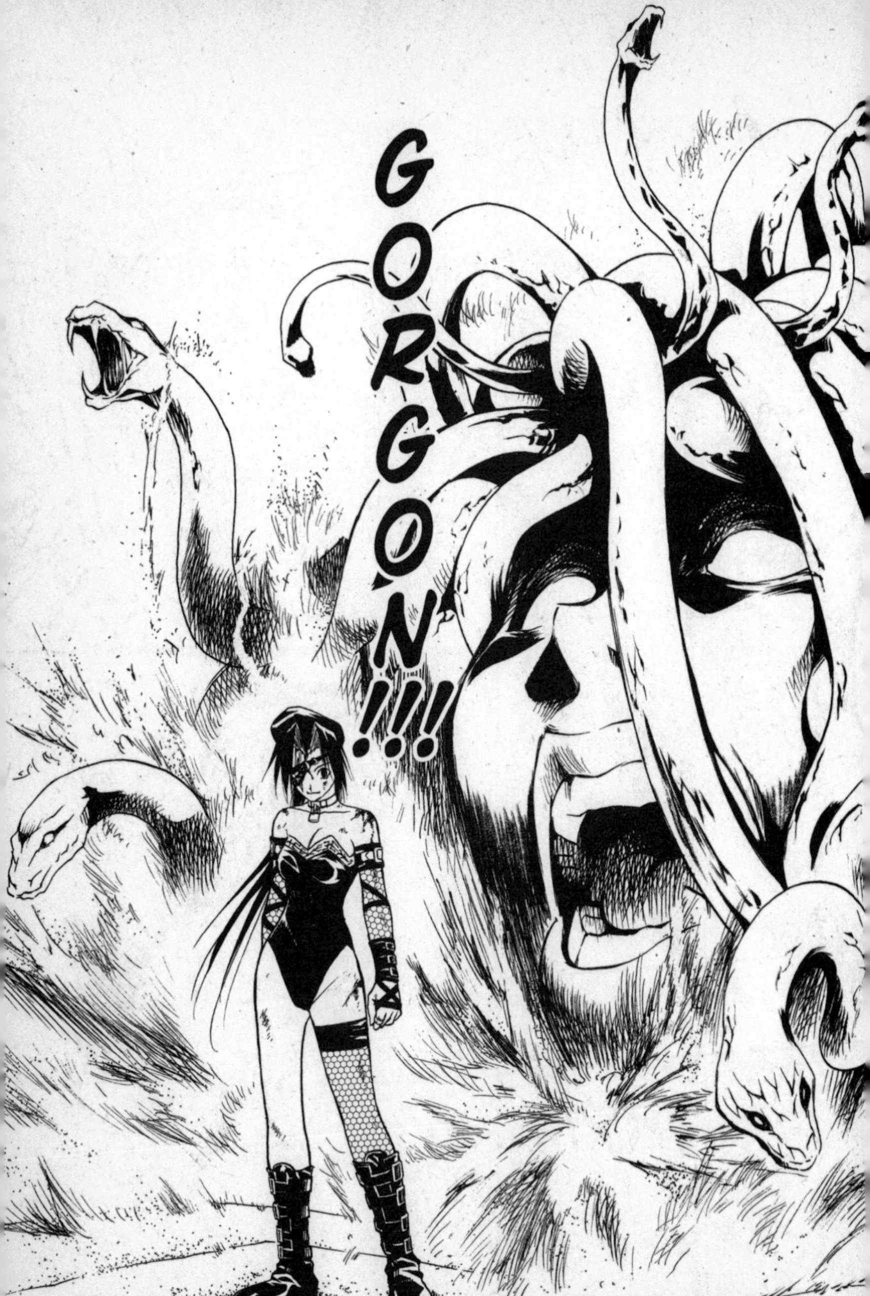
GORGON!!!!

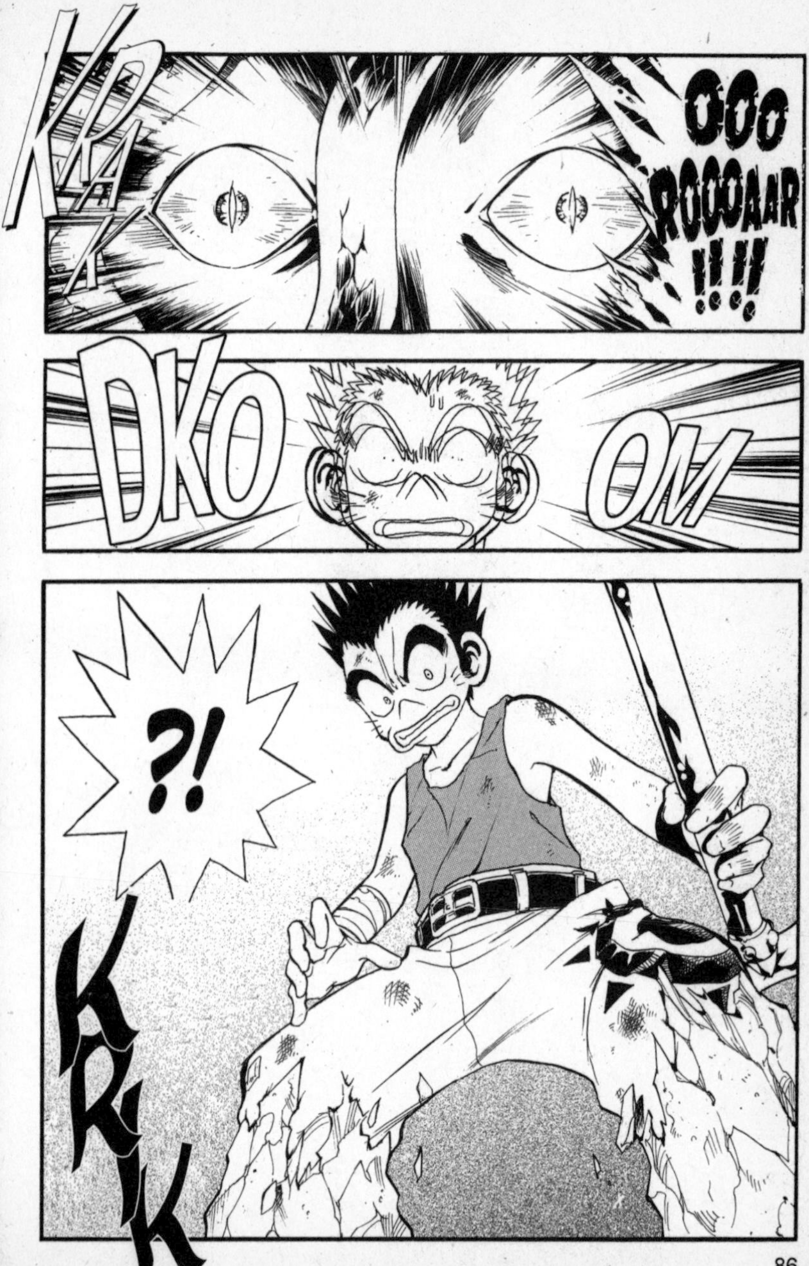
OOO ROOOAAR!!!!
KRAAK
DKOOM
?!
KRKK

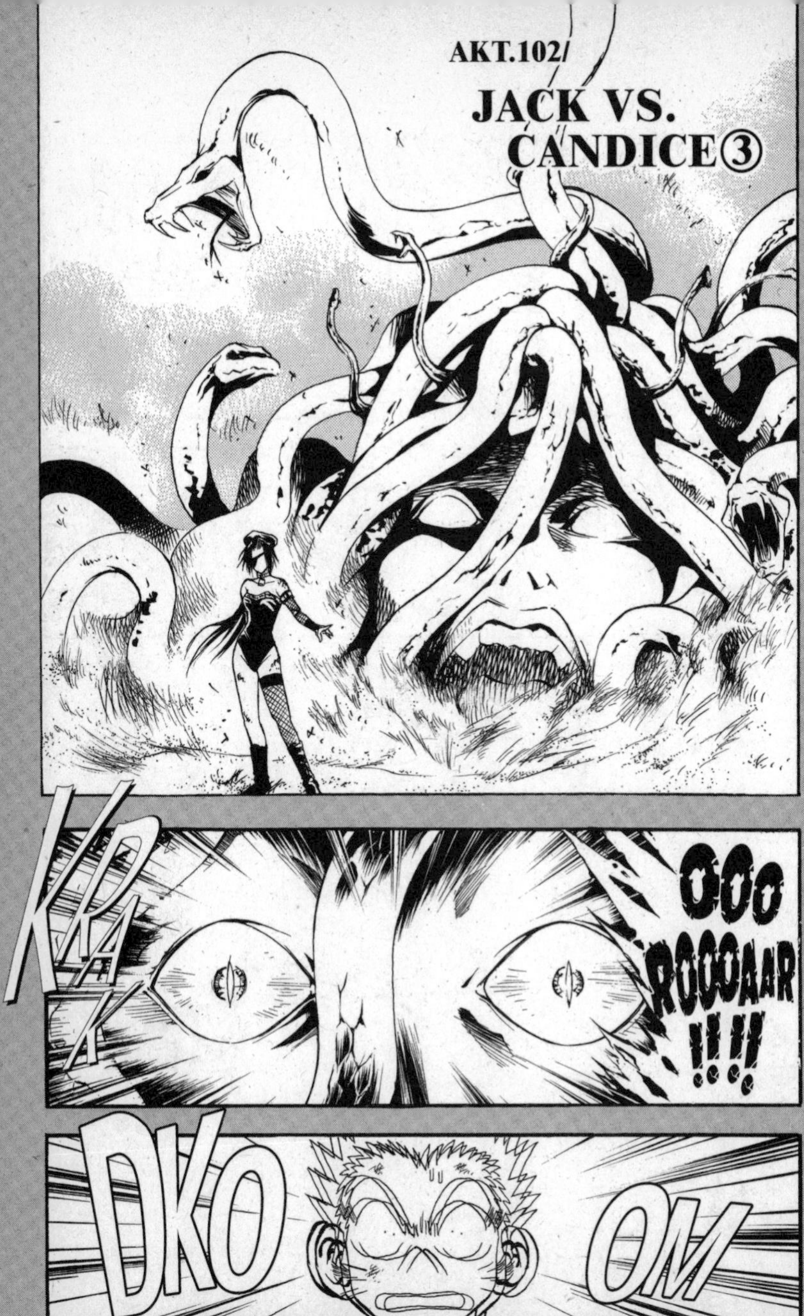

AKT.102/
JACK VS. CANDICE③
OOO ROOOAAR!!!!
KRAK
DKOOM

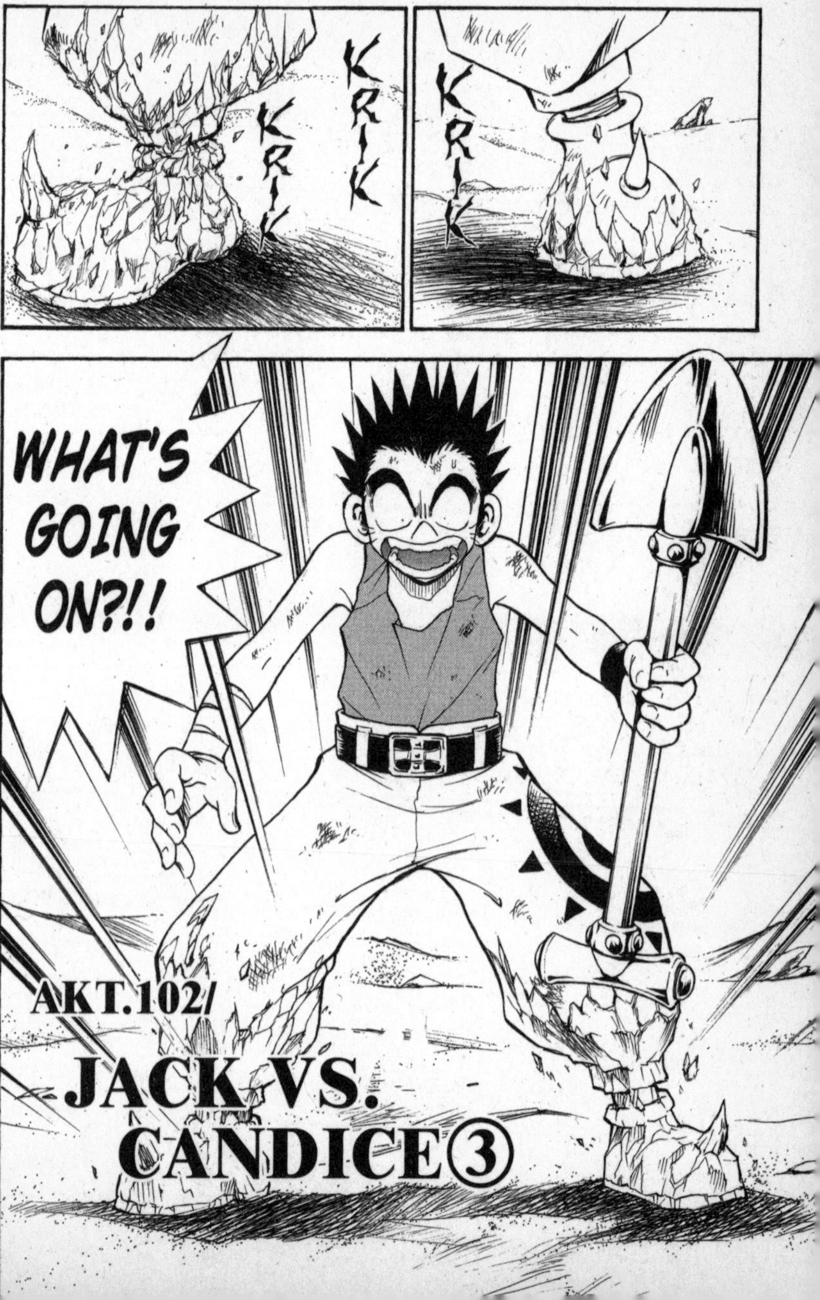
KRIK
KRIK
KRIK
WHAT'S GOING ON?!!
AKT.102/
JACK VS. CANDICE③

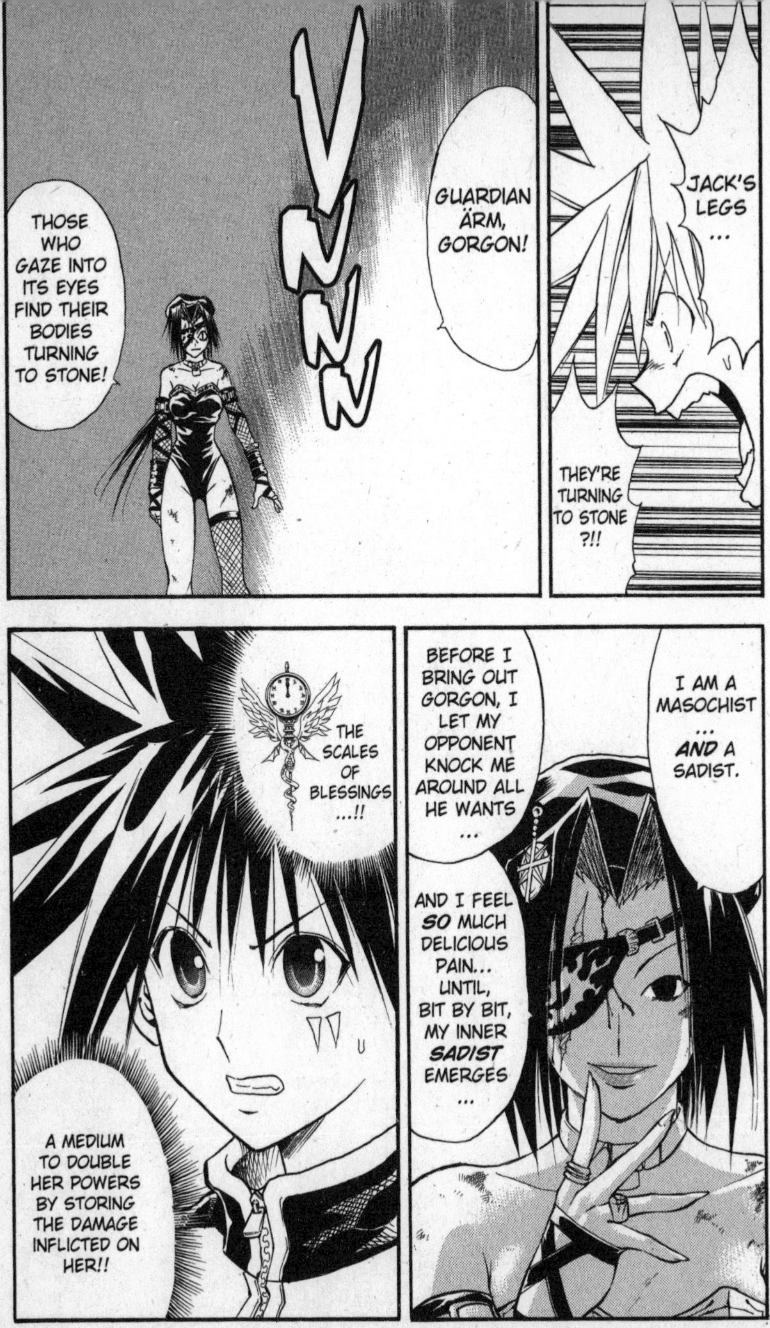
JACK'S LEGS ...
THEY'RE TURNING TO STONE ?!!
GUARDIAN ÄRM, GORGON!
VNNNN
THOSE WHO GAZE INTO ITS EYES FIND THEIR BODIES TURNING TO STONE!
I AM A MASOCHIST ... *AND* A SADIST.
BEFORE I BRING OUT GORGON, I LET MY OPPONENT KNOCK ME AROUND ALL HE WANTS ...
AND I FEEL *SO* MUCH DELICIOUS PAIN... UNTIL, BIT BY BIT, MY INNER *SADIST* EMERGES ...
THE SCALES OF BLESSINGS ...!!
A MEDIUM TO DOUBLE HER POWERS BY STORING THE DAMAGE INFLICTED ON HER!!

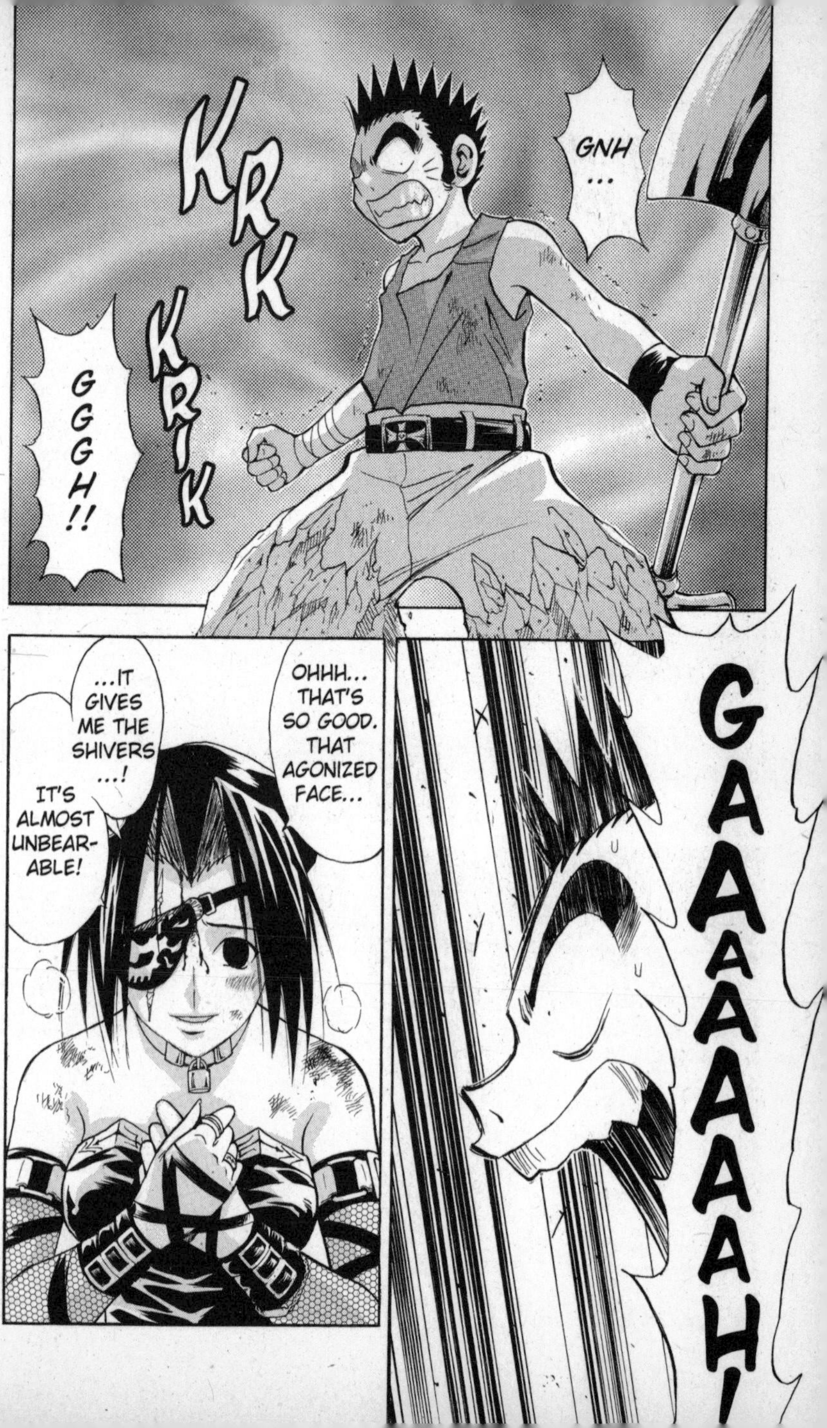
GNH...
KRK
KRIK
GGGH!!
GAAAAAAH!
OHHH... THAT'S SO GOOD. THAT AGONIZED FACE...
...IT GIVES ME THE SHIVERS...!
IT'S ALMOST UNBEAR-ABLE!

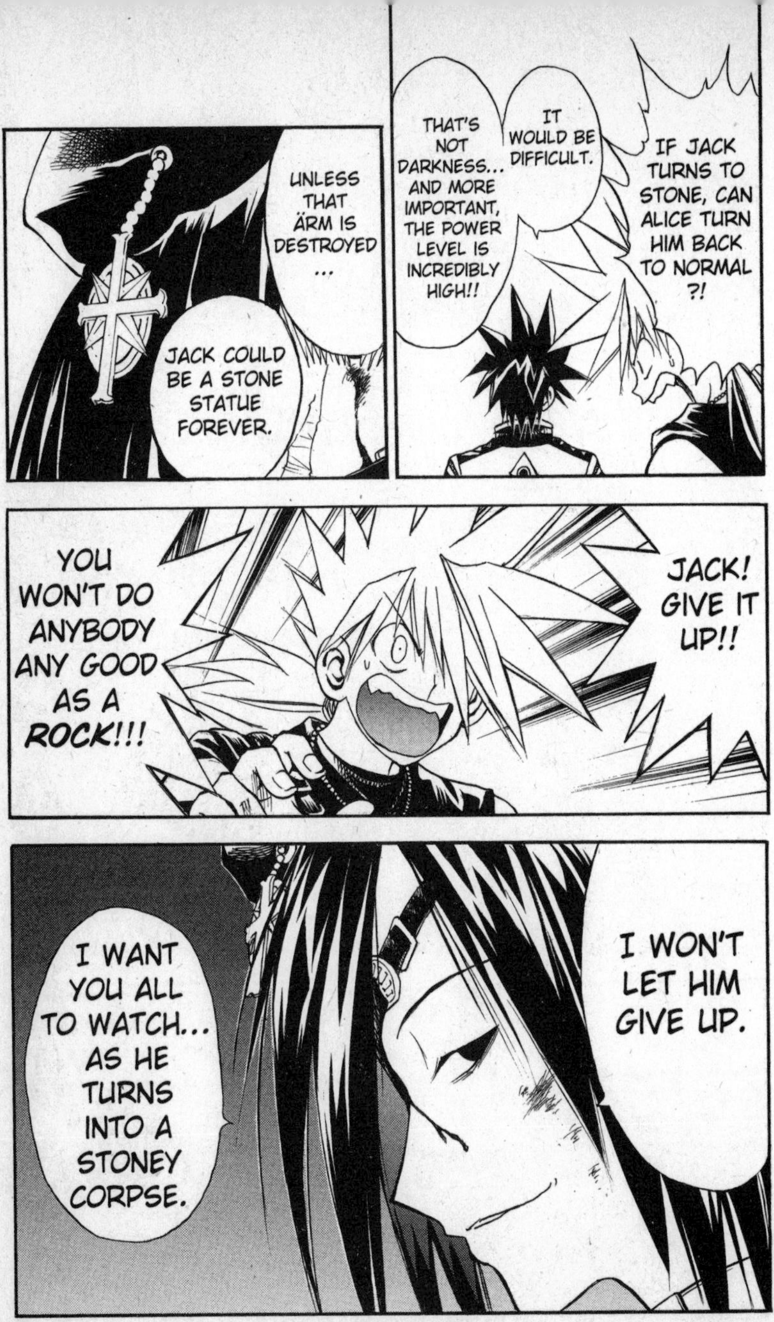
IF JACK TURNS TO STONE, CAN ALICE TURN HIM BACK TO NORMAL?!
IT WOULD BE DIFFICULT.
THAT'S NOT DARKNESS... AND MORE IMPORTANT, THE POWER LEVEL IS INCREDIBLY HIGH!!
UNLESS THAT ÄRM IS DESTROYED...
JACK COULD BE A STONE STATUE FOREVER.
JACK! GIVE IT UP!!
YOU WON'T DO ANYBODY ANY GOOD AS A *ROCK*!!!
I WON'T LET HIM GIVE UP.
I WANT YOU ALL TO WATCH... AS HE TURNS INTO A STONEY CORPSE.

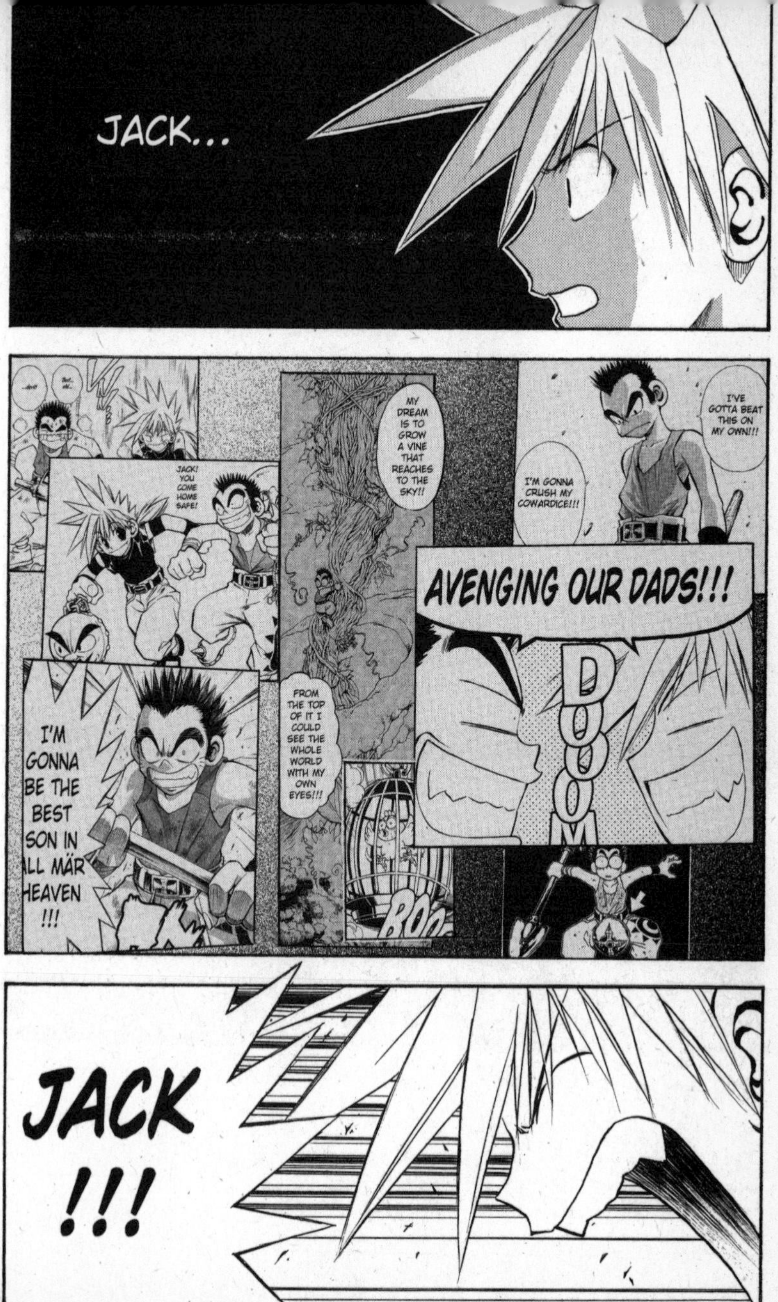
JACK...
I'VE GOTTA BEAT THIS ON MY OWN!!!
I'M GONNA CRUSH MY COWARDICE!!!
AVENGING OUR DADS!!!
DOOOOM
MY DREAM IS TO GROW A VINE THAT REACHES TO THE SKY!!
FROM THE TOP OF IT I COULD SEE THE WHOLE WORLD WITH MY OWN EYES!!!
JACK! YOU COME HOME SAFE!
I'M GONNA BE THE BEST SON IN ALL MÄR HEAVEN!!!
JACK!!!

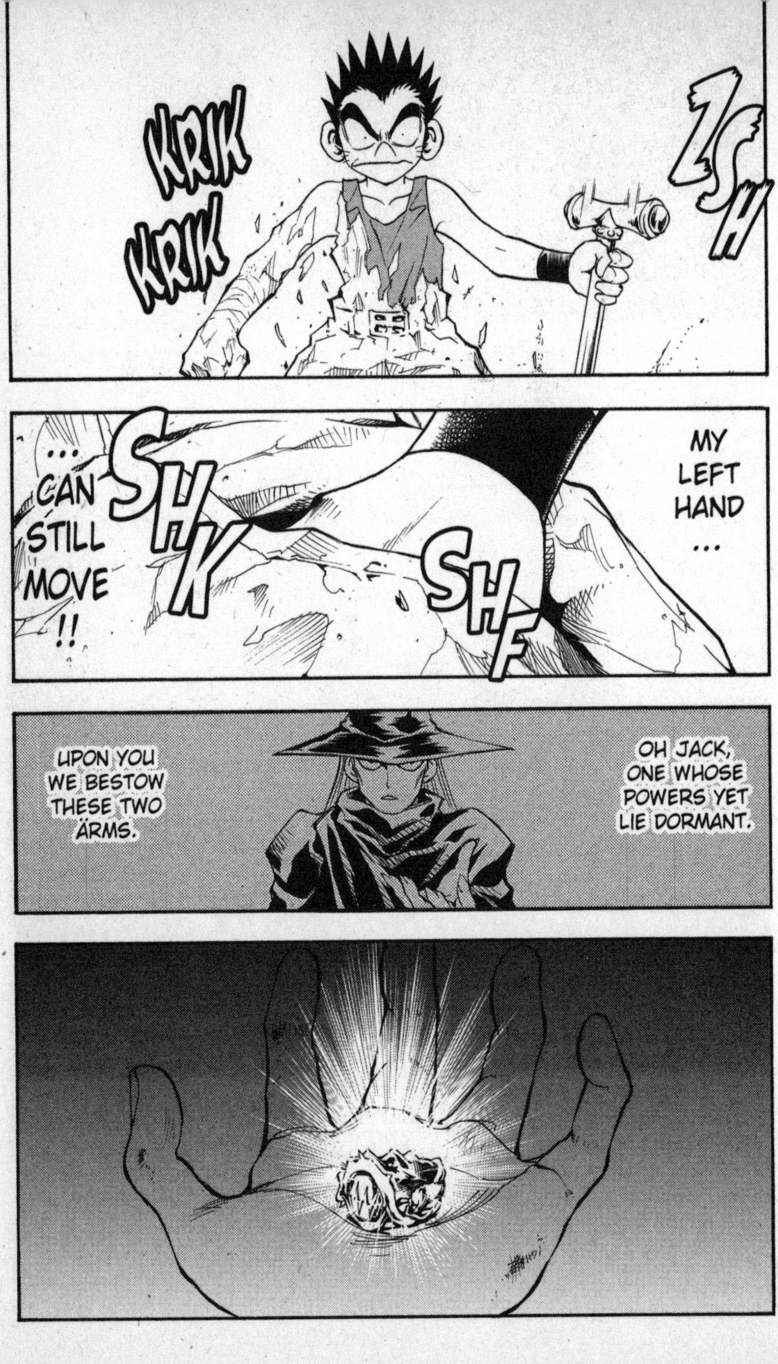
ZSH
KRIK KRIK
MY LEFT HAND ...
SHF
SHK
... CAN STILL MOVE !!
OH JACK, ONE WHOSE POWERS YET LIE DORMANT.
UPON YOU WE BESTOW THESE TWO ÄRMS.

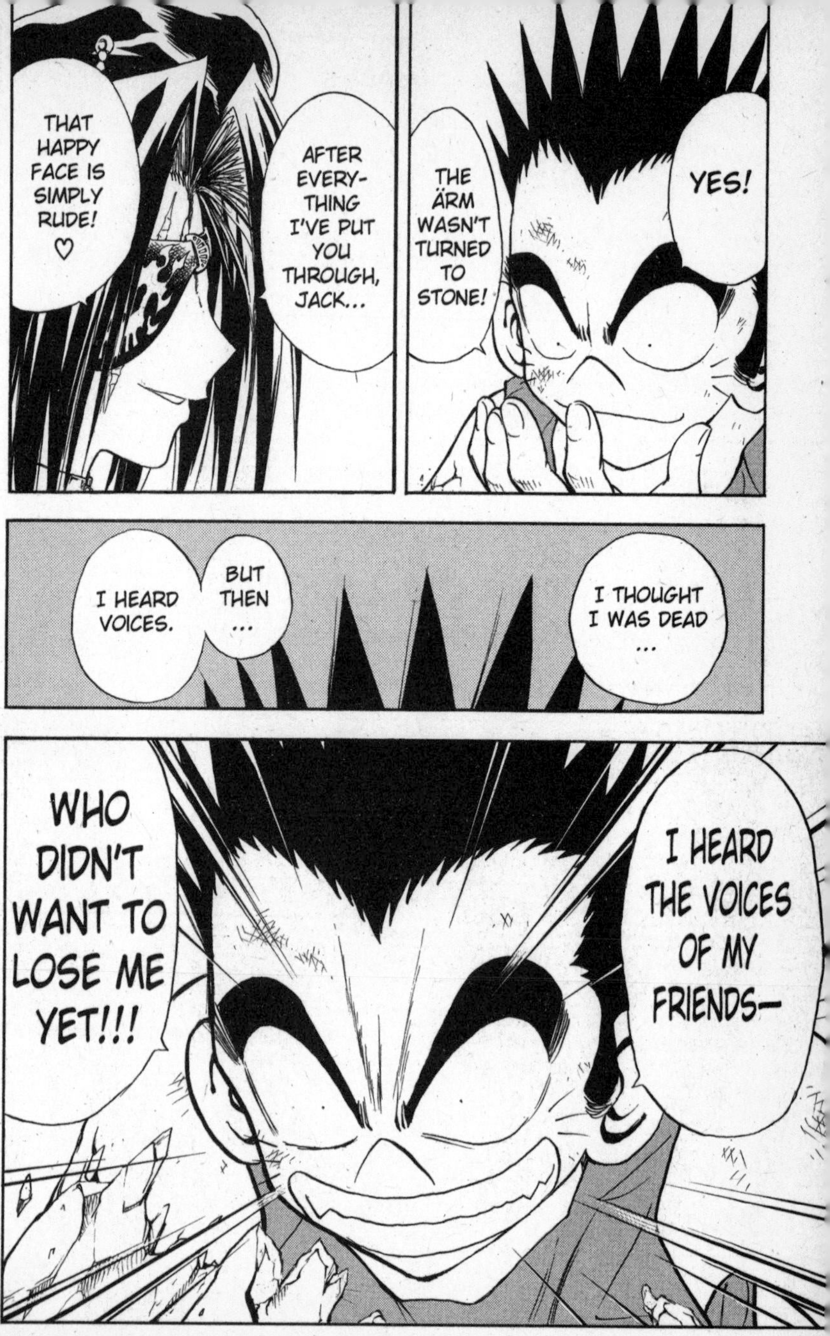
YES!
THE ÄRM WASN'T TURNED TO STONE!
AFTER EVERY-THING I'VE PUT YOU THROUGH, JACK...
THAT HAPPY FACE IS SIMPLY RUDE! ♡
I THOUGHT I WAS DEAD ...
BUT THEN ...
I HEARD VOICES.
I HEARD THE VOICES OF MY FRIENDS—
WHO DIDN'T WANT TO LOSE ME YET!!!

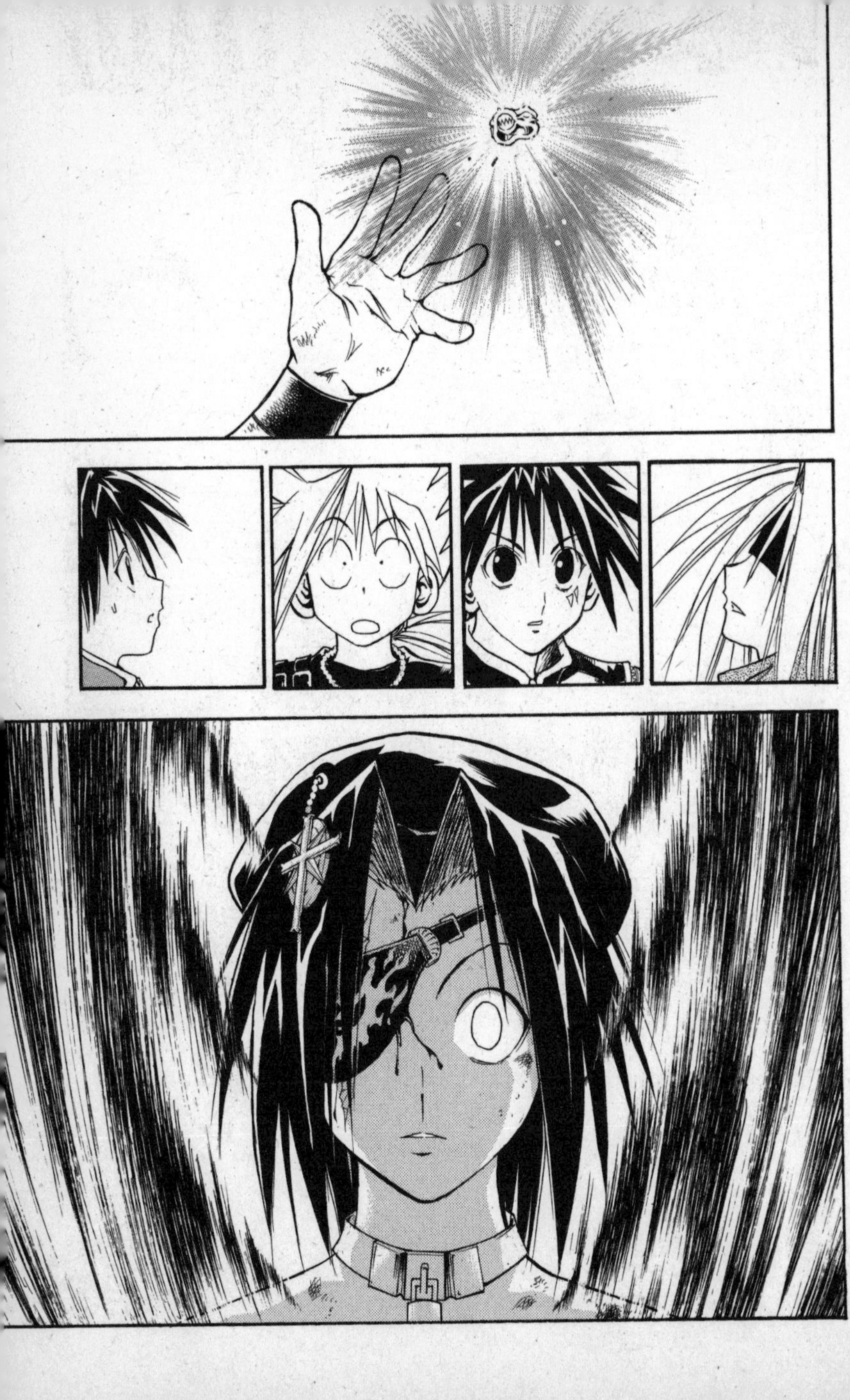

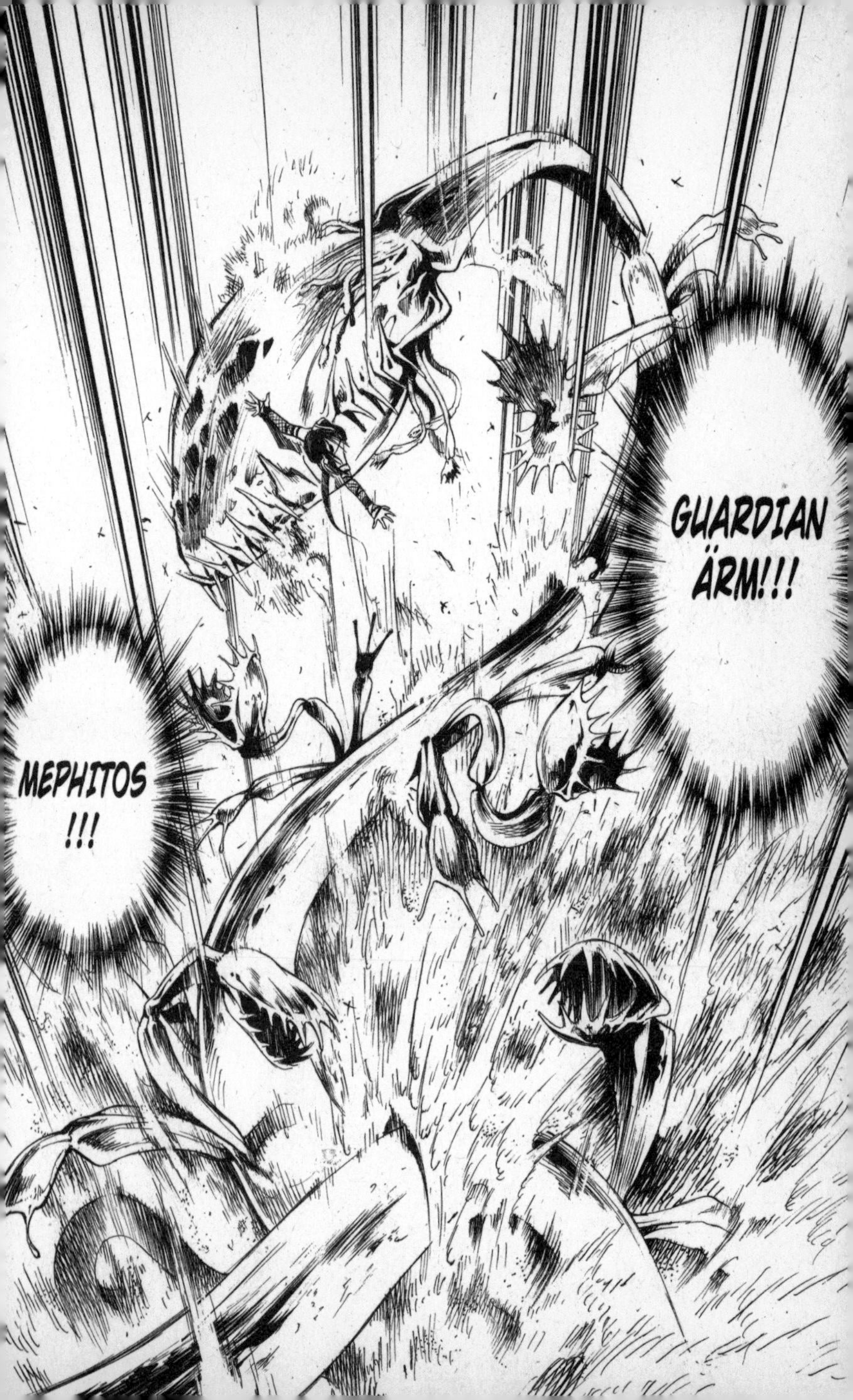
GUARDIAN ÄRM!!!
MEPHITOS !!!

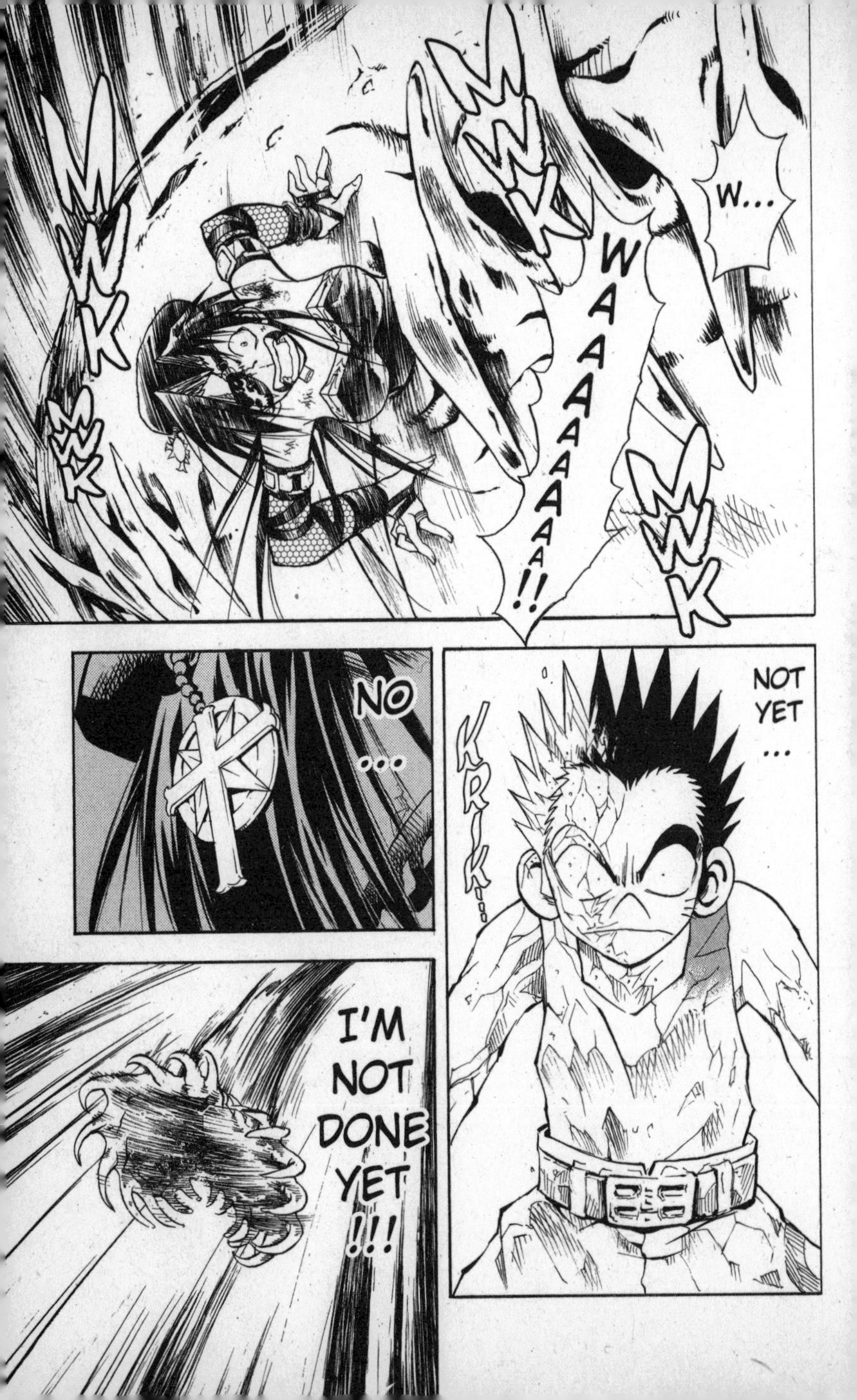
W...
WWK
WAAAAAAAAAA!!
WWK
WWWK
WWK
NOT YET ...
KRIK...
NO ...
I'M NOT DONE YET !!!

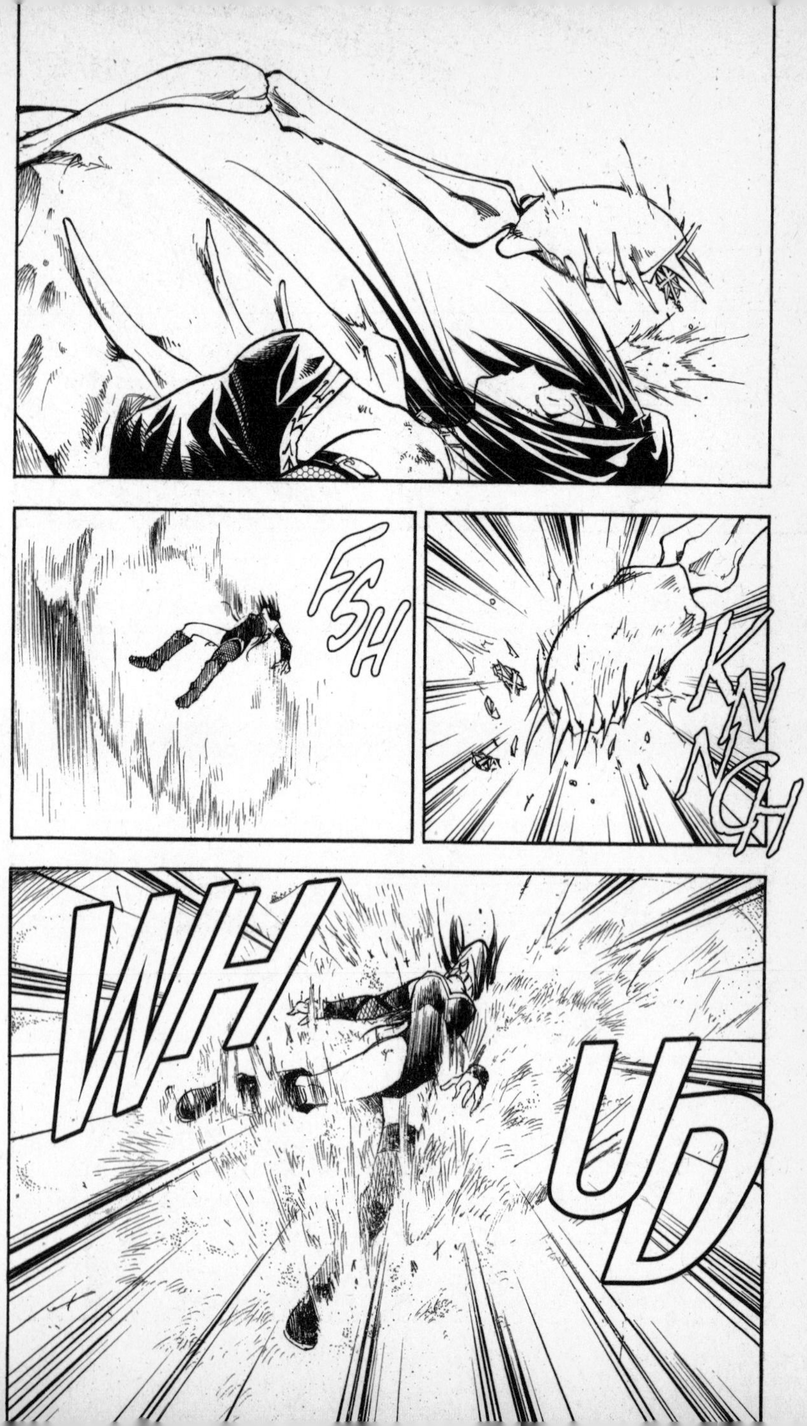
KNNCH
FSH
WHUD

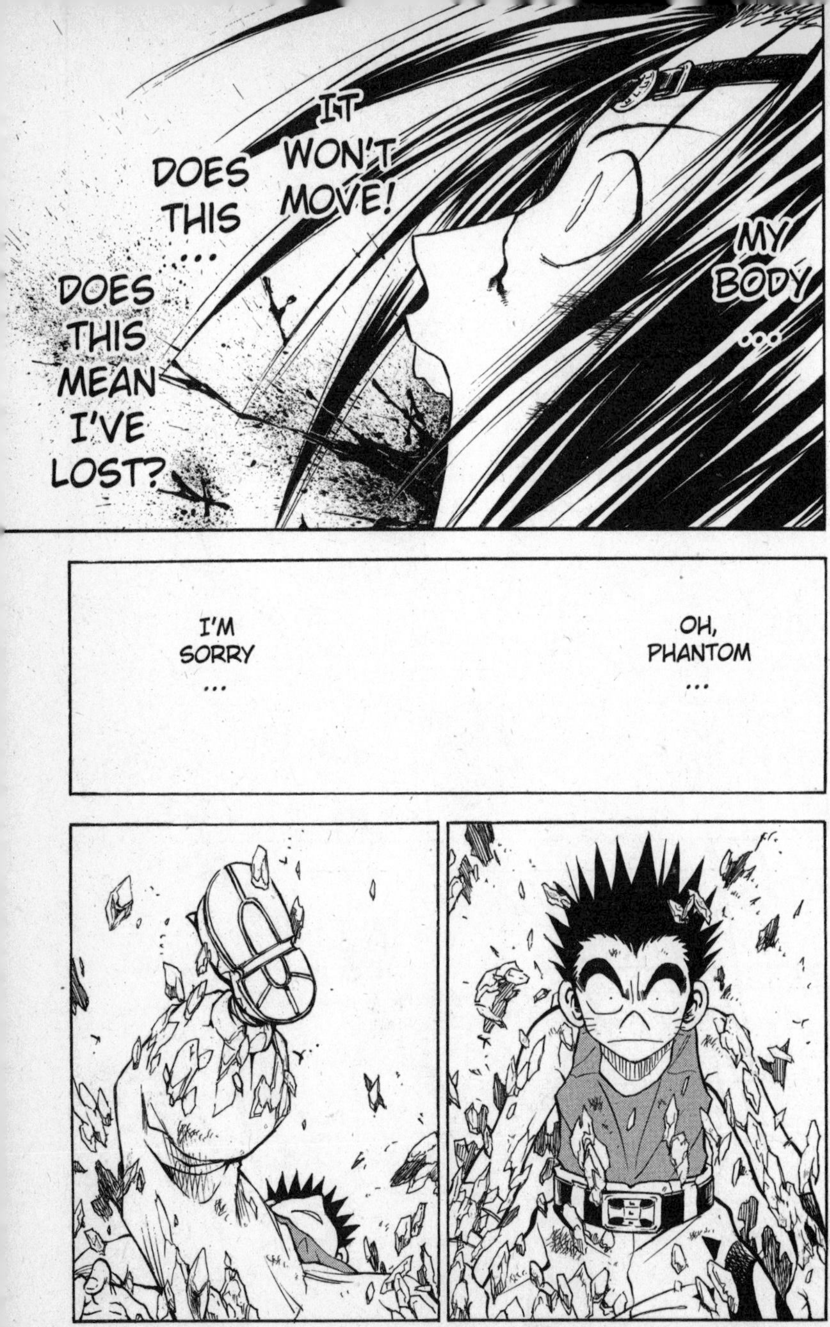
MY BODY...
IT WON'T MOVE!
DOES THIS... DOES THIS MEAN I'VE LOST?
OH, PHANTOM...
I'M SORRY...

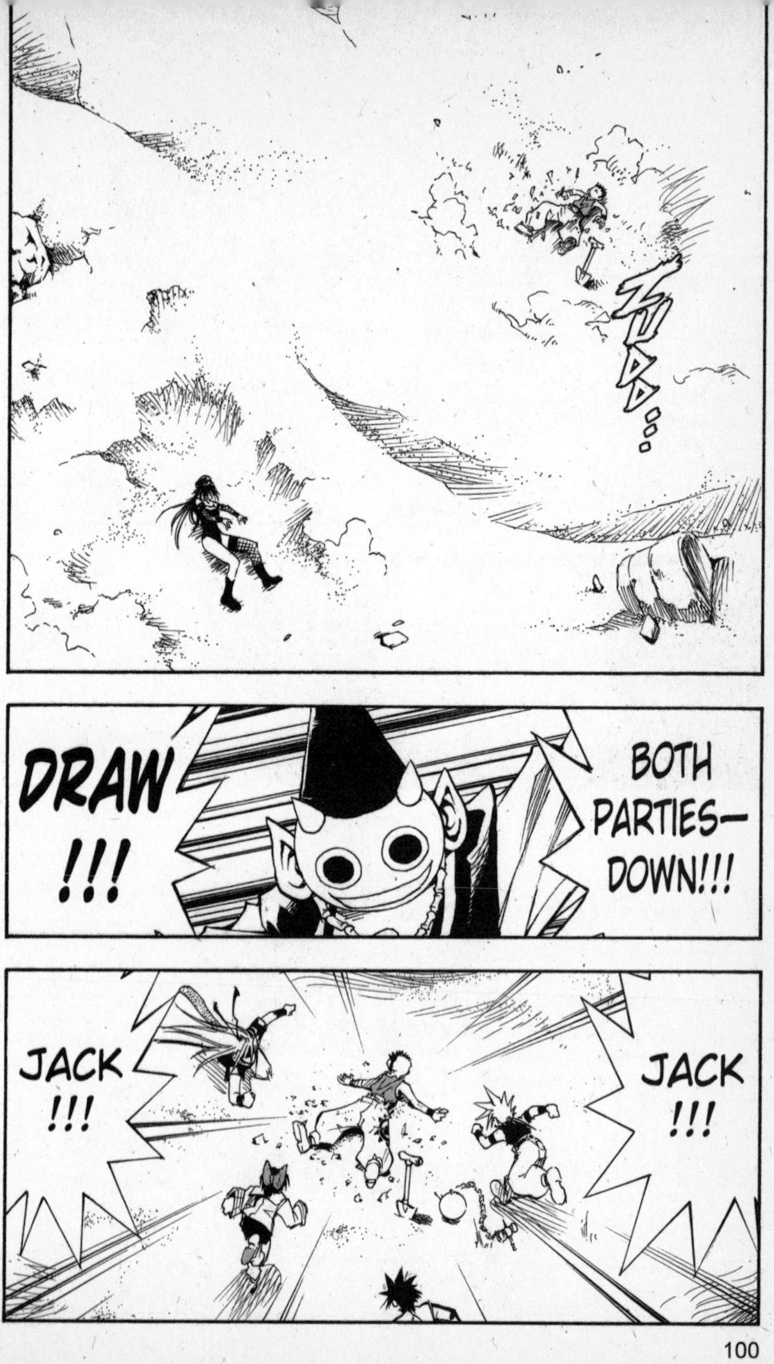
ZUDA...
BOTH PARTIES—DOWN!!!
DRAW!!!
JACK!!!
JACK!!!

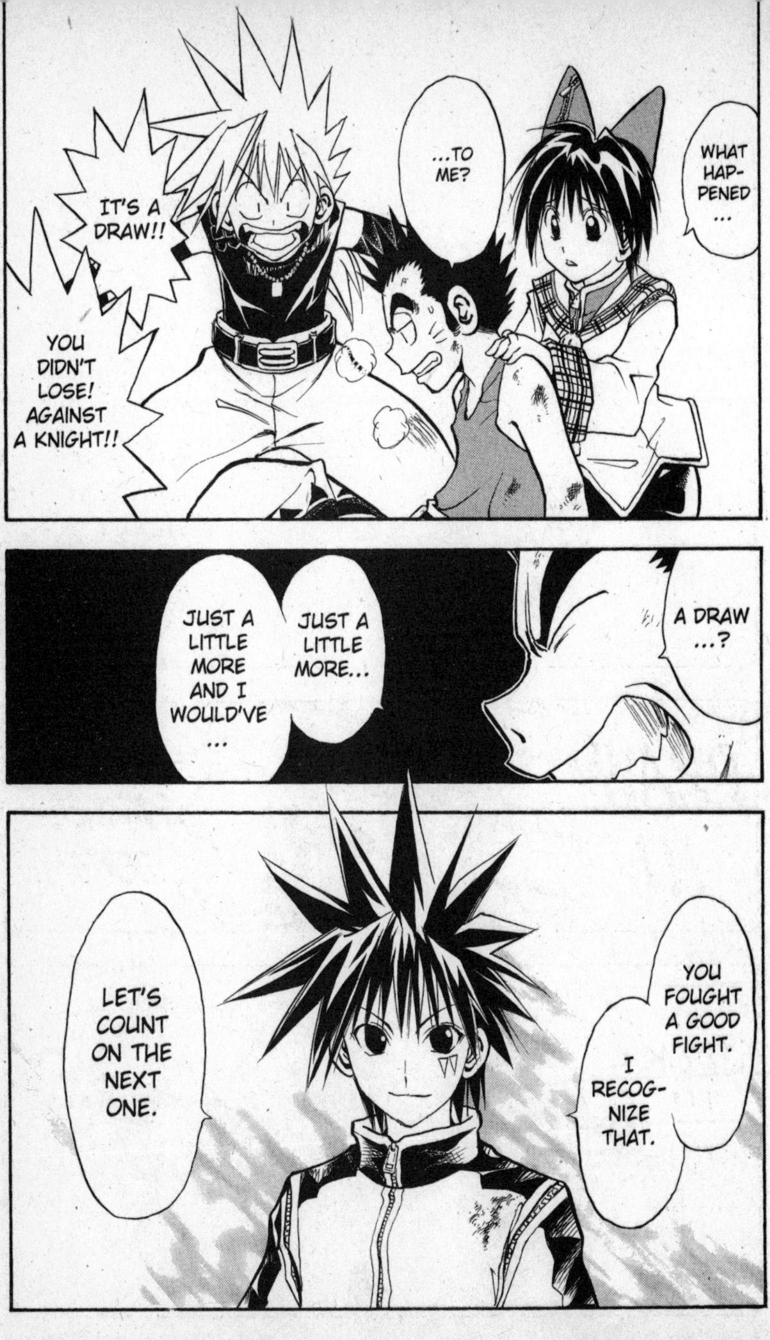
WHAT HAP-PENED ...
...TO ME?
IT'S A DRAW!!
YOU DIDN'T LOSE! AGAINST A KNIGHT!!
A DRAW ...?
JUST A LITTLE MORE...
JUST A LITTLE MORE AND I WOULD'VE ...
YOU FOUGHT A GOOD FIGHT.
I RECOG-NIZE THAT.
LET'S COUNT ON THE NEXT ONE.

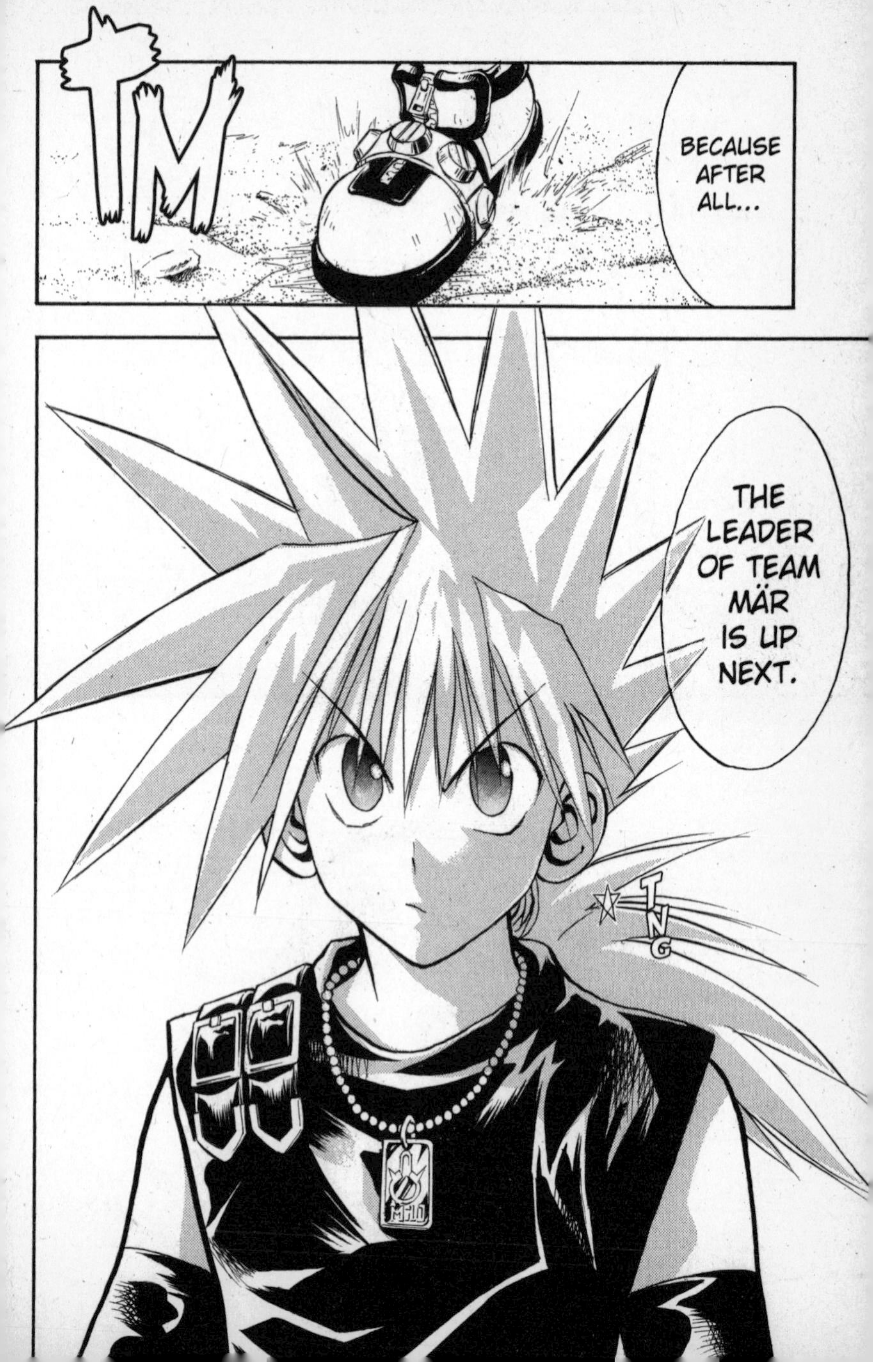
TM
BECAUSE AFTER ALL...
THE LEADER OF TEAM MÄR IS UP NEXT.
TING

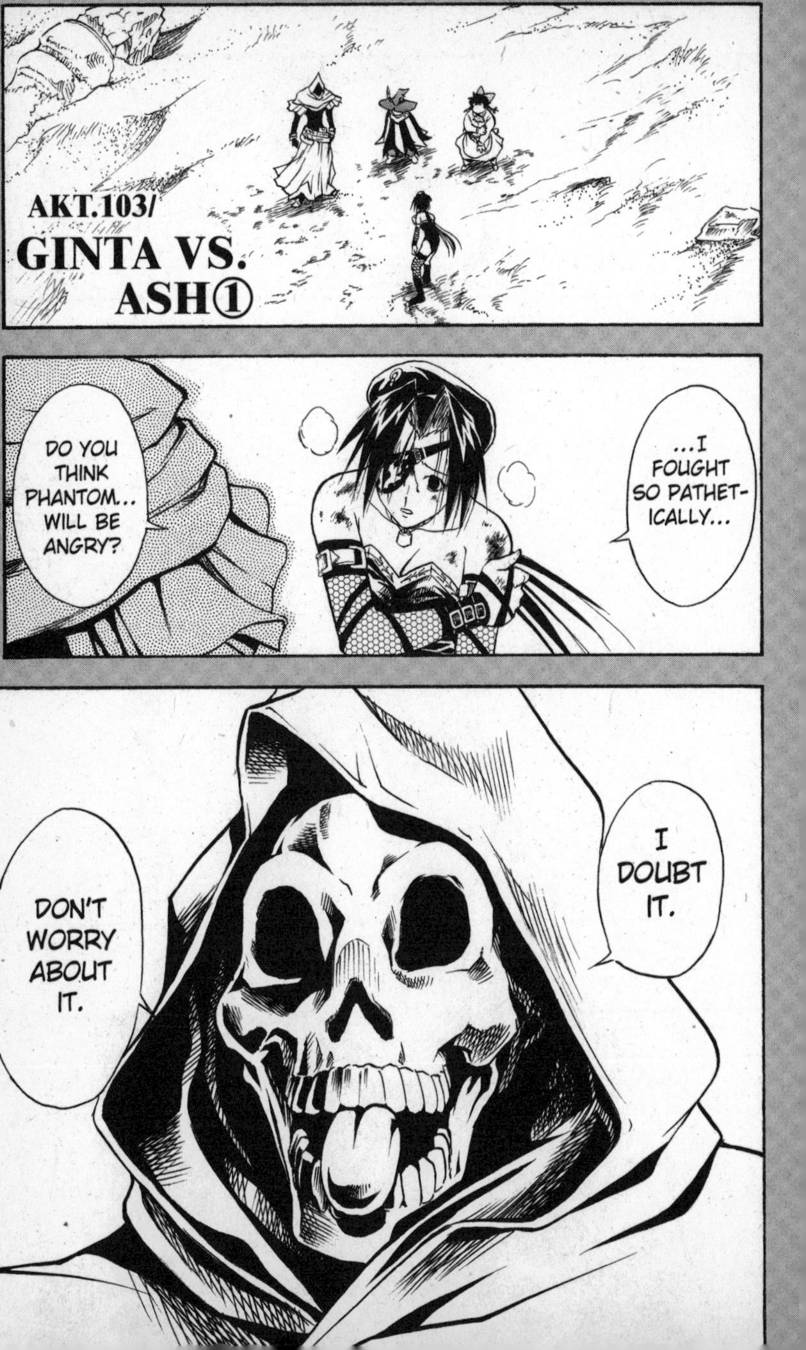
AKT.103/
GINTA VS. ASH①
...I FOUGHT SO PATHETICALLY...
DO YOU THINK PHANTOM... WILL BE ANGRY?
I DOUBT IT.
DON'T WORRY ABOUT IT.

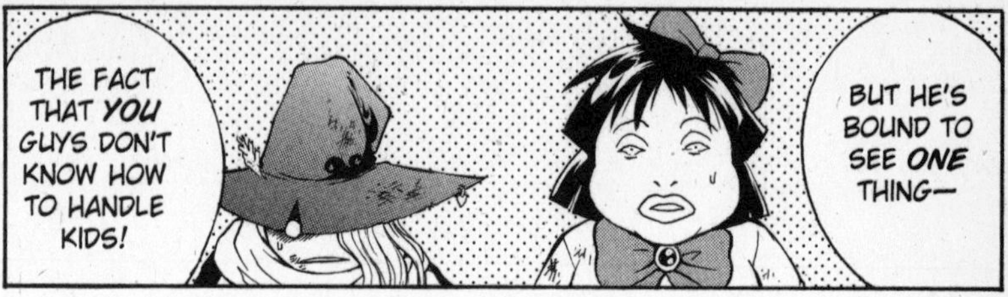
BUT HE'S BOUND TO SEE *ONE* THING—
THE FACT THAT *YOU* GUYS DON'T KNOW HOW TO HANDLE KIDS!

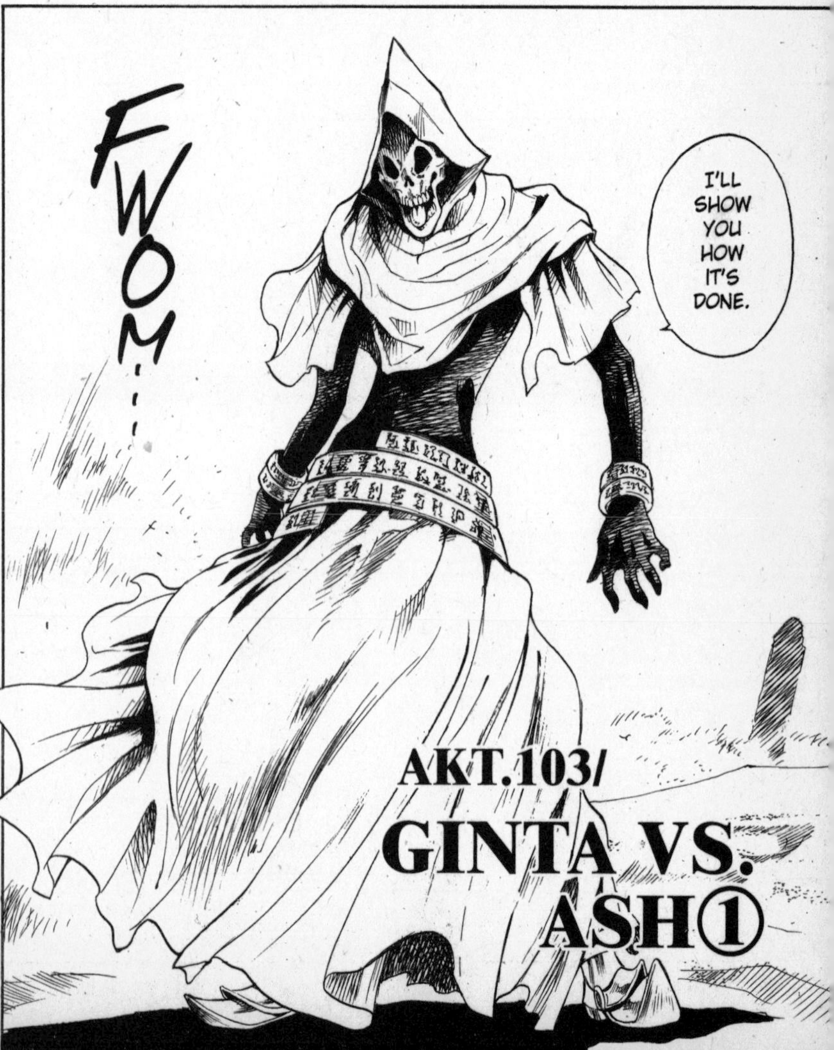
I'LL SHOW YOU HOW IT'S DONE.
FWOM...

AKT.103/ GINTA VS. ASH①

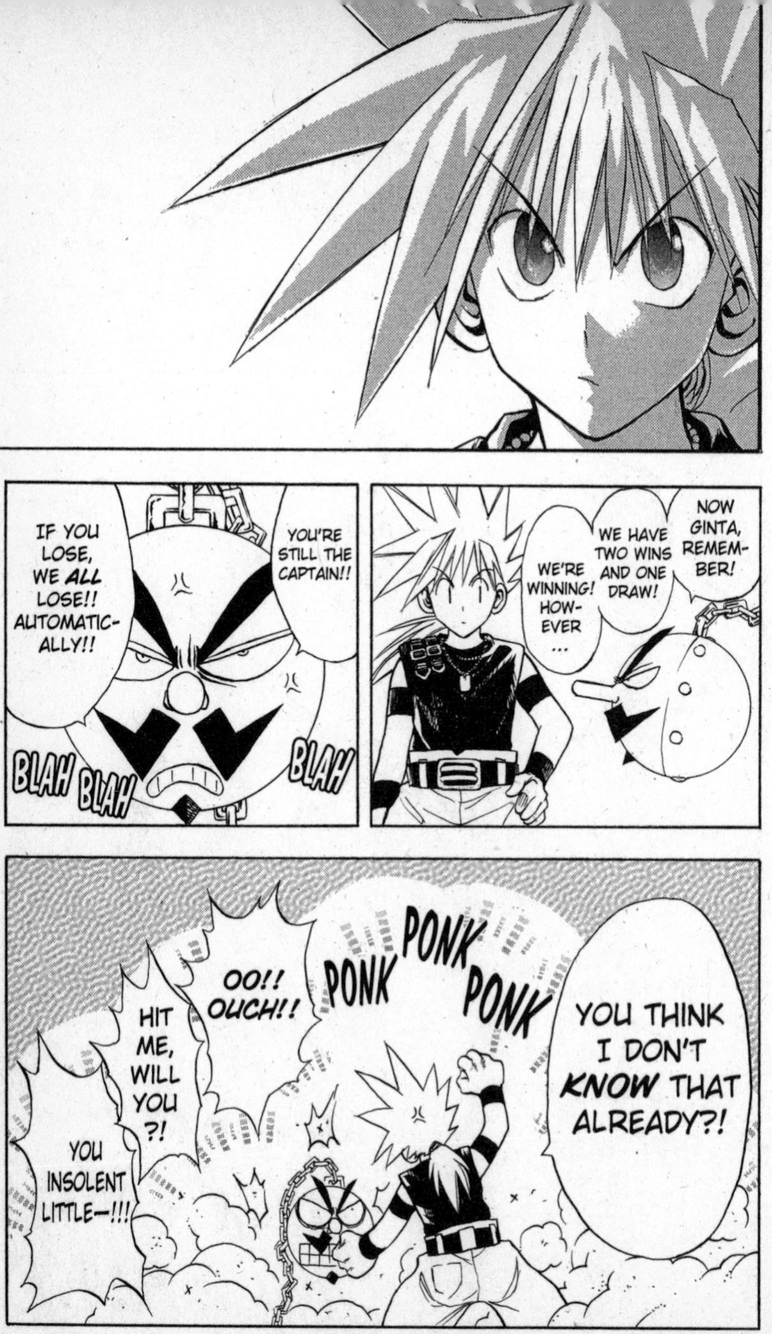
NOW GINTA, REMEMBER!
WE HAVE TWO WINS AND ONE DRAW!
WE'RE WINNING! HOWEVER ...
YOU'RE STILL THE CAPTAIN!!
IF YOU LOSE, WE ALL LOSE!! AUTOMATICALLY!!
BLAH
BLAH BLAH
YOU THINK I DON'T KNOW THAT ALREADY?!
PONK PONK PONK
OO!! OUCH!!
HIT ME, WILL YOU?!
YOU INSOLENT LITTLE—!!!

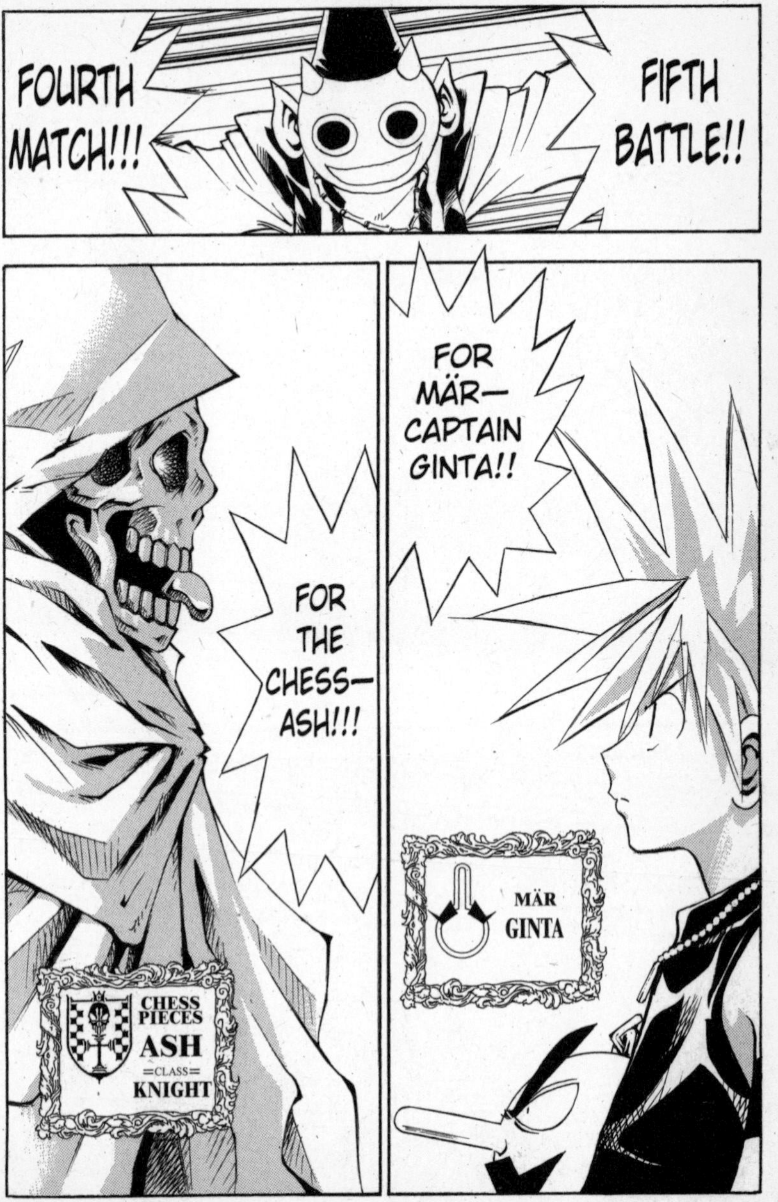
FIFTH BATTLE!!
FOURTH MATCH!!!
FOR MÄR—CAPTAIN GINTA!!
MÄR GINTA
FOR THE CHESS—ASH!!!
CHESS PIECES ASH =CLASS= KNIGHT

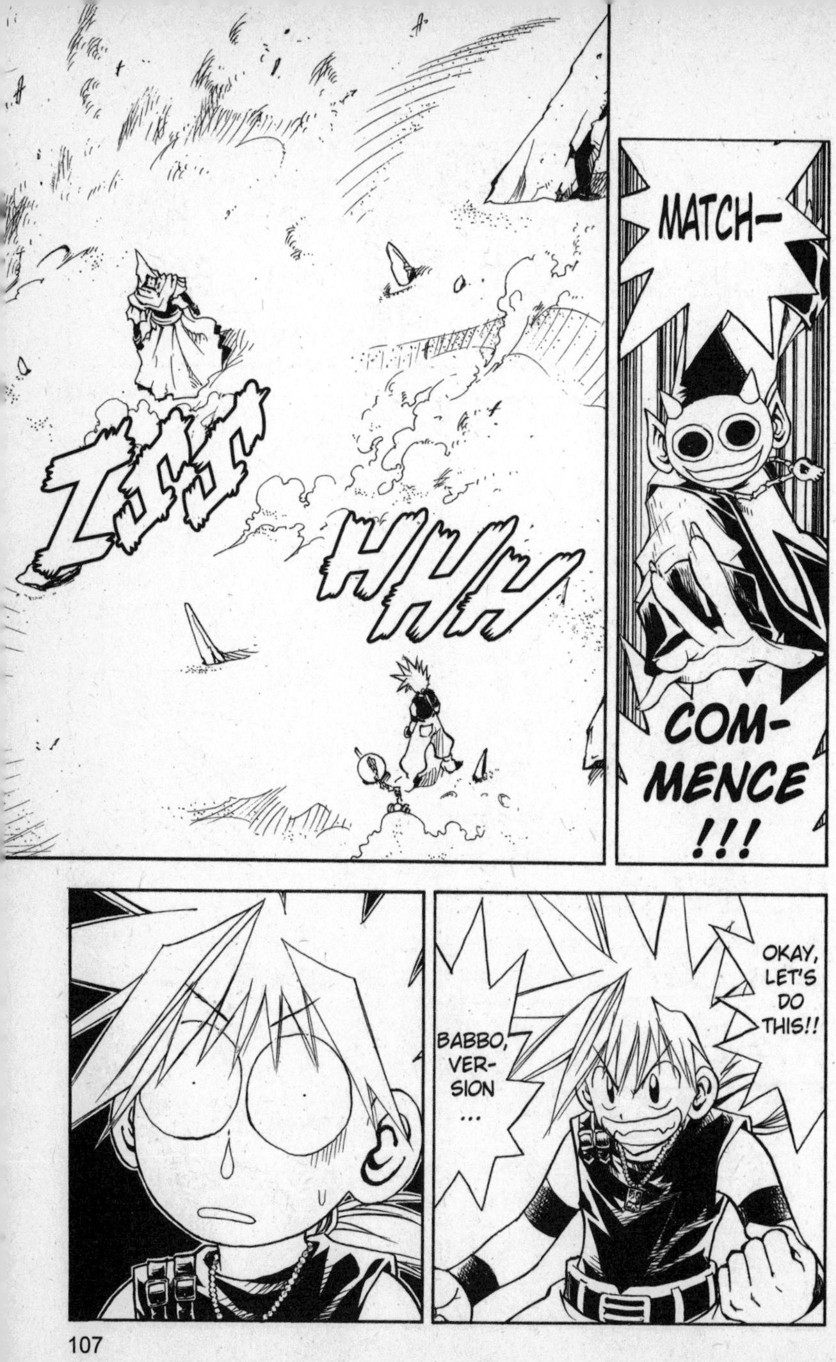
MATCH—
COM-
MENCE
!!!
OKAY, LET'S DO THIS!!
BABBO, VER-
SION
...

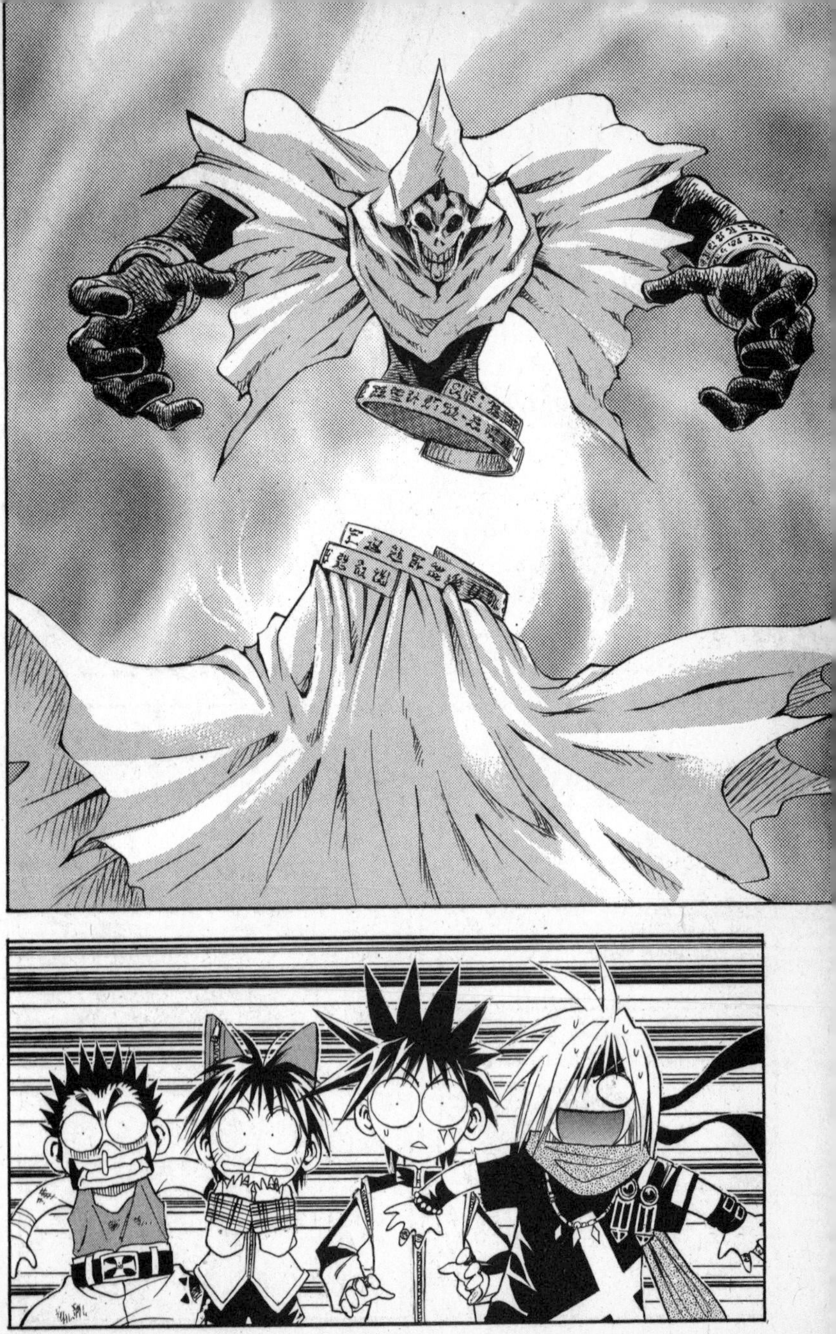

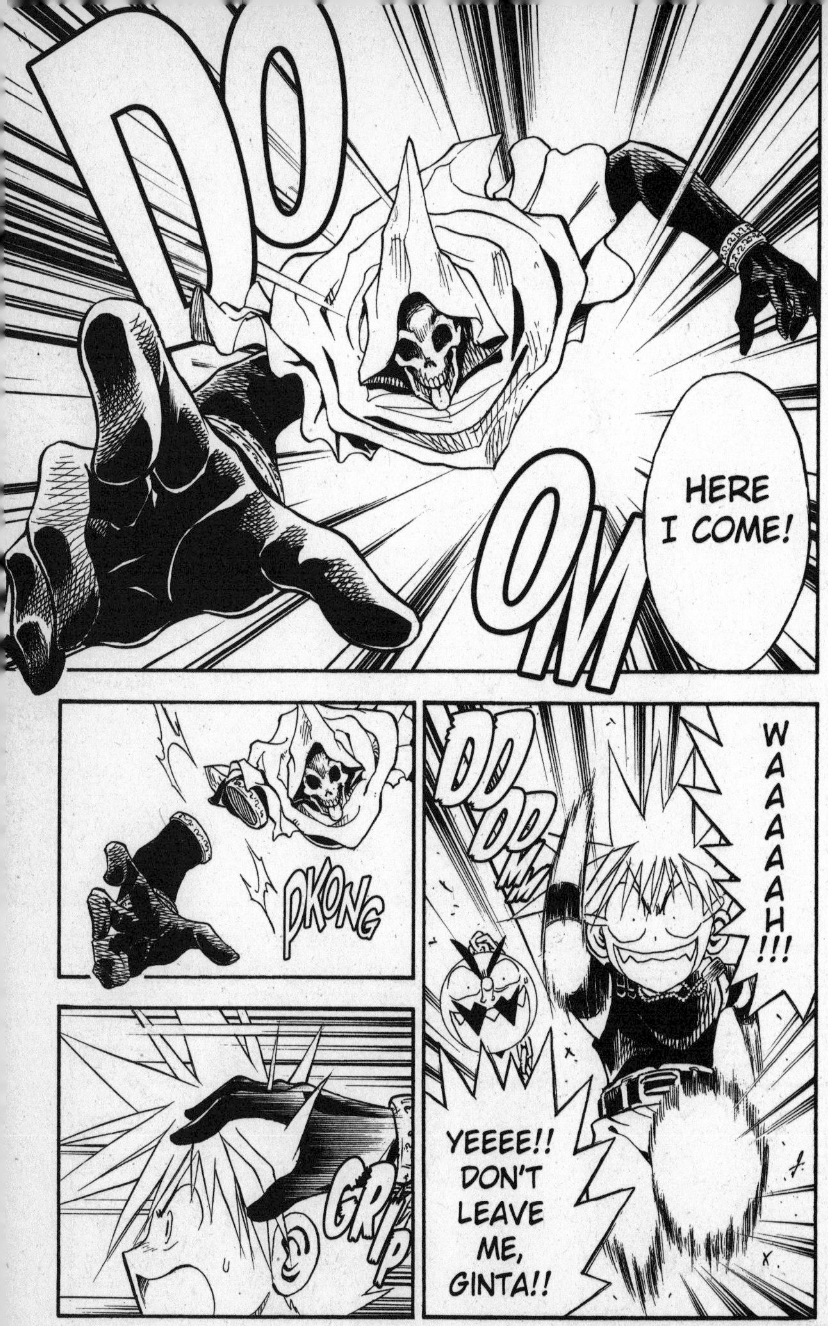
HERE I COME!
DOOM
WAAAAAAH!!!
DDDDM
YEEEE!! DON'T LEAVE ME, GINTA!!
DKONG
GRIP

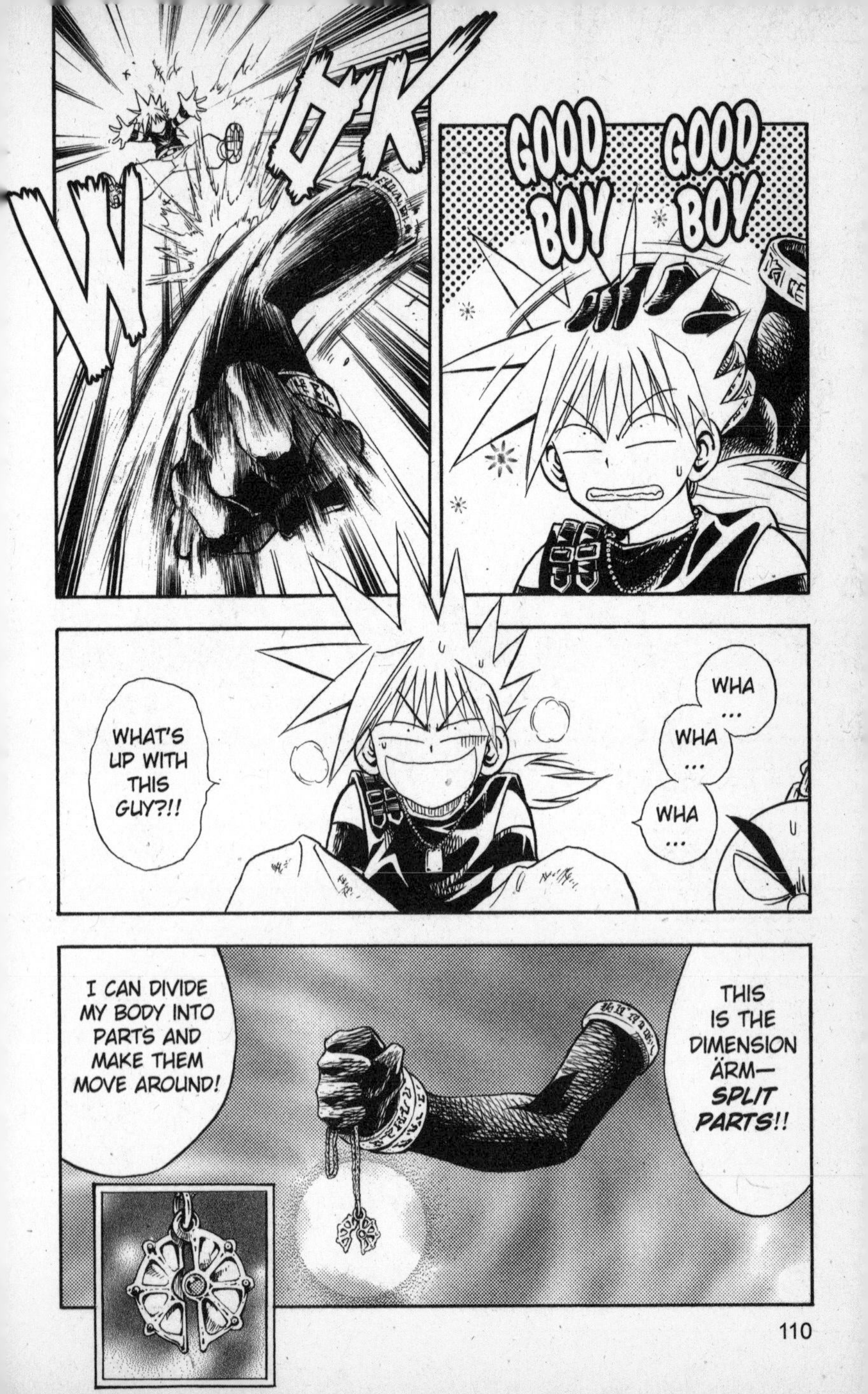
GOOD BOY GOOD BOY
WHA ...
WHA ...
WHA ...
WHAT'S UP WITH THIS GUY?!!
THIS IS THE DIMENSION ÄRM—*SPLIT PARTS*!!
I CAN DIVIDE MY BODY INTO PARTS AND MAKE THEM MOVE AROUND!

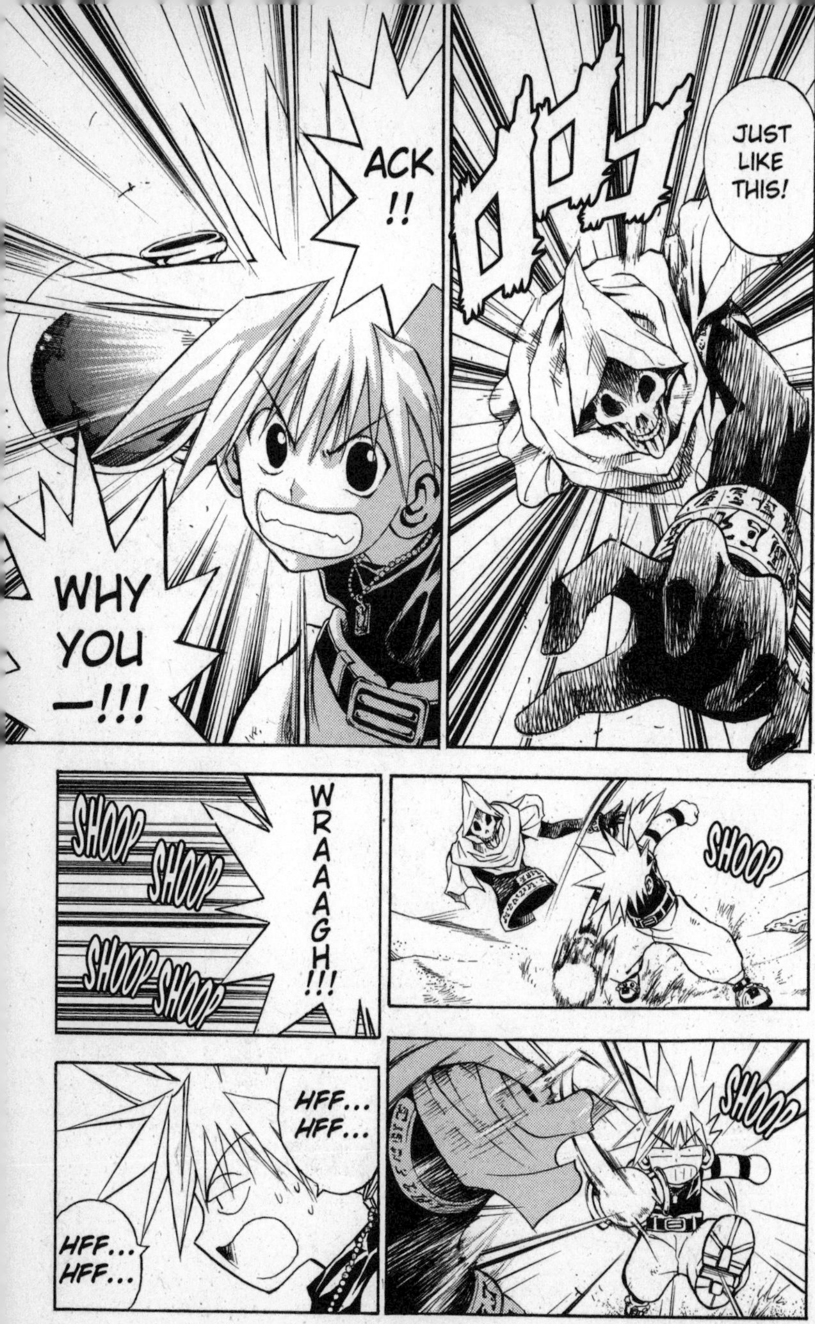
JUST LIKE THIS!
ACK!!
WHY YOU—!!!
SHOOP
WRAAAGH!!!
SHOOP
SHOOP
SHOOP
SHOOP
SHOOP
HFF... HFF...
HFF... HFF...

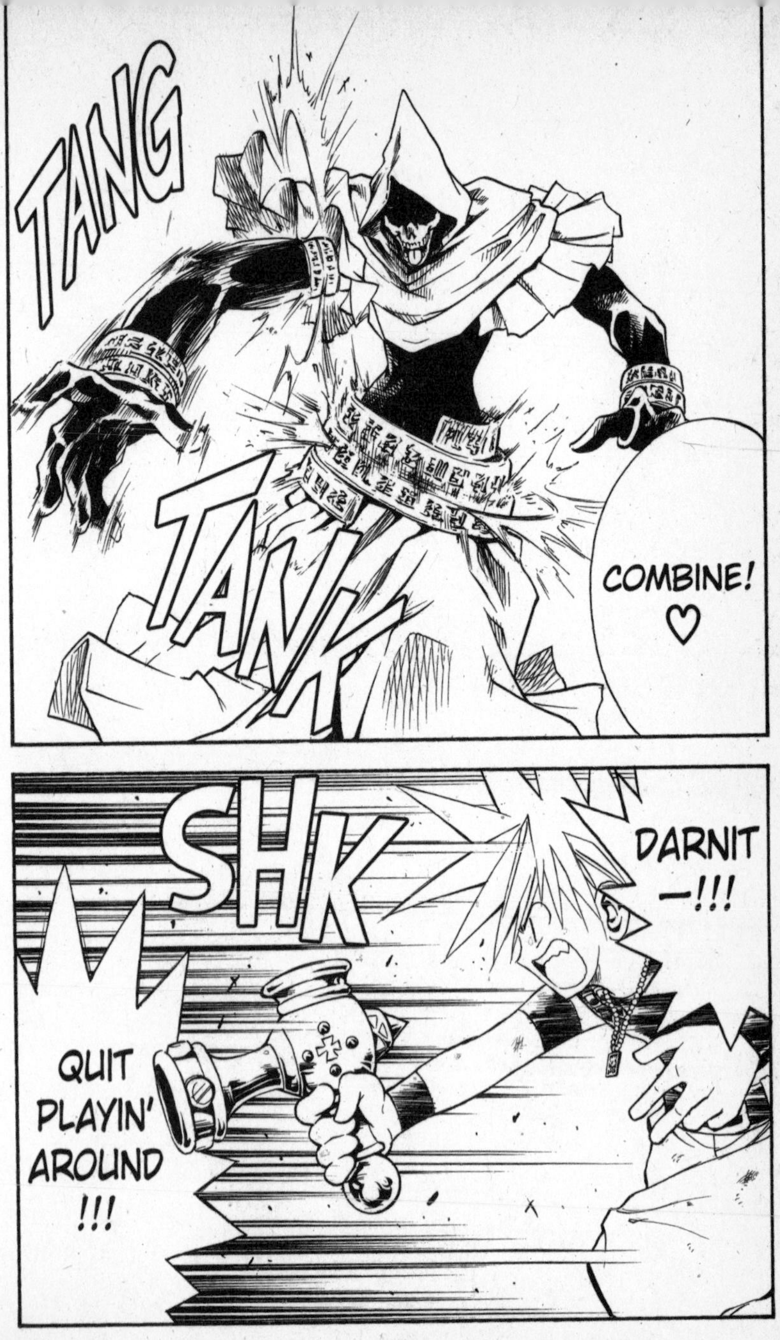
TANG
COMBINE! ♡
TANK
DARNIT—!!!
SHK
QUIT PLAYIN' AROUND !!!

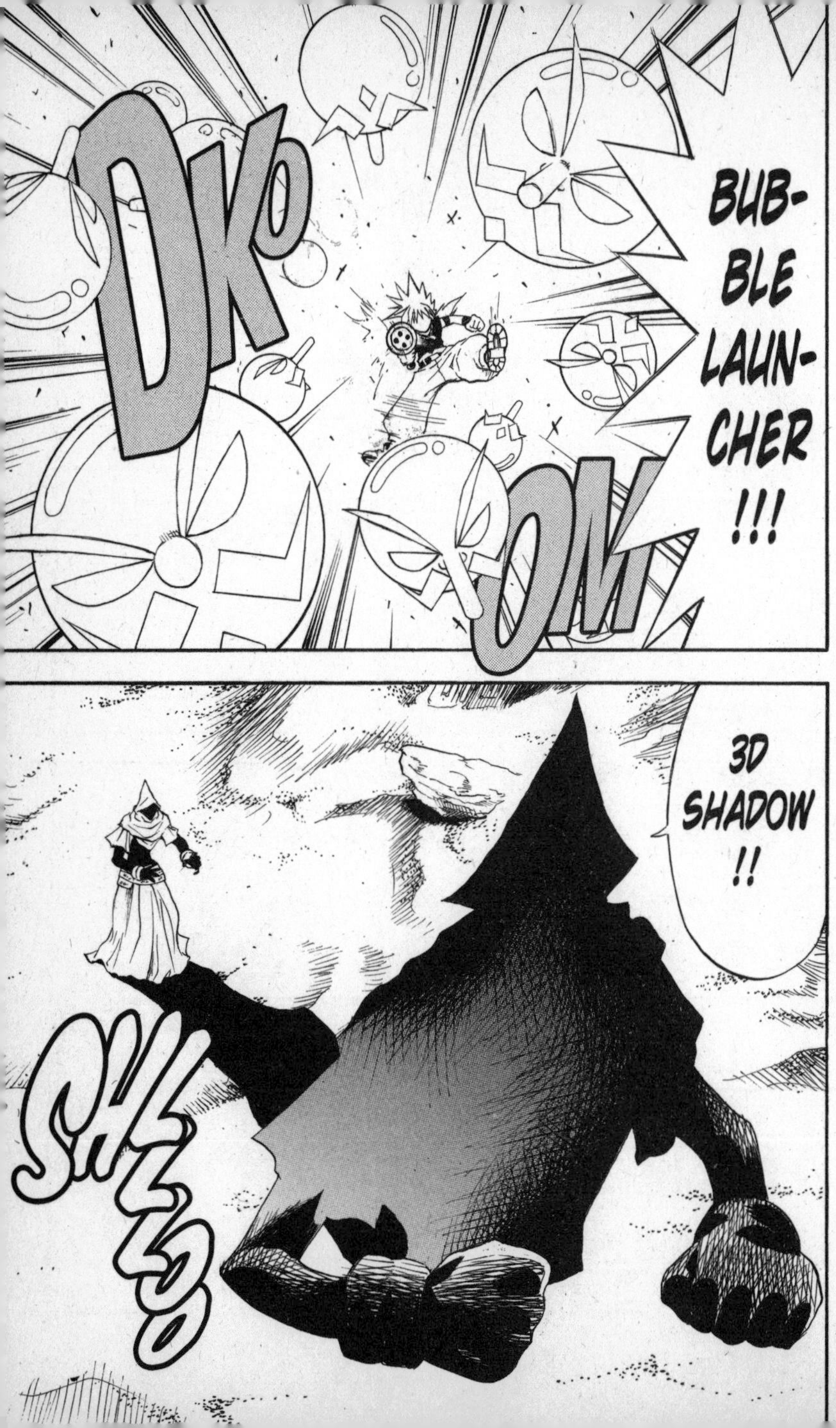
DKOOM
BUBBLE LAUNCHER!!!
3D SHADOW!!

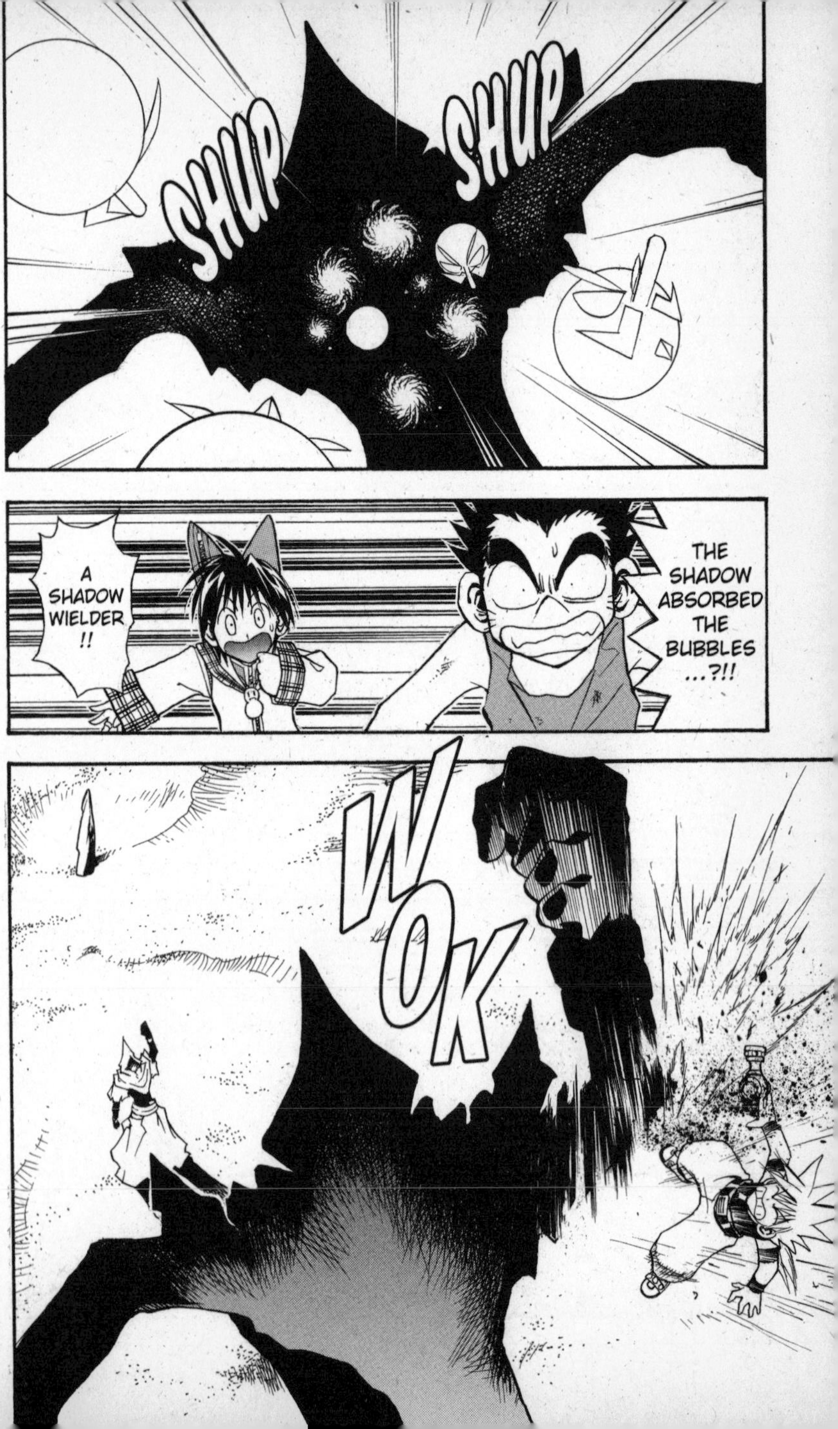
SHUP
SHUP
THE SHADOW ABSORBED THE BUBBLES ...?!!
A SHADOW WIELDER !!
WOK

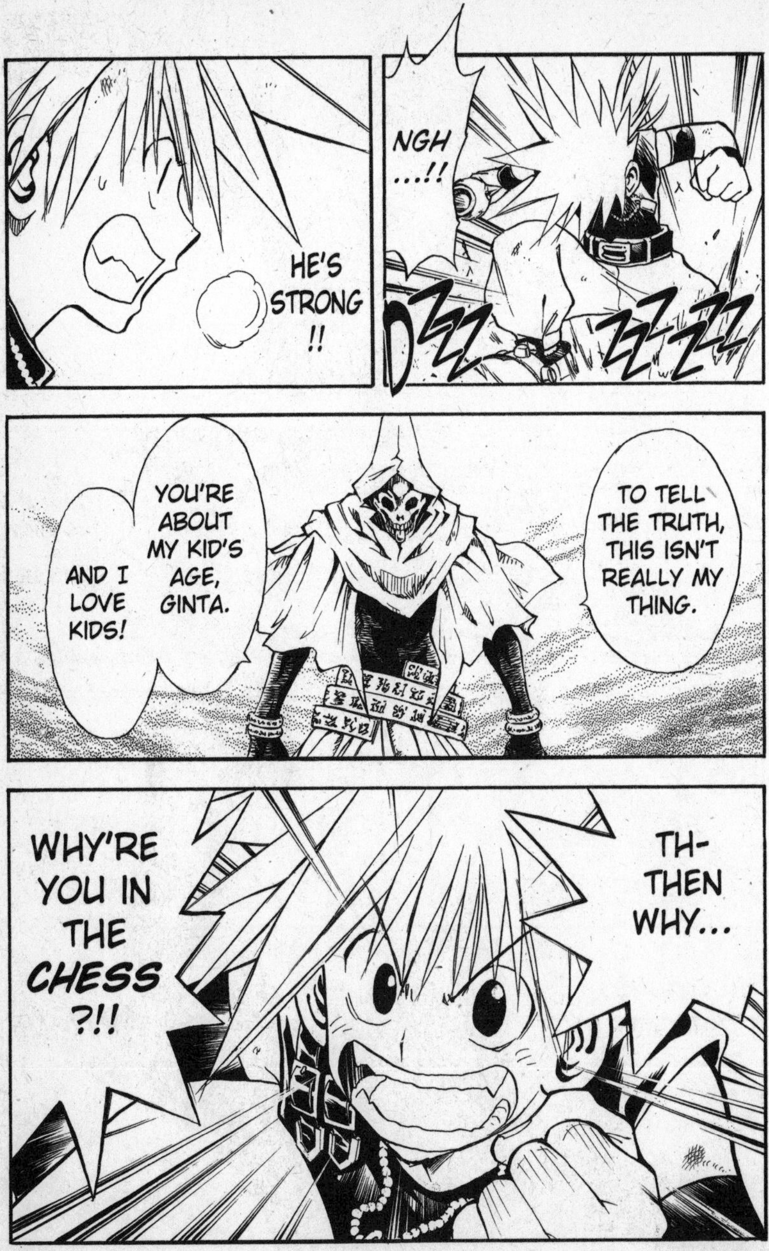
NGH ...!!
HE'S STRONG !!
TO TELL THE TRUTH, THIS ISN'T REALLY MY THING.
YOU'RE ABOUT MY KID'S AGE, GINTA.
AND I LOVE KIDS!
TH- THEN WHY...
WHY'RE YOU IN THE CHESS ?!!

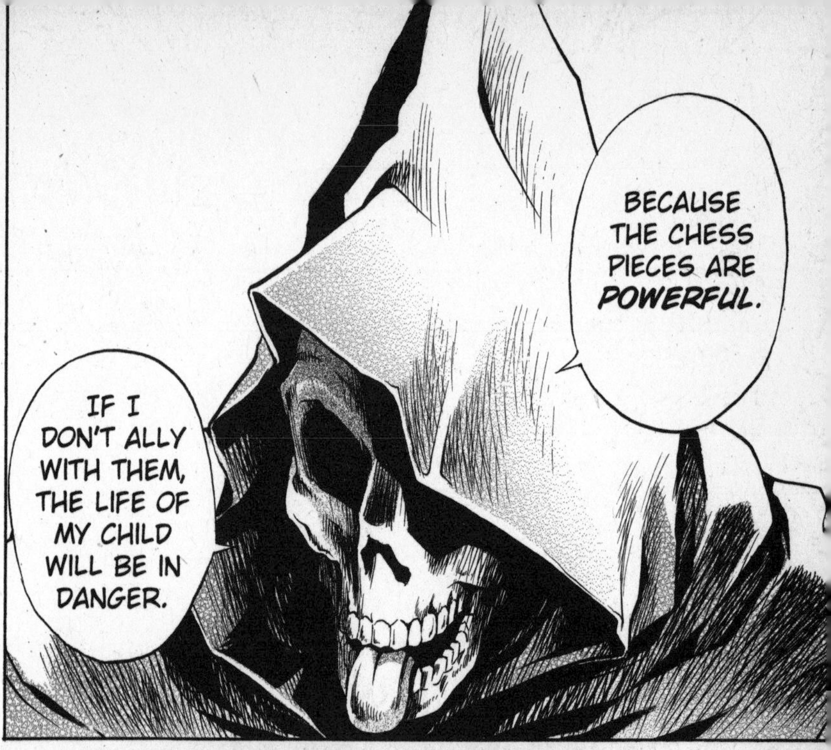
BECAUSE THE CHESS PIECES ARE POWERFUL.
IF I DON'T ALLY WITH THEM, THE LIFE OF MY CHILD WILL BE IN DANGER.

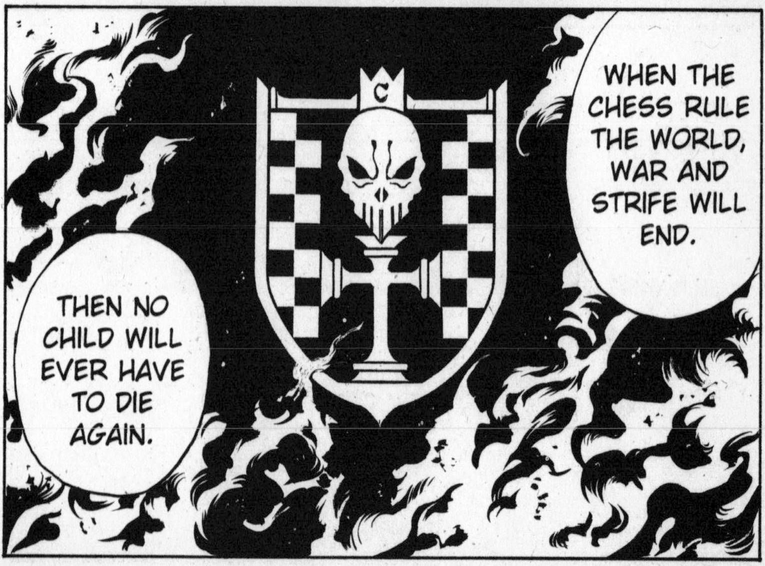
WHEN THE CHESS RULE THE WORLD, WAR AND STRIFE WILL END.
THEN NO CHILD WILL EVER HAVE TO DIE AGAIN.

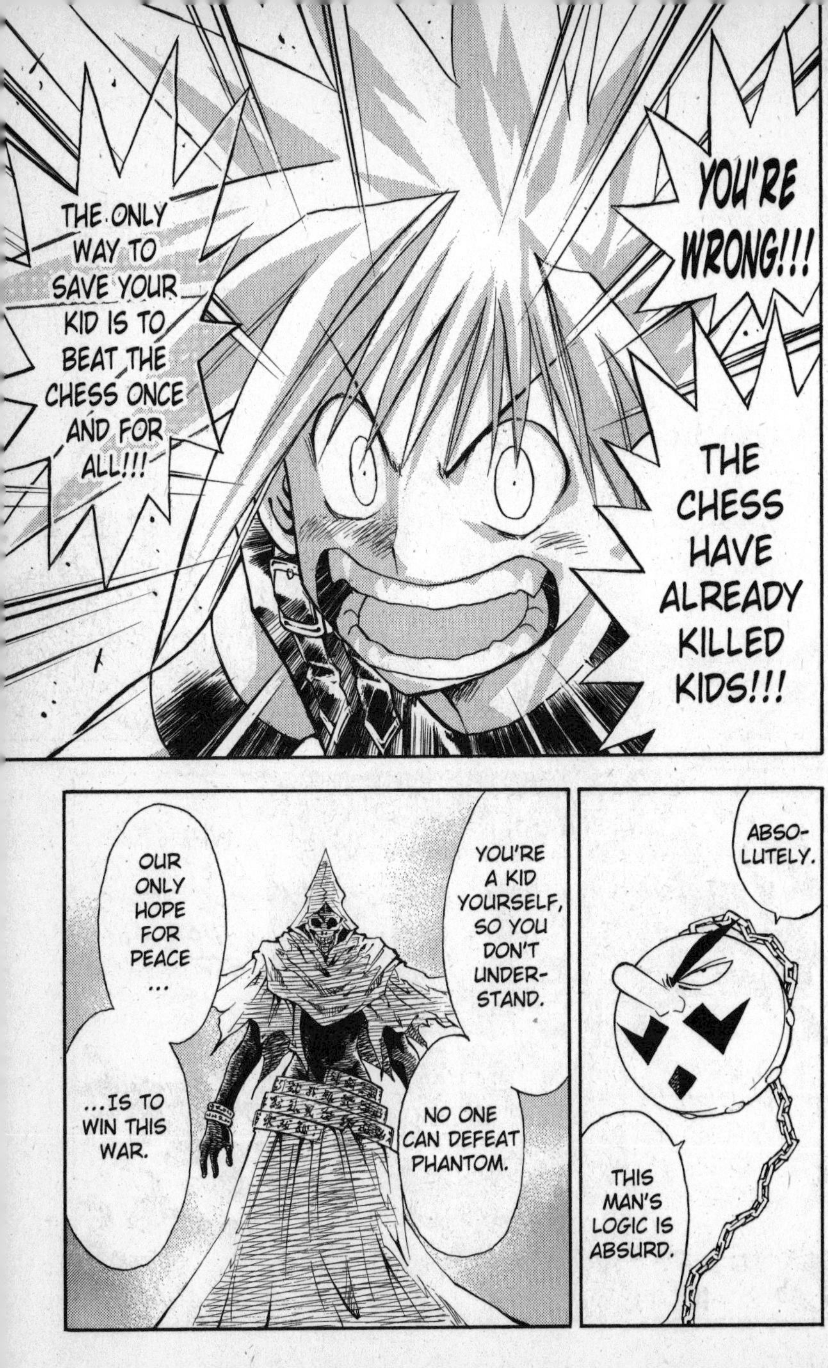
YOU'RE WRONG!!!
THE ONLY WAY TO SAVE YOUR KID IS TO BEAT THE CHESS ONCE AND FOR ALL!!!
THE CHESS HAVE ALREADY KILLED KIDS!!!
ABSO-LUTELY.
THIS MAN'S LOGIC IS ABSURD.
YOU'RE A KID YOURSELF, SO YOU DON'T UNDER-STAND.
OUR ONLY HOPE FOR PEACE ...
NO ONE CAN DEFEAT PHANTOM.
...IS TO WIN THIS WAR.

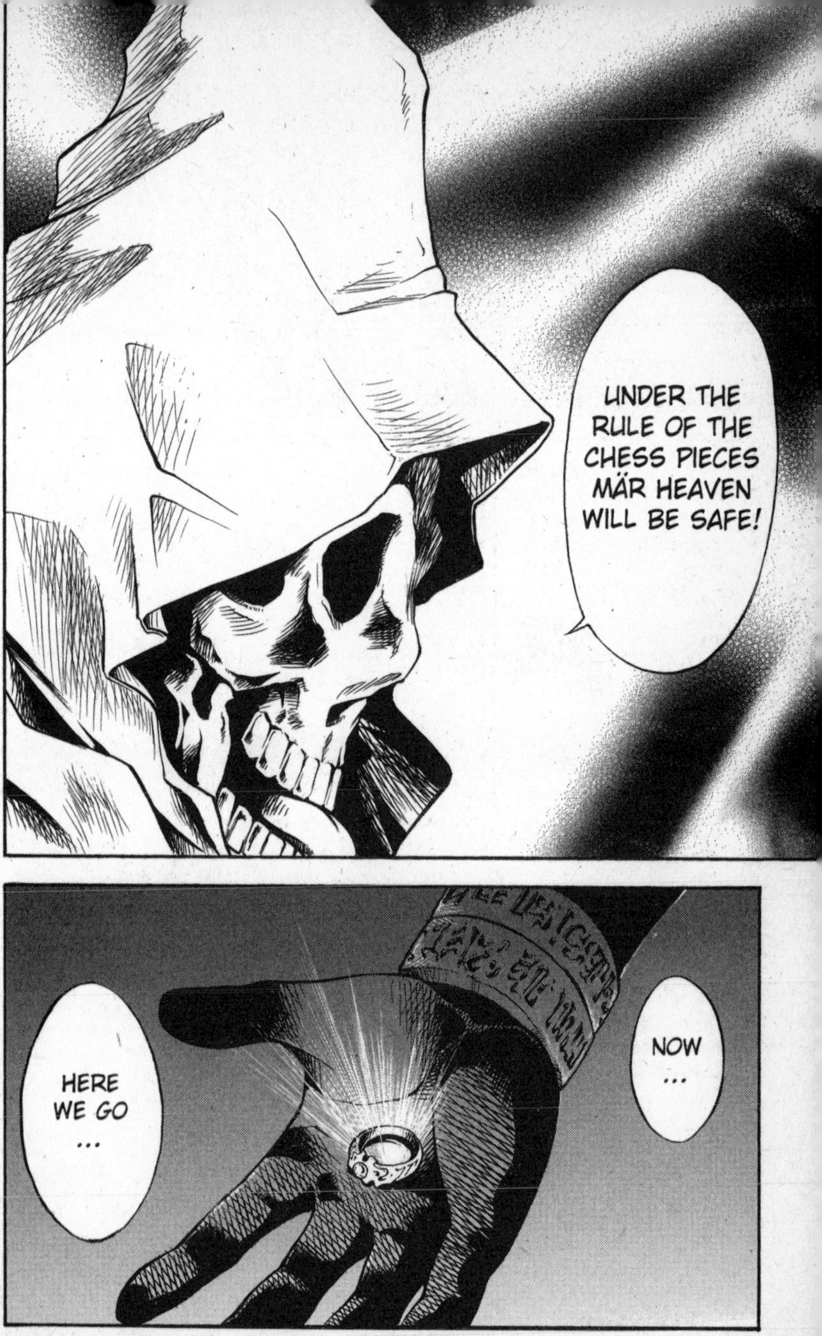
UNDER THE RULE OF THE CHESS PIECES MÄR HEAVEN WILL BE SAFE!
NOW ...
HERE WE GO ...

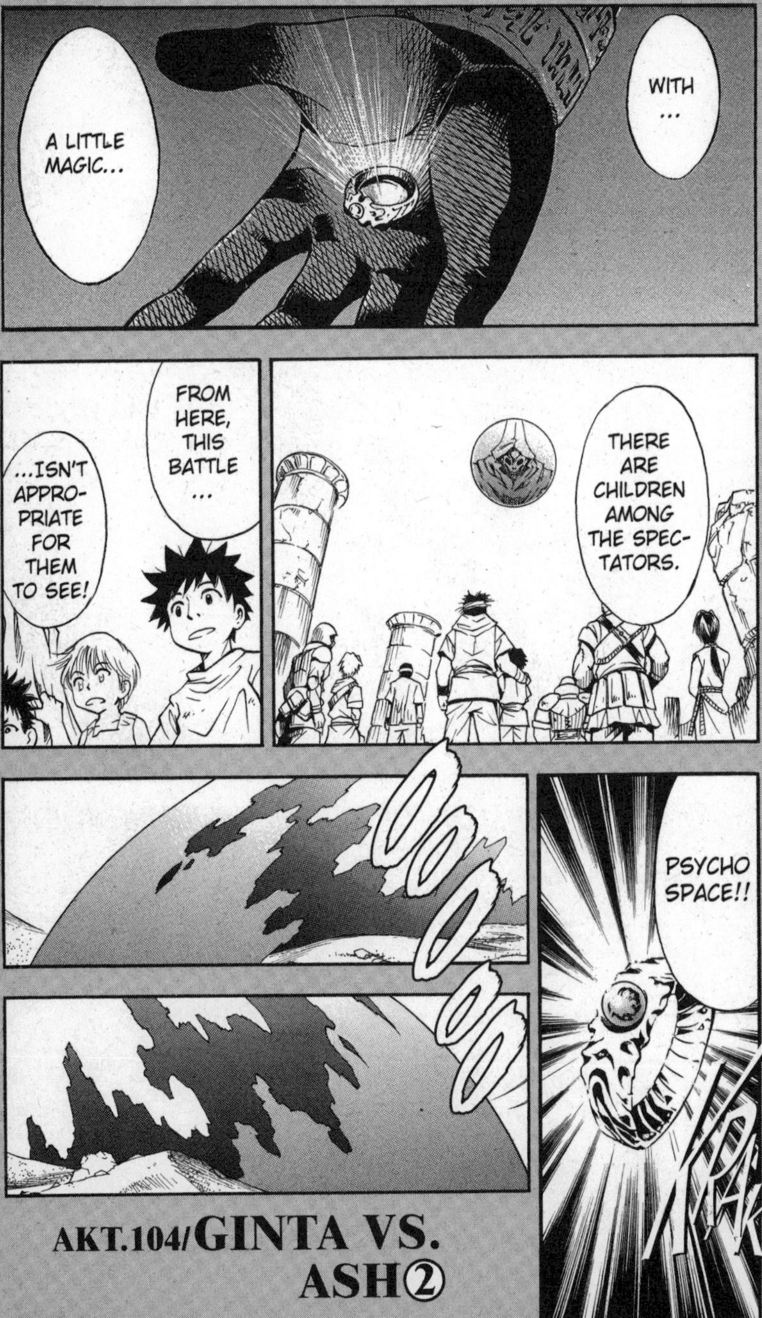
WITH...
A LITTLE MAGIC...
THERE ARE CHILDREN AMONG THE SPEC-TATORS.
FROM HERE, THIS BATTLE...
...ISN'T APPRO-PRIATE FOR THEM TO SEE!
PSYCHO SPACE!!
KRAK

AKT.104/GINTA VS. ASH②

AKT.104/ GINTA VS. ASH②

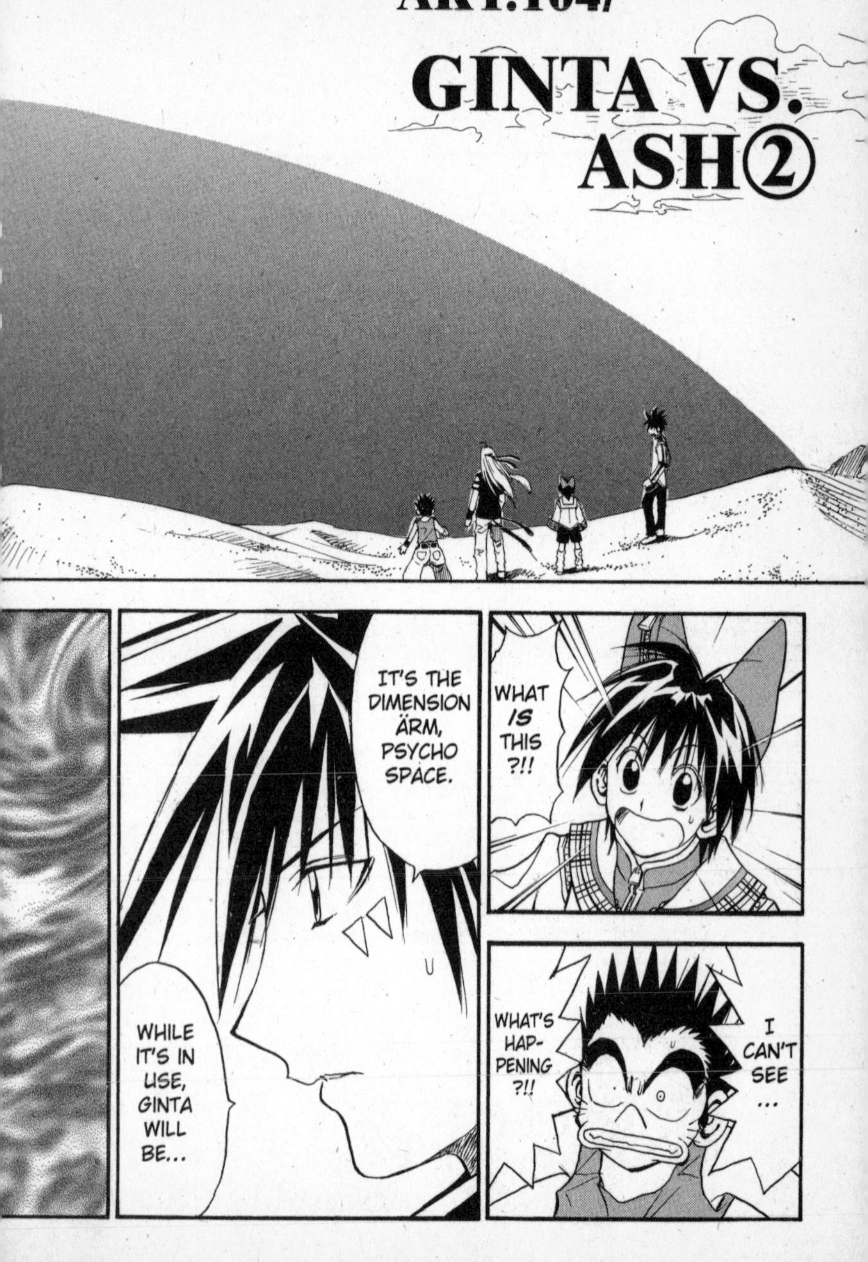
WHAT IS THIS?!!
I CAN'T SEE...
WHAT'S HAPPENING?!!
IT'S THE DIMENSION ÄRM, PSYCHO SPACE.
WHILE IT'S IN USE, GINTA WILL BE...

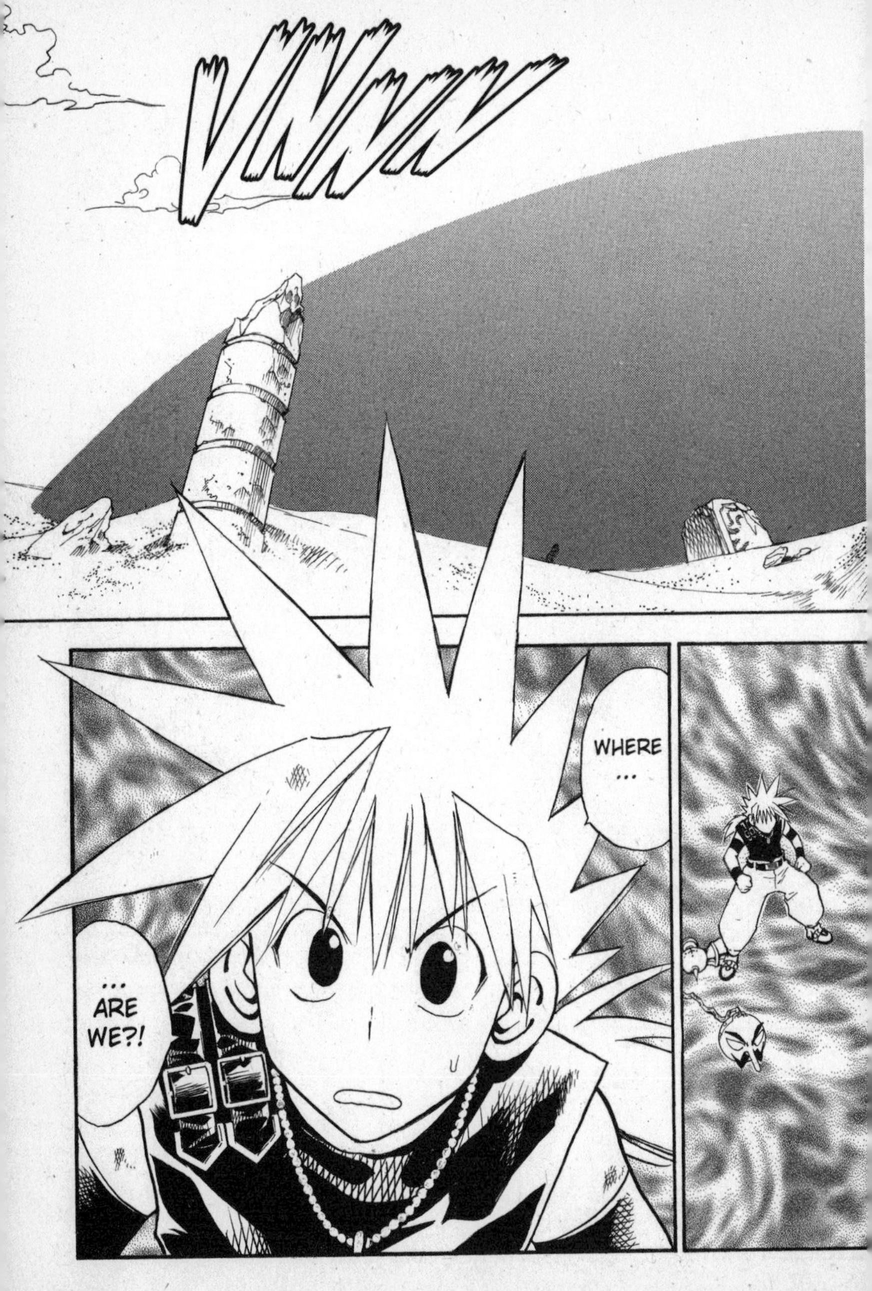
VNNN
WHERE ...
... ARE WE?!

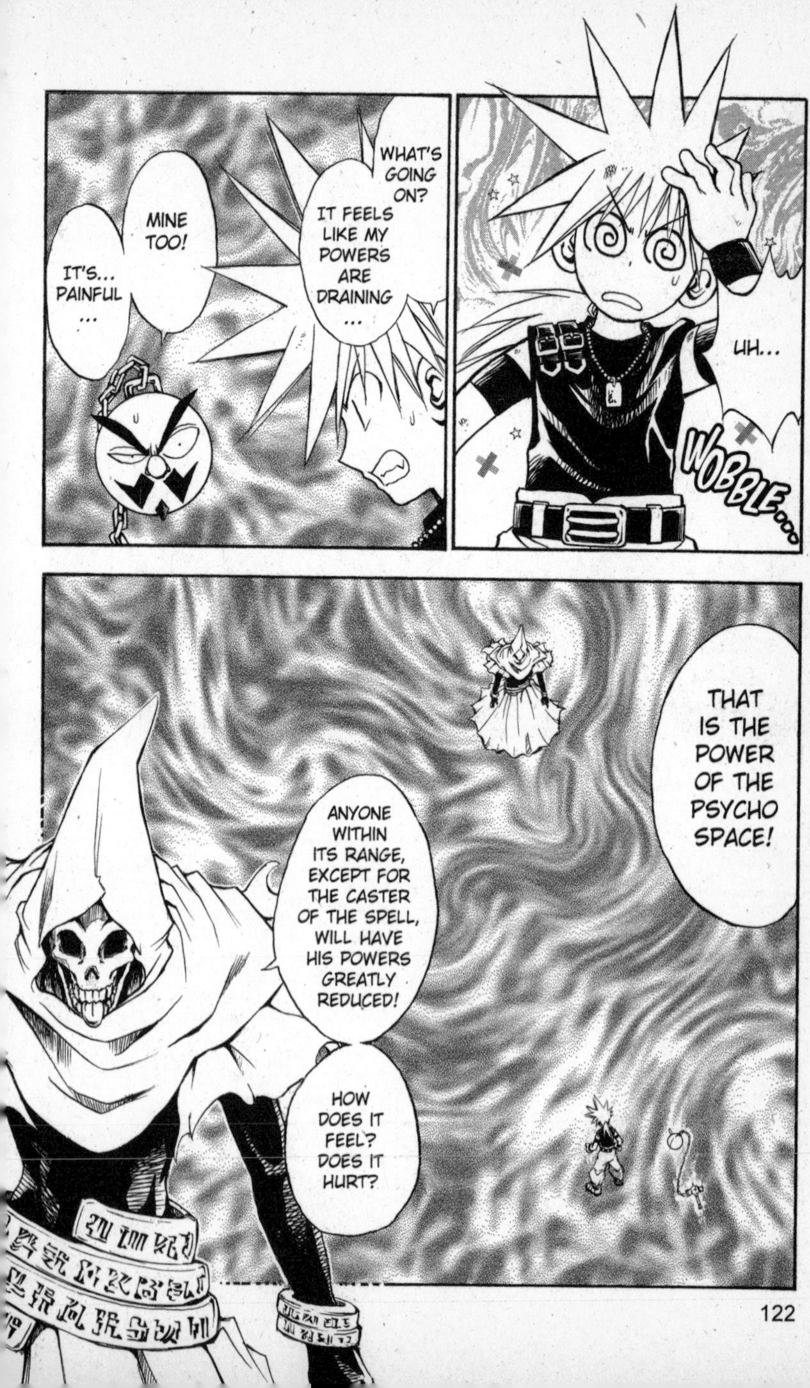
UH...
WOBBLE...
WHAT'S GOING ON?
IT FEELS LIKE MY POWERS ARE DRAINING...
MINE TOO!
IT'S... PAINFUL...
THAT IS THE POWER OF THE PSYCHO SPACE!
ANYONE WITHIN ITS RANGE, EXCEPT FOR THE CASTER OF THE SPELL, WILL HAVE HIS POWERS GREATLY REDUCED!
HOW DOES IT FEEL? DOES IT HURT?

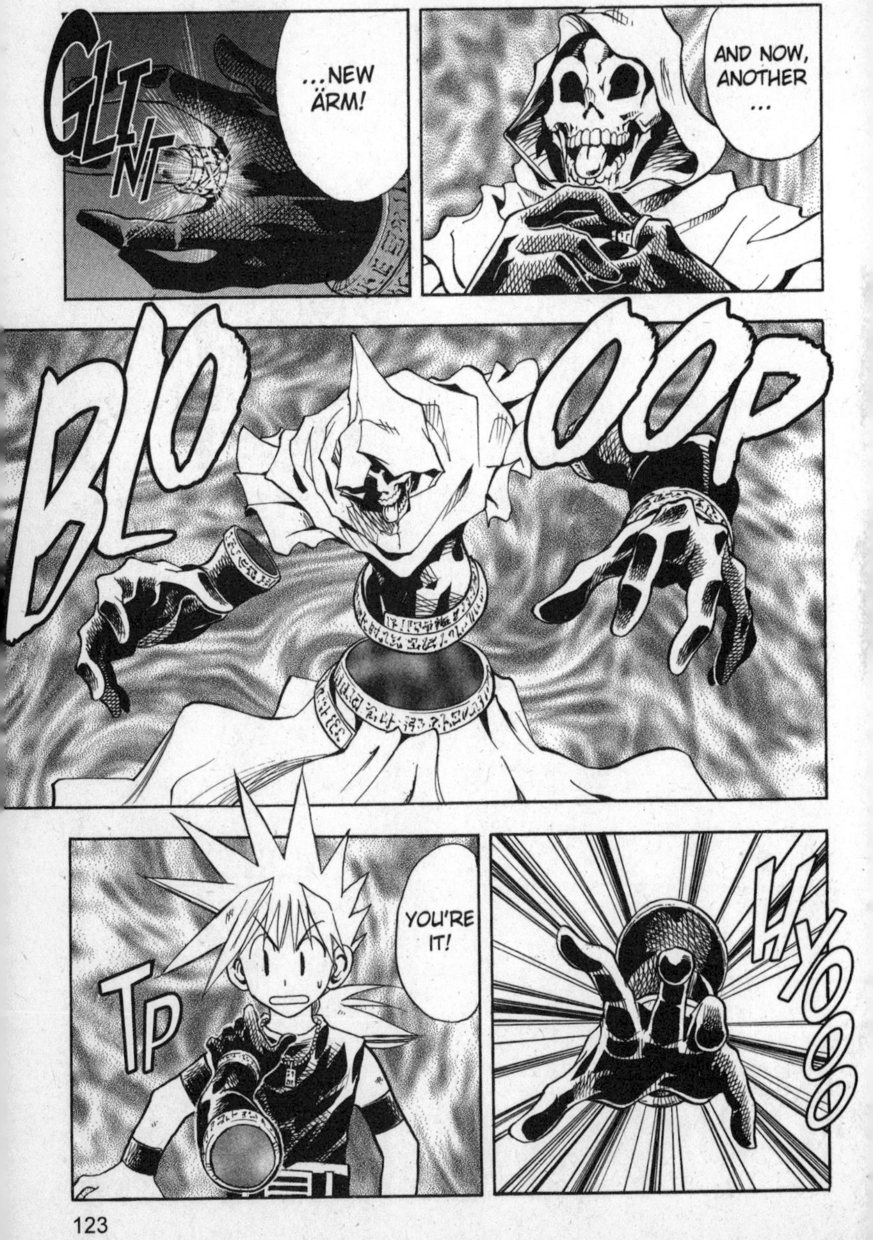
AND NOW, ANOTHER ...
...NEW ÄRM!
GLINT
BLOOOP
HYOOOO
YOU'RE IT!
TP

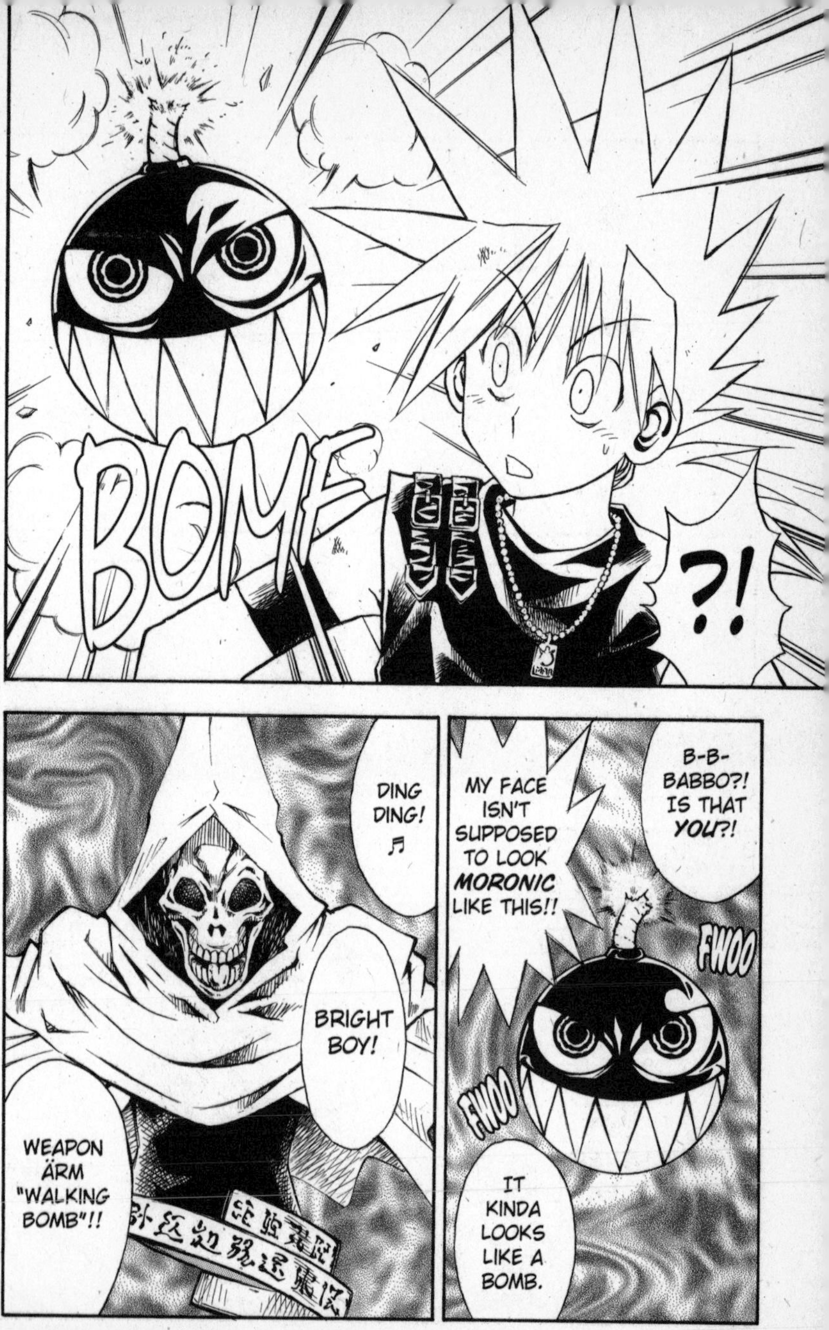
BOMF
?!
B-B-BABBO?! IS THAT *YOU*?!
MY FACE ISN'T SUPPOSED TO LOOK **MORONIC** LIKE THIS!!
FWOO
FWOO
IT KINDA LOOKS LIKE A BOMB.
DING DING! ♬
BRIGHT BOY!
WEAPON ÄRM "WALKING BOMB"!!

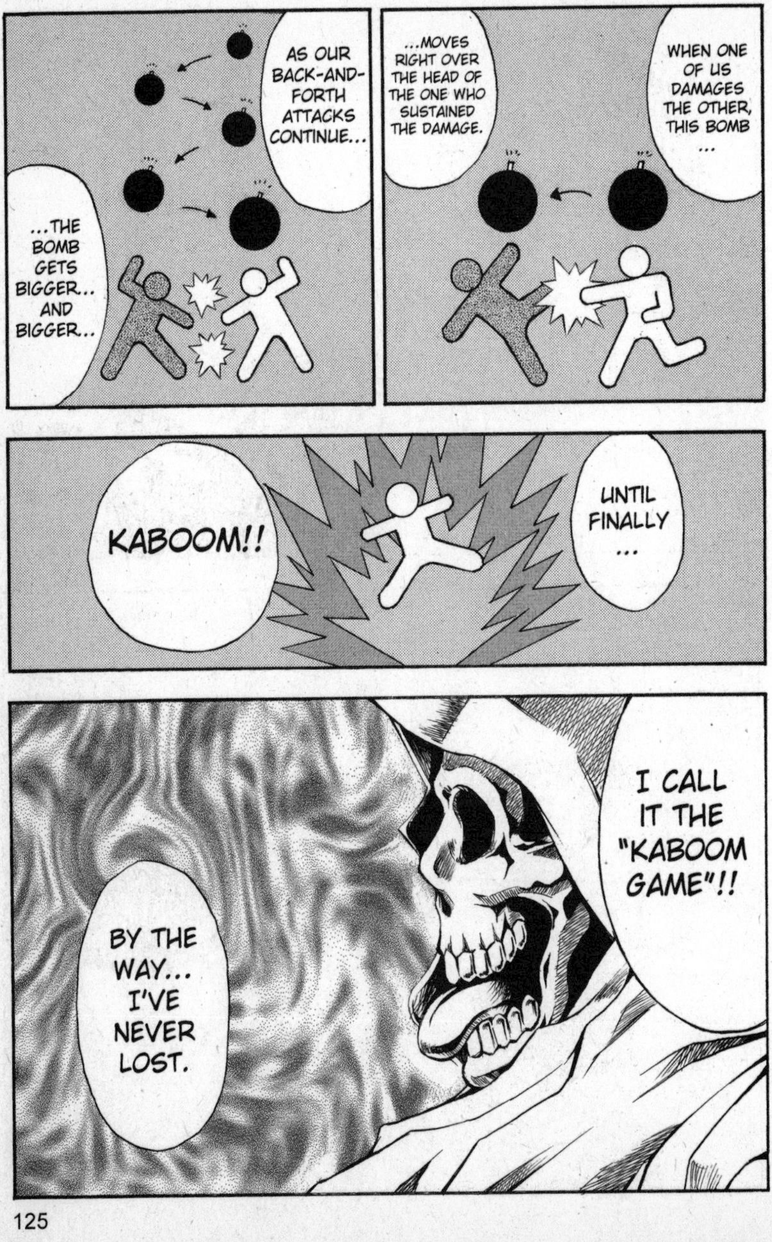
WHEN ONE OF US DAMAGES THE OTHER, THIS BOMB ...
...MOVES RIGHT OVER THE HEAD OF THE ONE WHO SUSTAINED THE DAMAGE.
AS OUR BACK-AND-FORTH ATTACKS CONTINUE...
...THE BOMB GETS BIGGER... AND BIGGER...
UNTIL FINALLY ...
KABOOM!!
I CALL IT THE "KABOOM GAME"!!
BY THE WAY... I'VE NEVER LOST.

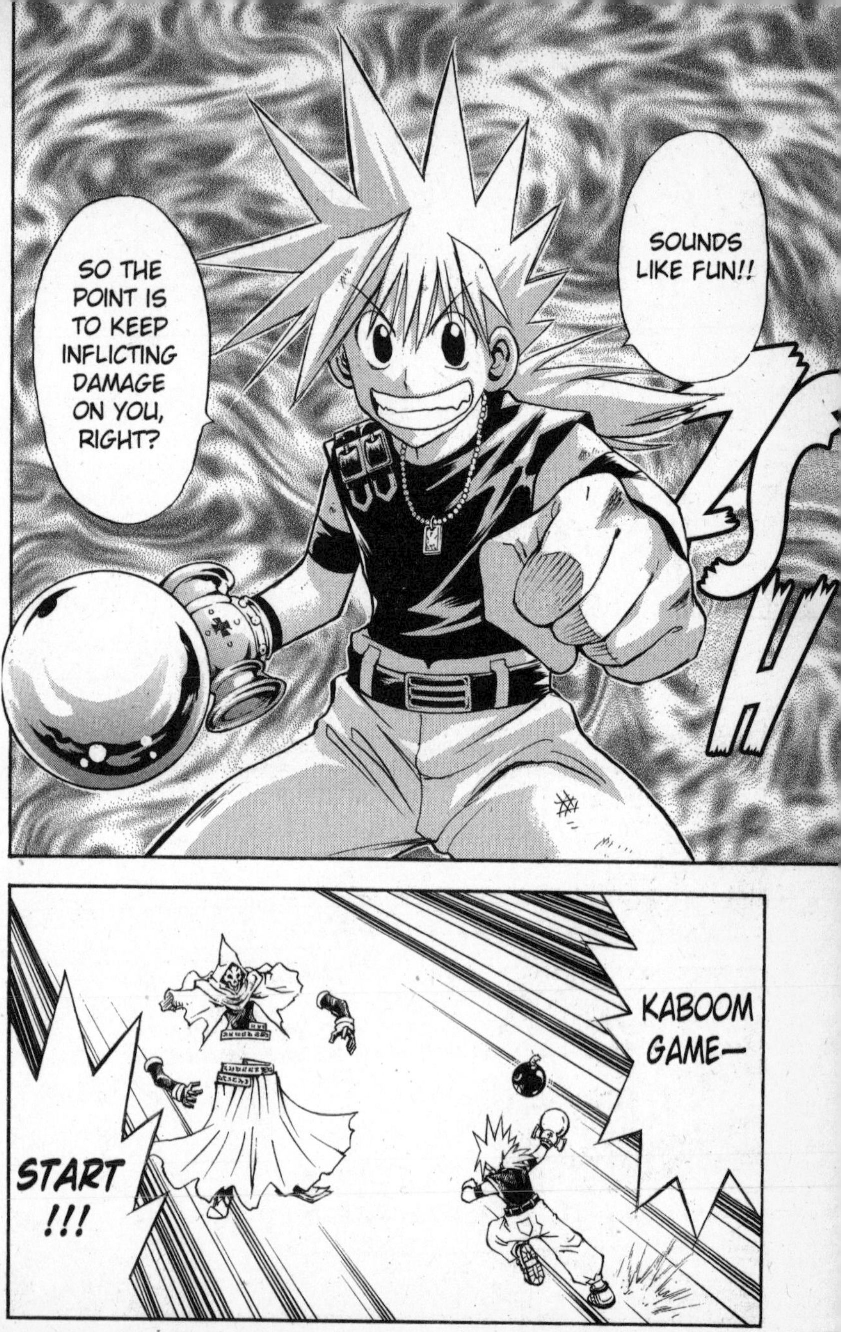
SOUNDS LIKE FUN!!
SO THE POINT IS TO KEEP INFLICTING DAMAGE ON YOU, RIGHT?
KABOOM GAME—
START !!!

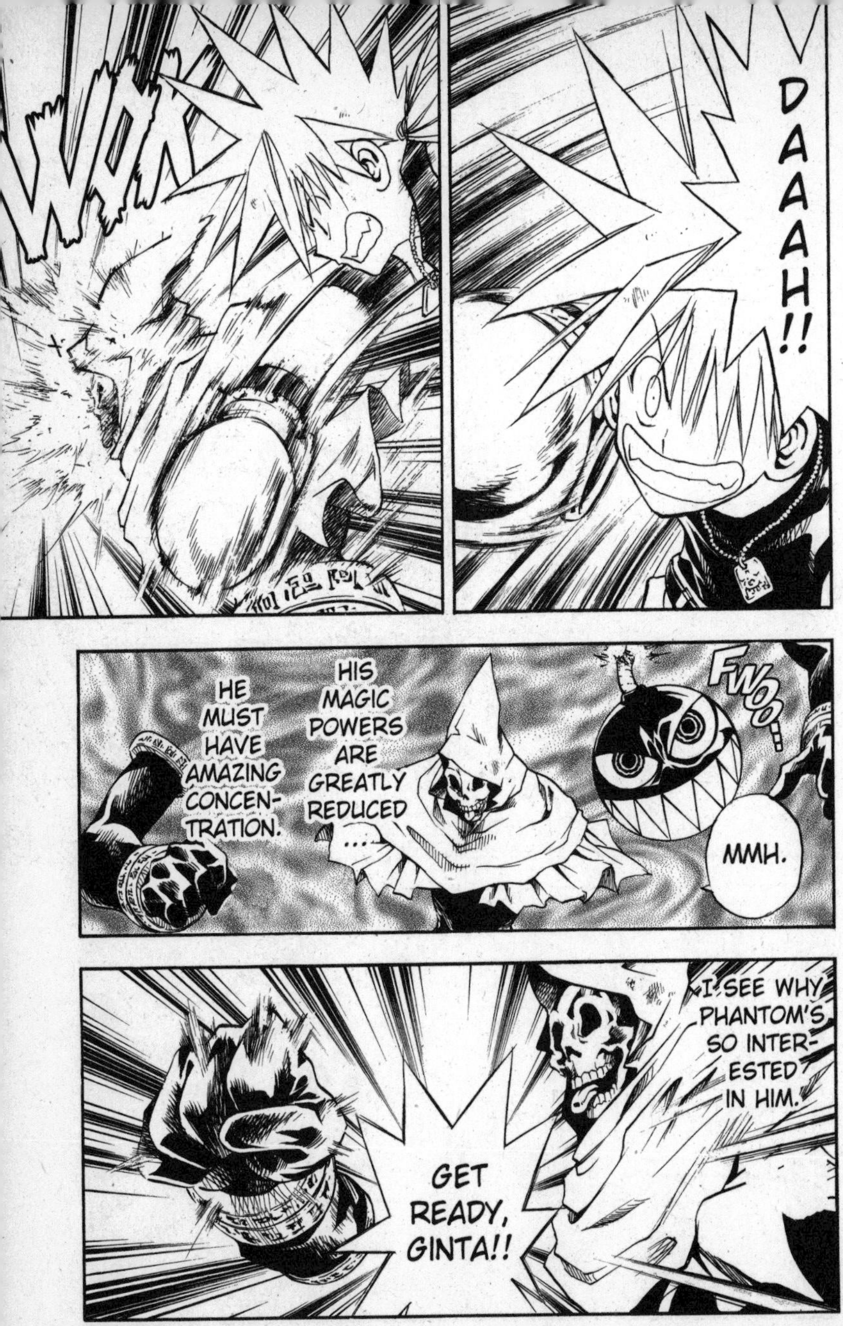
DAAAH!!
FWOO...
MMH.
HIS MAGIC POWERS ARE GREATLY REDUCED ....
HE MUST HAVE AMAZING CONCEN-TRATION.
I SEE WHY PHANTOM'S SO INTER-ESTED IN HIM.
GET READY, GINTA!!

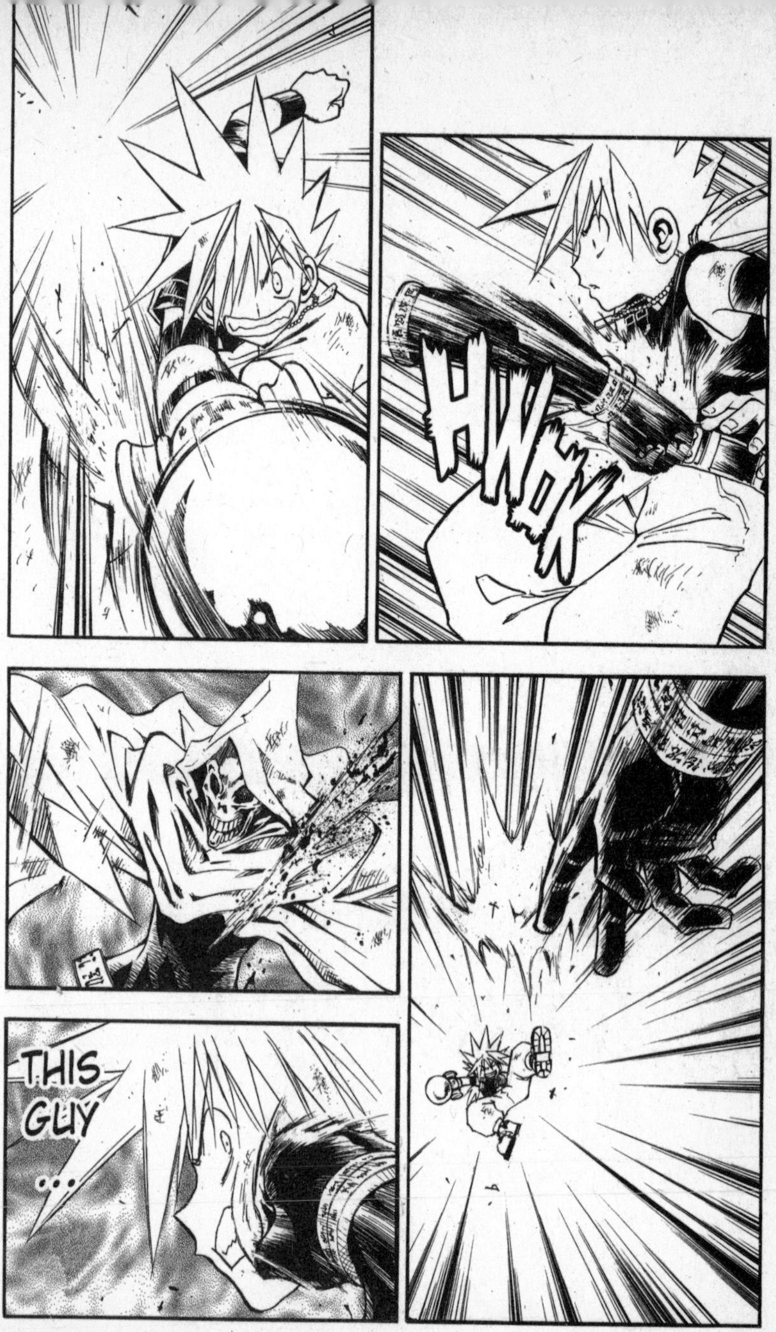
HWOK
THIS GUY ...

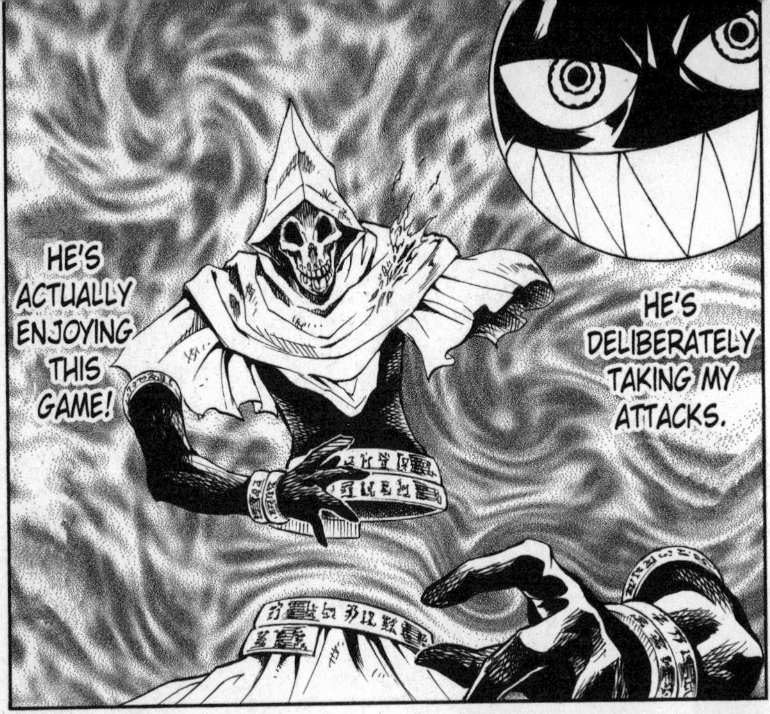
HE'S DELIBERATELY TAKING MY ATTACKS.
HE'S ACTUALLY ENJOYING THIS GAME!

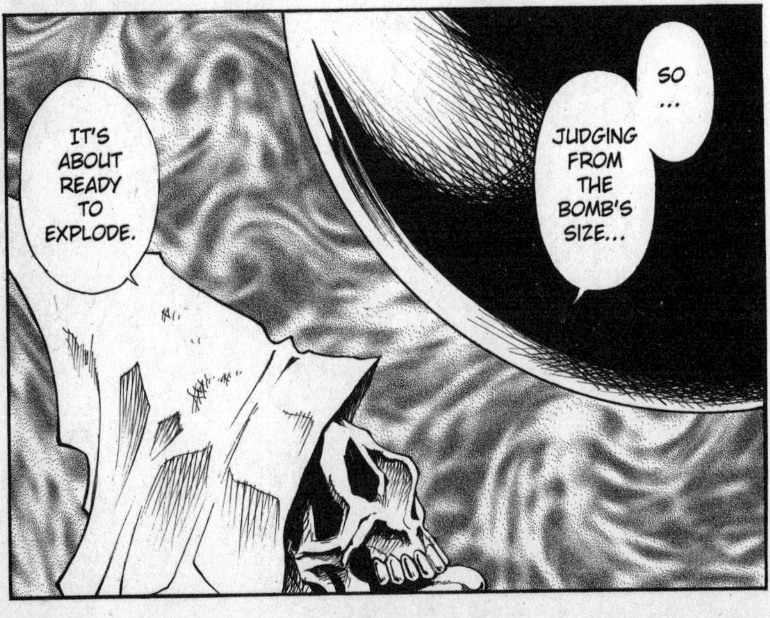
SO ...
JUDGING FROM THE BOMB'S SIZE...
IT'S ABOUT READY TO EXPLODE.

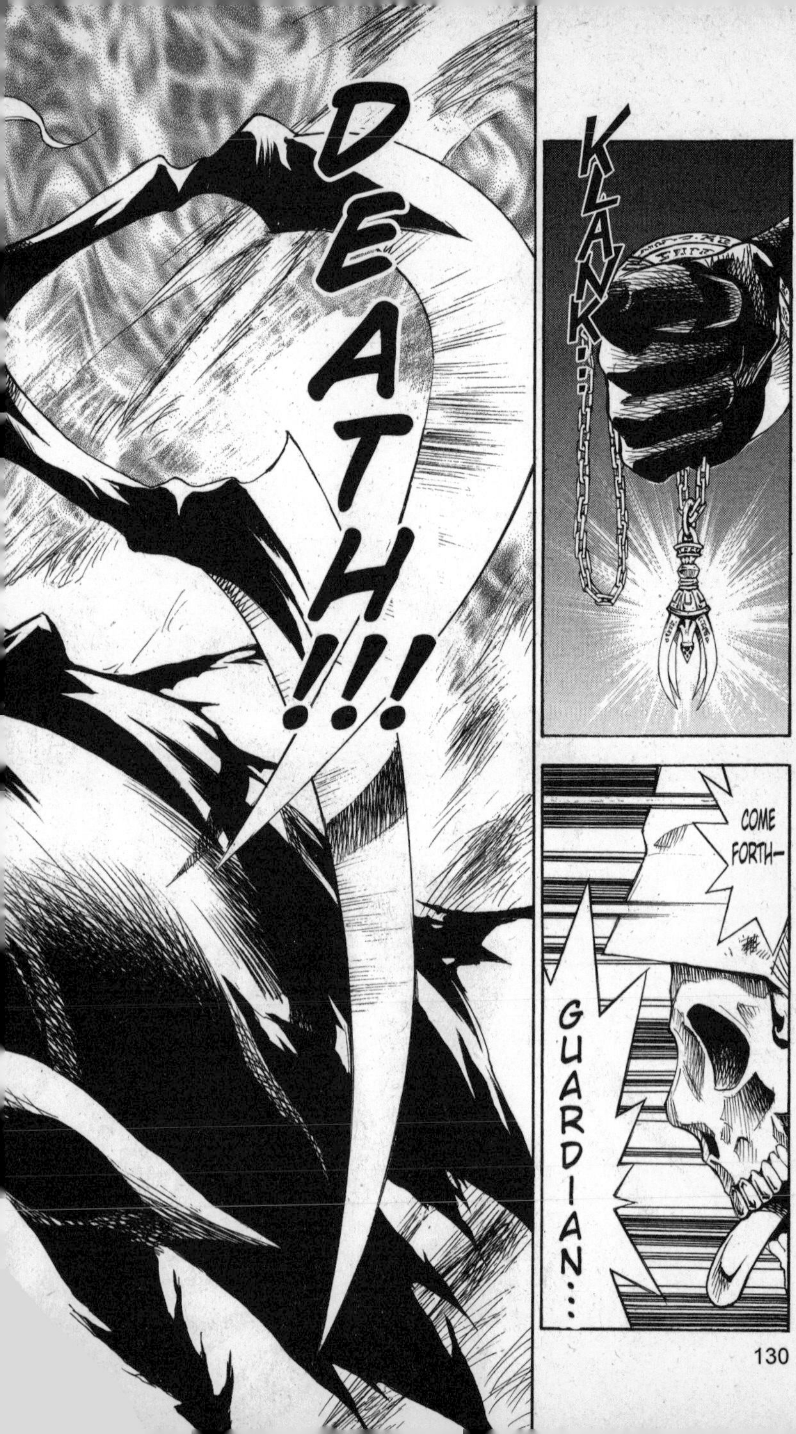
KLANK...
COME FORTH-
GUARDIAN...
DEATH!!!

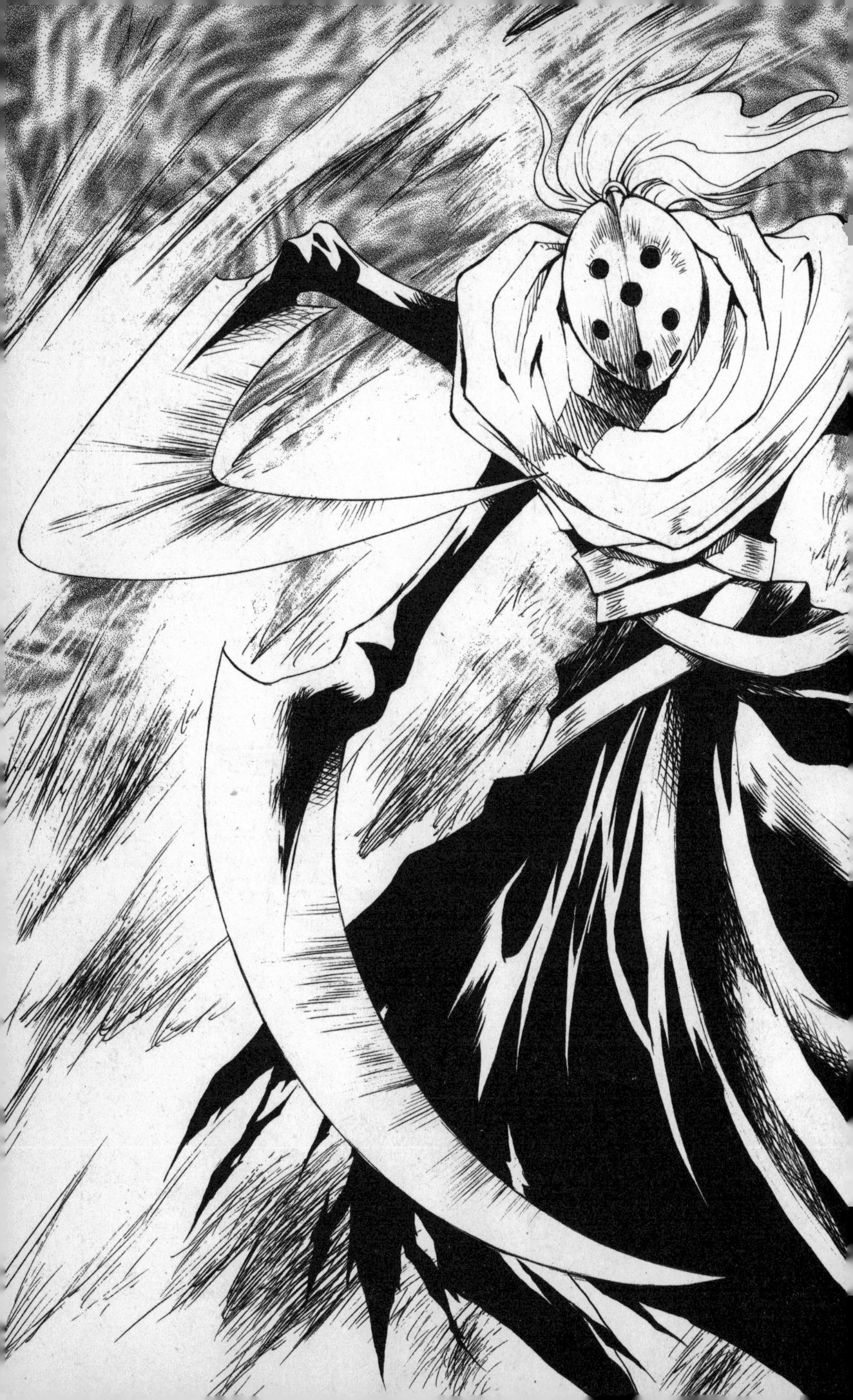

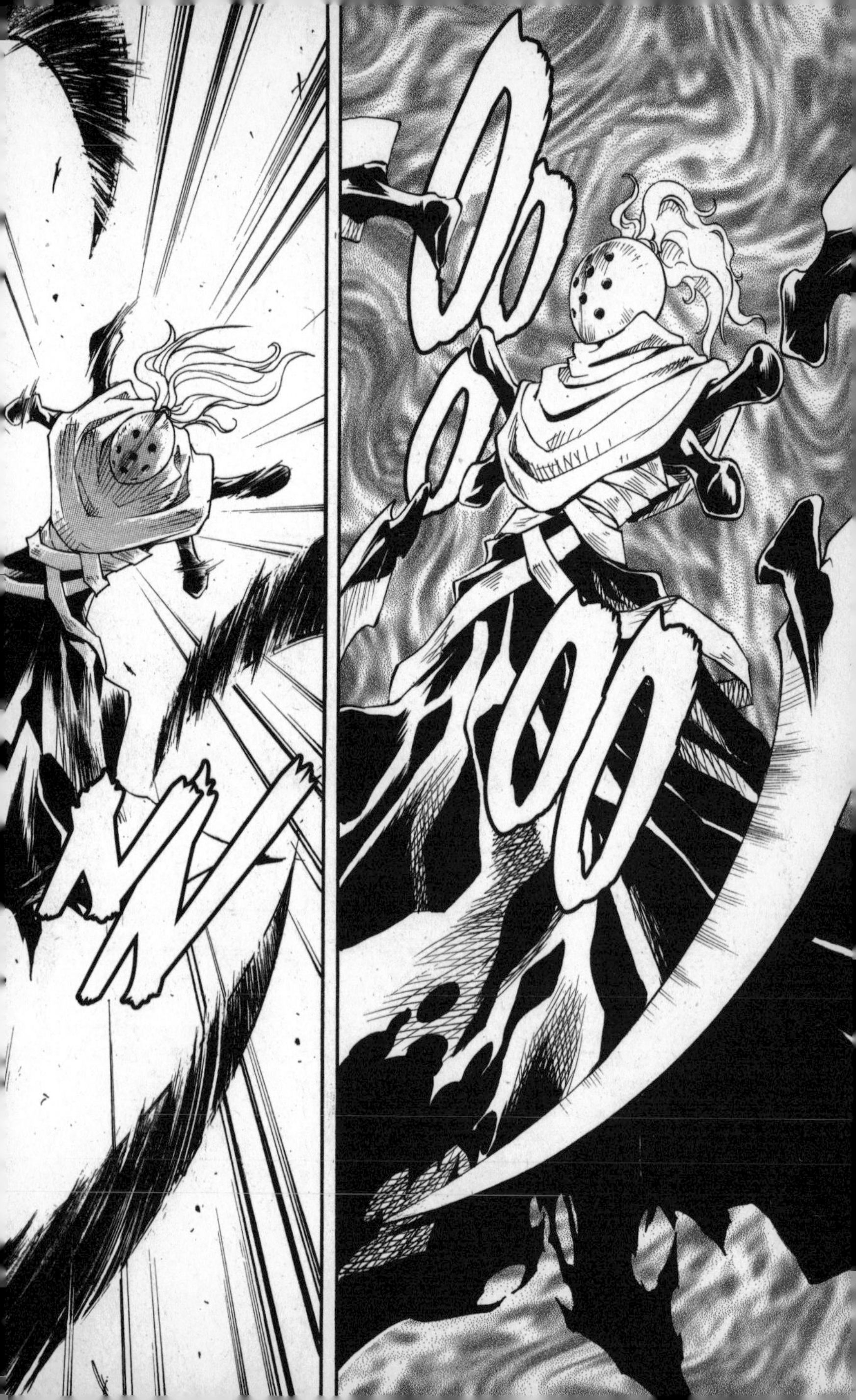

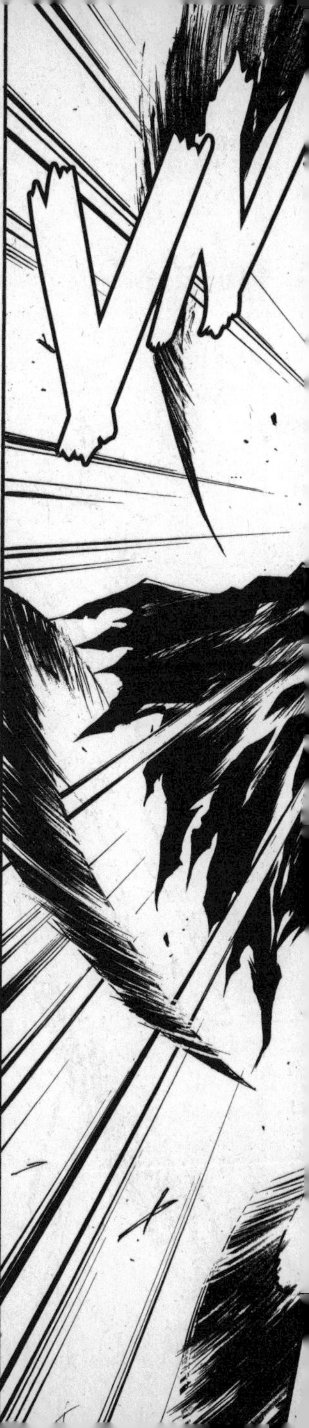
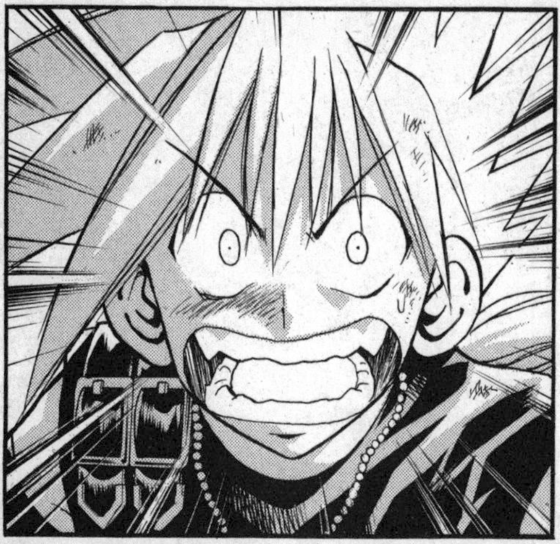
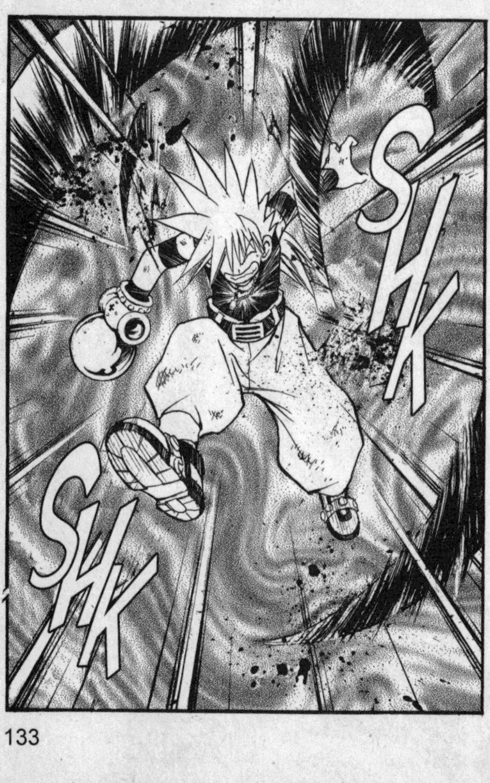
SHK
SHK

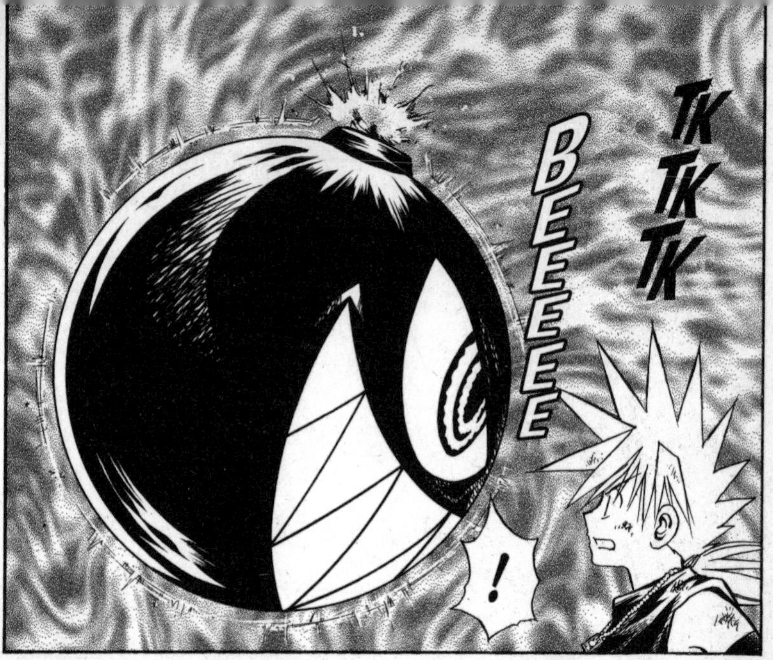
TK TK TK
BEEEEEE
!

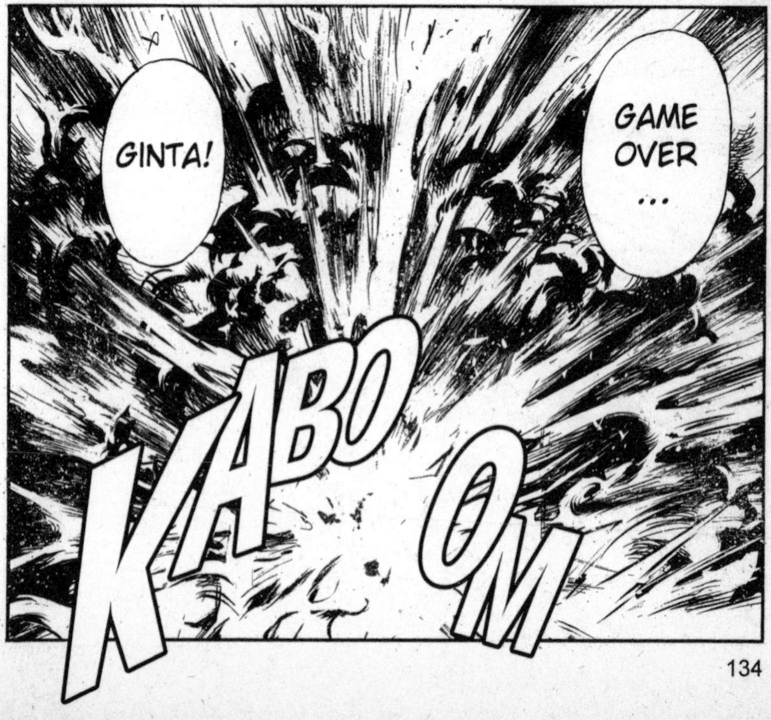
GAME OVER ...
GINTA!
KABOOM

AKT.105/ GINTA VS. ASH ③

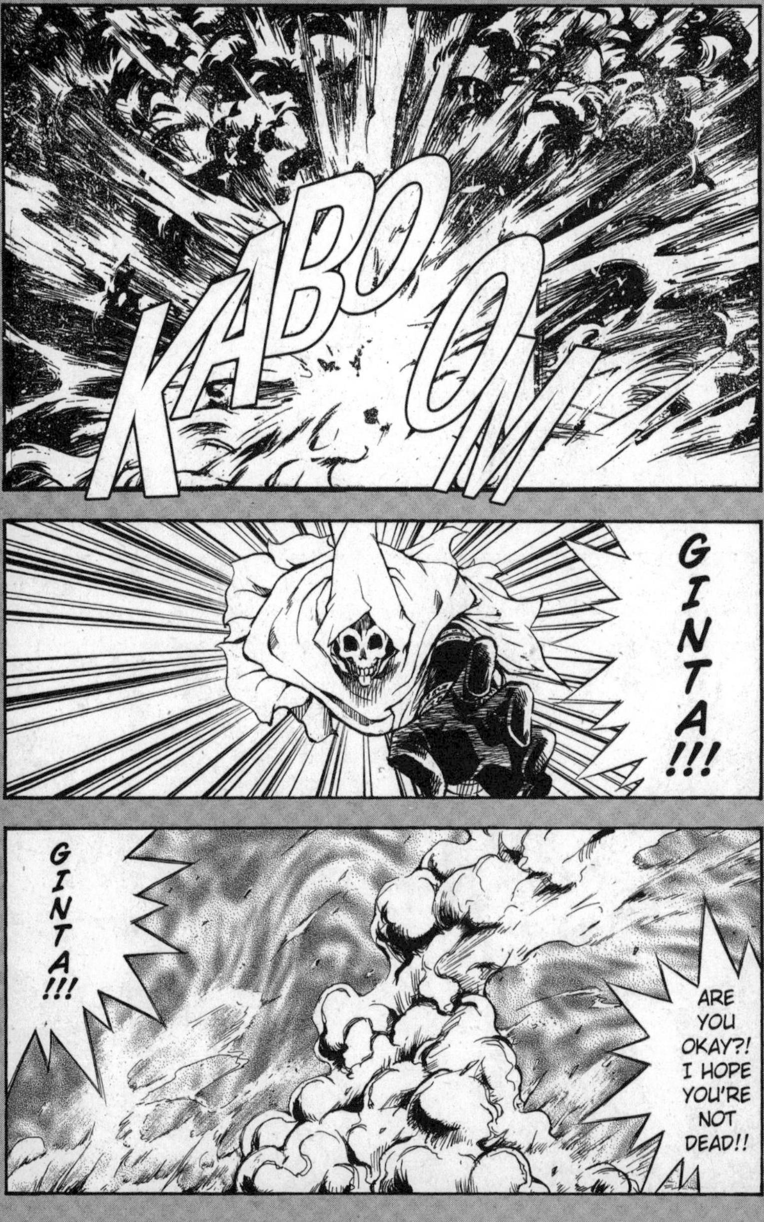
KABOOM
GINTA!!!
ARE YOU OKAY?! I HOPE YOU'RE NOT DEAD!!
GINTA!!!

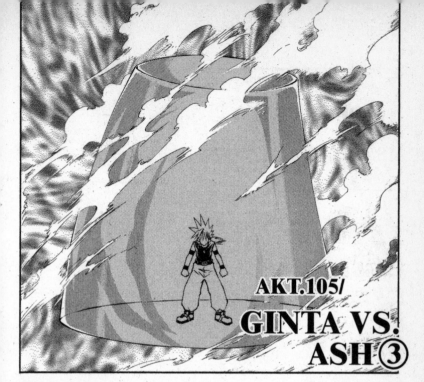

AKT.105/
GINTA VS.
ASH ③

I'M
ALIVE.

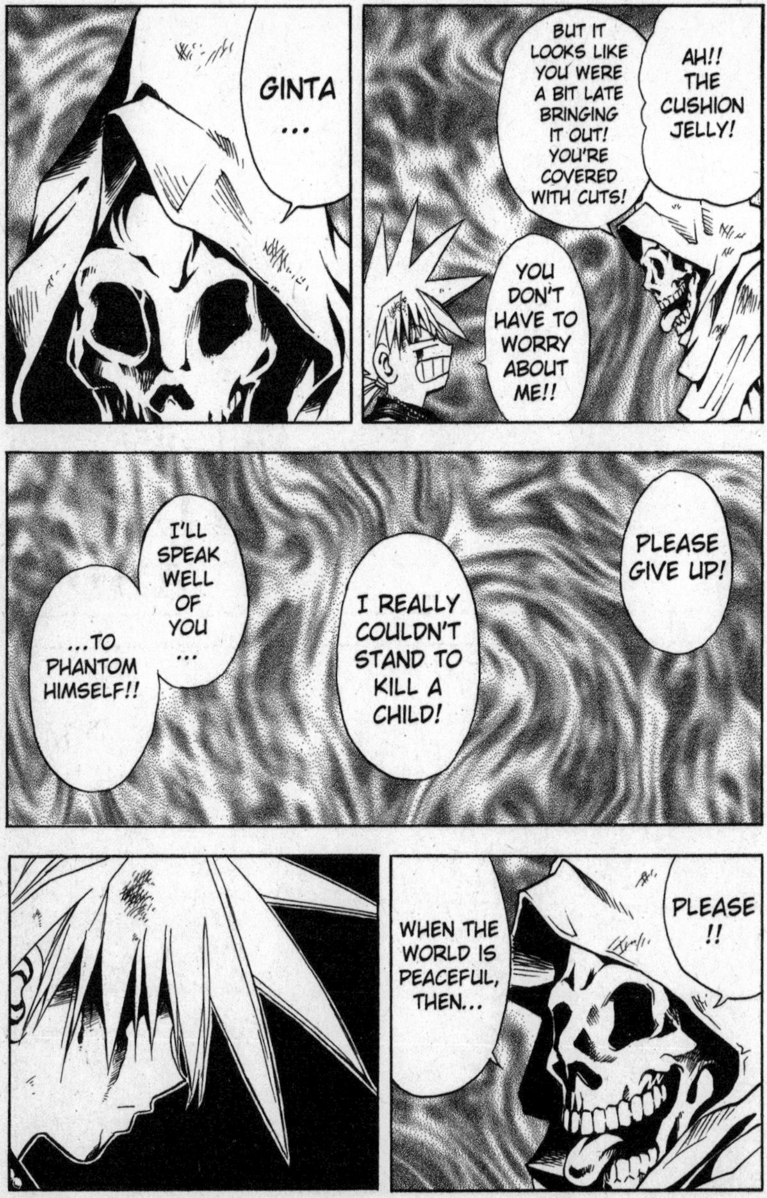
AH!! THE CUSHION JELLY!
BUT IT LOOKS LIKE YOU WERE A BIT LATE BRINGING IT OUT! YOU'RE COVERED WITH CUTS!
YOU DON'T HAVE TO WORRY ABOUT ME!!
GINTA ...
PLEASE GIVE UP!
I REALLY COULDN'T STAND TO KILL A CHILD!
I'LL SPEAK WELL OF YOU ...
...TO PHANTOM HIMSELF!!
PLEASE !!
WHEN THE WORLD IS PEACEFUL, THEN...

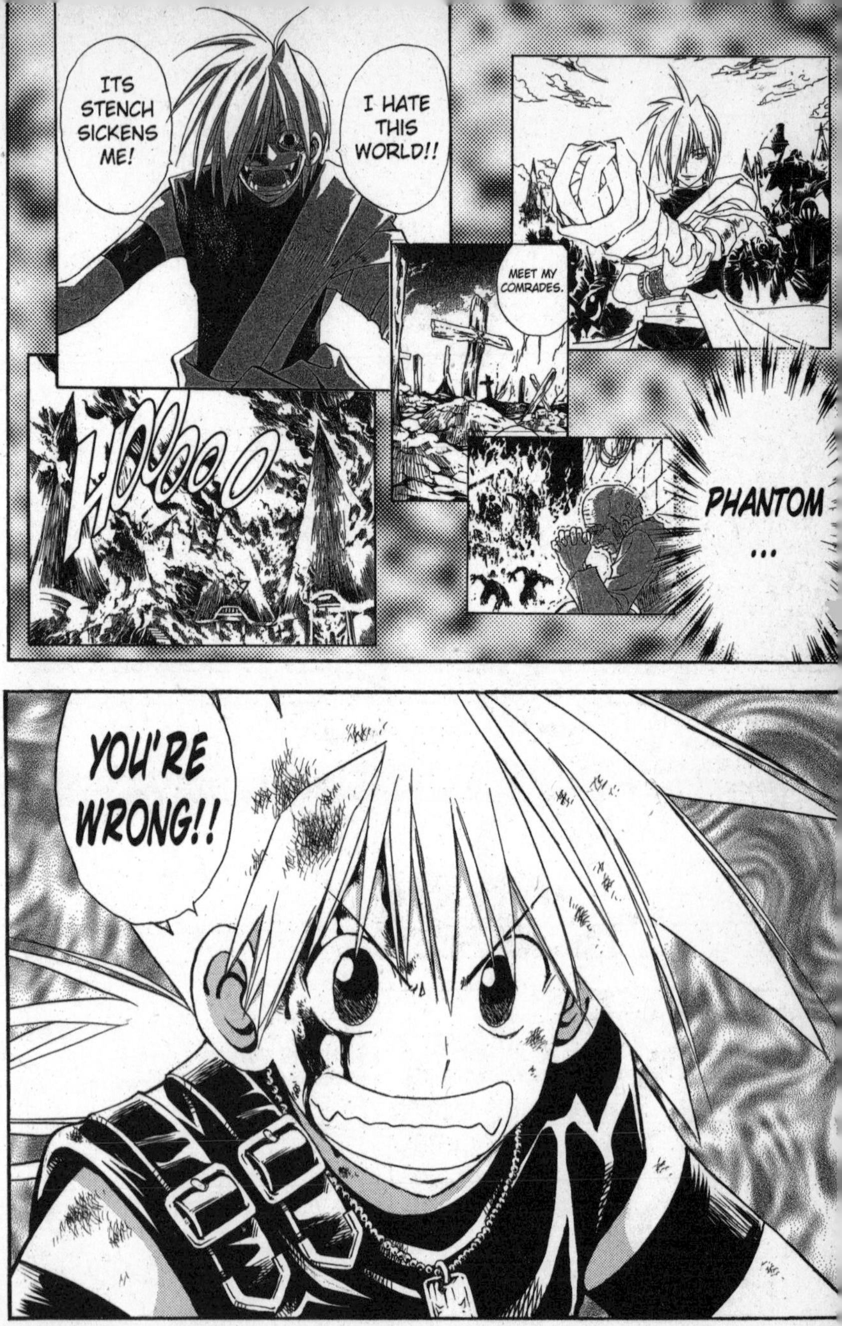
I HATE THIS WORLD!!
ITS STENCH SICKENS ME!
MEET MY COMRADES.
PHANTOM ...
HOOOOO
YOU'RE WRONG!!

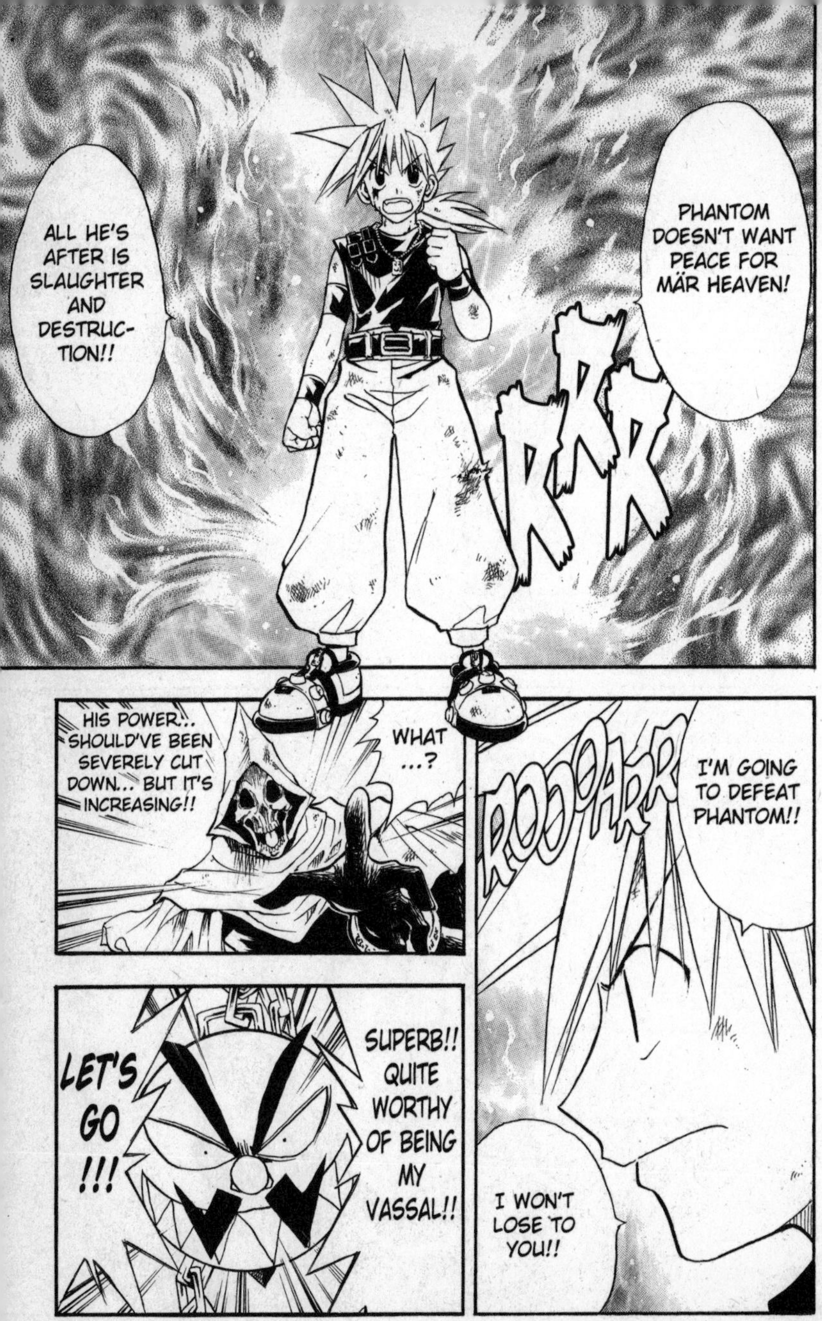
PHANTOM DOESN'T WANT PEACE FOR MÄR HEAVEN!
RRR
ALL HE'S AFTER IS SLAUGHTER AND DESTRUC-TION!!
ROOOARR
I'M GOING TO DEFEAT PHANTOM!!
I WON'T LOSE TO YOU!!
WHAT ...?
HIS POWER... SHOULD'VE BEEN SEVERELY CUT DOWN... BUT IT'S INCREASING!!
SUPERB!! QUITE WORTHY OF BEING MY VASSAL!!
LET'S GO !!!

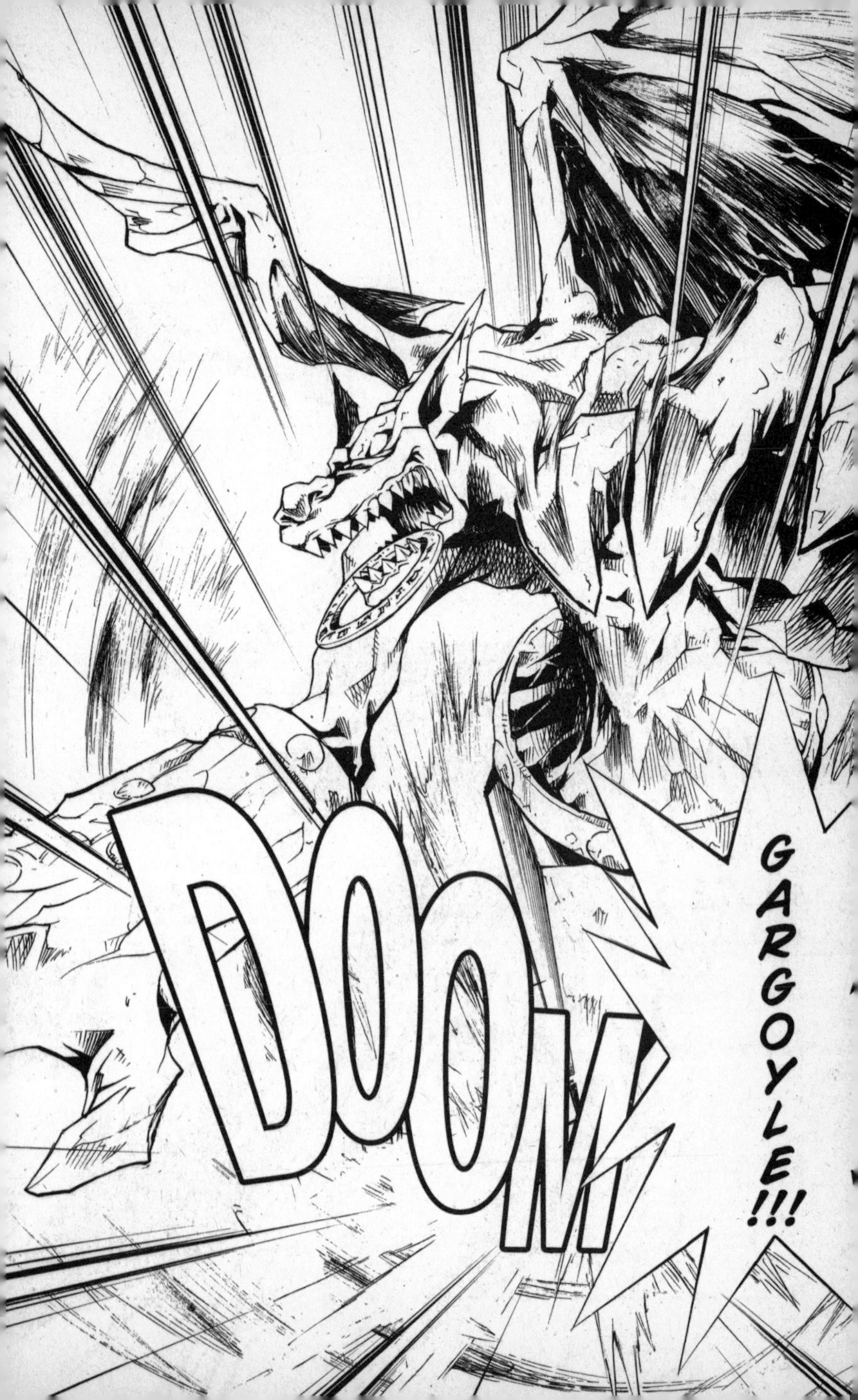
DOOM
GARGOYLE!!!

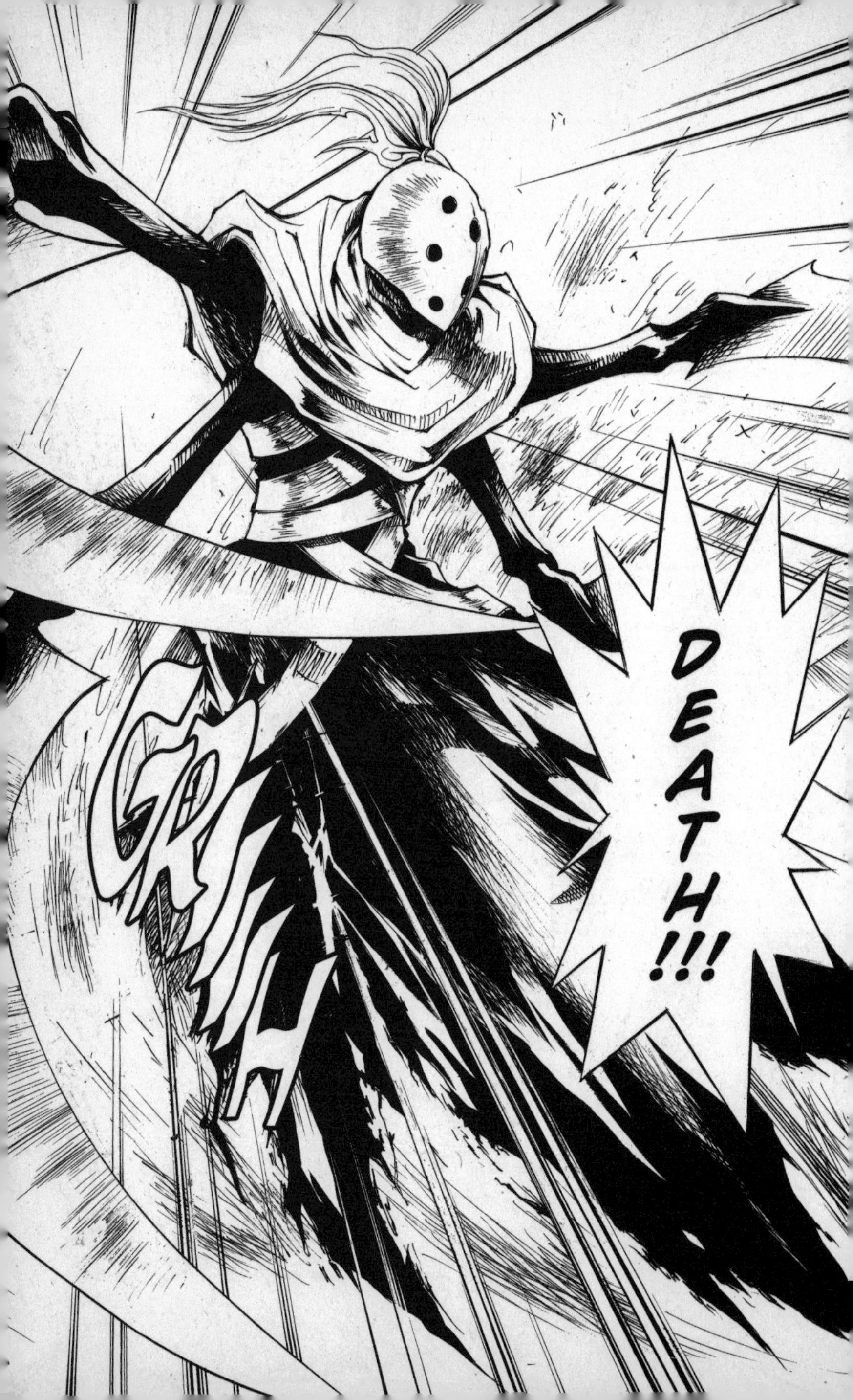
DEATH!!!

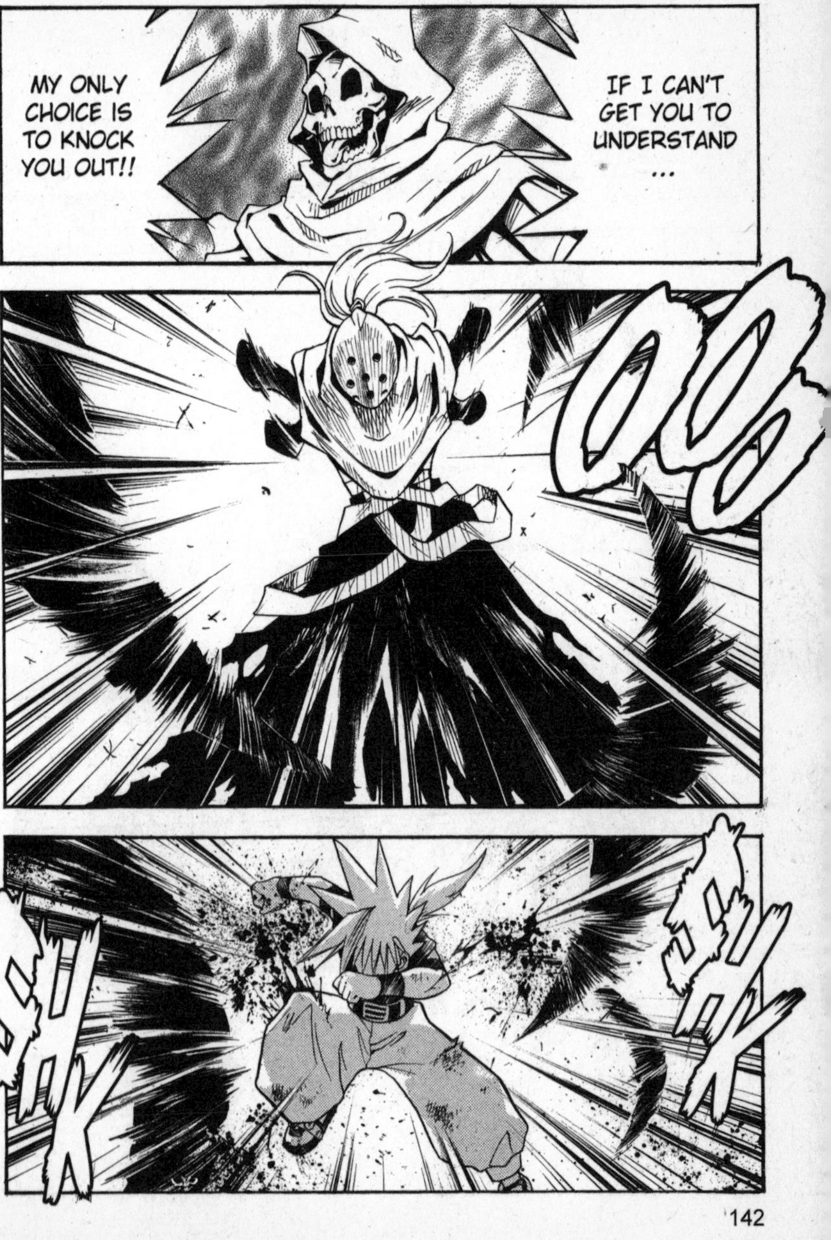
IF I CAN'T GET YOU TO UNDERSTAND ...
MY ONLY CHOICE IS TO KNOCK YOU OUT!!

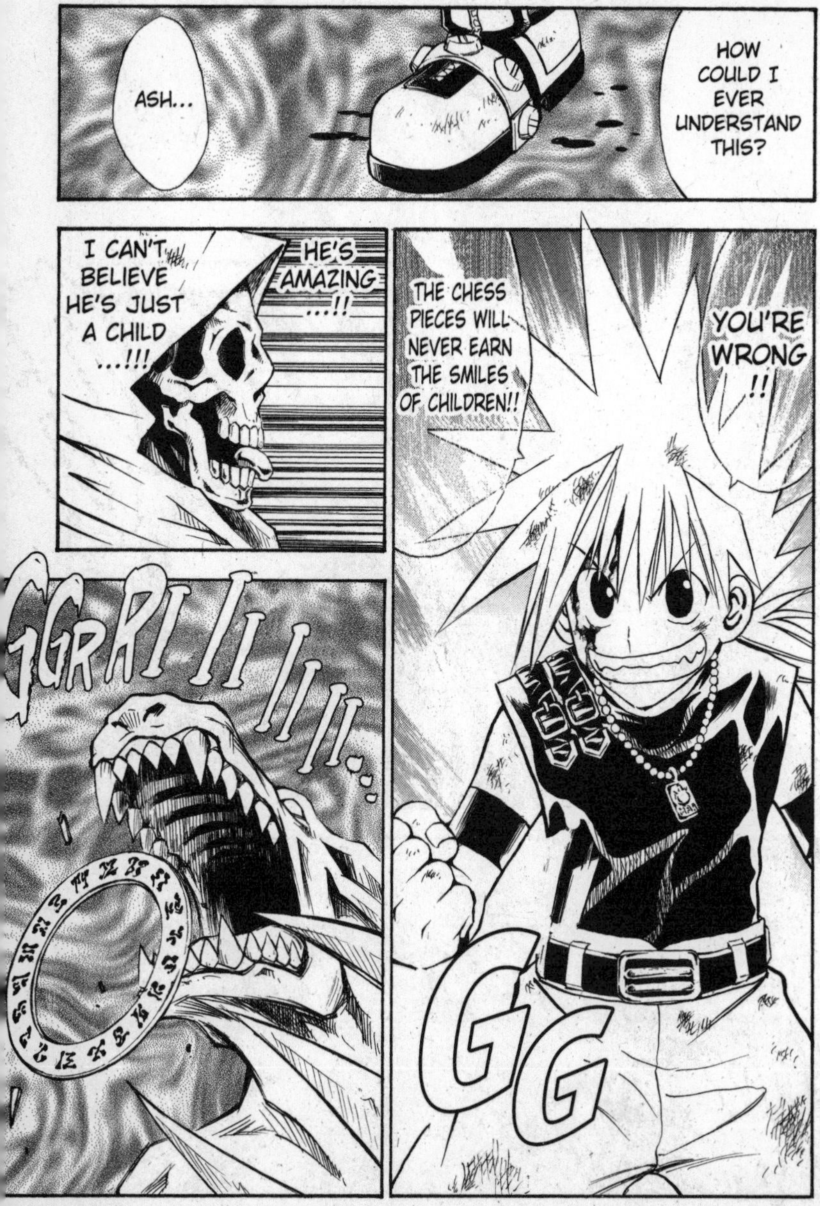
HOW COULD I EVER UNDERSTAND THIS?
ASH...
YOU'RE WRONG!!
THE CHESS PIECES WILL NEVER EARN THE SMILES OF CHILDREN!!
GG
HE'S AMAZING...!!
I CAN'T BELIEVE HE'S JUST A CHILD...!!!
GGRIIIIII...

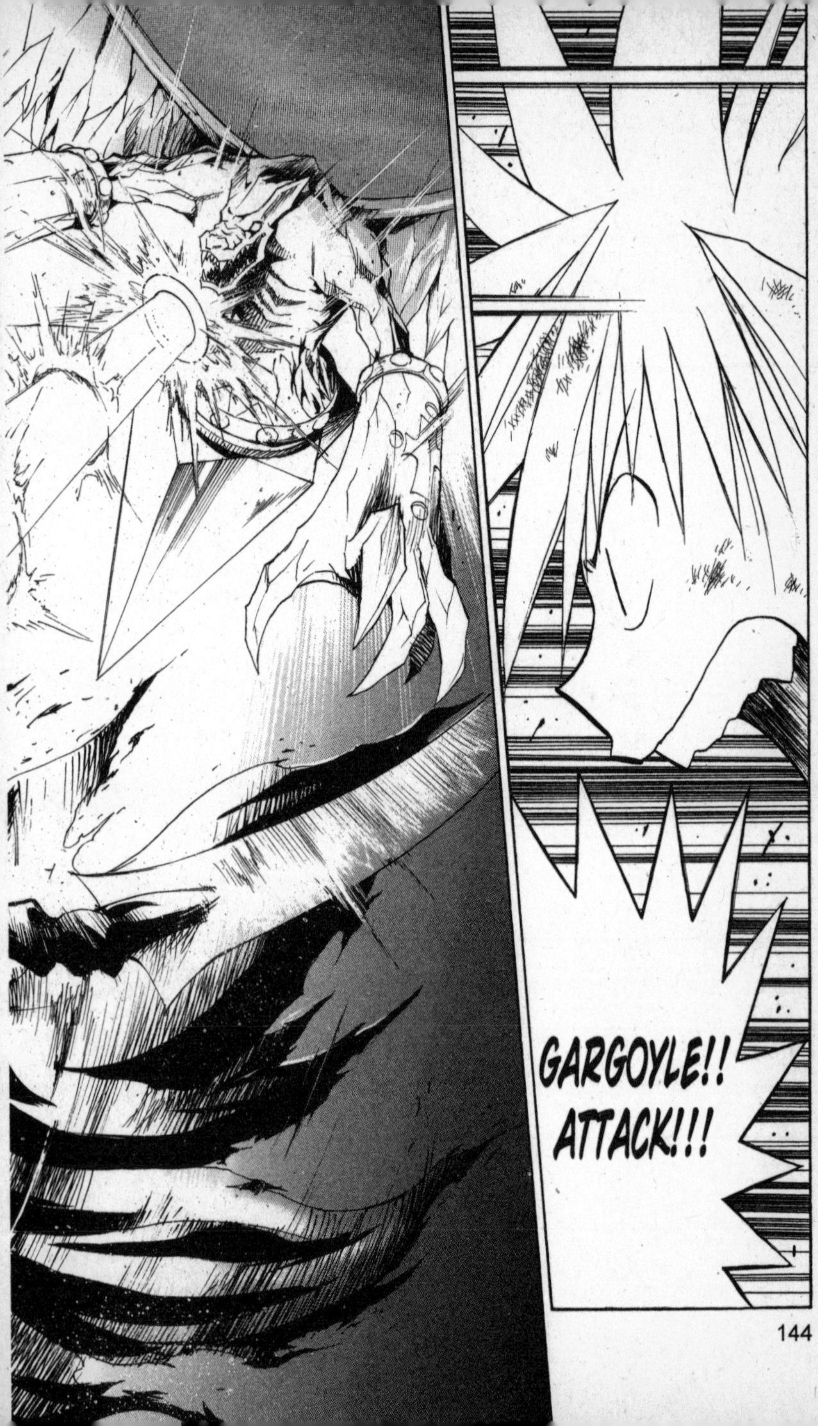
GARGOYLE!!
ATTACK!!!

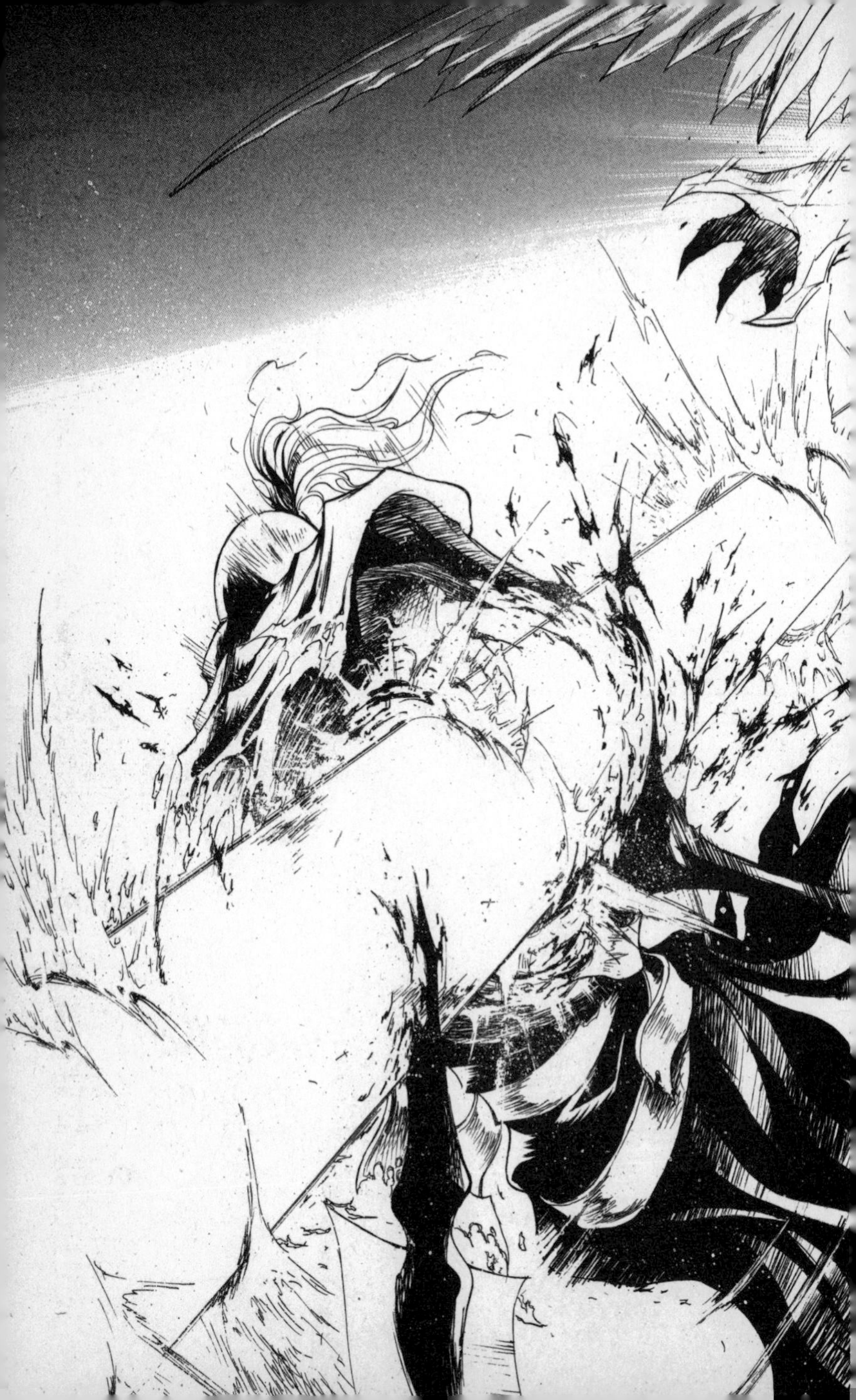

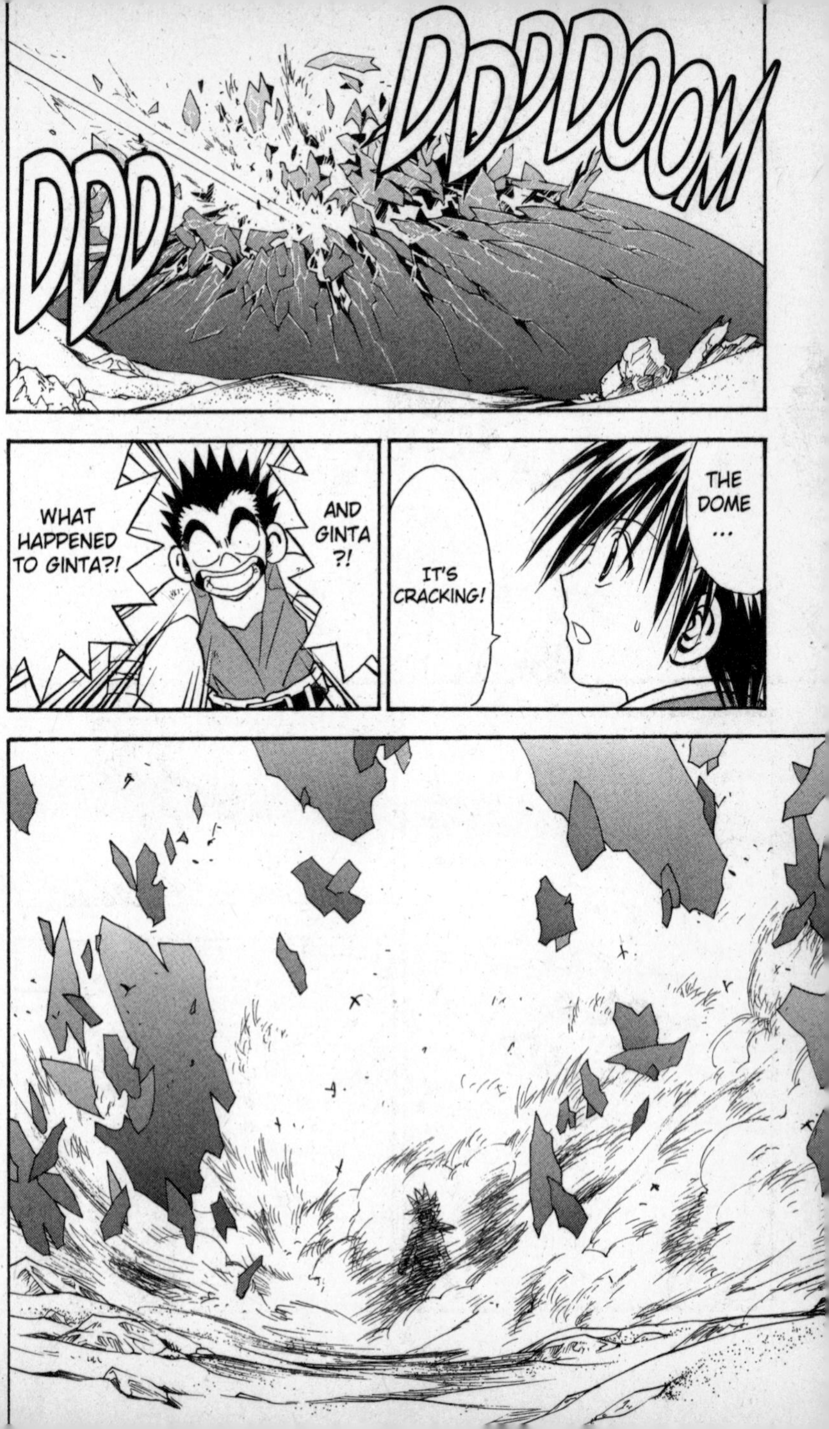
DDD
DDDDOOM
THE DOME ...
IT'S CRACKING!
AND GINTA ?!
WHAT HAPPENED TO GINTA?!

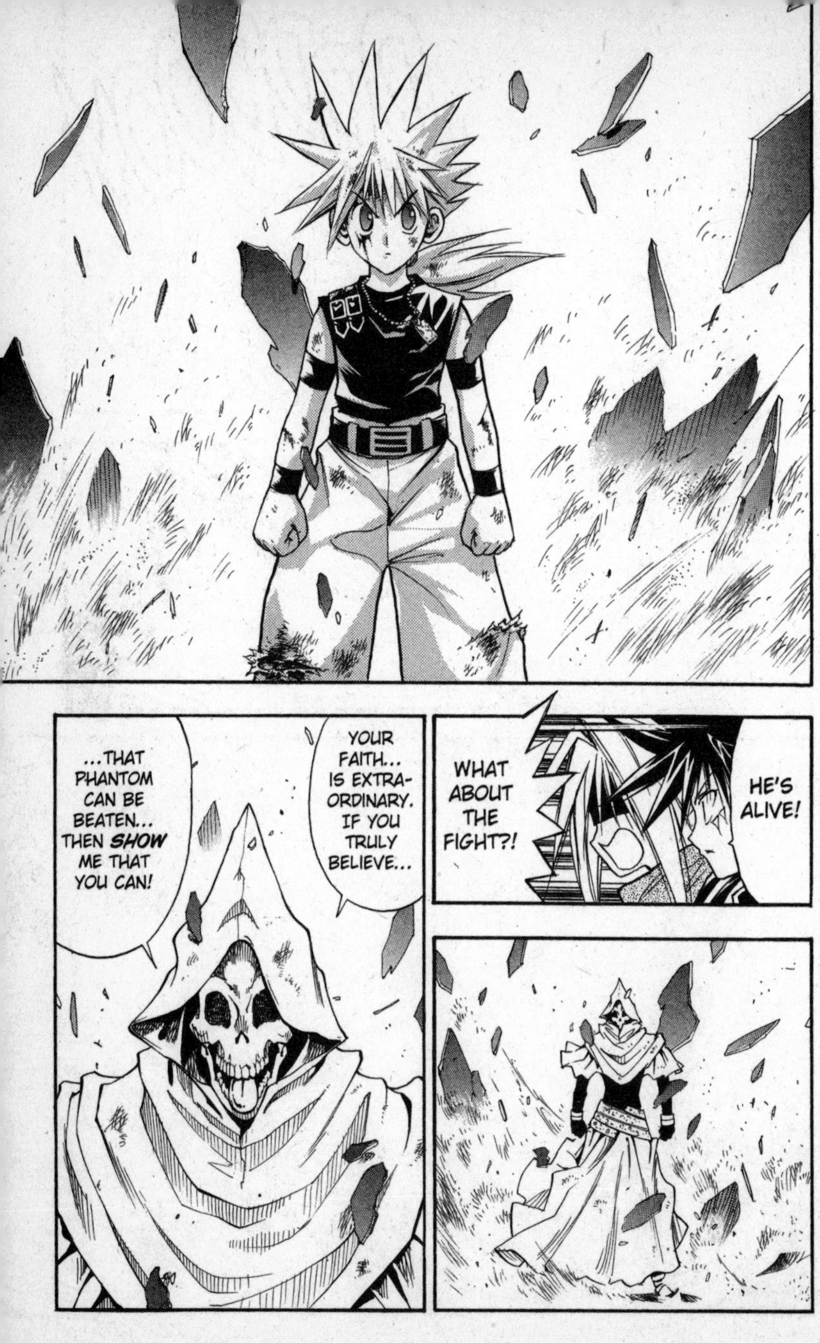
HE'S ALIVE!
WHAT ABOUT THE FIGHT?!
YOUR FAITH... IS EXTRA-ORDINARY. IF YOU TRULY BELIEVE...
...THAT PHANTOM CAN BE BEATEN... THEN *SHOW* ME THAT YOU CAN!

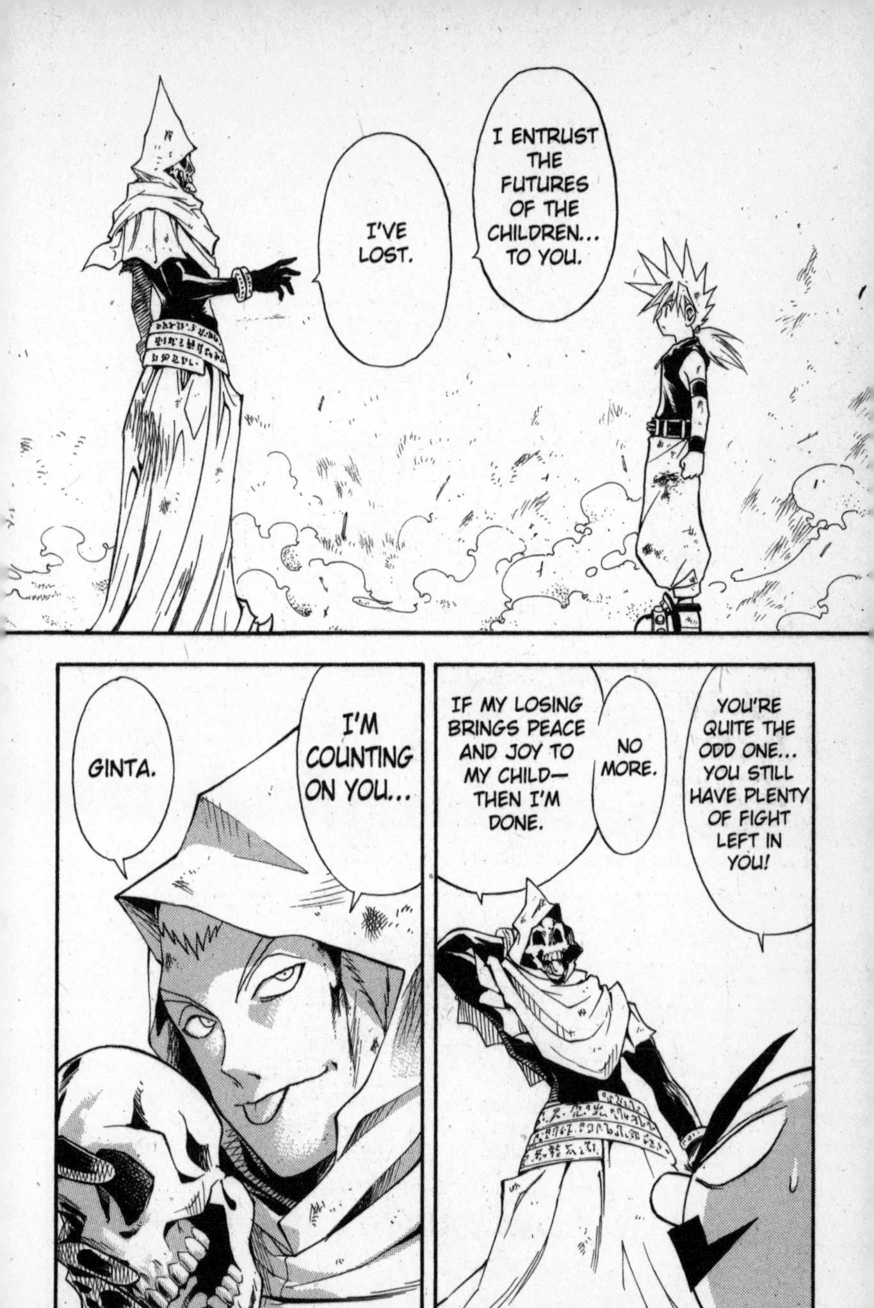
I ENTRUST THE FUTURES OF THE CHILDREN... TO YOU.
I'VE LOST.
YOU'RE QUITE THE ODD ONE... YOU STILL HAVE PLENTY OF FIGHT LEFT IN YOU!
NO MORE.
IF MY LOSING BRINGS PEACE AND JOY TO MY CHILD—THEN I'M DONE.
I'M COUNTING ON YOU...
GINTA.

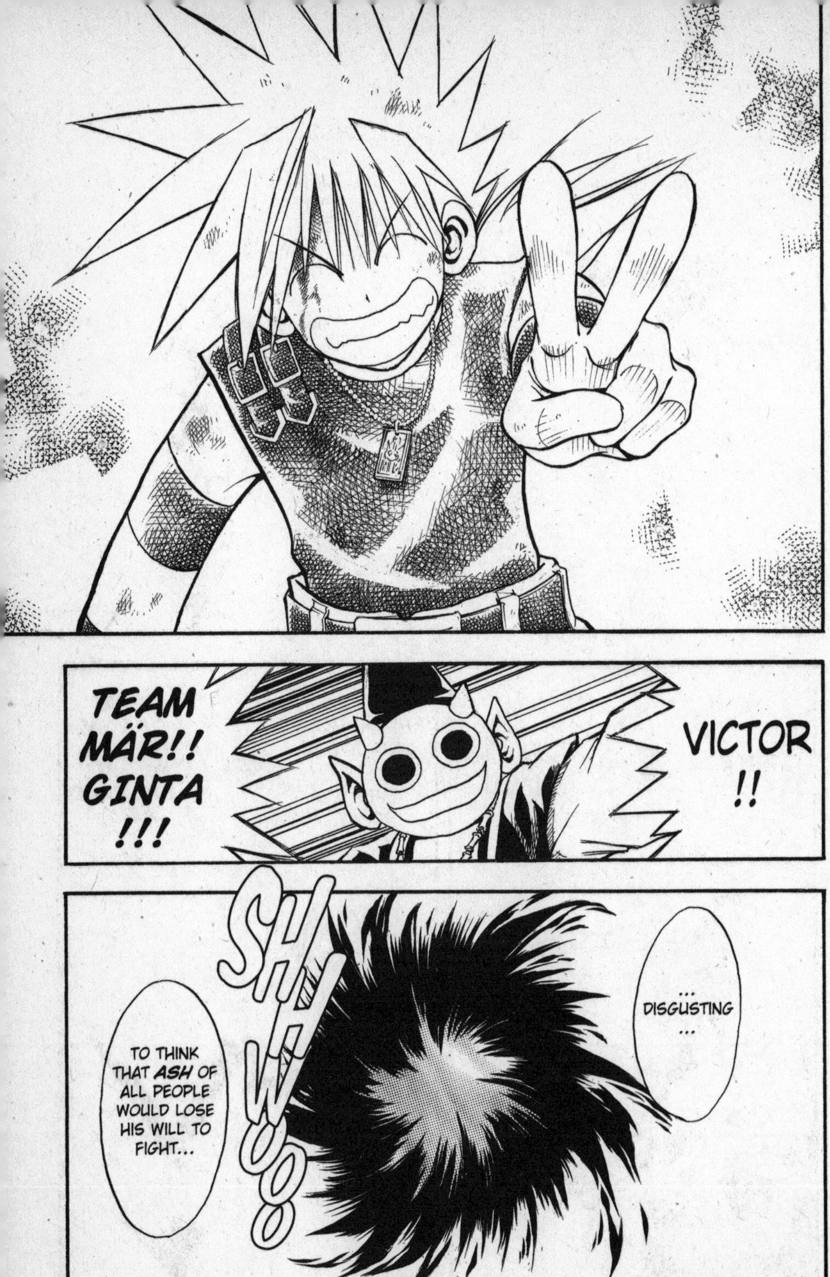
VICTOR !!
TEAM MÄR!! GINTA !!!
... DISGUSTING ...
SHWOOO
TO THINK THAT ASH OF ALL PEOPLE WOULD LOSE HIS WILL TO FIGHT...

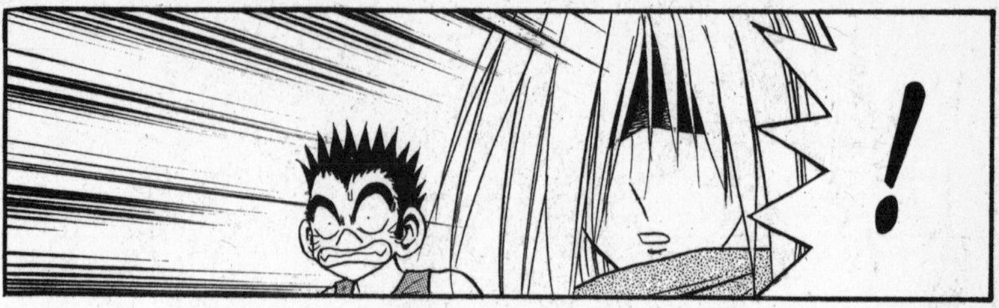
!

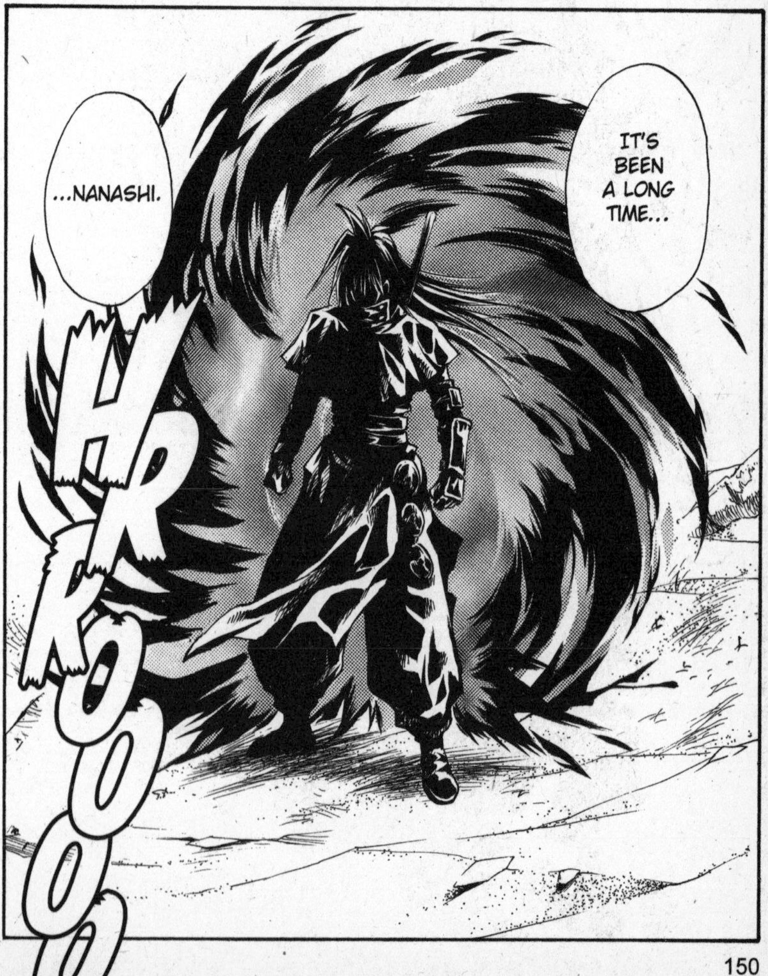
IT'S BEEN A LONG TIME...
...NANASHI.
HRROOOO

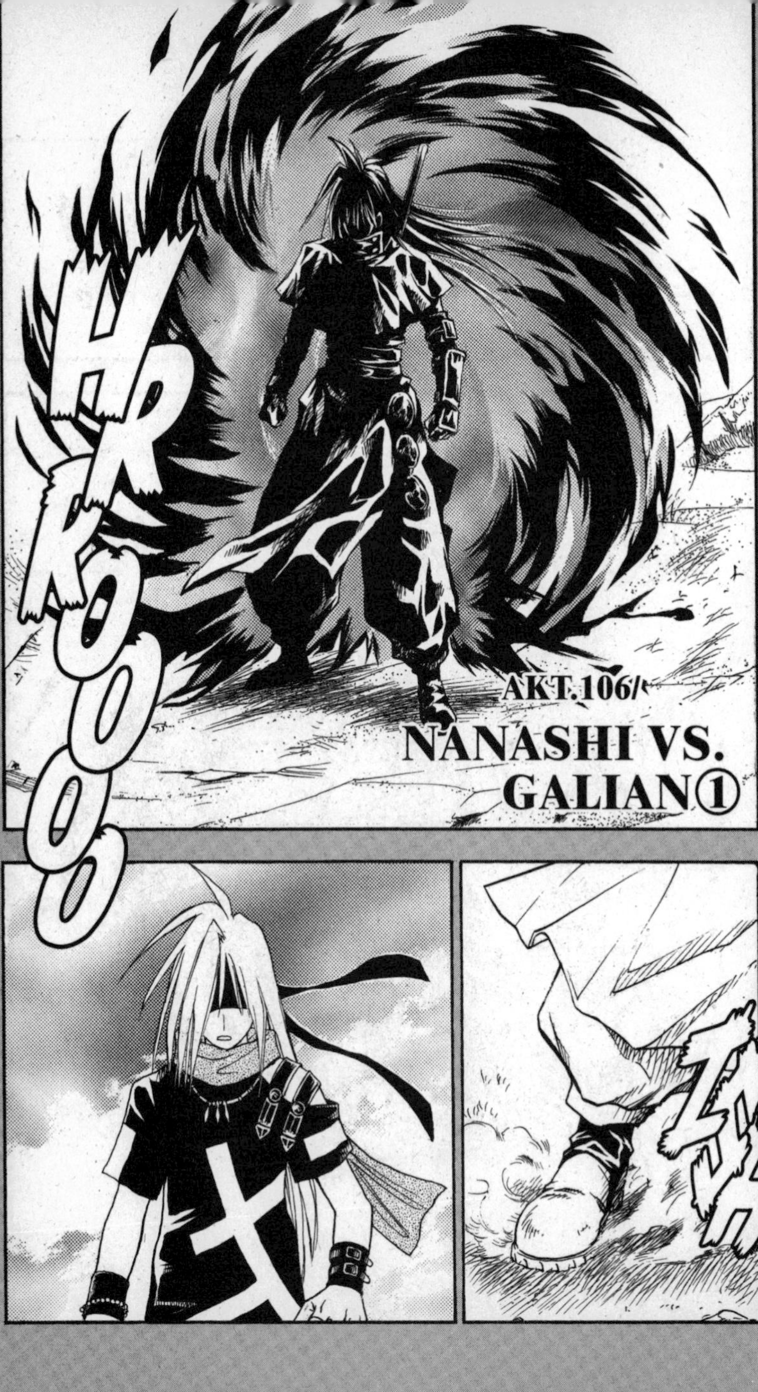
HRROOOOO
AKT.106/
NANASHI VS. GALIAN①
ZAH

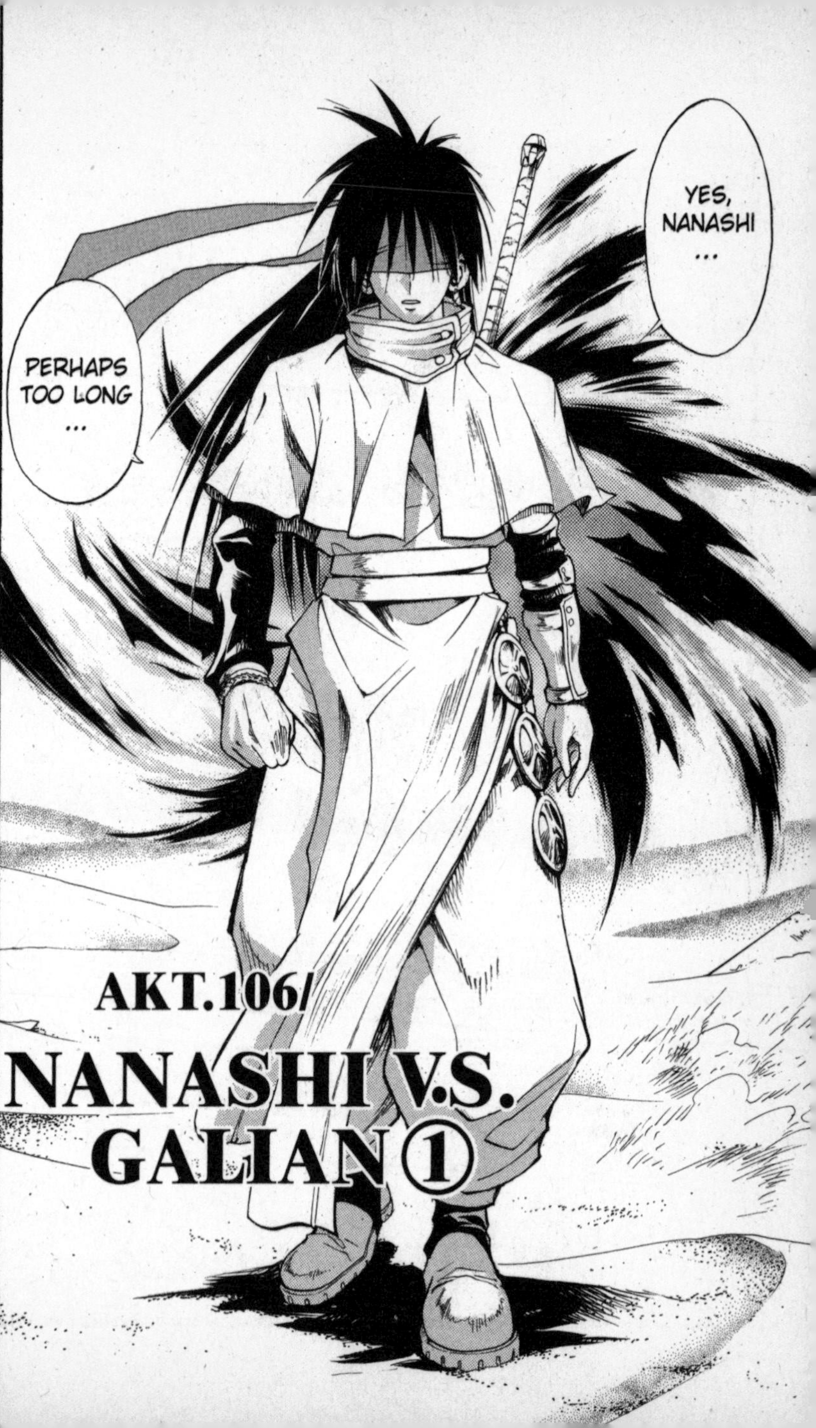
YES, NANASHI ...
PERHAPS TOO LONG ...
AKT.106/
NANASHI V.S. GALIAN ①

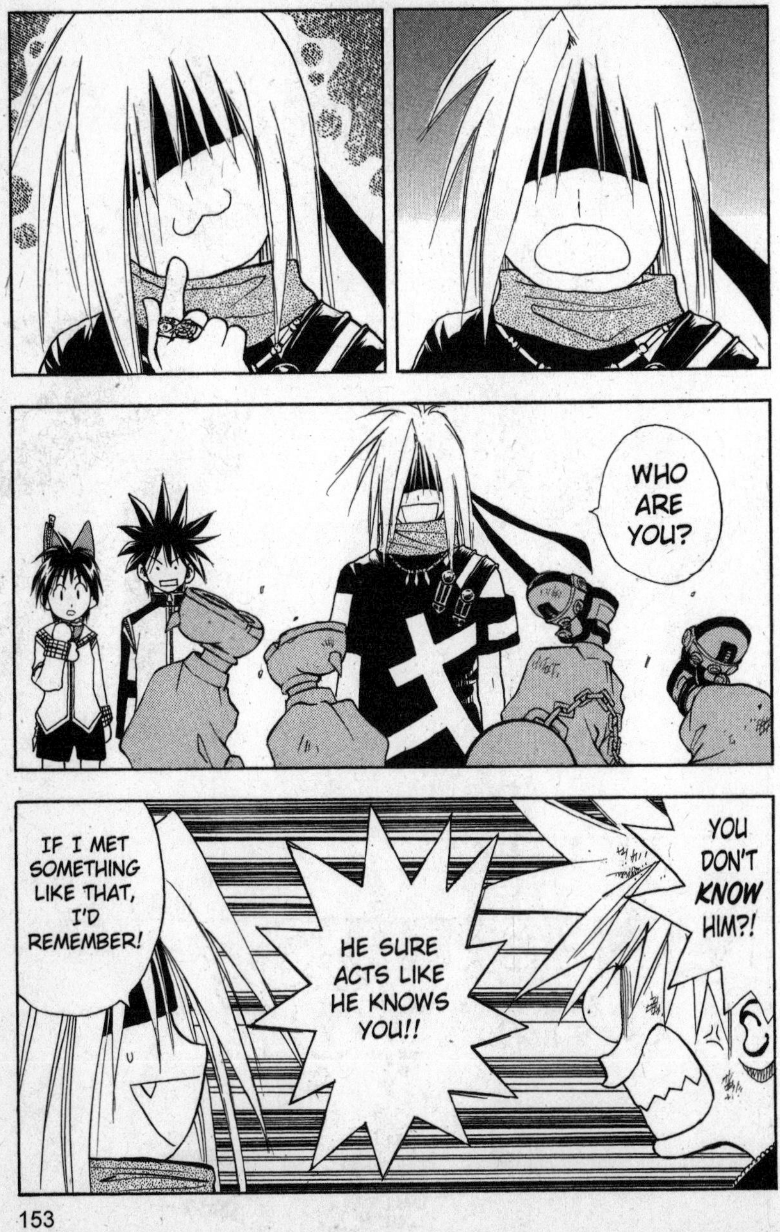
WHO ARE YOU?
YOU DON'T KNOW HIM?!
HE SURE ACTS LIKE HE KNOWS YOU!!
IF I MET SOMETHING LIKE THAT, I'D REMEMBER!

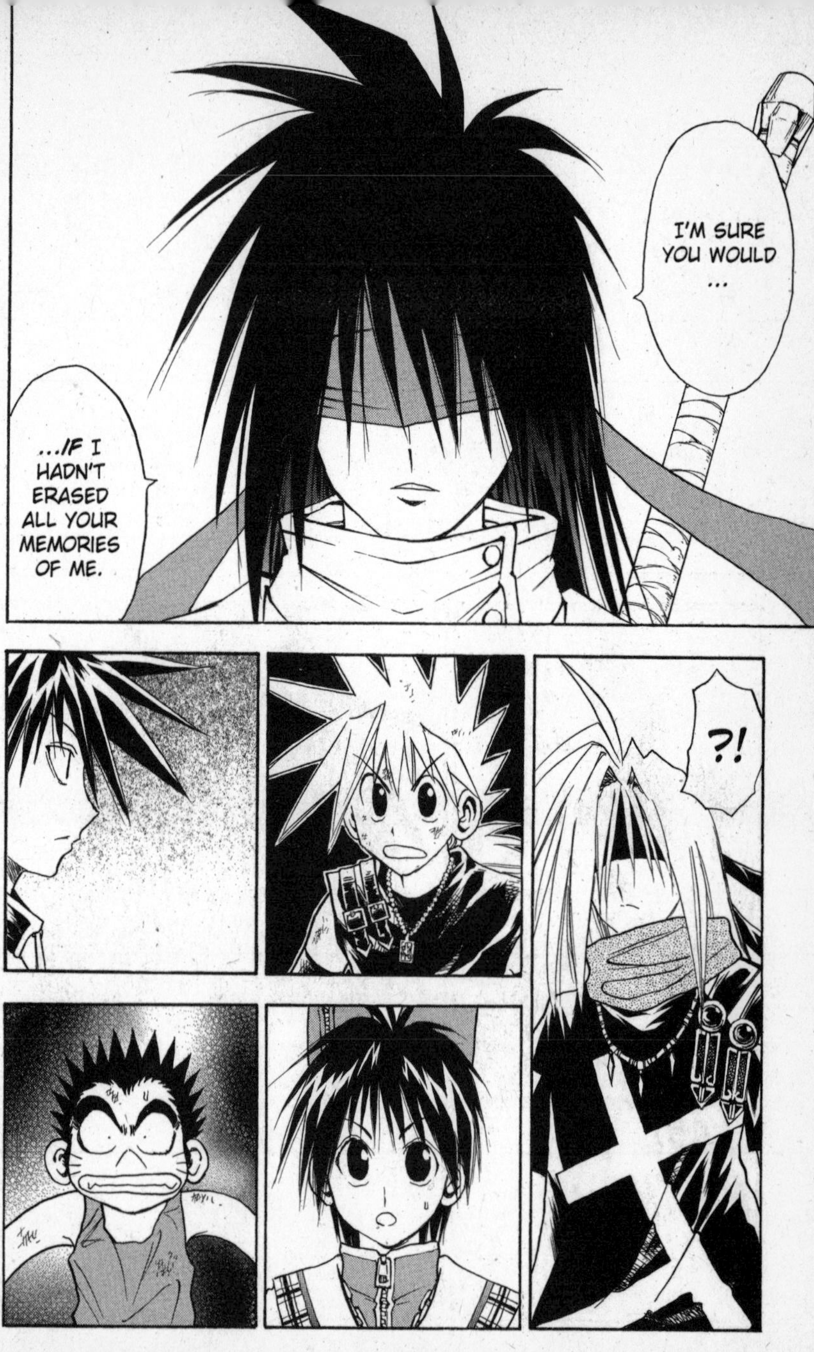
I'M SURE YOU WOULD ...
...IF I HADN'T ERASED ALL YOUR MEMORIES OF ME.
?!

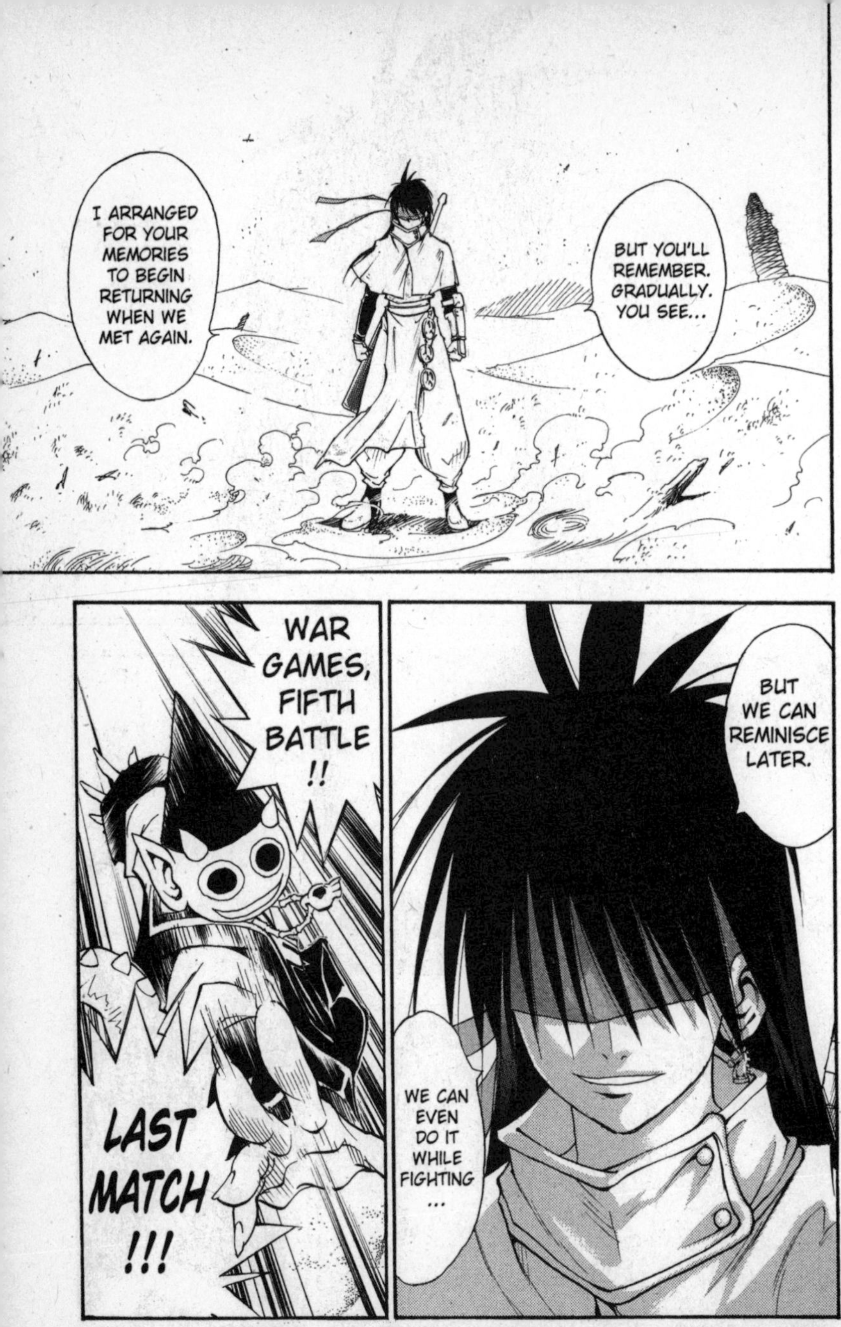
BUT YOU'LL REMEMBER. GRADUALLY. YOU SEE...
I ARRANGED FOR YOUR MEMORIES TO BEGIN RETURNING WHEN WE MET AGAIN.
BUT WE CAN REMINISCE LATER.
WE CAN EVEN DO IT WHILE FIGHTING ...
WAR GAMES, FIFTH BATTLE !!
LAST MATCH !!!

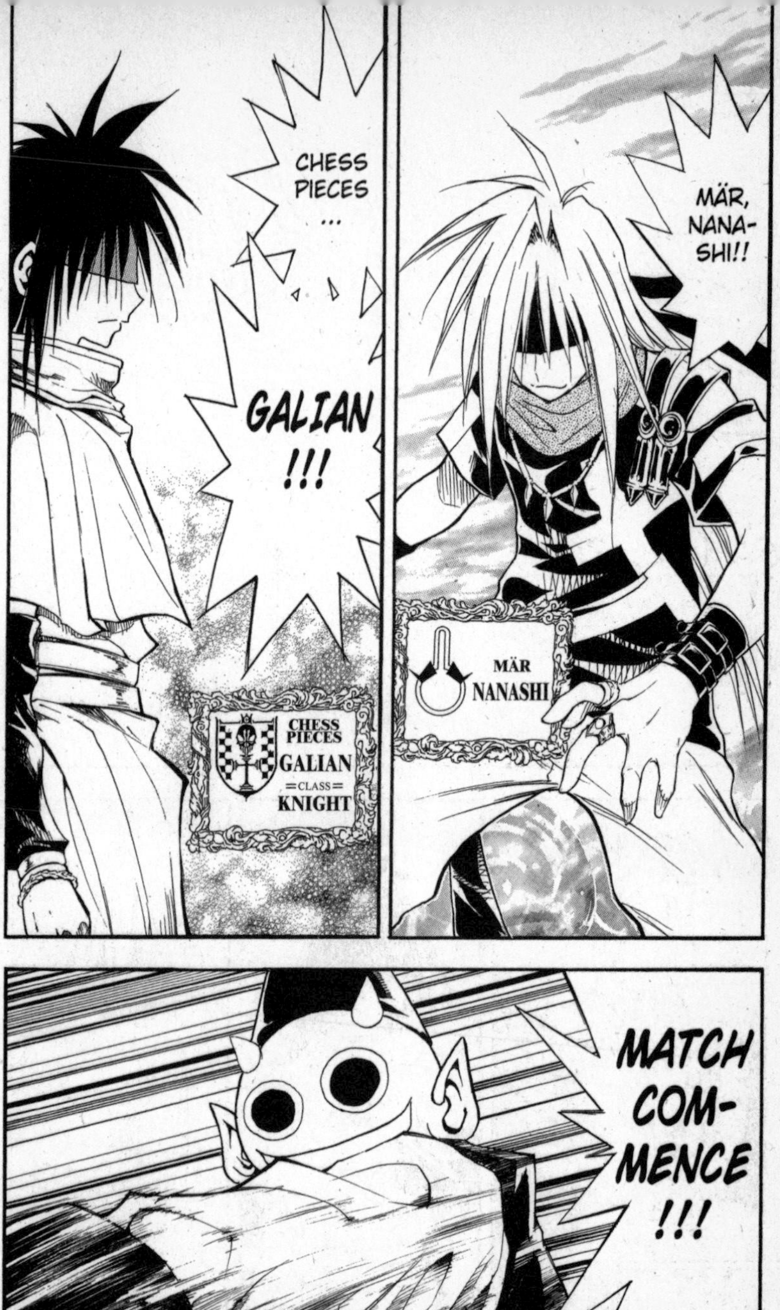
MÄR, NANA-SHI!!
MÄR
NANASHI
CHESS PIECES ...
GALIAN !!!
CHESS PIECES
GALIAN
=CLASS=
KNIGHT
MATCH COM-MENCE !!!

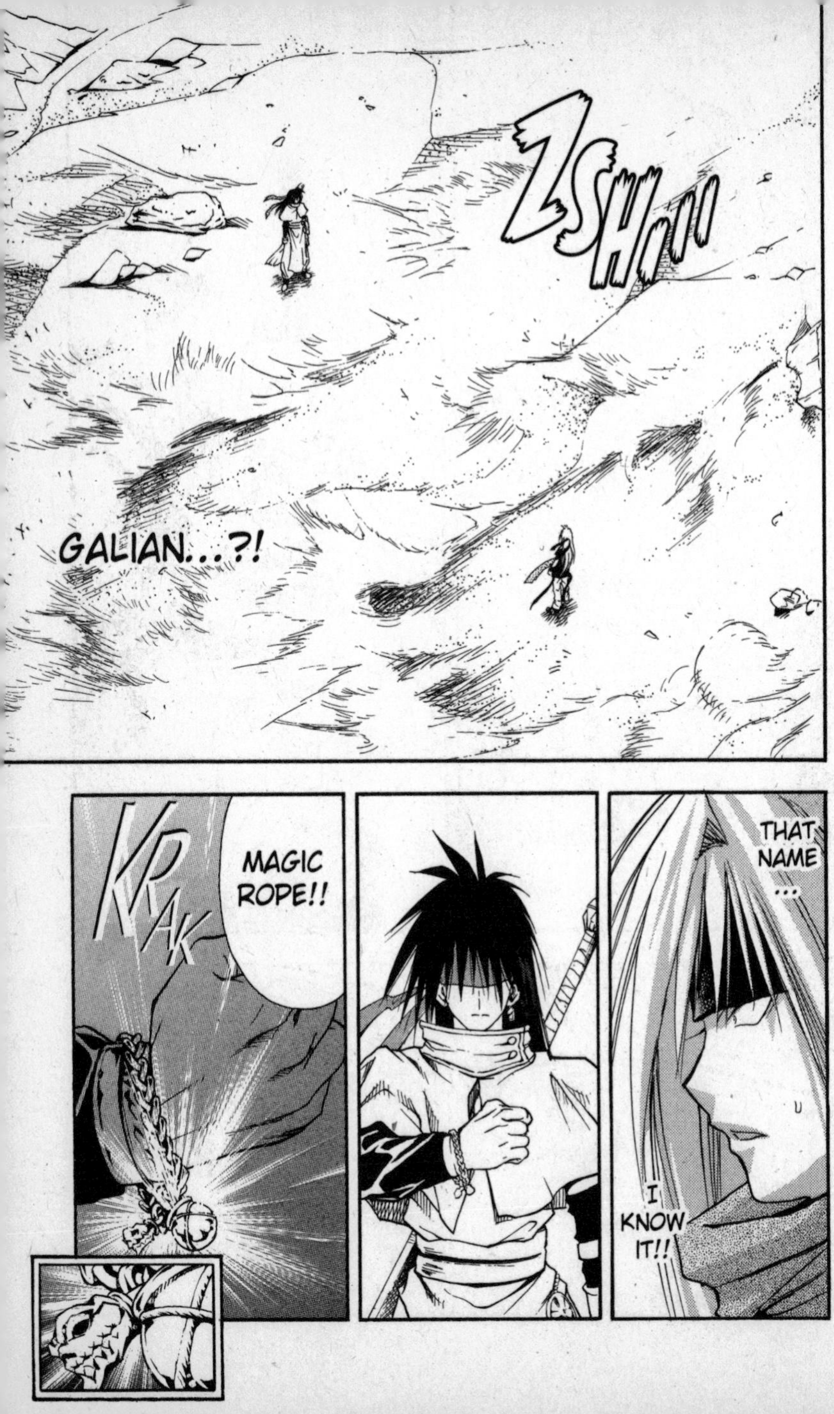
ZSHOOO
GALIAN...?!
THAT NAME...
I KNOW IT!!
MAGIC ROPE!!
KRAK

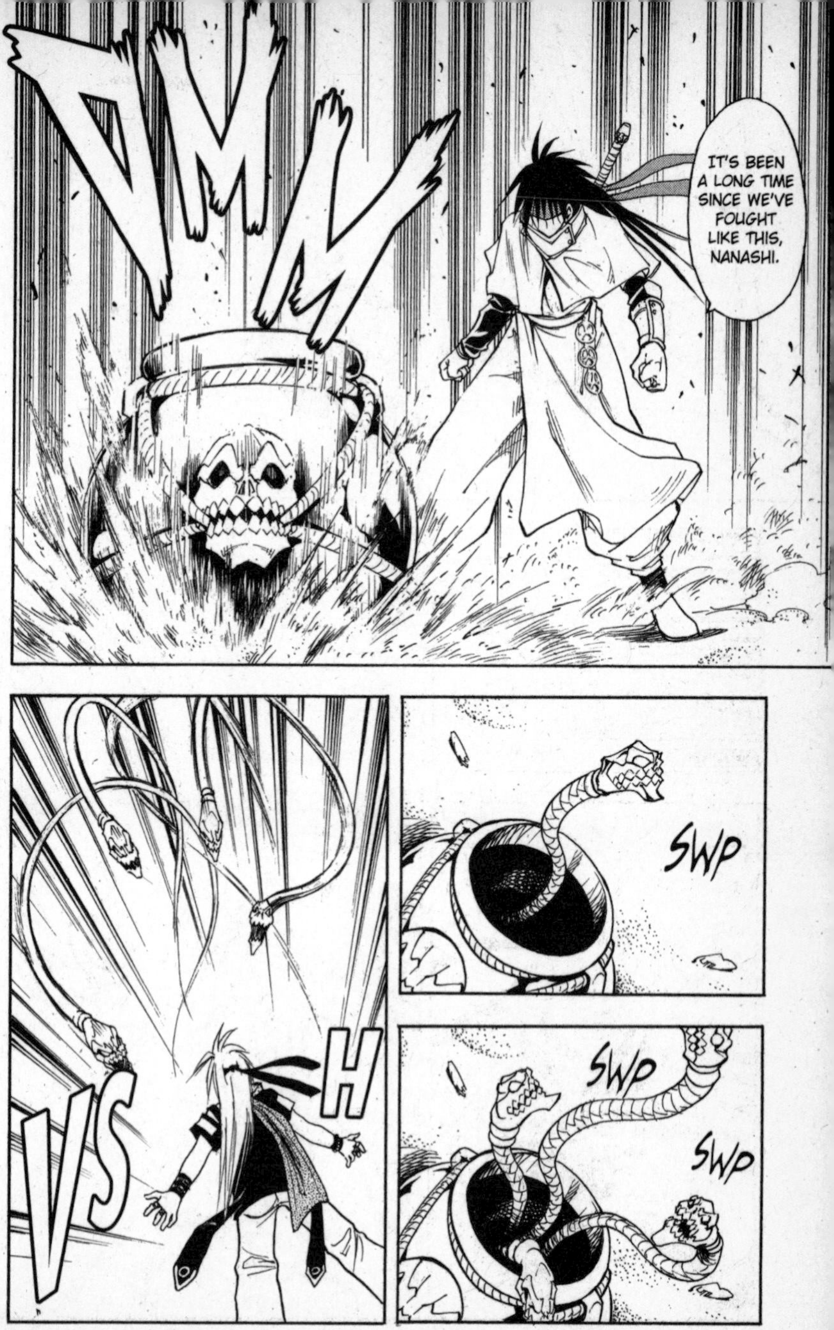
IT'S BEEN A LONG TIME SINCE WE'VE FOUGHT LIKE THIS, NANASHI.
SWP
SWP
SWP

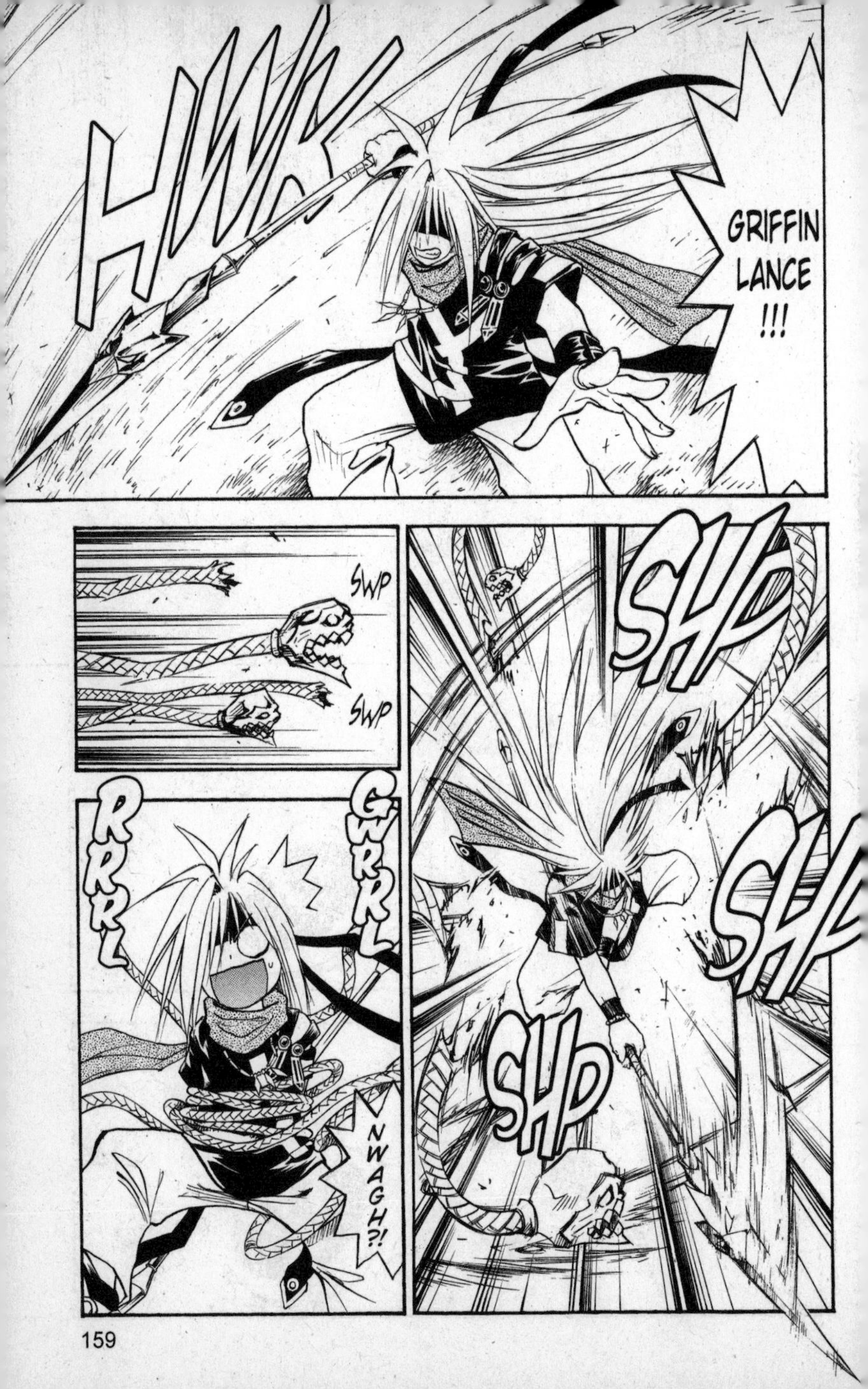
HWAM
GRIFFIN LANCE !!!
SHP
SHP
SHP
SWP
SWP
RRRL
GWRRL
NWAGH?!

I'VE GOT TO DESTROY IT!!

THAT POT...

GRR...

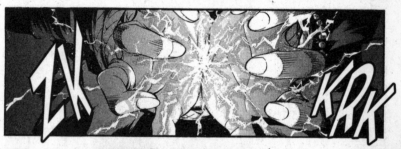

ZK

KRK

ELEC-TRIC EYE!!!

KRAH

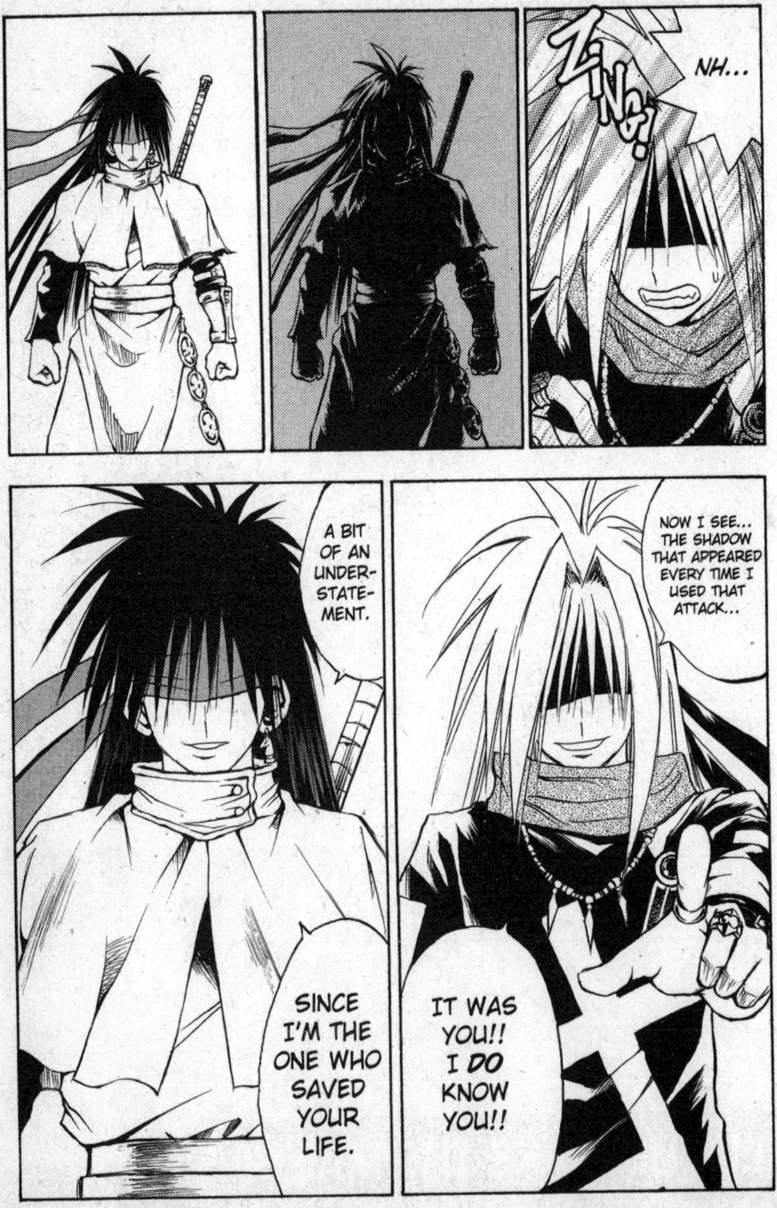
ZING!
NH...
NOW I SEE... THE SHADOW THAT APPEARED EVERY TIME I USED THAT ATTACK...
IT WAS YOU!! I *DO* KNOW YOU!!
A BIT OF AN UNDER-STATE-MENT.
SINCE I'M THE ONE WHO SAVED YOUR LIFE.

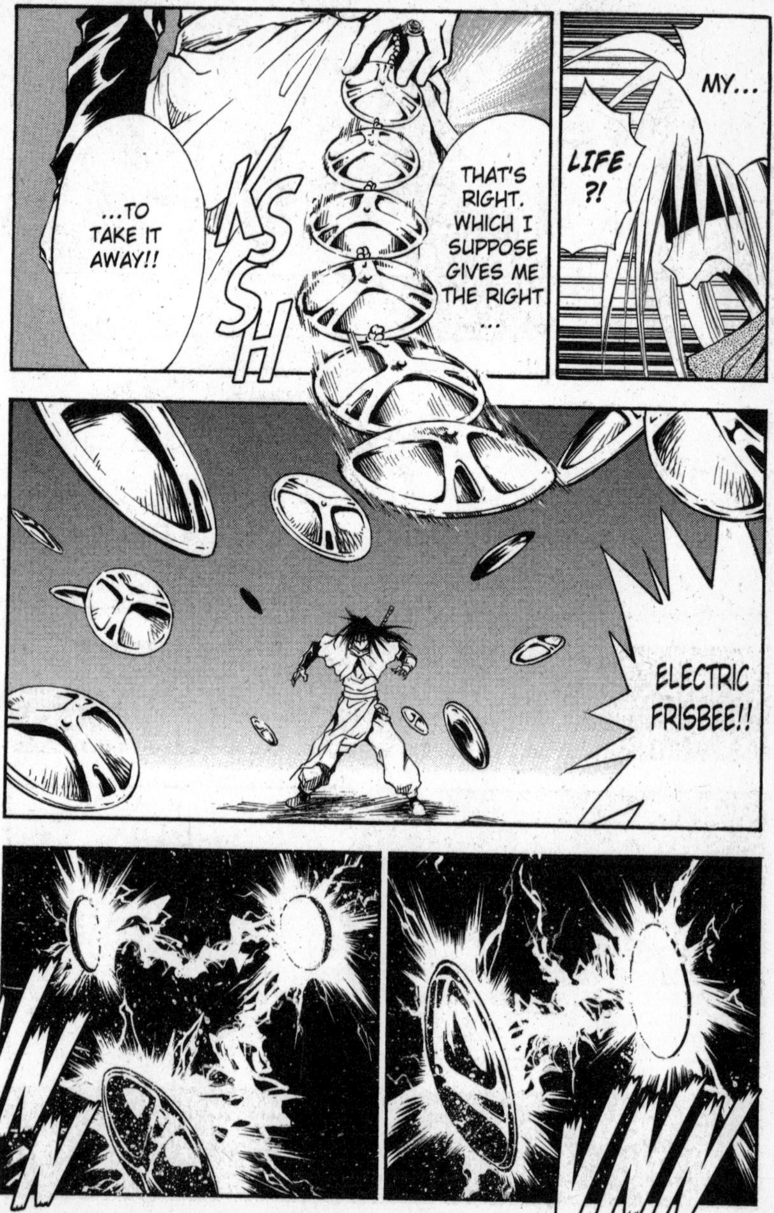
MY...
LIFE ?!
THAT'S RIGHT. WHICH I SUPPOSE GIVES ME THE RIGHT ...
KSSH
...TO TAKE IT AWAY!!
ELECTRIC FRISBEE!!

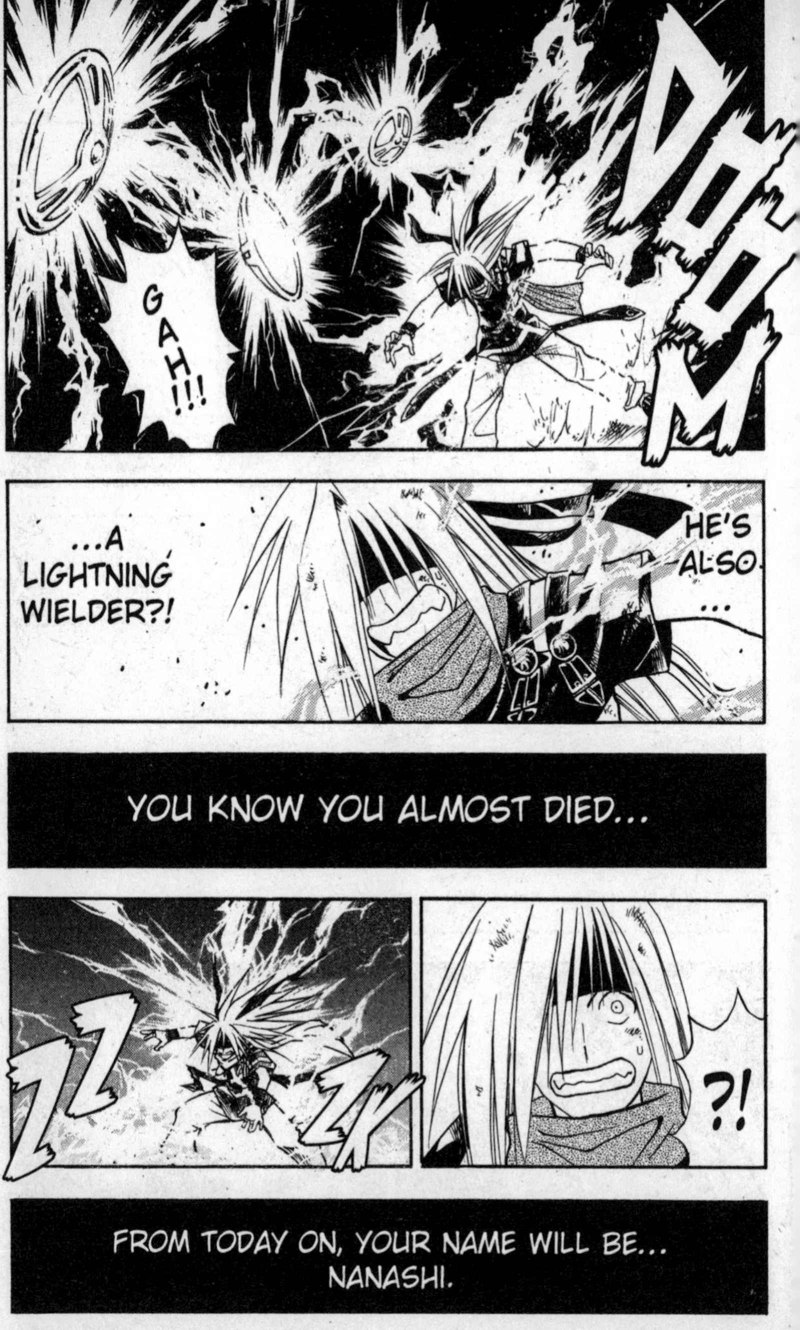
GAH!!!
HE'S ALSO...
...A LIGHTNING WIELDER?!
YOU KNOW YOU ALMOST DIED...
?!
FROM TODAY ON, YOUR NAME WILL BE... NANASHI.

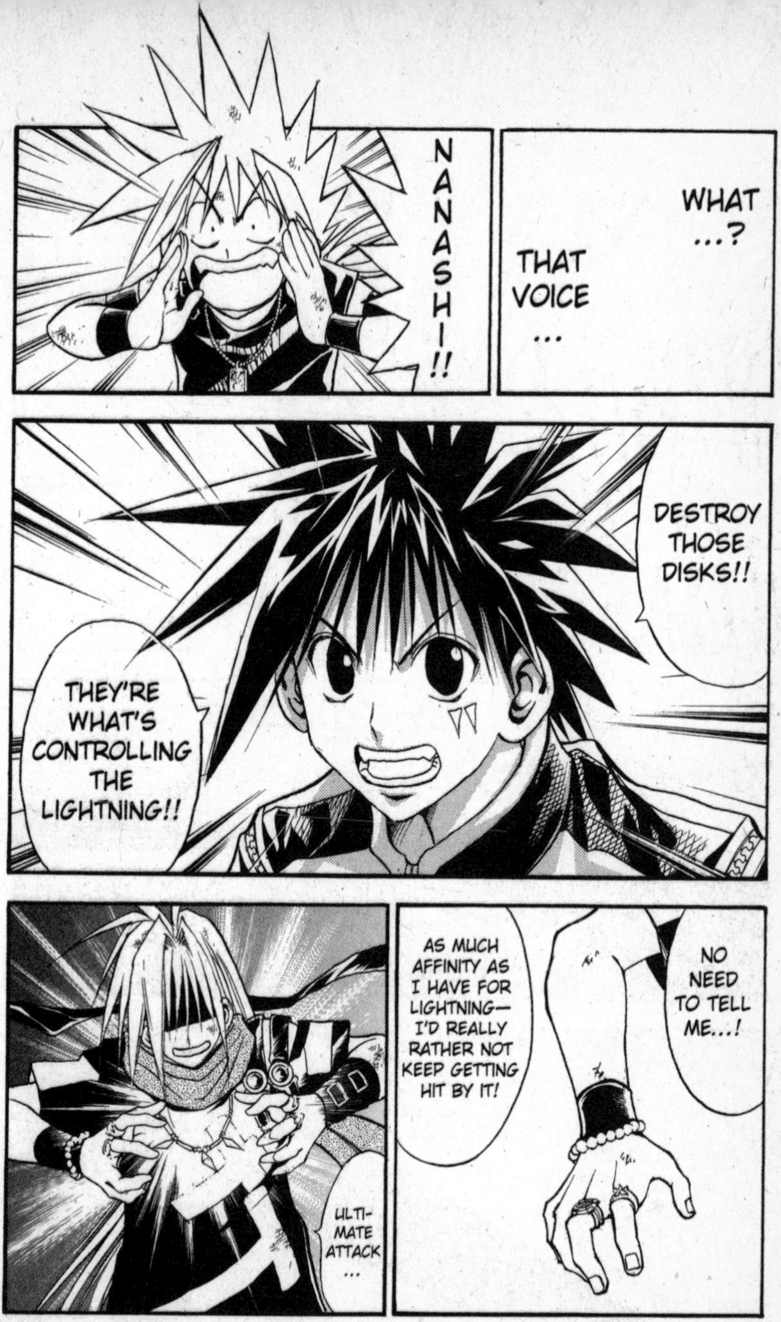
WHAT ...?
THAT VOICE ...
NANASHI!!
DESTROY THOSE DISKS!!
THEY'RE WHAT'S CONTROLLING THE LIGHTNING!!
NO NEED TO TELL ME...!
AS MUCH AFFINITY AS I HAVE FOR LIGHTNING— I'D REALLY RATHER NOT KEEP GETTING HIT BY IT!
ULTI-MATE ATTACK ...

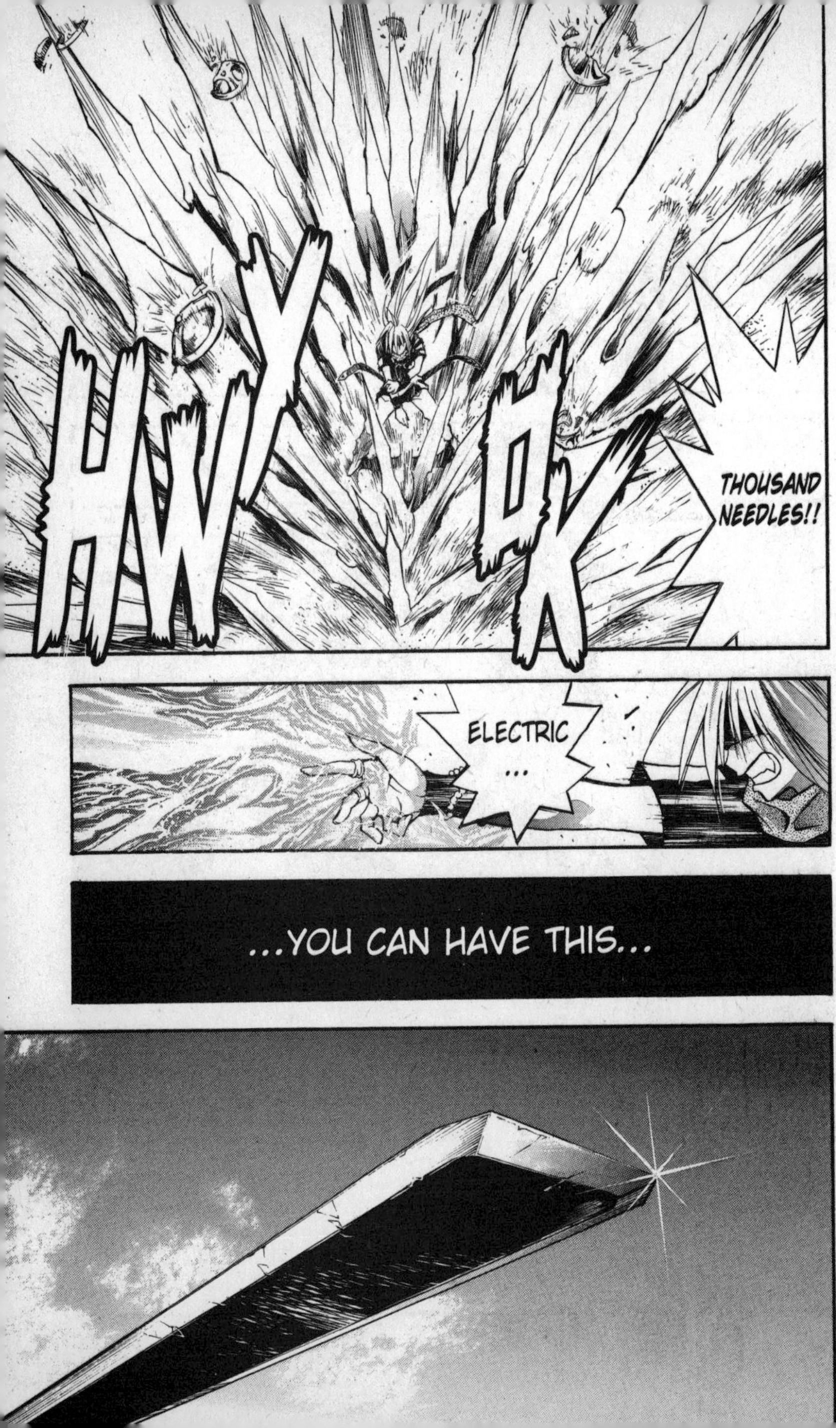
THOUSAND NEEDLES!!
ELECTRIC ...
...YOU CAN HAVE THIS...

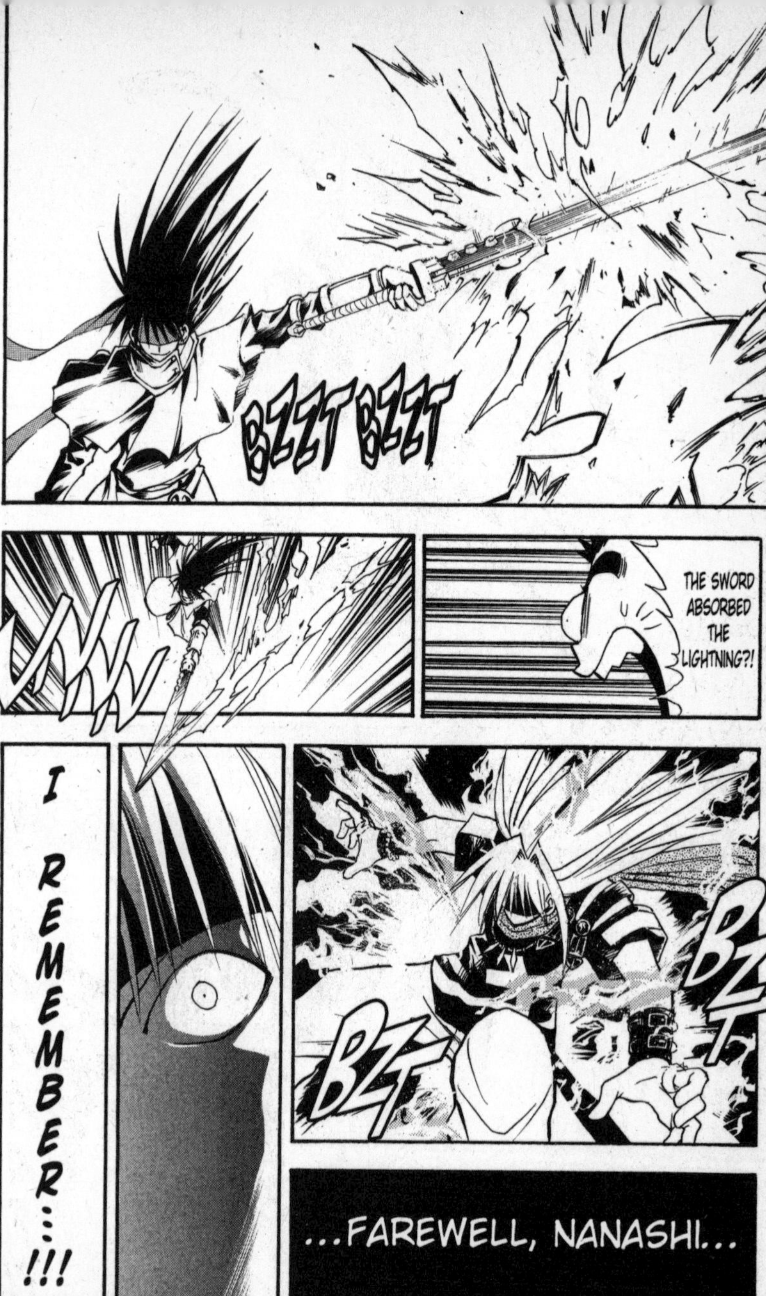
BZZT BZZT
THE SWORD ABSORBED THE LIGHTNING?!
BZT BZT
...FAREWELL, NANASHI...
I REMEMBER...!!!

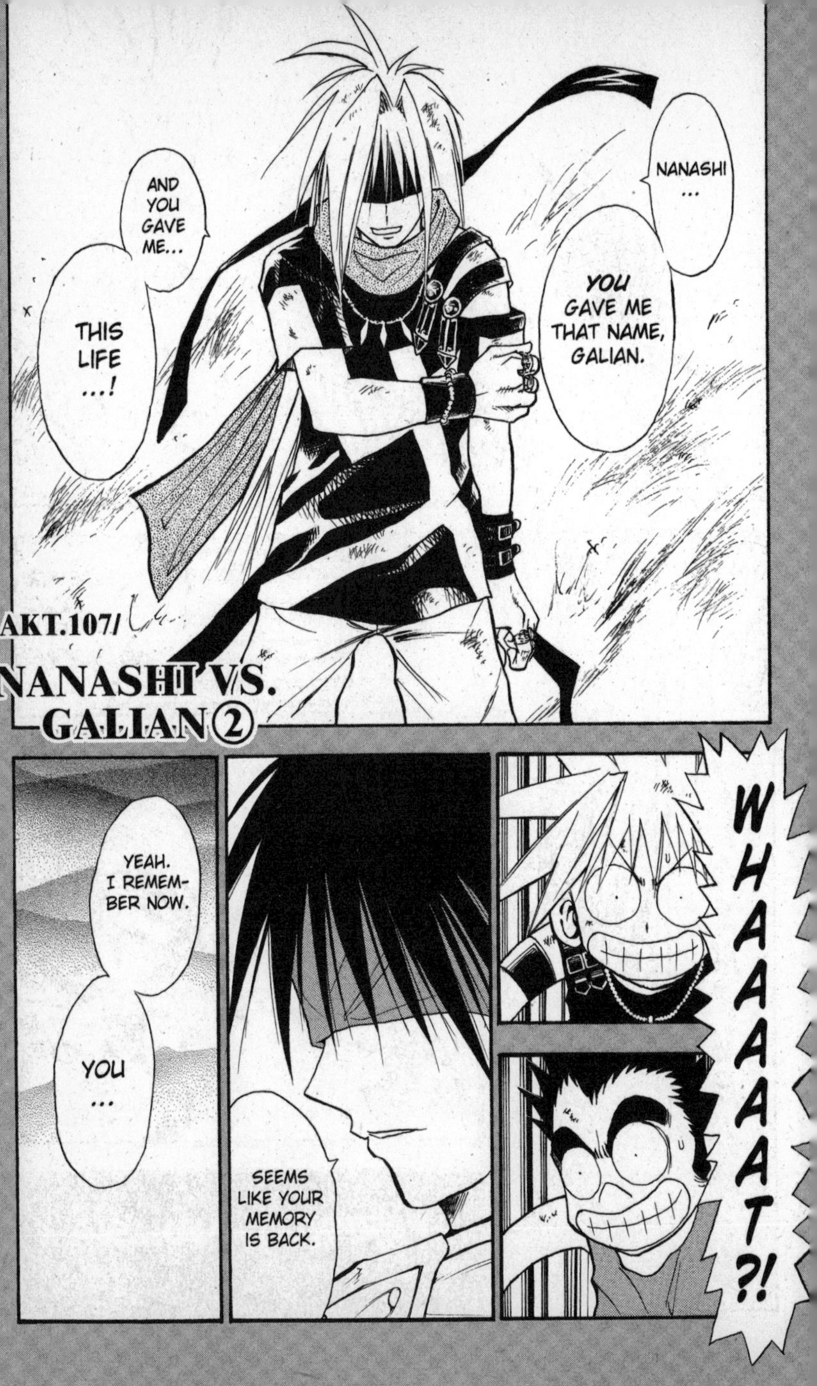
NANASHI ...
YOU GAVE ME THAT NAME, GALIAN.
AND YOU GAVE ME...
THIS LIFE ...!
AKT.107/
NANASHI VS. GALIAN ②
WHAAAAAAT?!
SEEMS LIKE YOUR MEMORY IS BACK.
YEAH. I REMEM-BER NOW.
YOU ...

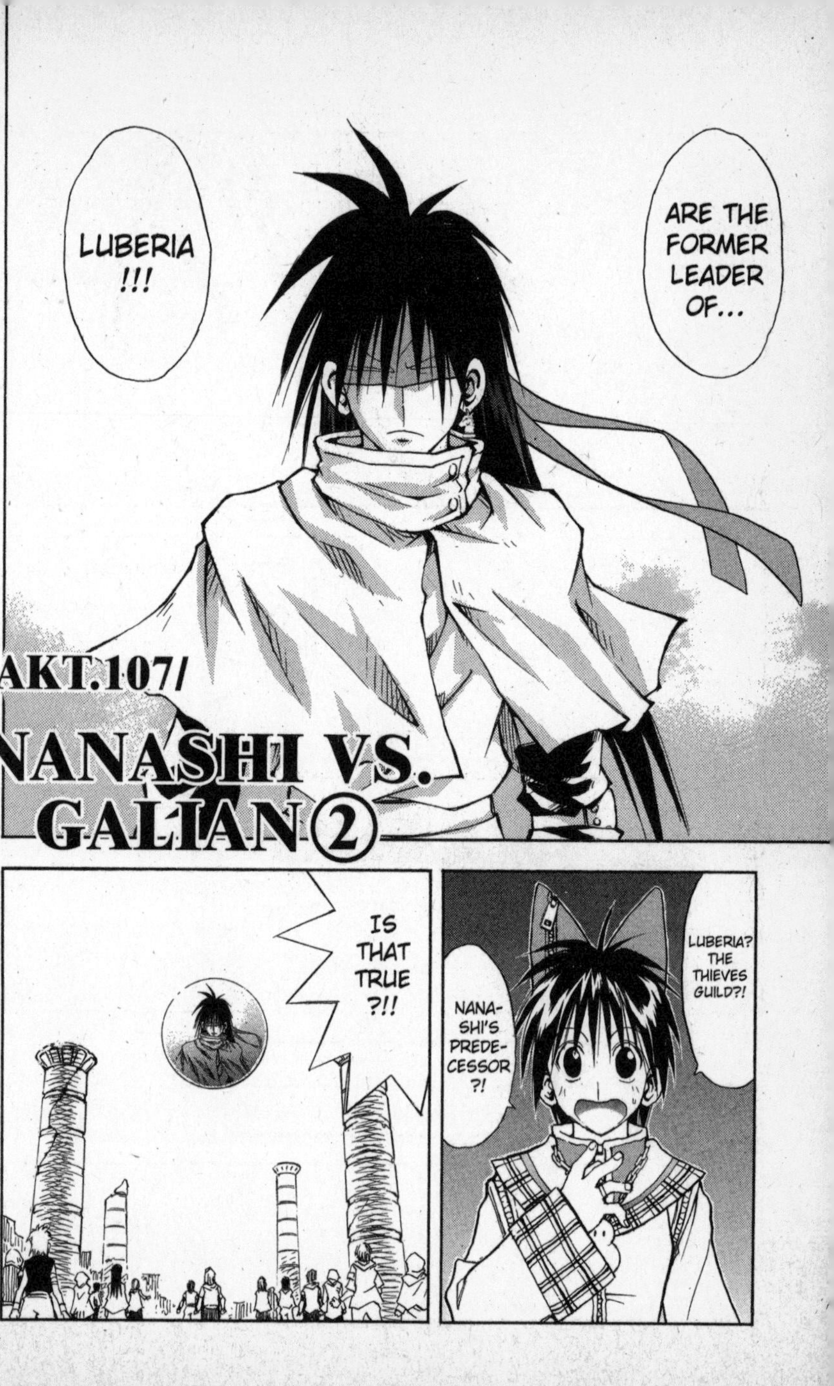
ARE THE FORMER LEADER OF...
LUBERIA !!!
AKT.107/
NANASHI VS. GALIAN 2
LUBERIA? THE THIEVES GUILD?!
NANA-SHI'S PREDE-CESSOR ?!
IS THAT TRUE ?!!

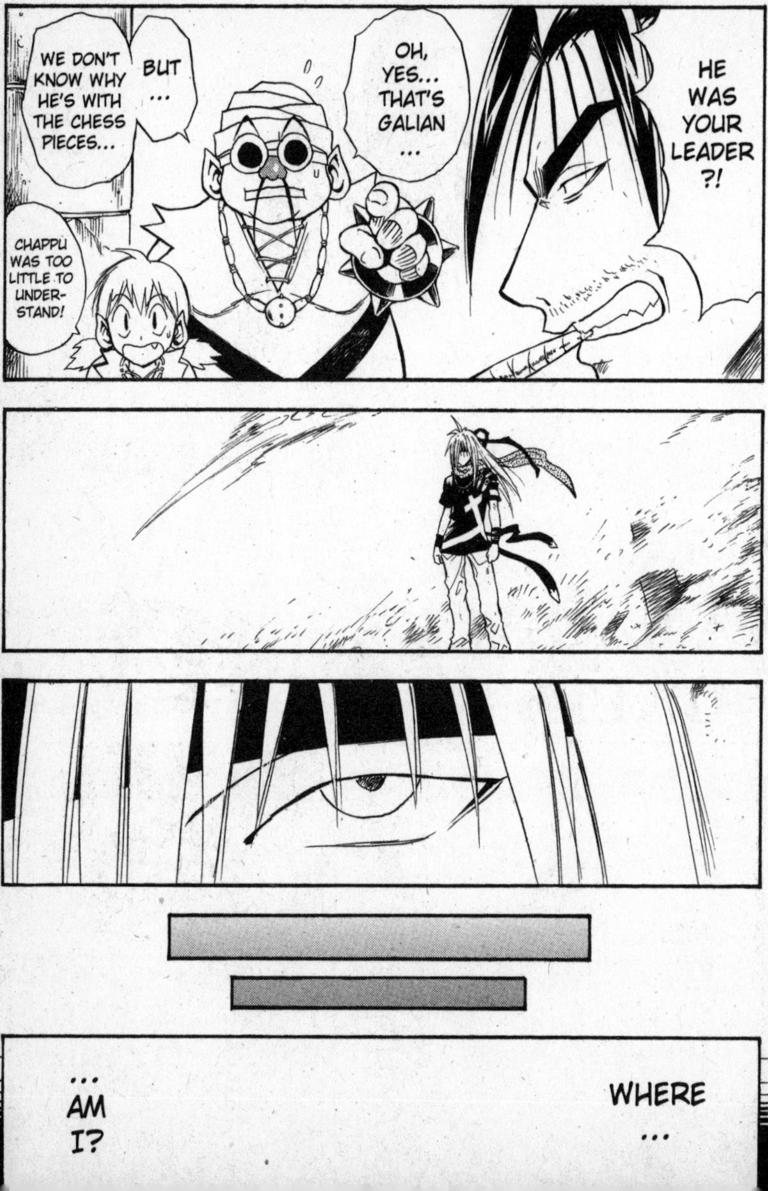
HE WAS YOUR LEADER ?!
OH, YES... THAT'S GALIAN ...
BUT ...
WE DON'T KNOW WHY HE'S WITH THE CHESS PIECES...
CHAPPU WAS TOO LITTLE TO UNDER-STAND!
WHERE ...
... AM I?

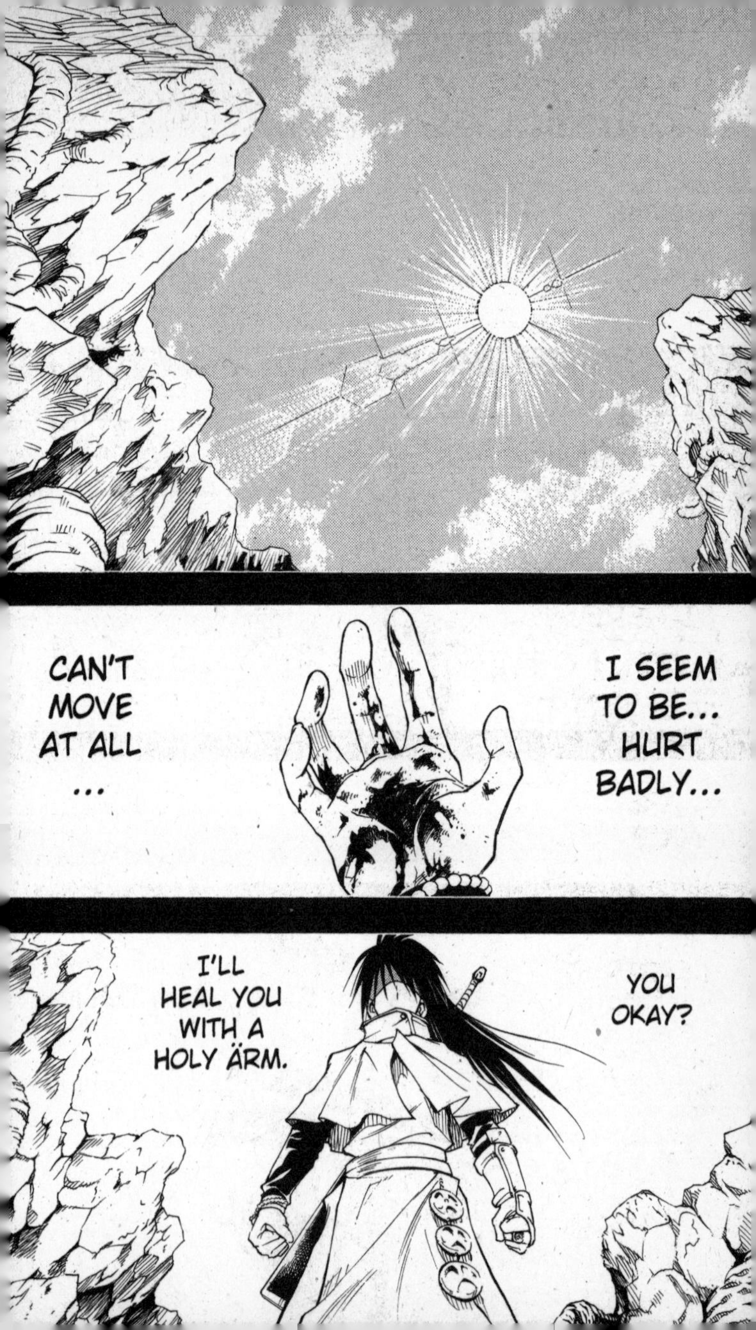
I SEEM TO BE... HURT BADLY...
CAN'T MOVE AT ALL ...
YOU OKAY?
I'LL HEAL YOU WITH A HOLY ÄRM.

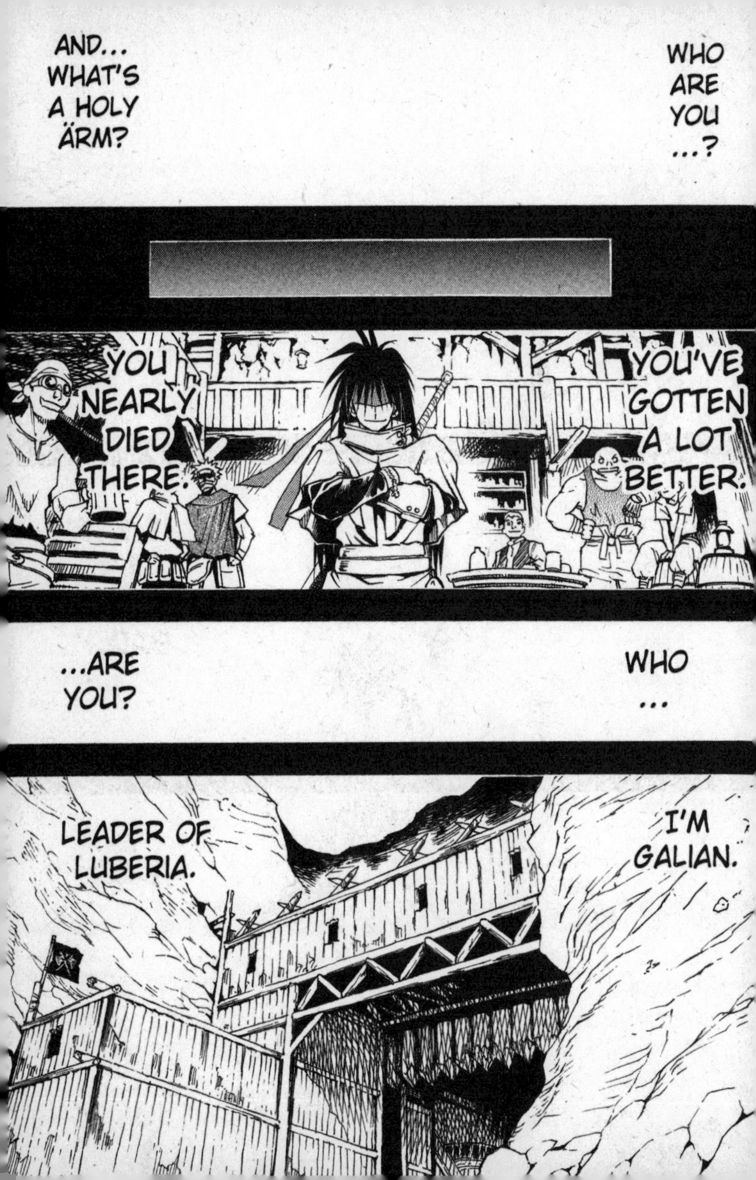
WHO ARE YOU ...?
AND... WHAT'S A HOLY ÄRM?
YOU'VE GOTTEN A LOT BETTER.
YOU NEARLY DIED THERE.
WHO ...
...ARE YOU?
I'M GALIAN.
LEADER OF LUBERIA.

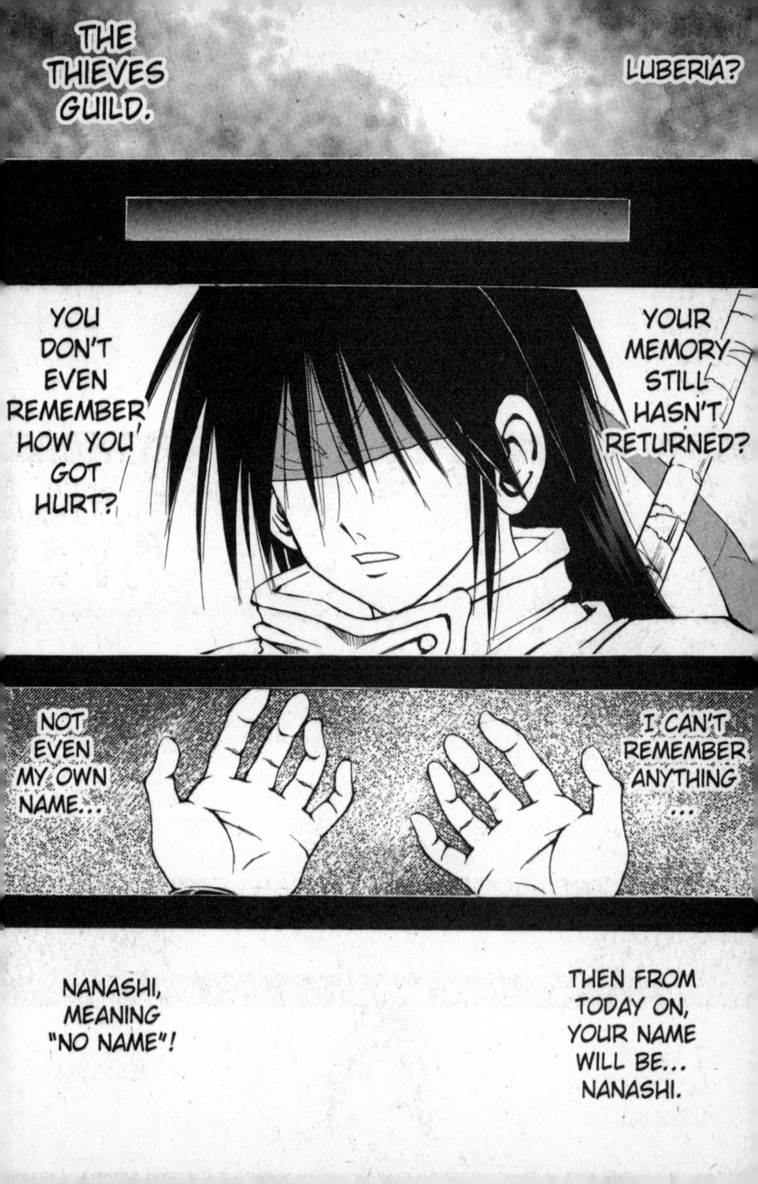
LUBERIA?
THE THIEVES GUILD.
YOUR MEMORY STILL HASN'T RETURNED?
YOU DON'T EVEN REMEMBER HOW YOU GOT HURT?
I CAN'T REMEMBER ANYTHING ...
NOT EVEN MY OWN NAME...
THEN FROM TODAY ON, YOUR NAME WILL BE... NANASHI.
NANASHI, MEANING "NO NAME"!

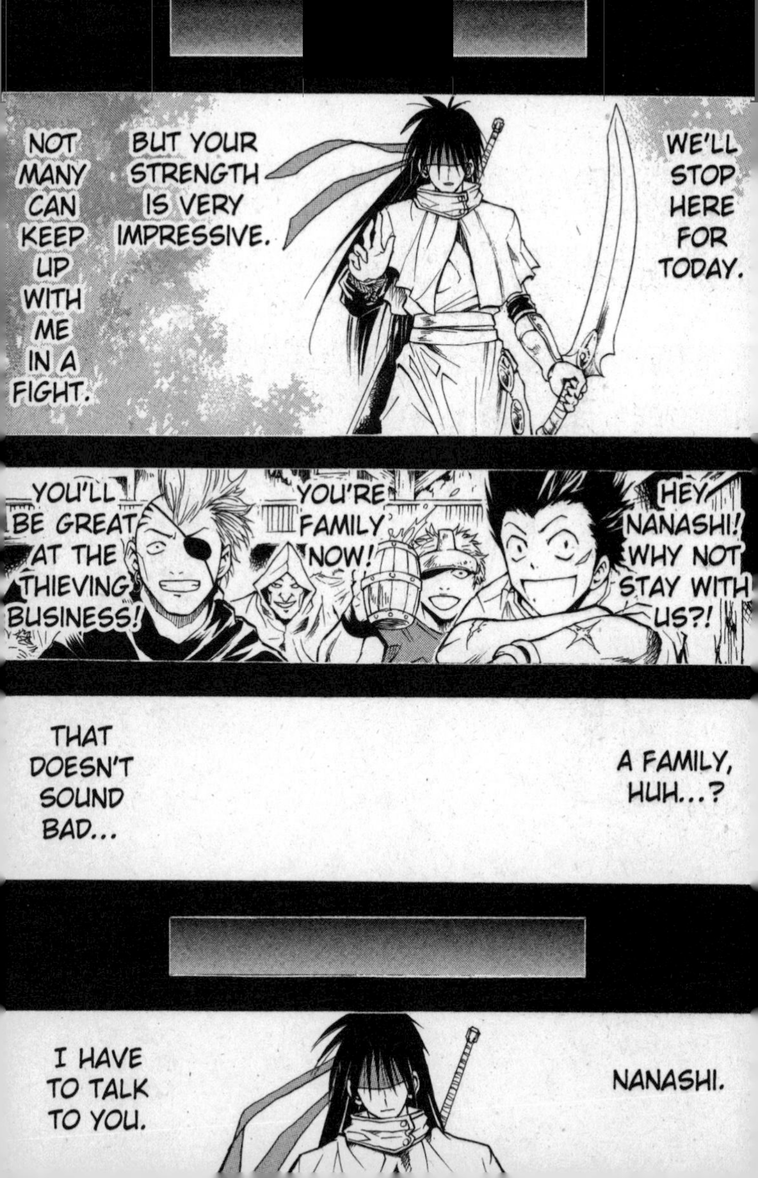
WE'LL STOP HERE FOR TODAY.
BUT YOUR STRENGTH IS VERY IMPRESSIVE.
NOT MANY CAN KEEP UP WITH ME IN A FIGHT.
HEY NANASHI! WHY NOT STAY WITH US?!
YOU'RE FAMILY NOW!
YOU'LL BE GREAT AT THE THIEVING BUSINESS!
A FAMILY, HUH...?
THAT DOESN'T SOUND BAD...
NANASHI.
I HAVE TO TALK TO YOU.

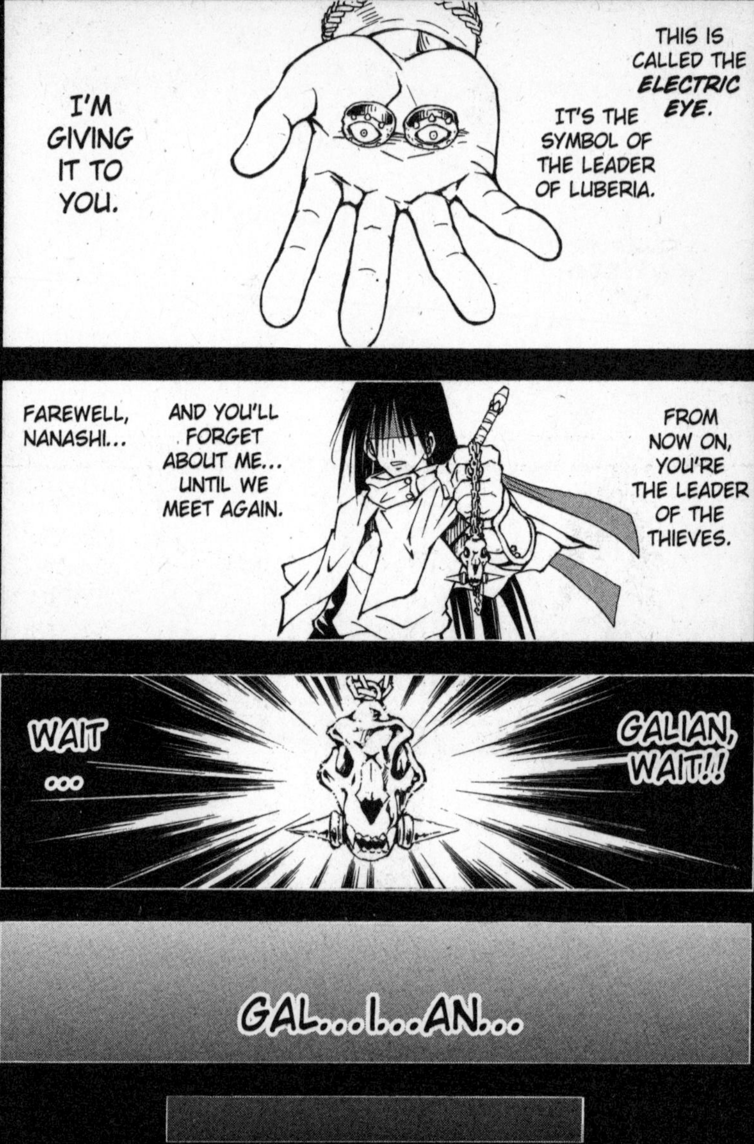
THIS IS CALLED THE *ELECTRIC EYE*.
IT'S THE SYMBOL OF THE LEADER OF LUBERIA.
I'M GIVING IT TO YOU.
FROM NOW ON, YOU'RE THE LEADER OF THE THIEVES.
AND YOU'LL FORGET ABOUT ME... UNTIL WE MEET AGAIN.
FAREWELL, NANASHI...
GALIAN, WAIT!!
WAIT ...
GAL...I...AN...

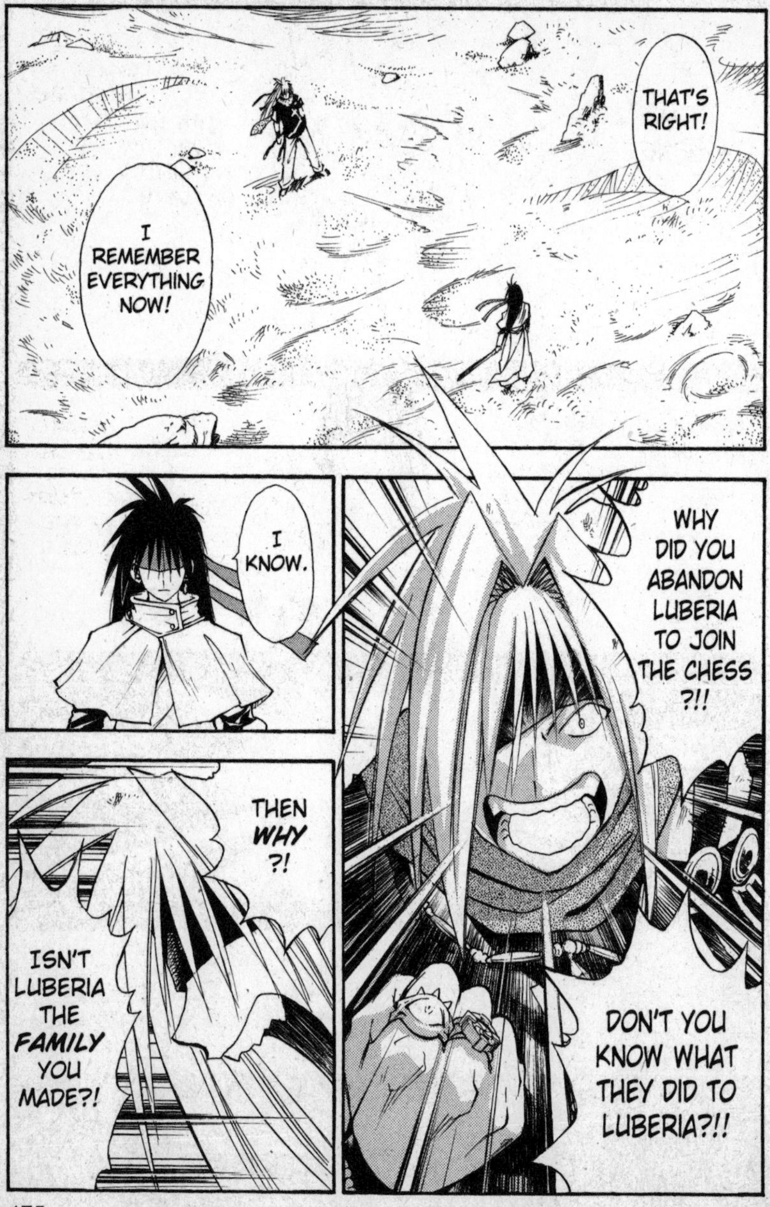
THAT'S RIGHT!
I REMEMBER EVERYTHING NOW!
WHY DID YOU ABANDON LUBERIA TO JOIN THE CHESS?!!
DON'T YOU KNOW WHAT THEY DID TO LUBERIA?!!
I KNOW.
THEN *WHY*?!
ISN'T LUBERIA THE *FAMILY* YOU MADE?!

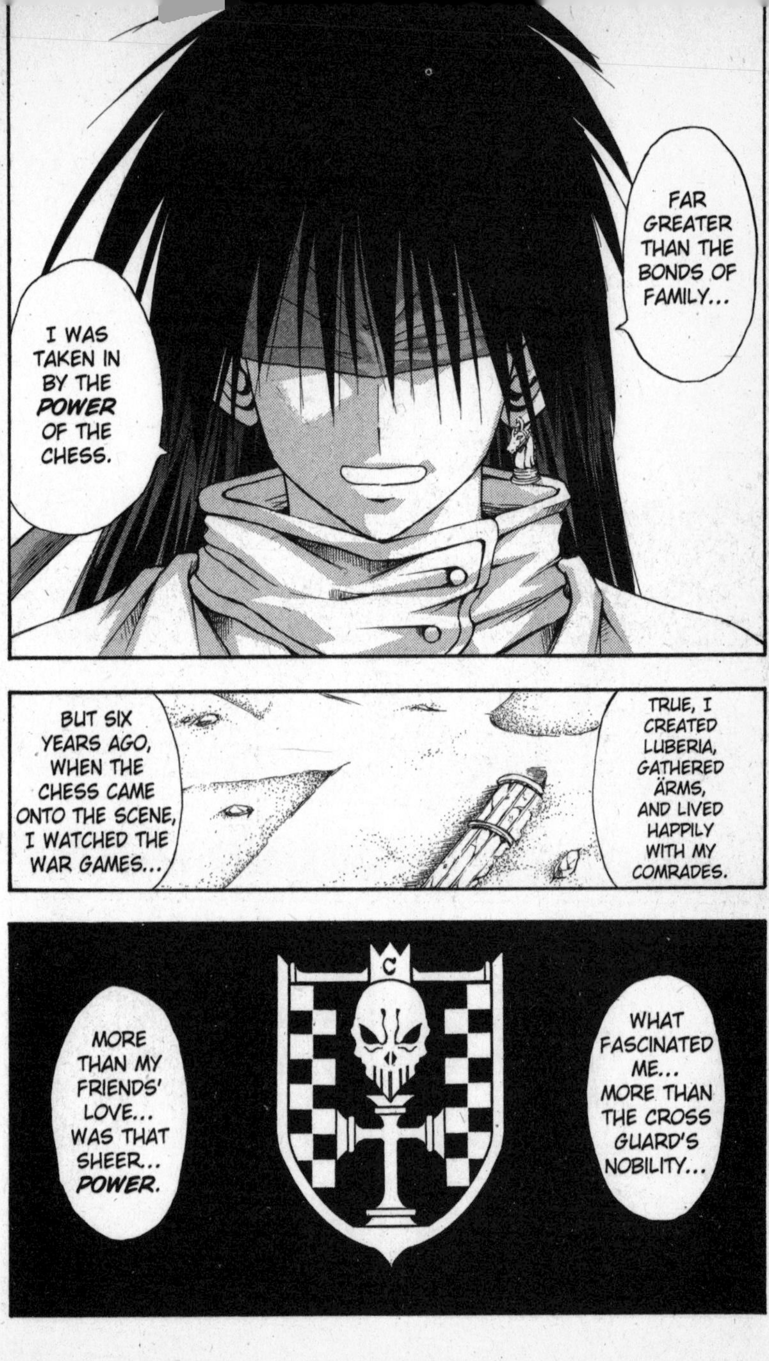
FAR GREATER THAN THE BONDS OF FAMILY...
I WAS TAKEN IN BY THE *POWER* OF THE CHESS.
TRUE, I CREATED LUBERIA, GATHERED ÄRMS, AND LIVED HAPPILY WITH MY COMRADES.
BUT SIX YEARS AGO, WHEN THE CHESS CAME ONTO THE SCENE, I WATCHED THE WAR GAMES...
WHAT FASCINATED ME... MORE THAN THE CROSS GUARD'S NOBILITY...
MORE THAN MY FRIENDS' LOVE... WAS THAT SHEER... *POWER*.

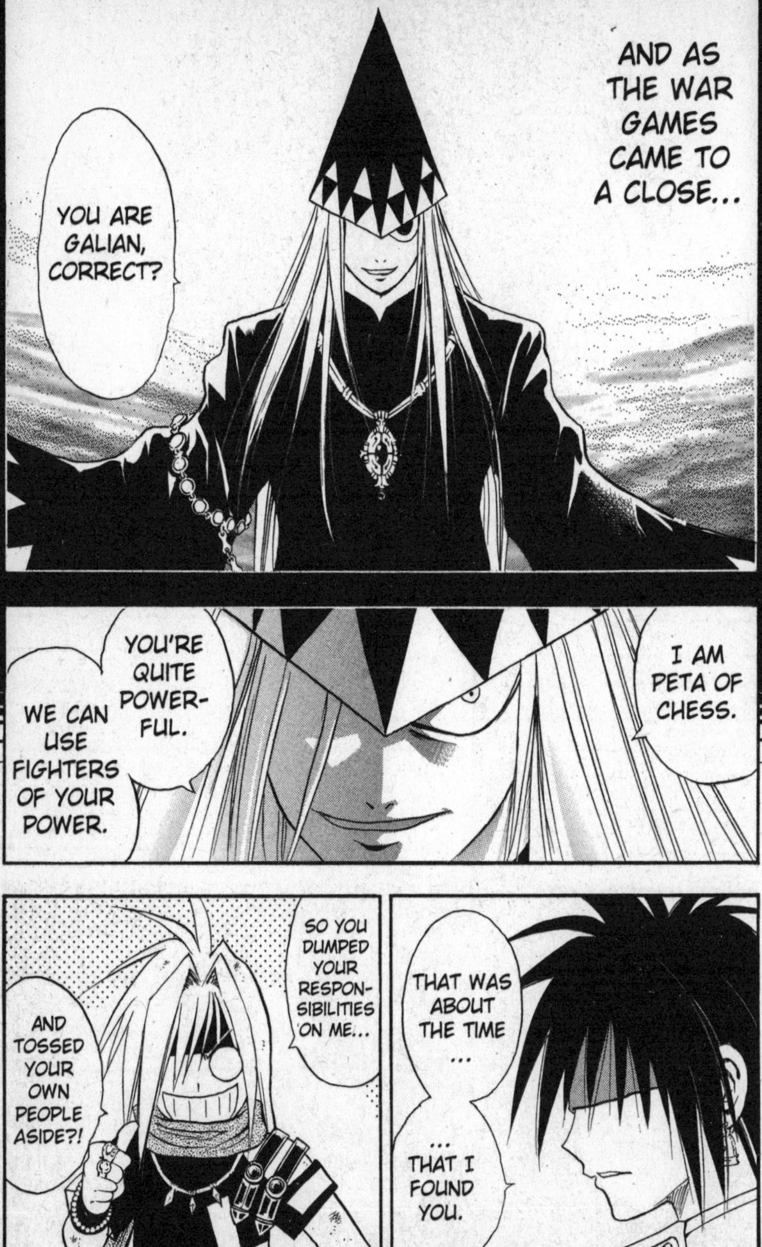
AND AS THE WAR GAMES CAME TO A CLOSE...
YOU ARE GALIAN, CORRECT?
I AM PETA OF CHESS.
YOU'RE QUITE POWER-FUL.
WE CAN USE FIGHTERS OF YOUR POWER.
THAT WAS ABOUT THE TIME ...
... THAT I FOUND YOU.
SO YOU DUMPED YOUR RESPON-SIBILITIES ON ME...
AND TOSSED YOUR OWN PEOPLE ASIDE?!

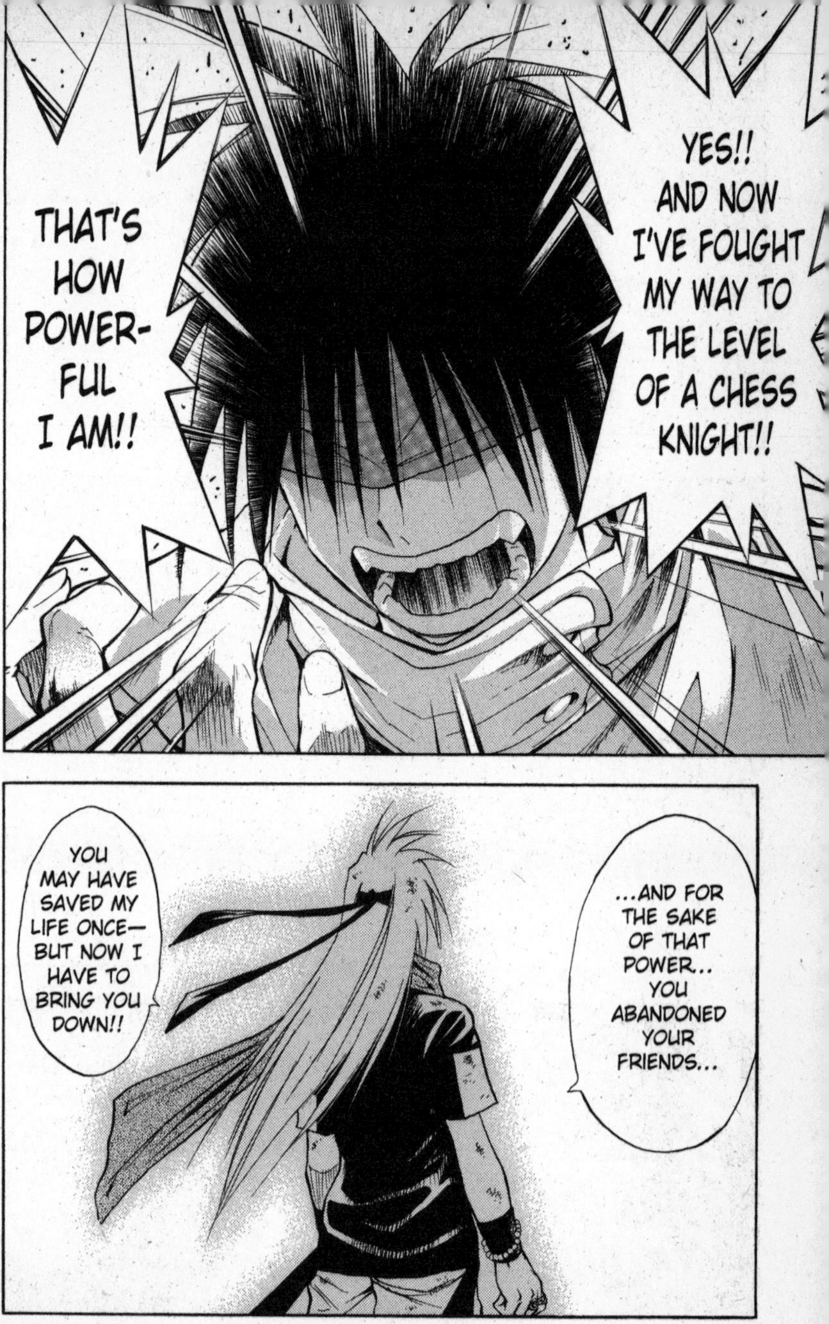
YES!! AND NOW I'VE FOUGHT MY WAY TO THE LEVEL OF A CHESS KNIGHT!!
THAT'S HOW POWER-FUL I AM!!
...AND FOR THE SAKE OF THAT POWER... YOU ABANDONED YOUR FRIENDS...
YOU MAY HAVE SAVED MY LIFE ONCE— BUT NOW I HAVE TO BRING YOU DOWN!!

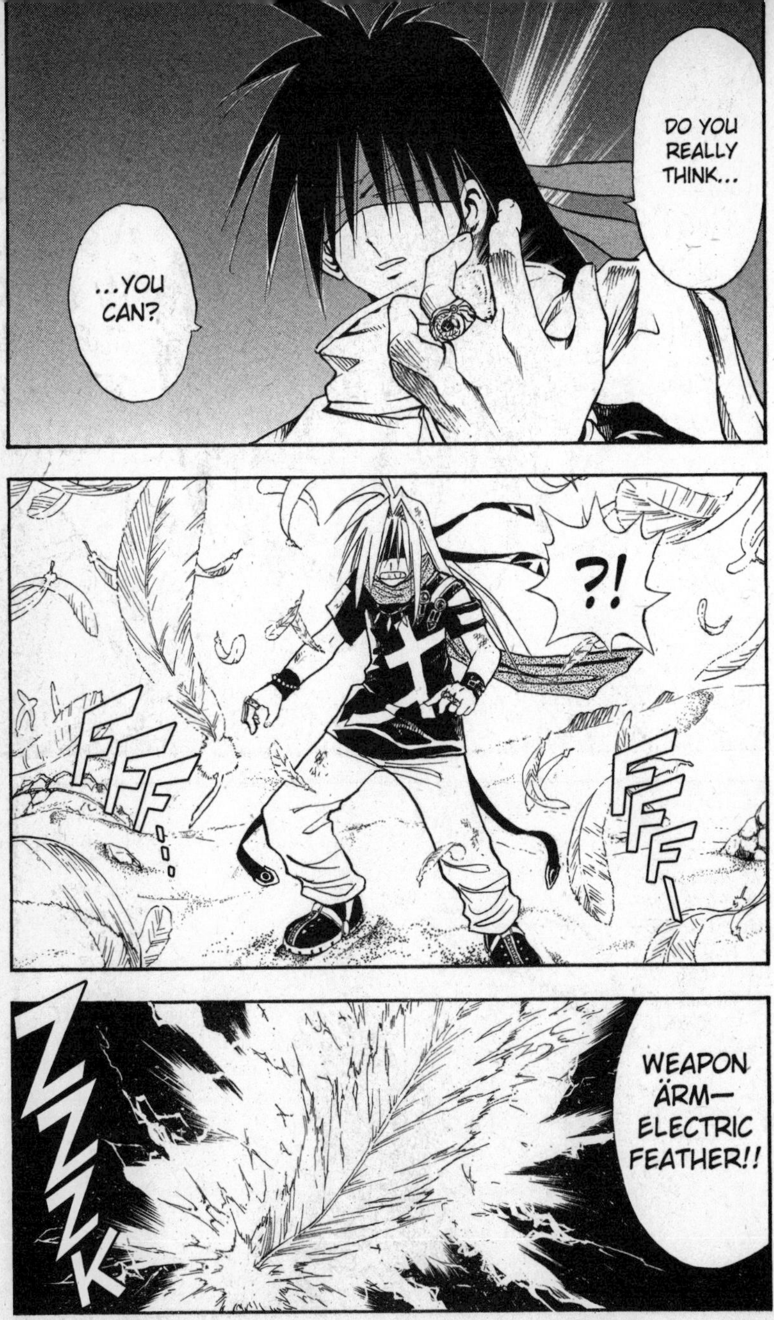
DO YOU REALLY THINK...
...YOU CAN?
?!
FFFF—
FFFF...
WEAPON ÄRM— ELECTRIC FEATHER!!

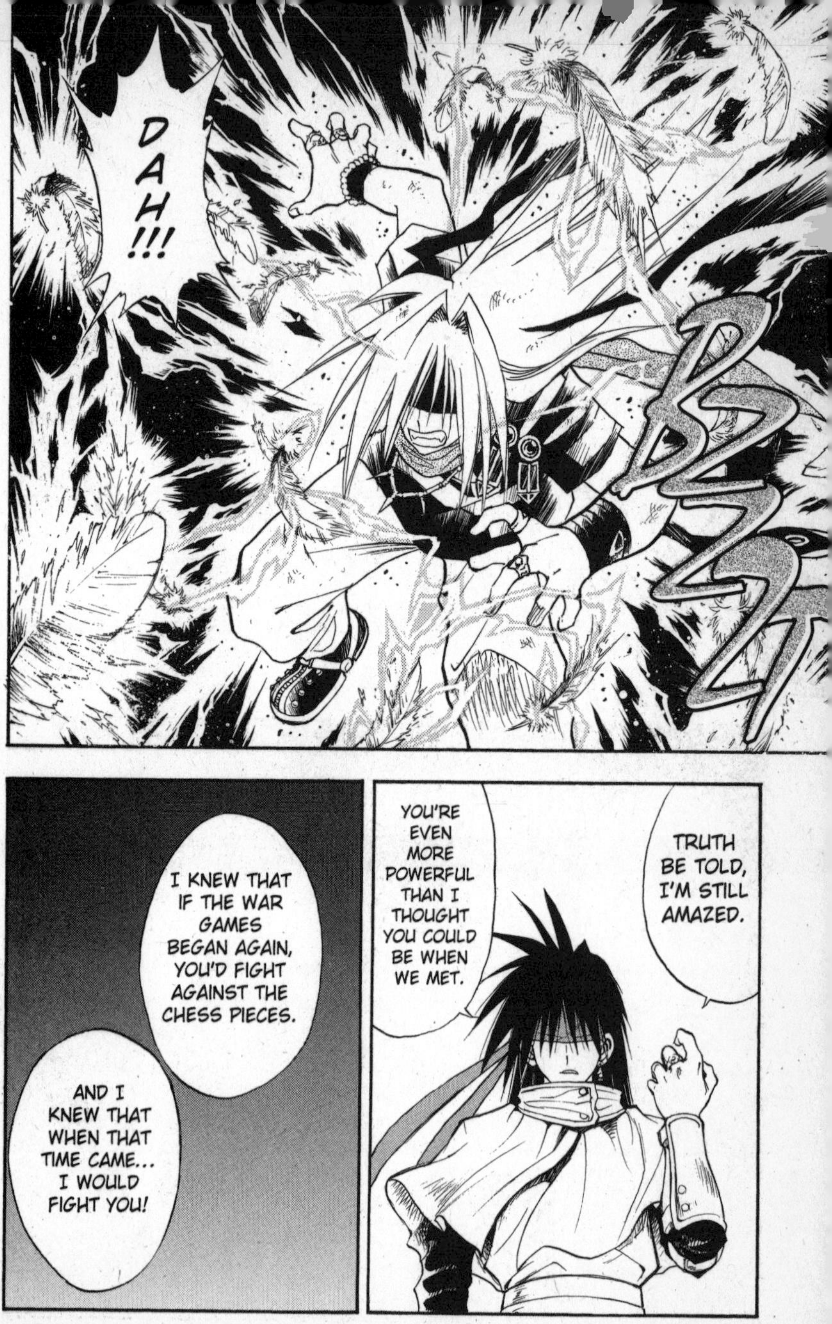
DAH!!!
BZZT
TRUTH BE TOLD, I'M STILL AMAZED.
YOU'RE EVEN MORE POWERFUL THAN I THOUGHT YOU COULD BE WHEN WE MET.
I KNEW THAT IF THE WAR GAMES BEGAN AGAIN, YOU'D FIGHT AGAINST THE CHESS PIECES.
AND I KNEW THAT WHEN THAT TIME CAME... I WOULD FIGHT YOU!

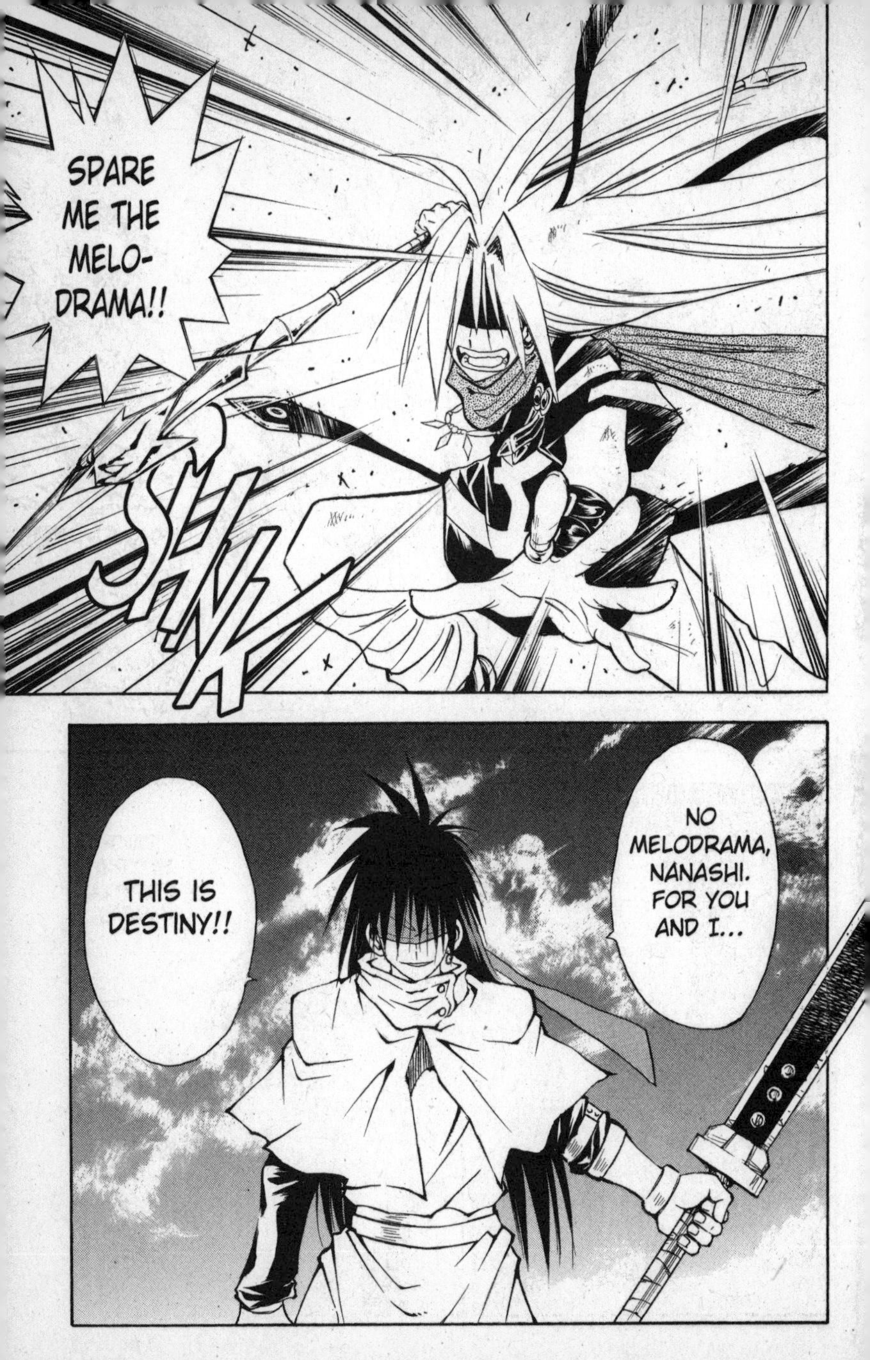
SPARE ME THE MELO-DRAMA!!
SHINK
NO MELODRAMA, NANASHI. FOR YOU AND I...
THIS IS DESTINY!!

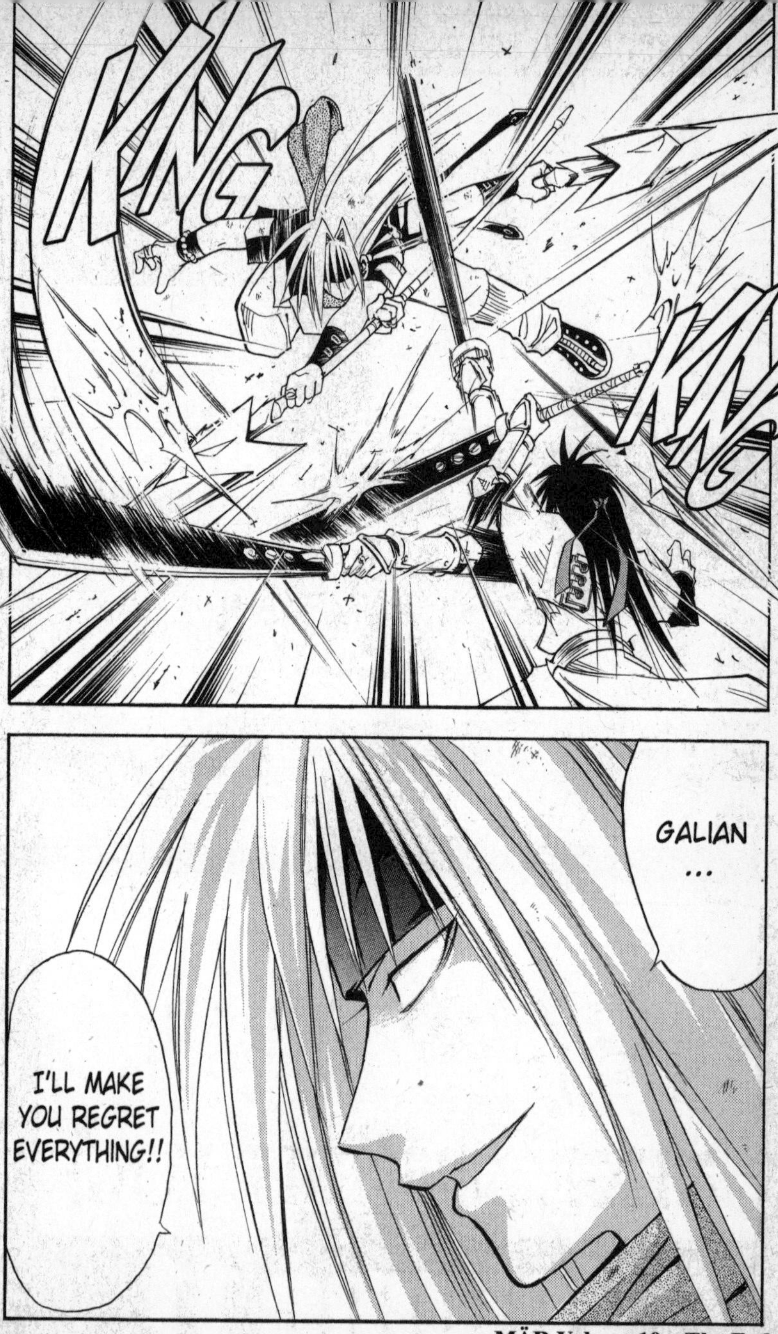
KING
KING
GALIAN ...
I'LL MAKE YOU REGRET EVERYTHING!!

MÄR Volume 10 – The End

THE EXCITEMENT BUILDS...

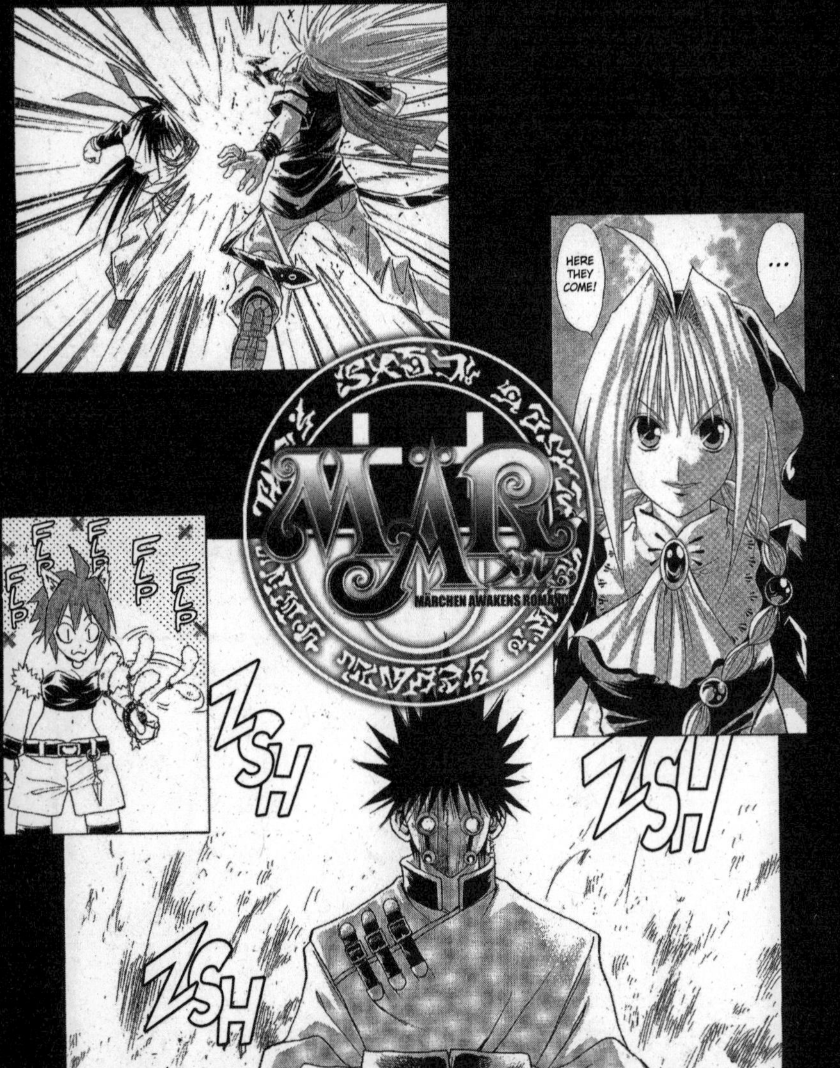

...
HERE THEY COME!
MÄR
MÄRCHEN AWAKENS ROMANCE
FLP FLP FLP FLP FLP
ZSH
ZSH
ZSH
NEXT... I'LL KILL YOU!

Volume 11

COMING SOON!

AREN'T THE POWERS OF IMAGINATION GREAT? IT'S THE BEST THING ABOUT BEING HUMAN!

Hoshino

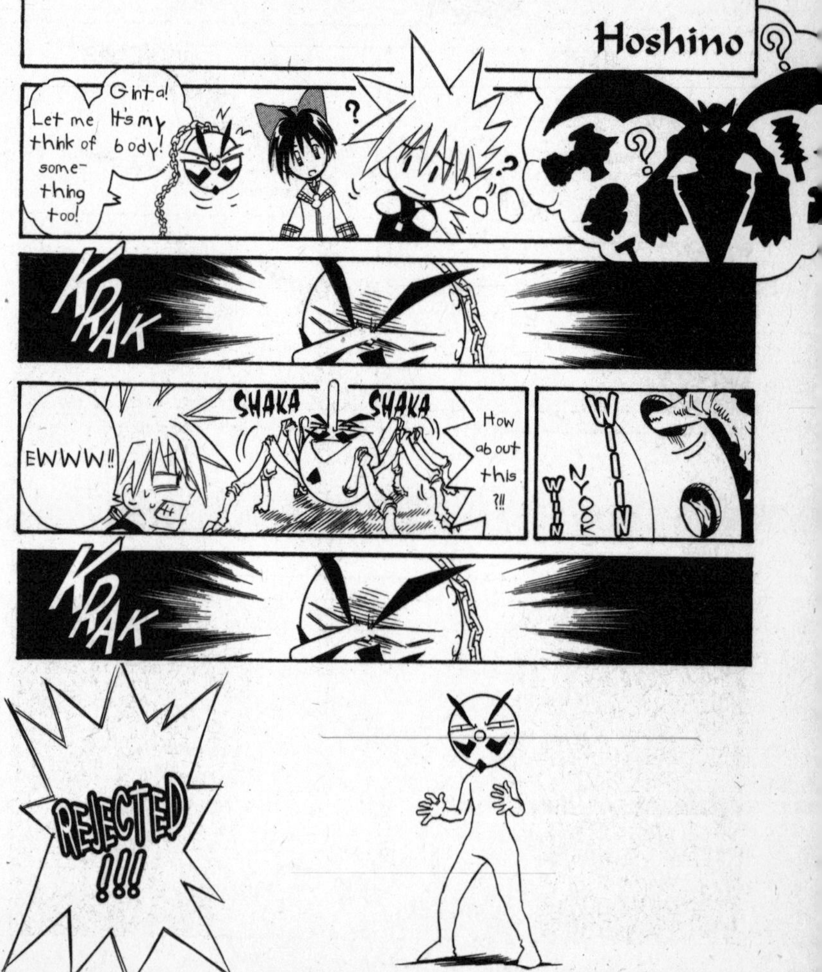
Ginta! It's my body!
Let me think of something too!
KRAK
WIIIN
NYOOK
WIIIN
SHAKA SHAKA
How about this?!!
EWWW!!
KRAK
REJECTED!!!

TITLE: "Yeah, I do understand...but still..."

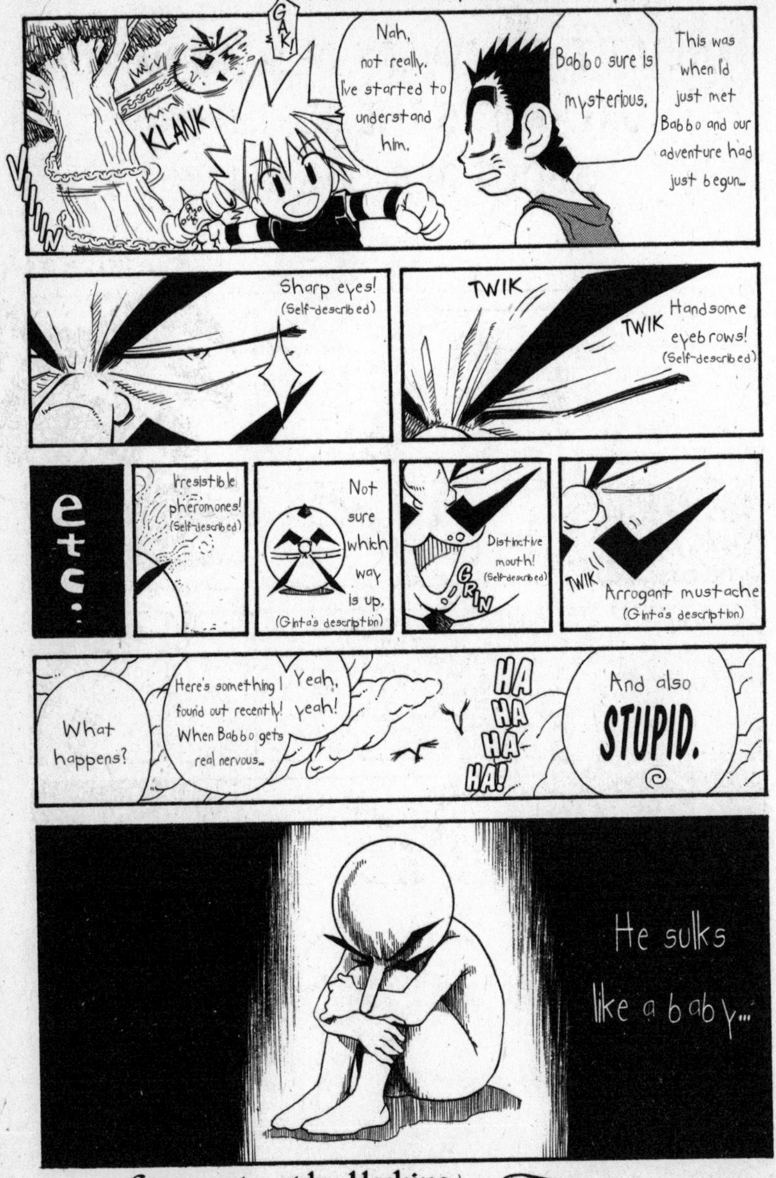
This was when I'd just met Babbo and our adventure had just begun...
Babbo sure is mysterious.
Nah, not really. I've started to understand him.
GAK!
KLANK
VIIIIN
TWIK
TWIK
Handsome eyebrows! (Self-described)
Sharp eyes! (Self-described)
Arrogant mustache (Ginta's description)
TWIK
Distinctive mouth! (Self-described)
GRIN
Not sure which way is up. (Ginta's description)
Irresistible pheromones! (Self-described)
etc.
And also STUPID.
HA HA HA HA!
Yeah, yeah!
Here's something I found out recently! When Babbo gets real nervous...
What happens?
He sulks like a baby...

Story and art by Hoshino

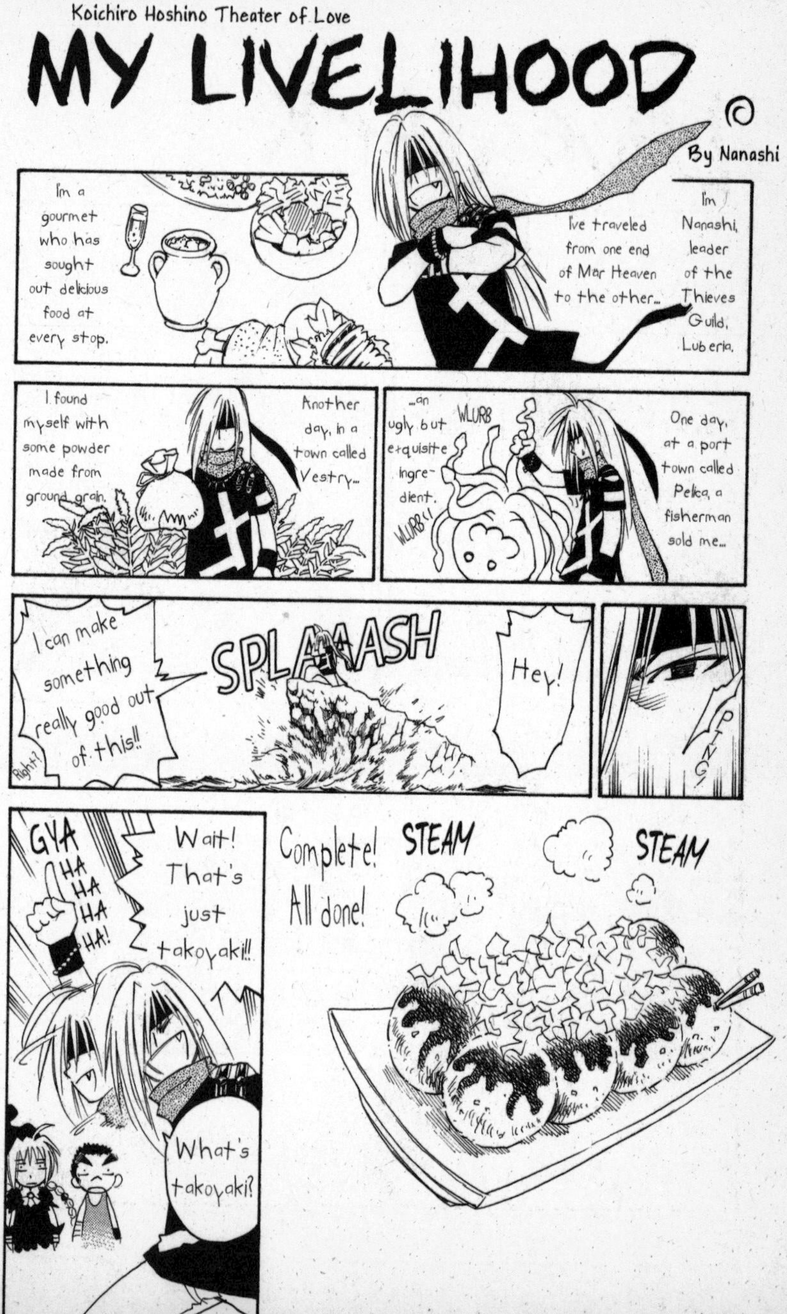
Koichiro Hoshino Theater of Love
MY LIVELIHOOD ©
By Nanashi
I'm Nanashi, leader of the Thieves Guild, Luberia.
I've traveled from one end of Mär Heaven to the other...
I'm a gourmet who has sought out delicious food at every stop.
One day, at a port town called Pelica, a fisherman sold me...
WLURB
...an ugly but exquisite ingredient.
WLURB
Another day, in a town called Vestry...
I found myself with some powder made from ground grain.
PING!
Hey!
SPLAAASH
I can make something really good out of this!!
Right!?
Complete! All done!
STEAM
STEAM
Wait! That's just takoyaki!!
GYA HA HA HA HA!
What's takoyaki?

LOVE JACK

Story and Art by Fuse

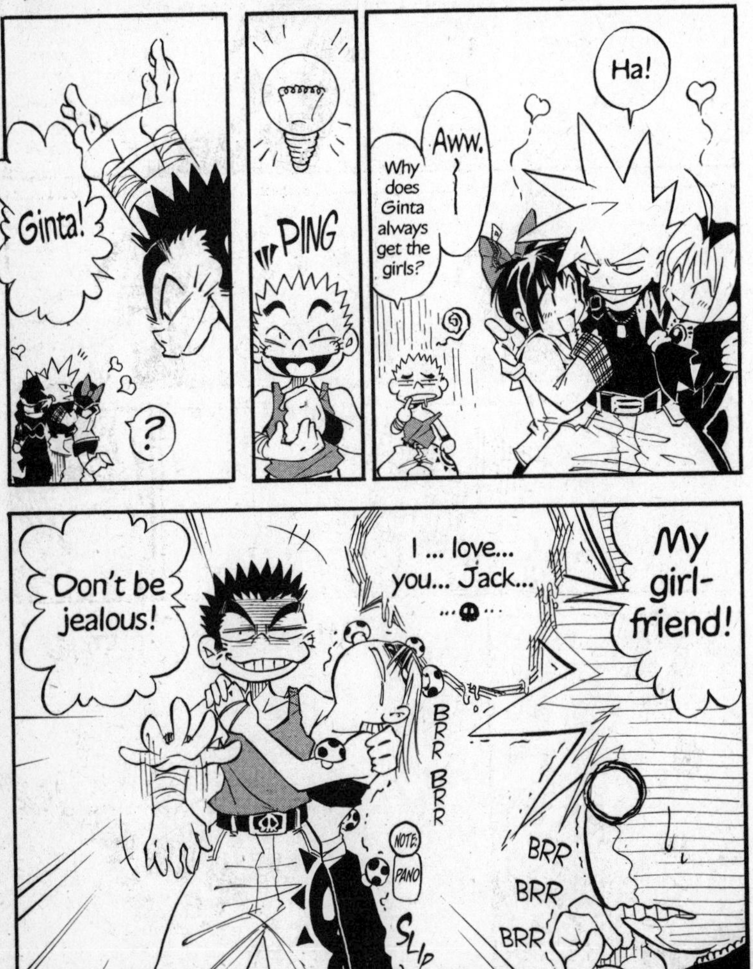

Ha!
Aww.
Why does Ginta always get the girls?
PING
Ginta!
?
My girl-friend!
I ... love... you... Jack... ...
Don't be jealous!
BRR BRR BRR
BRR BRR BRR
NOTE: PANO
SLIP...

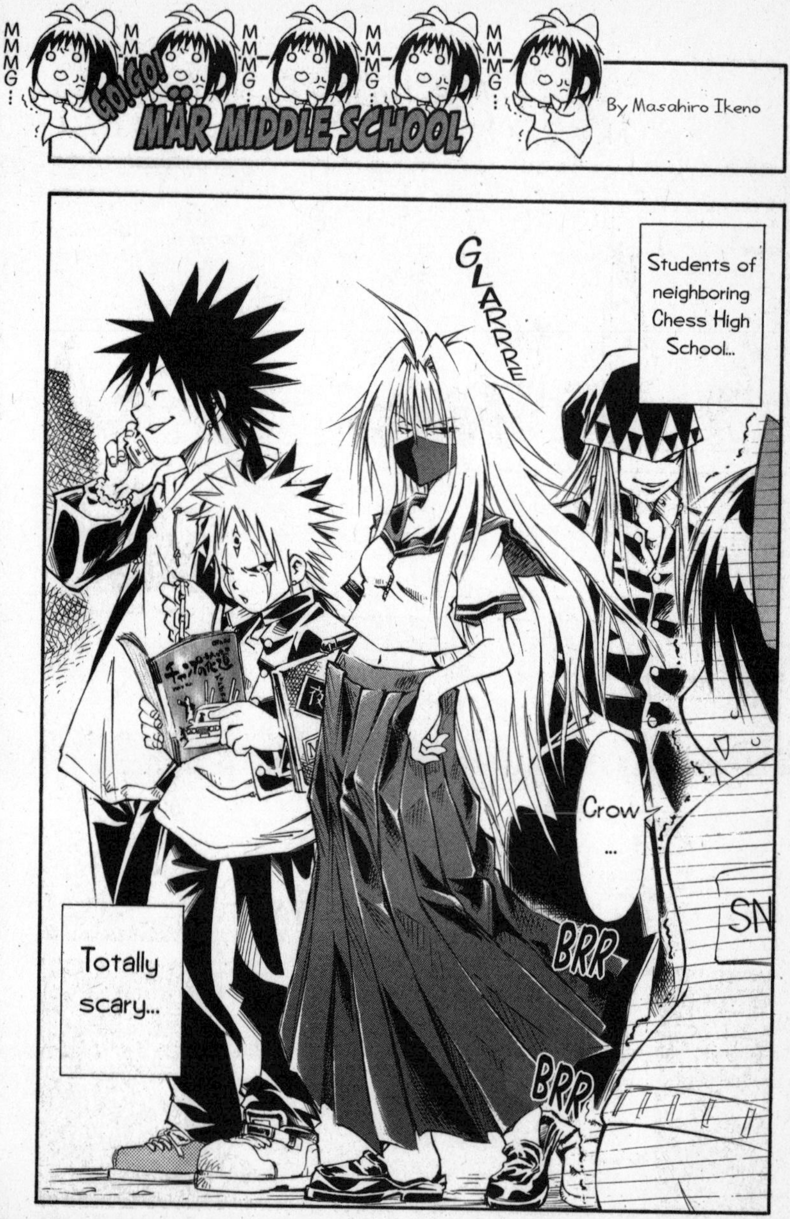
GO!GO! MÄR MIDDLE SCHOOL
By Masahiro Ikeno
MMMG...
MMMG...
MMMG...
MMMG...
MMMG...
Students of neighboring Chess High School...
GLARRRE
Crow...
SN
BRR
BRR
Totally scary...

ACID VOMIT

THE TOTAL WASTE EXPRESS

By G.B.

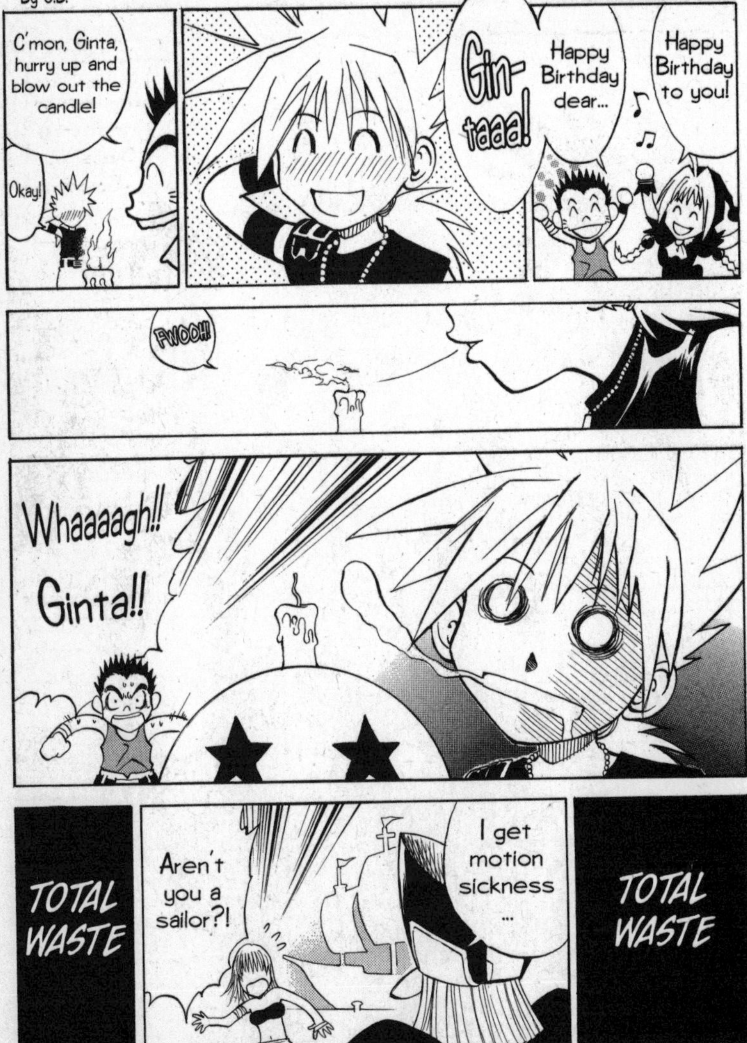

Happy Birthday to you!
Happy Birthday dear...
Gin-taaa!
C'mon, Ginta, hurry up and blow out the candle!
Okay!
FWOOH!
Whaaaagh!!
Ginta!!
TOTAL WASTE
I get motion sickness ...
Aren't you a sailor?!
TOTAL WASTE

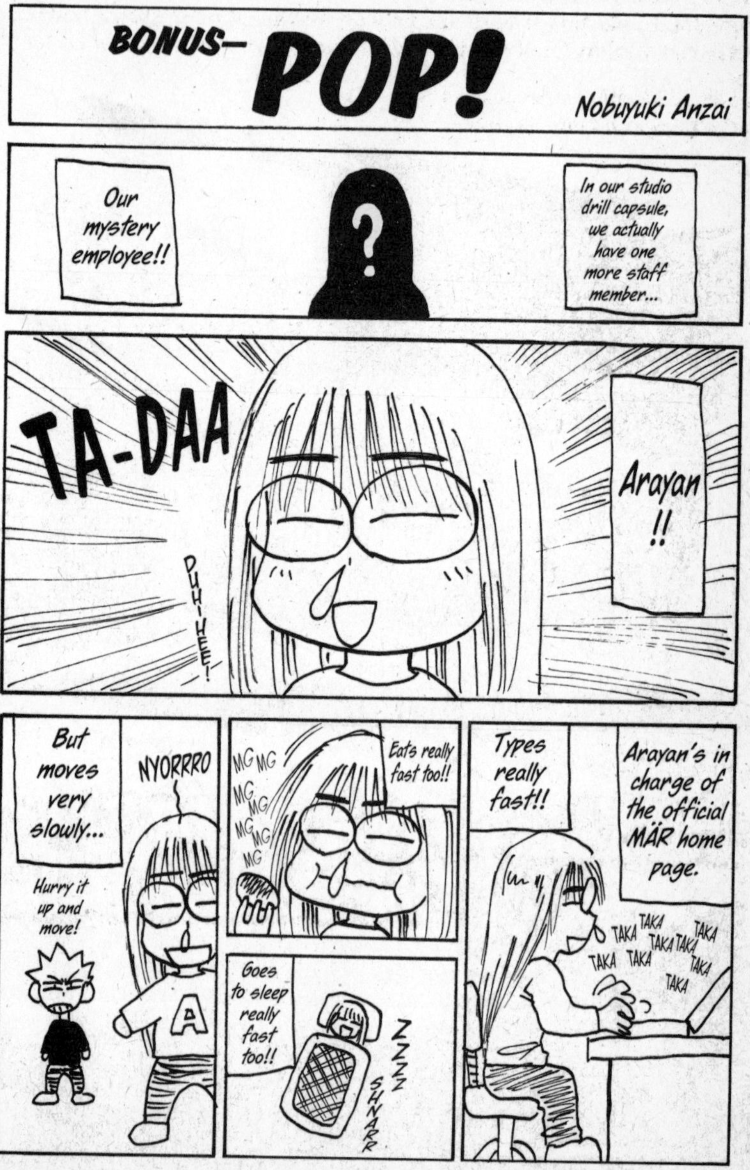
BONUS—
POP!
Nobuyuki Anzai
In our studio drill capsule, we actually have one more staff member...
Our mystery employee!!
?
Arayan!!
TA-DAA
PUHIHEE!
Arayan's in charge of the official MÄR home page.
Types really fast!!
TAKA TAKA TAKA TAKA TAKA TAKA TAKA TAKA TAKA
Eats really fast too!!
MG MG MG MG MG MG MG
Goes to sleep really fast too!!
ZZZZ
SHNARR
But moves very slowly...
NYORRRO
Hurry it up and move!
A